S. (Sabine) Baring-Gould

A study of St. Paul

His character and opinions

S. (Sabine) Baring-Gould

A study of St. Paul
His character and opinions

ISBN/EAN: 9783741142963

Manufactured in Europe, USA, Canada, Australia, Japa

Cover: Foto ©ninafisch / pixelio.de

Manufactured and distributed by brebook publishing software (www.brebook.com)

S. (Sabine) Baring-Gould

A study of St. Paul

A STUDY OF ST. PAUL

A

STUDY OF ST. PAUL

HIS CHARACTER AND OPINIONS

BY

S. BARING-GOULD M.A.

AUTHOR OF
"THE TRAGEDY OF THE CÆSARS" "MEHALAH" ETC.

LONDON
ISBISTER AND COMPANY Limited
15 & 16 TAVISTOCK STREET COVENT GARDEN
1897

Printed by BALLANTYNE, HANSON & Co.
London & Edinburgh

CONTENTS

CHAP.		PAGE
	PREFACE	vii
	CHRONOLOGICAL INTRODUCTION	13
I.	THE TWELVE	21
II.	TARSUS	41
III.	THE DEATH OF STEPHEN	58
IV.	THE CONVERSION	81
V.	ARABIA AND JERUSALEM	92
VI.	ANTIOCH	111
VII.	CYPRUS	140
VIII.	GALATIA	153
IX.	THE COUNCIL AT JERUSALEM	176
X.	THE SECOND JOURNEY—GALATIA	197
XI.	,, ,, —MACEDONIA	210
XII.	,, ,, —ATHENS	225
XIII.	,, ,, —CORINTH	241
XIV.	THE LAW AND THE GOSPEL	257
XV.	THE GOSPEL AND THE NATURAL LAW	277
XVI.	THE THIRD JOURNEY—EPHESUS	287
XVII.	THE PERIOD OF CONFLICT	299
XVIII.	ST. PAUL'S MODE OF ARGUMENT	318
XIX.	THE RIOT AT EPHESUS	337

CONTENTS

CHAP.		PAGE
XX.	THE EPISTLE TO THE ROMANS	343
XXI.	THE VOYAGE TO JERUSALEM	367
XXII.	THE RIOT AT JERUSALEM	381
XXIII.	CÆSAREA	398
XXIV.	ROME	412
XXV.	THE LAST YEARS	428

ADDENDA:

THE APOSTOLATE (p. 65)	439
RELIGIOUS ECSTASY (p. 116)	443
ANATOLIAN POLYANDRY (p. 160)	445
THE GREEKS (p. 165)	448
"MULIERES SUBINTRODUCTÆ" (p. 174)	450
CIRCUMCISION AMONG THE COPTS (p. 199)	452
THE "ROBUR" (p. 219)	452
THE UNKNOWN GOD (p. 233)	453
PROPHECIES AND UNKNOWN TONGUES (p. 249)	453
PAULINE ANOMIA (p. 310)	457

INDEX 463

MAPS:

I. THE FIRST JOURNEY OF ST. PAUL.

II. THE SECOND JOURNEY OF ST. PAUL.

ERRATUM.—P. 181: *for* "Crete" *read* "Cyprus."

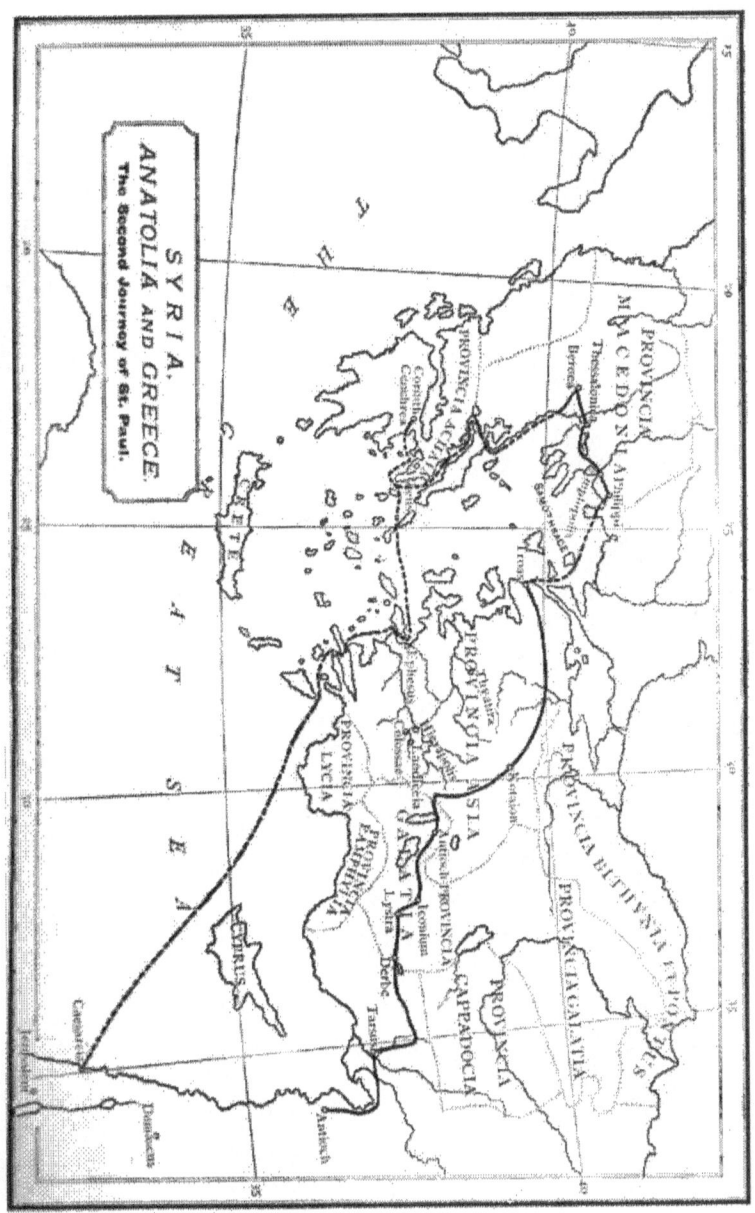

PREFACE

THE question has been put to me—I have asked it of myself—Is there room for another Life of St. Paul?

I venture to answer that there is.

Whether I was the proper man to undertake it—that is another question altogether. I did not seek to write it. It was, so to speak, forced upon me. Paul, like Shakespeare and Napoleon, are men of whom the world is never weary, who are ever in its mind, of whom it is always desirous to know more.

I do not pretend to add anything to the vast accumulation of detail that has been piled about the central figure of the Apostle, till his personality is buried under the mass of material collected. For this I have not the learning.

For original research, a study of the localities, their relation to the narrative in the Acts, and for the rehabilitation of the credibility of the book that had been sharply assailed, Professor Ramsay's works have been epoch-making.[1] I have made no explorations in Asia Minor, and so can add nothing. There have been studies of St. Paul, as a figure in a stained glass window, in which drawing and colouring are unreal, and the setting is lead. Such studies may be said to be of the past.

But there are others which combine much archæological detail and local colour with a treatment of the Apostle such

[1] "The Church in the Roman Empire," 4th ed., 1895; "St. Paul the Traveller and the Roman Citizen," 1896.

as a Roman client used towards his patron, and a seventeenth century author employed to the nobleman to whom he dedicated his book. He is fawned upon, adulation is "laid on with a trowel," he is exhibited as incapable of errors of judgment, of feebleness in argument, of doing anything but what is faultlessly right. Unctuous expletives are poured over him, till the precious balms break his head.

For such a work I have no stomach.

There have been studies, mainly German, in which the critics have treated the great Apostle as the Neolithic men treated a dead chieftain. They have first exposed him to the birds of prey, then have collected his disjointed bones, scraped them, and rearranged them according to their several idiosyncrasies—now adjusting a leg-bone to an arm-socket, and then rejecting a tibia as too stout or too slim, and relegating it to some other subject.

There have been studies, and these French, in which effort has been expended in arranging a stagey effect; the Apostle has been made to assume picturesque attitudes, surrounded with crowds artistically grouped, in scenery appropriate if somewhat gorgeous.

Then there have been studies of Paul by such as were resolved to find in his writings a complete ecclesiastical and theological system, and others by such as were equally determined to see in them nothing but what is amorphous.

The line I have adopted is that of a man of the world, of a novelist with some experience of life, and some acquaintance with the springs of conduct that actuate mankind.

A novelist, it will be objected, with a shrug, is the last man who should treat such a subject. The historian dreads the play of his imagination, altering facts; the religious man fears irreverence in handling them; and the critic disputes his acumen in investigation. His hand is unaccustomed to the scalpel say these, unused to the censer say others.

But this is due to a misconception of what a novelist really is, or should be. He is not properly an enchanter, calling up fantastic visions, a creator of startling situations, and an elaborator of ingenious plots; least of all is he a mechanical reproducer of moving photographs.

He is rather one who seeks to sound the depths of human nature, to probe the very heart of man, to stand patiently at his side with finger on pulse. He seeks to discover the principles that direct man's action, to watch the development of his character, and to note the influence the surroundings have on the genesis of his ideas, and the formation of his convictions.

This, then, is the point of view adopted by me. I treat the great Apostle as a man. I put aside detail unnecessary to my purpose, archæological, epigraphical, historical, geographical. My book is not, therefore, a life of St. Paul, if incidents and accidents make up a man's life, but a study of his mind, the formation of his opinions, their modification under new conditions, and the direction taken by his work, under pressure of various kinds, and from different sides.

At the same time I have used my best endeavour to be accurate in such details as were to my purpose to mention, having had recourse to the latest and best authorities. If I have here and there had occasion to refer to the Talmud, it is because that is accessible to every one, in the translation by Moses Schwab, and that of Beracoth by Chiarini. I have been sparing of references that encumber the foot of a page, like barnacles on the keel of a vessel, and delay progress.

With regard to the divine element in the narrative, I hold that to eliminate that is to misconceive the story of Paul altogether, to throw away the only key that can unlock the many problems of his life and labours. But I am indisposed to obtrude the divine and miraculous, wherever the facts of the narrative can be explained without forcible intervention with the natural order.

I think that certain good people, whose opinions I respect, whose faith I reverence, and whose piety I love, are disposed to misconceive the nature and function of inspiration, and to regard it as overmastering those who are inspired, neutralising their wills and suppressing their individuality.

There are two sorts of action in the world productive of results—that which is vital, and that which is mechanical. The first contains in itself almost infinite possibilities of development and adaptation. The second is formal and invariable. The first is a divine gift, the second is a contrivance of man.

Wherever and whenever God acts, it is in the first way, by the infusion of life, the production of germs in which the power of expansion, of selection, and of accommodation to shifting conditions, is found to exist. In a word, life as given by God contains in itself the faculty of growth. And I take it that inspiration is of like nature, and that we radically misunderstand it, if we reduce it to a mere mechanical force, like steam, that sets certain human wheels in motion to produce a certain predestined amount of work, according to a certain pre-ordained pattern.

From the point of view I have elected, I am bound to consider St. Paul mainly from the human side. I do not deny the other, the spiritual side (God forbid!), but I think that this latter has been unduly studied to the neglect of the human aspect. A biography that does not take both into account must be a limping and incomplete production. But this is not all.

Not only does an examination of St. Paul's life in its human aspect assist us in understanding the man himself, but, if the same method be applied to those among whom he moved, whom he gained by his teaching, or won by his abundant charity, and those whom he exasperated by his peculiar tactics, then they cease to pass before us like marionettes, but are seen as living men, alive to the smallest interference with

PREFACE

their interests; men very much like ourselves, prejudiced, touchy, tenacious of traditional rights. So we comprehend better than we could otherwise the secondary causes of Paul's successes, as well as the main motives that produced opposition.

The method I propose to follow moreover assists us in penetrating to the root of some of the problems that beset the student of Primitive Church history.

The Tübingen school *a fait fortune* out of its discovery of a supposed fiery antagonism between St. James and St. Peter on one side, and St. Paul on the other, resulting in an angry schism that was healed over in the second century, in such a manner as to leave a scar discernible only under the microscope. To conceive of such a reconciliation is to suppose a violation of the law governing all schisms, which drives the fractions ever further apart, hardening their peculiarities, and rendering the raw edges too irritable ever to reunite.

All the indications of heat noted by the thermometer and keen eye of the Tübingen scholars, and interpreted by them in one way, are capable of interpretation, more naturally, in another.

With respect to the chronology of Paul's career there is but one period about which there is any real difficulty. I have ventured to suggest a solution of what has been a *crux* to his biographers, and which reconciles all difficulties in a very simple manner.

I must express my gratitude to the Rev. R. Gwynne, Vicar of St. Mary's, Charing Cross Road, and to the Rev. J. B. Hughes, late Master of Blundel School, Tiverton, and Vicar of Staverton, Devon, for kindly looking through my proof sheets.

S. BARING-GOULD.

LEW TRENCHARD, DEVON.

CHRONOLOGICAL INTRODUCTION

In considering the chronology of St. Paul's history we soon discover that there are in it two epochs, one that can be determined with tolerable nicety, the other very difficult to arrange.

We have to settle everything between the year 35, when his conversion took place, and 63, when the narrative in the Acts closes. We must take the second half of his life first, and work backwards.

We know that Paul sailed, a prisoner, for Rome, in the autumn after the appointment of Porcius Festus as procurator, which took place early in 60. He, therefore, sailed in the fall of 60. He had been a prisoner in Cæsarea for three years, from the riot in Jerusalem at Pentecost. That, therefore, took place in 58. At Easter in 58 he was at Philippi. He arrived there from Corinth, where he had spent the winter of 57–58.

He had come to Corinth in the autumn of 57, from Ephesus, where he had tarried three years—that is to say, from the spring of 55.

He had arrived at Ephesus from Antioch through Galatia, having spent the winter of 54–55 in Antioch.

To Antioch he had returned from his second missionary journey through Asia, Macedonia, and Achaia, which had lasted probably from 52. We can check this date by that of the proconsulship of Gallio in Achaia.

14 CHRONOLOGICAL INTRODUCTION

The Council of Jerusalem took place some time in the winter of 51-52.

So far is fairly certain.

The chronology of the earlier portion of St. Paul's career is more difficult to settle satisfactorily.

It is generally agreed that his conversion took place in 35. Then he spent three years in Arabia, and after that came up to Jerusalem, in 38.

"Then, fourteen years after," he wrote to the Galatians, "I went up again to Jerusalem with Barnabas."

Are we to deduct the three years in Arabia from these fourteen? Probably so. Then this gives us the date 49 for the second visit. He was fetched from Tarsus by Barnabas in 48.

Now comes the difficulty.

We are told (Acts xi. 22-24) that Barnabas was sent by the Apostles to Antioch, and that, perplexed as to his course, he went on to Tarsus, and fetched Paul thence (xi. 25, 26). Then we hear of prophets foretelling a famine, which famine takes place in the reign of Claudius Cæsar. The brethren at Antioch resolve on sending relief to the believers in Jerusalem (xi. 27-29), and Barnabas and Paul take it up to Jerusalem (xi. 30).

Then comes in—parenthetically—the account of Herod's persecution and of the death of Herod (xii. 1-19; 22-23). Then follows the return of Barnabas and Paul to Antioch (xii. 25).

All commentators make Paul and Barnabas go twice to Jerusalem, with an interval of some three years between, and because Paul distinctly asserts that he had *not* been in Jerusalem till 48, they suppose he went part of the way, and turned back for some unknown reason.

They have been led to this impotent conclusion because satisfied that the prophesied famine took place in 44. But is it not possible, nay, probable, that the famine continued for several years, and the distress prevailed for as many as five; that the Church in Antioch sent up alms annually, but only by the hands of Barnabas and Paul in the last year, 49?

When Luke set to work to string his notes together into a consecutive record, it was at a distance from Palestine, and many years after the events related. His notes had been taken down from various persons, at different times and occasions, and what he had to do was to piece them together to the best of his ability. All the earlier portion of the Acts was thus composed. The only portion of which he could be sure of the chronological sequence was that in which he had been a companion of the Apostle.

The account of the fetching of Paul by Barnabas, he had doubtless heard from the former. That of the persecution and the death of the persecutor he had from some Jewish believer; but how to dovetail this in with Paul's reminiscences was a matter of pure conjecture; and when he did it—it was clumsily done.

Nowadays we can check dates by reference to the files of the *Times*, or to "Year Books." Luke had no such opportunities. If, as Professor Ramsay supposes, the Acts were written about 78, then this was some thirty or thirty-four years after the famine.

This was his collection of notes:

    a. Barnabas sent to Antioch (xi. 22-24).

    β. Barnabas fetches Paul (xi. 25-26).

    γ. Arrival of Prophets at Antioch foretelling famine (xi. 27-28).

δ. A collection made (xi. 29).
ε. Barnabas and Saul carry it to Jerusalem (xi. 30).
[ζ. *Persecution of the Church by Herod* (xii. 1–19).
η. *Death of the Persecutor* (xii. 20–23)].
θ. Barnabas and Saul return from Jerusalem (xii. 25).

Is it not obvious that paragraphs ζ and η are intruded where they have no right, and that the narrative should continue straightway from ε to θ, showing how Barnabas and Saul go up to Jerusalem and then return to Antioch? Before α we have first the long story of St. Peter and Cornelius, which was no part of Paul's reminiscences, but which Luke probably obtained from Mark. Then comes another note from another source (xi. 19–21) relative to the dispersion of the believers after the persecution in which Stephen perished. Then comes the mission of Barnabas, and then, suggested by the scattering after the first persecution in 35, comes the scattering after the persecution in 44, which sends Agabus and other prophets to Antioch.

The re-arrangement of the text that I propose would be this:—

Persecution of the Church by Herod. **Spring of 44.**

In consequence of the persecution, the prophets driven from Jerusalem arrive in Antioch, where they foretell the approaching failure of the harvest and subsequent famine. A collection resolved on.

Death of Herod, 44.

News of the progress of the Gospel in Antioch reaches the Apostles.

They are now in tranquillity, "The Church has rest," 45–48, and they are able to consider the matter; they send Barnabas to Antioch, 48.

CHRONOLOGICAL INTRODUCTION 17

Barnabas goes to Tarsus and fetches Paul, 48.

Barnabas, ready with his report, takes up the contribution, and associates Paul with him, when he makes his report to the Apostles, 49.

The report considered; Barnabas and Paul return to Antioch, 49.

The persecution accounts for the coming of the prophets to Antioch, flying from the wrath of Herod.

It is inconceivable that the Apostles should have been able to consider the state of affairs in Antioch at the very time that persecution raged. It is far more likely that when it was over, and the period of security had set in, they began to apply their minds to the difficulties of the situation at Antioch, and that it was then, and then only, in 48, that they deputed Barnabas to report on it.

Josephus by no means limits the famine to one year. He says, "Then came Tiberius Alexander as successor to Fadus. . . . Under these procurators that great famine happened in Judea, in which queen Helena bought corn in Egypt at great expense, and distributed it to those that were in want, as I have already related" (Antiq. xx. c. 5). This is plain enough. If it began so early as 44, it lasted on for several years.

The prophet Agabus foretold it in 44, and the Church in Antioch sent annual contributions till 49, during which time the dearth was chronic. In the last year only did Barnabas and Saul take it up. There is nothing in the text that militates against the supposition that the contribution was made annually during the period of distress, and that it was only on the last occasion of transmitting it that the two Apostles conveyed the money to Jerusalem.

It seems to me that this simple supposition, coupled

with that of the misplacement of the account of the persecution and death of Herod, explains every difficulty. I append a table of the chronology I propose to follow.

Date.	Events in St. Paul's Life.	Contemporary Events.	Composition of Epistles.
circa 4	Saul *alias* Paul born.		
,, 18	At Jerusalem under Gamaliel (xxii. 3).		
,, 25	Returns to Tarsus.		
30		The Crucifixion.	
35	Paul returns to Jerusalem (vii. 58; viii. 1). Stephen stoned (vi.; vii.). Conversion of Paul (ix. 1–8). He retires into Arabia (Gal. i. 17).		
37		Pilate deposed, 16th March.	
38	Paul re-visits Damascus; obliged to fly (ix. 20–25). First visit to Jerusalem after conversion (ix. 26; Gal. i. 18). Then returns to Tarsus (ix. 26–30; Gal. i. 18).		
44		Persecution at Jerusalem (xii. 1–19). Prophets dispersed by persecution come to Antioch and foretell a famine (xi. 27, 28). Harvest fails and famine begins, and lasts intermittently for six years. Death of Herod Agrippa (xii. 20–23). Fadus procurator till 46. Then Tiberius Alexander till 48.	

CHRONOLOGICAL INTRODUCTION 19

Date.	Events in St. Paul's Life.	Contemporary Events.	Composition of Epistles.
48	Barnabas sent to Antioch by the Apostles (xi. 22-24). In the autumn he goes to Tarsus and fetches Paul, who spends with him the winter in Antioch (xi. 25, 26).	Ventidius Cumanus procurator till 52.	
49	Barnabas and Paul go up with alms to Jerusalem (xi. 30). Thence they return to Antioch (xi. 30; xii. 25); but previous to their return Paul has a vision in the Temple (xxii. 17-20).		
50	In the spring the ordination of Barnabas and Paul (xiii. 1-3). Then they undertake the first missionary journey to Cyprus and Galatia (xiii. 4-52; xiv. 1-25).	Jews expelled Rome.	
51	Paul and Barnabas in Galatia. They return in the fall of the year to Antioch (xiv. 26-28).		
52	In the winter the Council of Jerusalem (xv. 1-30; Gal. ii. 1). After it return of Paul and Barnabas to Antioch (xv. 30). In the spring Paul starts on his second missionary journey, through Galatia to Macedonia and Achaia (xvi.-xviii.).	Felix procurator till 60.	
53	Paul at Corinth (xviii. 1-18).		Epistles to the Thessalonians.
54	Return to Palestine in the spring (xviii. 18). Winter of 54-55 spent in Antioch (xviii. 22).	Gallio Proconsul of Achaia, 53-54. Death of Claudius. Accession of Nero.	
55	Paul starts on his third missionary journey, and arrives in Ephesus (xviii. 23; xix. 1).		Epistle to the Galatians. Epistles to the Corinthians.

Date.	Events in St. Paul's Life.	Contemporary Events.	Composition of Epistles.
56	At Ephesus (xix.; xx. 1).		Epistle to the Romans.
57	At Ephesus, but in autumn goes to Corinth, where he winters (xx. 1–3).		
58	At Easter in Philippi, then sails for Jerusalem (xx. 3–38). Riot at Jerusalem at Pentecost, and Paul is conveyed a prisoner to Cæsarea (xxi.–xxiii.).		
59	In prison at Cæsarea (xxiv.).		Epistles to Philemon, to Colossians and to Ephesians. The Gospel of St. Luke composed at the advice of St. Paul.
60	In the autumn sails for Rome (xxv.–xxvii.).	Festus procurator, 60–62.	
61	In spring arrives in Rome (xxviii.).		
62	Detained prisoner in Rome (xxviii. 30).		Epistle to Philippians. Pastoral epistles.
63	Record in Acts closes.		
64	(Release of Paul before the burning of Rome.)	Burning of Rome, July 19–25. Persecution in Rome.	
65	Confirming the Churches.		
(?) 66	Paul beheaded.		
circ. 79	Date of the composition of the Acts of the Apostles.		

CHAPTER I

THE TWELVE

The Twelve limited in their education—The Pentecostal Gift gave zeal and spiritual force, but could not supply educational defects—A possible scheme suggested—The important work effected by the Twelve—Paul's work supplemented theirs—The history of Rabbinism—Training of the memory among the Jews—Importance of this for the Twelve—And that they should remain in Jerusalem—Further account of Rabbinism—Illustration of Rabbinic interpretation—The great achievement of the Pharisees—To them was due the unique position of the Jewish nation—Defects in their system—Hatred of the Gentiles—The degradation of the High-priesthood—This tended to make the Synagogue the religious centre—May have helped on the progress of the Gospel—The material on which the Twelve had to work—The proselytes—Cause of the attraction of Mosaism—Few heathens became fully incorporated—Proselytes of the Gate—Spread of Jewish customs in the Old World—The Diaspora—Jews in Alexandria—In Rome—Relaxation of strictness of observance—The fitness of Paul for the office of Apostle to the Diaspora and their converts.

THE Apostles of Jesus Christ were drawn from the humblest class: some were fishermen, one a tax-gatherer, all without more education than such as was afforded in the Jewish schools, an education calculated to contract the brain and envelop the heart in a cobweb of prejudice that would impede its pulsation.

They had never been brought into contact with the men outside the prickly hedge of the Law; they knew nothing of the practical common-sense of the Roman, the subtle and searching mind of the Greek. They had probably never heard of the great river of philosophy that flowed through the classic world. Plato, that searcher after God, was unknown to them even by name, and their early training had been such as to wholly unfit them to understand the nature and to measure the force of that stream when brought to look upon it.[1]

At Pentecost, indeed, the souls of the Eleven had been flushed with the Holy Ghost, and the divine illumination had lifted their mental and spiritual powers to the highest degree of exaltation attainable by them. But a vessel cannot be filled with more fluid than it is calculated to hold. The gift could not have supplied them with what they had not previously gained—experience of the Gentile mind, knowledge of its cravings, experience bred of association, and with that, sympathy, which springs out of such association.

Had the extension of the "kingdom" been left to the first Apostles, it might have assumed a very different form from that it took in the sequel.

In a future chapter I will endeavour to show how that *possibly* the divine intention may have been to retain the Jewish nation as the great evangelising power in the world, so that through the seed of Abraham all generations of men, all the nations on earth, might be blessed in a fuller and more perfect manner than actually took place. For such a work the Twelve would have sufficed. But as

---

[1] In Acts iv. 13, the Apostles are spoken of as "unlearned" and "ignorant." The word ἰδιῶται is incorrectly translated "ignorant," as it really means "laymen." The Jews regarded all those who were not trained in the schools of the rabbis as uneducated, although they might have picked up some knowledge of the Law in the village schools which, by a law enacted by Simon Ben Shelach, all Jewish children were bound to attend.

the divine plan, supposing it was such, was frustrated by the stubbornness wherewith the Jew refused to accept the glorious mission, then the work of evangelisation had to be effected by other means; and an apostle of another description from that of the Twelve became necessary.

Paul, indeed, was not quite all that could have been desired, for he was out of touch with the intellectual life of the classic world; but he had sympathies wider than the other Apostles, and a somewhat more vigorous intellect. Above all, he was a Hellenic Jew, one born out of Judea, and, in addition, a Roman citizen; so that, if out of intellectual, he was at all events in political, sympathy with the ruling power.

It would have been vastly difficult for the Apostles at Jerusalem to overcome their prejudice against the Gentiles, and they had not the experience in dealing with inquirers from among the heathen that was possessed by the Hellenic Jews.

In the sequel I trust to be able to show how very important a work was really effected by the Twelve, for which they are not given credit—how that, in fact, Paul's work was supplemental to theirs. He has had the advantage, not shared by them, of having a biographer, devoted in his admiration. Consequently he has been given a position in the history of the development of the Church to their disadvantage.

It is necessary, in order to understand the mental condition of the Jew when the Gospel was first preached, to take a survey of the rise of Rabbinism. In China but one daughter in a family has her feet systematically deformed to prevent her from walking. In Jewry every man-child had his brains contracted till they became incapable of liberal thought and of generous emotion.

In one of Marryat's novels, the father of the hero is represented as the inventor of an apparatus by means of which certain non-existent bumps in the head might be artificially raised, and certain existing protuberances might also be reduced. The entire energy and ingenuity of the sopherim or scribes, since the Captivity, had been directed to the contrivance of a similar moral and intellectual apparatus; and this apparatus was the school, with its continuation, the synagogue.

There was nothing wanton and arbitrary in this. It was forced on the rulers as the only method attainable for the preservation of the national religion and character. Before the Captivity, the people had shown a strange hankering for the paganism that surrounded them. They were mingled with the heathen and learned their manners. But after the return from exile, all this ceased. Having no political independence, and living under a governor, they sought in the Law the support of their nationality, and zealously carried out its precepts as far as was practicable. But the conditions were different from what they had been. Formerly they were an agricultural people: their life had been simple and the horizon of their ideas limited. They had been unreflective and unphilosophical. In Babylon they were brought into connexion with a people standing on the higher intellectual stage, a people of many sciences, of splendid culture, of great political importance, and of considerable commercial energy. Inevitably this connexion altered their character. They were as surely humiliated by their sense of inferiority as by the fact of their captivity. They observed the commerce of the Babylonians, took it to heart, and when they returned to their own land it was with the resolve that they would become traders. The bed of their intellectual life had deepened; they became reflective, and in their impatience at their political humiliation built their hope, and satisfied their pride, on the prophecies of a coming Messiah and a restoration of their political splendour and importance.

On the return to the land of Covenant, the first measures adopted by Ezra and Nehemiah were to require the people to put away their strange wives, and then in combination to rebuild the wall of Jerusalem. This was a figure of the direction thenceforth given to the national character: the Jew was to be cut off from all association with the heathen, every thread of sympathy was to be snapped, and he was to labour at the erection of an impenetrable hedge about him, not so much as a protection against the irruptions of the Gentiles as to prevent the breaking forth of those within. The prophet was no more, he was supplanted by the schoolmaster, and what the prophet had failed to effect by the blast of inspired declamation, that the schoolmaster achieved by dry routine.

In olden times, while the children of Israel still possessed a national kingdom, they had felt their isolation keenly; the Law had been an oppressive yoke to them, which they bore impatiently, and endeavoured repeatedly to shake off. They wanted to live as did those about them, to eat, drink and intermarry with them. But now there ensued a complete change in this respect, they devoted their entire energy to the erection of an insurmountable barrier between them and the nations around, and this barrier was "the hedge of the Law."

In consequence of the break-up of the Persian empire, Judæa in time became an integral portion of the Syrian empire under Seleucus Philopator and Antiochus. These kings promoted the settlement of Greeks and Syrians in Palestine, and a party of Jews threw off more or less of their national customs and their exclusiveness and soon became total renegades. The office of High Priest was trafficked for, and was bought by the highest bidder. Consequently the High-priesthood fell into contempt; but the scribes were looked upon as the upholders of the Jewish nationality and guardians of the law.

The Law was given to the Hebrews when they were a pastoral and agricultural people, and it was no longer applicable to them in their new condition as citizens and merchants and handicraftsmen. Life had become more complicated and its conditions were changed. The scribes now undertook to explain the Law so as to meet every contingency. Their judgments were like the precedents in English law courts; they were, however, transmitted orally, and the memory of the scholars was loaded with this mass of traditional interpretation. In later times this was committed to writing and was called the Mishna.

But as the precedents or rather explanations in the Mishna were some times conflicting, at others obscure, and as moreover fresh questions arose demanding further consideration, an additional compilation was made, and this, attached to the Mishna, was entitled the Gemara.

As certain rabbis nevertheless did not understand and explain the Law alike, schools came into existence advocating the principles of particular teachers.

What tended pre-eminently to the popularity of this

teaching was that the office of rabbi or scribe was open to every one, and was not restricted, like the priesthood, to a single tribe. Thence arose the saying that the crown of the kingdom rested in Judah, that of the priesthood was with the seed of Aaron, but that the diadem of the Law was common to all Israel.

The sphere in which the scribe performed his functions was the school first, and then the synagogue. What was brought into life in the former was ripened in the latter.

In the school, the scribe read the text of the Law, and then translated it into the vulgar tongue. Then followed the explanation, according to the tradition of the elders. He exacted of his pupils a retentive memory, and when from the school they passed to become teachers themselves, then it was laid upon them to abstain from independent exegesis. No scripture was of any private interpretation; all was traditional.

"Every disciple is bound to teach in the same words in which his master has taught"; and the highest praise that could be accorded to a scholar was that he resembled a cemented cistern which retained every single drop of water that distilled into it.

In Hindustan, in like manner, that which was required by the Brahmins of their pupils was memory and not reason—memory developed and trained to such exactitude as to preserve intonation and accent as well as the text of the Vedas.

This marvellous discipline of the memory must be considered in relation to the Gospel record and the office of the Twelve. They had accompanied Christ Jesus as disciples, and, like all pupils under a rabbi, they hung on His lips, and retained His teaching to the very words employed. Their great function then, in Jerusalem, was to act as the living depository of the Gospel of Jesus Christ, to repeat with one voice what they had been taught. They were a living Book, twelve synoptic Gospels; and till the Church had begun to expand it was all important that they, as witnesses to Christ's acts, and guardians of His words, should remain in the Holy City.

I do not think that we take sufficiently into consideration the fact of the energy of a nation for several generations being directed towards the discipline of the memory—and its bearing on the formation of the Four Gospels. Through the incessant reading of newspapers and new books, the memory of man in a civilised European nation is reduced to powerlessness. But the Jew was trained to concentrate his attention on every word that fell from his teacher. He was not allowed to write down even notes, everything must be stored in the mind, and everything preserved there literally as spoken by the teacher.

If Rabbinism had done nothing else, we have to thank it for having made accuracy of memory an heriditary power among the Jews, and so given to us a guarantee of the substantial accuracy of the Gospel record.

And we can at once realise what a tremendous testimony to Christ was the presence of twelve certificated witnesses (if I may use the expression), together with some hundreds of others who had heard and seen Christ, but whose reports needed correction and approval by those chosen and set apart to give to the world the authentic record.

At first they no more thought of writing it down than did the Jewish rabbis think of consigning Mishna and Gemara to paper; but as the Church extended, and as the Gentiles were gathered in who had not undergone centuries of discipline to train their memories to accuracy, then it became necessary to issue authenticated narratives of Christ's sayings and doings in written form.

If the Twelve had scattered directly after Pentecost, the great force of their testimony would have been weakened. It was essential that they should remain as a college together for a while.

To return to the narrative of the development of Rabbinism.

The study of the Law became more and more general, and zealously cultivated as the oppression of the rulers became heavier. Indeed, the sole refuge open to the people was in the elucidation of their ancient literature; their only consolation in their sorrow and shame lay in the Messianic prophecies.

The desire to study grew so great, that every man whose circumstances allowed him, regarded it as his highest duty to devote himself to it.

"It was the chief care of the Israelites," says Josephus, "to educate their children aright, and so to imprint the Law in their hearts in childhood, that when asked by any one a question relative to it, every child would answer as readily as if questioned concerning its name."

The more the exegesis of the Law claimed the acuteness of the student to find out new logical subtleties, the greater occasion it gave to ambition to strive after distinction, and consequently it was the only ground on which the Jewish child could acquire fame, the sole field in which his intellectual faculties could exercise themselves. That a great deal of the interpretation was mere hair-splitting is indisputable, and much of the shaping of the Law to adapt it to the circumstances of life in a town was arbitrary and forced.

Nothing indeed was too trivial to be fitted with a rule. Life is made up of little matters. So also there is an unpleasant, animal side to life. The rabbis did not shrink from laying down maxims of conduct for this also—and a good deal of their teaching has to do with what is very disgusting. Yet as there is in man's animal condition such a fact, it had to be provided for.

But an example is better than description, and an illustration is therefore given of the method of scriptural interpretation as practised in the schools.

"It is written, *God is angry every day* (Ps. vii. 11). The question was mooted: For what length of time did His anger last? The reply given was: For a moment only. But then it was further inquired what is the duration of a moment. The answer given was, one 58,888th part of an hour, and this moment of time was conceivable by one man only, Balaam, of whom it is written (Numb. xxiv. 16) that he *knew the knowledge of the Most High*. But it was argued: How is it conceivable that he should know the mysteries of the Most High who could not understand what his ass said? . . . . For what length of time does God's anger endure? For a moment. But how long is that moment? The opinion of the Rabbi Arina is—So long as it takes to utter the word 'moment.' But how do we know that His anger endures for a moment? By the text (Ps. xxx. 5): *His anger endureth but a moment, but in His favour is life.* But at what period of the day or night is this moment of wrath? Afai answers: During the three first hours of the day, when the comb of the cock becomes white, and when he stands on one leg. But, it is further asked, When is it that he stands on one leg? The reply is, At every hour of the day the cock has got red veins in his comb, except only at one—and that is the moment when God is wroth. Then, and then only, those red veins do not show.

"A heretic living hard by the R. Jehoshua, son of Levi, worried him with captious citations from Scripture. Therefore he took a cock, and set the bird between his feet, and fixed his eyes on him, awaiting the proper moment in which to invoke the curse of God. But wearied with watching, Jehoshua fell asleep. Then he concluded from this that such a course is improper, for it is written, *His tender mercies are over all His works* (Ps. cxlv. 9).

"There is a tradition that the R. Meir asserted: When the sun rises, then the kings of the East and West assume their crowns and adore the planet, whereupon the wrath of the Holy One, blessed be He! flames up in a moment."[1]

War, subjection, persecution, had destroyed the buoyancy, had broken the youthful vigour of the Jewish nation, and as its political significance declined, the greater became its intensive activity.

Rabbinical scholasticism was accompanied by asceticism, generally sincere, but also sometimes simulated. The object aimed at was disengagement of the mind from sensual objects, that it might be wholly given up to study.

The Pharisees were not a sect; but the name was applied to those who stood forward in defence of the national religion, customs and existence, against every effort made to destroy them.

The people saw, and rightly appreciated, in the Pharisee the upholder of the national life, the bulwark of the law of

[1] Baracoth, f. 7.

God, and whenever a Pharisee was molested a tumult was provoked.

The splendid constancy of the Pharisees, their dauntless endurance of persecution, justified the respect shown them. During the troubles of the Asmonæan dynasty, and the infamy of the Herodian rule, the Pharisees had suffered frightfully for their conscientiousness. God's cause had been in their hands, and they had not proved unworthy of the trust. When Alexander Jannaeus, the Sadducee, exercised the office of High Priest (B.C. 95), he performed his sacerdotal functions with such ostentatious levity, that the patience of the people gave way, and they pelted him with citrons. Thereupon he charged them with his guards and killed six thousand men in the streets of Jerusalem.

The party of the Pharisees roused the people to resent the insults offered to Jehovah; civil war ensued, which in six years cost the lives of fifty thousand men. The High Priest was victorious in the end, and he caused eight hundred Pharisees to be crucified, and their wives and children to be massacred before their eyes as they hung on their crosses, whilst he caroused with his concubines and enjoyed the shrieks of his victims. It was, again, the Pharisees who had called the people to resistance under Herod the Idumæan, who sold the High-priesthood or thrust into it his own creatures, and then displaced them as his caprice directed; who, moreover, employed Jewish money to build heathen temples and for the solemnisation of games.

Amid all this, the Pharisees remained firm as rocks, and completed the fabric of traditional interpretation of the Law, and entirely preserved Judaism from intermixture with paganism. For this a lasting obligation was due to them; but at the same time they had elaborated such a net of ceremonial formalities as entangled the Jew and hampered his every movement of mind and body.

In Jerusalem, in Judæa, the sense of humiliation to which the Jew was subjected under foreign domination, the bitter wrongs he had undergone, even the interference of the Romans in his internecine quarrels, had bred a feeling of intense resentment, and hatred of the Gentile. There is none of this in the prophets—it was the outgrowth of oppression, and is like that felt by the British of Wales against their Saxon conquerors, in the time of Augustine of Canterbury.

Such then was the temper of mind in the Jewish nation at the time of the Apostles. Everything tended to attach them by every fibre of their hearts to the religion of Moses, and to make them cling to that party which had so nobly vindicated the honour of God, and the sacredness of the vocation of the nation. And this feeling must have been enhanced by the galling sense of the High-priesthood, and all the superior positions in the Temple, in fact the true spiritual headship of the nation, being in the power of the rationalistic, contemptuous and irreligious Sadducees. The situation was much like that of devout Catholics under Sixtus V., Alexander VI., and Julius II. In the abhorrence in which the Sadducean holders of the High-priesthood were held, there was undoubtedly a tendency manifest, though not declared, to form of the Synagogue the religious centre of life in place of the Temple. This was due partly to the disrepute into which the High-priesthood had fallen, partly to the fact that the vast bulk of the Jews no longer lived within access to the Temple, and could reckon on visiting it only occasionally, as Mussulmans visit Mecca.

We find after a few years many Pharisees and priests

joining the Apostles, when they found the disgrace of the condition of affairs in the Temple insupportable. No doubt many clergy and monks joined Luther, not because they believed in his doctrine of justification, but because they despaired of the Papacy. This is one explanation of the progress of the Gospel in Jerusalem.

We will next endeavour to see what was the material upon which it was the mission of the Apostles to work.

First came the Jews—the Pharisees and those who respected the Pharisee, nine-tenths of the population. Of them nothing further need be said. Outside these was the ring of proselytes.

In the attitude of hostility toward Gentiledom assumed by the Jews, one would have supposed that Judaism would have been unsympathetic and repulsive to the Greek and Roman. This, however, was by no means the case. It must be admitted that Judaism did achieve considerable missionary success, due solely to the efforts of the Pharisees, and this is acknowledged even by pagan writers. When Philo says, "The laws of Moses attract the whole world, the barbarian, stranger, and Greek, those who live on the continents and such as inhabit the islands, natives of east and west, of Europe and Asia," he may be suspected of exaggeration. Josephus more modestly says, " Many Greeks have embraced our laws," and he mentions numerous proselytes in Antioch and Damascus. In the latter city, he says, "almost all the women were attached to the Jewish religion." At Antioch in Pisidia the Jews stirred up the women of high rank against the Apostles.

The adoption of Israelitish customs became common in Greek cities. Heathen testimony is hardly open to suspicion. Horace, Dio Cassius, Tacitus remark on the fact that

Judaism possessed an attractive power, and that many pagans were drawn to adopt the laws of Moses. Persius and Juvenal tell us that the Romans themselves were quite as ready as the Greeks to be seduced. The Gospel speaks of the zeal of the Pharisee who compassed sea and land to make one proselyte, at the same time that it allows us to see that the quality of these converts was not good.

The Acts reveal to us the fact that throughout Asia Minor, wherever there was a synagogue, there numbers of pagans were assiduous in their attendance on the public prayers and instructions. Various causes favoured this propaganda: the superiority of monotheism over polytheism, of the Jewish moral code over religions without any ethic standards whatsoever, and the repulsion exercised on the nobler spirits by the licentiousness of the legends of their gods, and the same may be said of the rites connected with their cult. To the naturally modest and instinctively chaste soul of woman, a religion which branded all sensual indulgence possessed a rare attraction. Women who desired to be shielded from the universal corruption, virgins trembling and disgusted at the foulness of pagan life, fled to Mosaism, just as in the turbulent and lawless Middle Ages they hid themselves in the cloister.

Again, there was the attraction of novelty, always great to the idle and the dissatisfied. A fever of curiosity moreover had taken possession of the Roman world precisely at this period, a taste for magic, for occult sciences, clandestine ceremonies, and mystical initiations. To this must be added the effect produced by the forged Sibylline oracles, loudly proclaimed and appealed to, and the manifest sincerity with which the Jews expected the coming of the Messiah and the establishment of His kingdom over all the world.

To a large extent the proselytes were recruited from the lower ranks of the people, especially from those vagabond strangers to whom it offered a religion, a country, and a future. But that which chilled enthusiasm was the severity of the conditions. "The prescriptions of the Law," says Josephus, "are more difficult to endure than the legislation of Lacedæmon," and many converts grew lukewarm, then cold and relapsed. But this was not wholly the case. The Jews were not insensible to the advantage of having adherents among the noble and the rich, not only because of the political influence these could use in their favour, but also because of the money contributions to be exacted from them. Probably those proselytes " of righteousness," of whom Dio, Tacitus, Philo, and Juvenal write, men who divested themselves entirely of the old man to incorporate themselves into the Jewish nation, were few in number.

To become incorporated into the Jewish religion completely was to become antagonistic to the State, as the Roman mind conceived it, to refuse to take part in the customary sacrifices and to swear by the genius of the emperor and of Rome, to refuse homage to the eagles, and to the images of the prince, to abstain from a thousand matters of social and municipal and political custom so intimately linked with religion, that they were inseparable, and must inevitably bring on the Roman citizen who renounced them, the charge of atheism or treason. We do, indeed, hear of an occasional case of this sort, as that of Pomponia Græcina, and later of Flavius Clemens and Acilius Glabrio,[1] but

---

[1] These two latter were, however, Christians and not Jews. Flavia Domitilla, the wife, or perhaps the niece of Clemens, it is doubtful which, gave her vineyard for the use of the Christians as a cemetery. The hypoge of the Acilii has been found lately in connection with the catacomb of St. Priscilla. See " Römische Quartal-Schrift," iv. (1890), p. 305.

they were so rare, that we must conclude that the number of those who entirely united themselves to the Jews were very few indeed. Vastly more numerous were the proselytes " of the gate," uncircumcised, who were required only to believe in one God, and to observe the precepts given to Noah and his sons (Gen. ix. 2–7). The Jews of the straitest observance never looked with a favourable eye on these converts. One whole sect of the Pharisees, that of the disciples of Shammai, strongly opposed the making of proselytes, except of the highest order, who would submit to the whole Law, and they declared that it was due to the influx of these aliens that the delay was occasioned in the coming of the Messiah.

Judaic influence was not limited to the making of converts, it introduced certain of its customs among the heathen, which were adopted unintelligently and without inquiry as to their purport. The Sabbath was observed in Greece and Rome by the pagans, without their knowing wherefore. Josephus says: "One does not find a Greek town, or, for the matter of that, hardly any among the barbarians, in which men do not cease from work on the seventh day, do not light lamps and fast. Many abstain, like us, from eating certain meats, and strive to emulate our unity, our interchange of goods, our industry in the handicrafts, and our constancy in suffering for the observance of our laws." That this is not overdrawn is shown by Persius, and by a well-known saying of Seneca. The latter blames a custom which he admits has become almost universal.

And now—it may well be asked, "How is it possible that Jews, despising and hating the Gentiles, should labour to convert them?" To understand this we must remember that the Jewish people was cleft into two portions—that which remained in the Holy Land, and that which was of the Dispersion. All the missionary work was done by the latter.

The dispersion of the Hebrews through east and west was not a result of the destruction of Jerusalem. It dated, perhaps, from the conquests of Alexander, probably from before, and was an accomplished fact in the century of Augustus. The war of extermination under Titus, waged in Palestine, changed the general situation but slightly. The Macedonian conqueror, flushed with the victory he had gained over Tyre, came to Jerusalem, where he was received with acclamations, and the High Priest, with politic complaisance, showed him the Messianic prophecies, and interpreted them as finding their fulfilment in himself. The Jews eagerly invoked his aid to wreak their long harboured revenge against Babylon; they strengthened his hands by sending reinforcements to his aid, and inflated his confidence by assurances of success.

Whether Alexander divined the commercial aptitude of the Jews, or whether, as is more probable, he assisted and accelerated a movement of emigration already begun, can not be said; but when he founded the city to be called by his name, at the mouth of the Nile, in the depth of the Mediterranean basin, he invited to it a colony of Jews.

In Alexandria they speedily became so numerous, that they occupied two out of the five quarters of the city. They became vastly wealthy, monopolised the navigation of the Nile, and the corn trade. Antioch had been given the right of citizenship by Seleucus. The Jews had planted themselves there in considerable numbers, and drew to themselves the trade that passed through this town. They had spread into Asia Minor, and set up their counters wherever ran the lines of commerce, and where the counters were, large communities grew up with schools and synagogues.

Rome, the centre of the world, could not remain without a settlement of Jewish usurers and merchants. Horace had a friend who was a Jew, and the empress Livia a confidant who belonged to that nation. But in the imperial city they never became as wealthy and powerful as in Alexandria; they obtained a livelihood as actors, fortune-tellers, and engaged in petty trades.

The disrepute into which the High-priesthood had fallen had relaxed its controlling power over the Jew; and the Synagogue became the centre of religious life in place of the Temple. To the latter the Jew continued to make his annual pilgrimage, but it had ceased to engage his respect and affection, to a large degree, and the Synagogue had become the predominant factor in his religious life; and as a synagogue could be established anywhere, it served to give to the Jew a feeling that he was at home even in the midst of Gentiledom. He still, indeed, entertained a lofty contempt for the religion, manner of life, even the persons of the heathen; but for the sake of gain the Jew condescended to associate with them, and took their money without scruple, though stamped with idolatrous figures, and coming from contaminating hands.

Lucri bonus est odor ex re qualibet.

But the very fact of living in the midst of those of another race and creed, of daily exchange of courtesies, of occasional reception of good offices, must tend to corrode prejudice and soften harshness of feeling. And the evidence that such was the case is seen in the great numbers of converts made; for the Jew would not have striven to bring the Gentile within the fold, unless he had been moved towards him by pity and regard.

We are accordingly led to see that if, in the divine purpose, the Gentiles were to be gathered into the Church, the proper agent for carrying to them the summons, "Come, for all things are now ready," would be a man of the Diaspora (Dispersion), one who, though a Jew by birth, had been brought up among the Gentiles, and not only knew them, but had a heart full of tenderness towards them.

CHAPTER II

TARSUS

A.D. 4—20

The province of Cilicia—The delta of the Pyramus and Sarus—Tarsus —On the high road to the East—The manufacture of cilicium— Troubles from robbers and pirates—A municipium—Past history— Population mixed—The trade of Tarsus—The University—The Cydnus—Unhealthiness of the delta—Date of Paul's birth—Roman citizenship—Relic of St. Paul at Tarsus—The names of Saul and Paul—Early life at Tarsus—Jews kept apart from the Greeks— Strong anti-Gentile feeling—Paul unlikely to have associated with the Greek students—Importance of education to a Jew—Revulsion in later times in Paul's mind against Judaic strictness—Paul sent to Jerusalem for his education—The two schools of Hillel and Shammai—Gamaliel—Disputes between the schools—Mode of interpretation of Scripture.

LIKE the Swiss canton of Appenzell, the province of Cilicia is divided into two strongly characterised regions, the one Alpine, barren, culminating in snowy peaks tenanted by rugged mountaineers, pasturing droves of goats and wild Cappadocian cobs, with a disposition for brigandage, under favouring circumstances. The other is level, fertile as the Garden of Eden, dense with an agricultural and peaceful population. The latter is a Mesopotamia in miniature, a rich alluvial delta of two rivers, the Pyramus and Sarus.

At one time, very remote, the whole of this tract was sea, a gulf running deeper inland than that of Iskanderun, but that was at the dawn of the Drift period, before the rise of the veil of history.

The great plain of rich red deposit, dashed with black humus, and streaked, where the Cydnus rolls down its limestone rubble, with white, is watered by canals, these combed out into countless flossy rills, and was of inexhaustible fertility. In February it was flushed pink with almond blossom, and was fragrant with citron flowers. It produced groves of oaks and mulberries, the dark green foliage broken at intervals by the silvery grey of the olive, rising above the verdure like puffs of wood smoke.

The capital, Tarsus, to the west of this delta, planted on the Cydnus, that flowed athwart the city, was sheltered from the north by the serrated range now called the Bulghar Dagh. The town lay in a position of commanding importance for traffic. It had its port a few miles below, on the Mediterranean, through which trade was carried on with Egypt, Cyprus, and Palestine. It lay on the main road along which travelled the merchandise of the East to the markets of the West, and where marched the cohorts of Rome destined for the garrisons of Syria.

From Tarsus started the highway that threaded the mountain passes by the Cilician Gates—a natural portal—to Central Asia Minor, to Phrygia and Lycaonia on one side, and to Cappadocia on the other.

The paved road crossing the plain, straight as an arrow, passing by bridges over the two rivers, was trodden incessantly by caravans and by troops, by the imperial post, and by peasants and mountaineers laden with the produce of the plains and the yield of the rock fastnesses.

The suburbs of the town abounded in taverns, where sailors and soldiers, muleteers, and peasants roystered and drank; and Egyptian or Greek dancing-girls entertained them to the twanging of a rote or the tinkle of a systrum.

One whole quarter was devoted to the manufacture of hair-cloth, called cilicium, and to tanning. There sounded incessantly the rattle of the loom and the thumping of rolled river pebbles used by the fellers in making skins flexible.

The cloth made of goat's hair was a staple of manufacture in Tarsus, and this material took its name from the province which furnished both the raw material and the fabricated stuff. This dark cloth was employed almost universally for the coarse habits worn by fishermen and sailors, as being impervious to wet, and of imperishable endurance. It was likewise used for horsecloths, tents, and sacks. Gaily dyed, it was the substance of which the Phrygian cap was shaped.

The mountains of Cilicia maintained vast herds of long-haired goats, that furnished the cloth-weavers of Tarsus with the hair, the tanners with the skins, and the victuallers with cheese.

Cyprian copper found its way to Tarsus for combination with tin from the mines inland, to make the precious amalgam bronze.

At one time wickerwork helmets, covered with felt, and the whole studded with bronze rosettes, formed a peculiar manufacture in this portion of the peninsula, and these caps travelled far into the centre of Europe.[1]

But the prosperity of Tarsus had long been held in check by the pirates who infested the Pamphylian sea, cruising up and down the Cilician straits, and falling on the merchant vessels that slipped across the Gulf of Issus; also by the organised bands of robbers in the mountains, who plundered the caravans, or took toll of such as they suffered to wend their way through the fastnesses.

[1] "L'Anthropologie," 1896, t. vii. p. 270.

The strong hands of Augustus and Cyrenius had tamed the insolence of the mountaineers; Pompey and Cæsar had destroyed the piratical fleets, and had hung and crucified the pirates. Consequently, in the first century, Tarsus was enjoying unexampled tranquillity and the prosperity that ensues from it. The wealthy citizens could retire from the heats of summer to their villas on the high ground without fear of molestation, and the passes guarded by forts were open to the trader.

It was not surprising that the city looked with gratitude to the imperial house, and was staunch in its loyalty. The Cæsars in return made Tarsus a *municipium*, but did not accord it the rights of a colony; it was given the same privileges as Antioch in Syria—it elected its own magistrates and was not burdened with a garrison. Cilicia had passed under many masters; it had at one time been held by Egypt, then by the Assyrian, next by the Persian; it had become a portion of the Græco-Syrian kingdom, and had finally been incorporated as a province into the Roman Empire. The population was mixed. An Argive colony was planted there under the mythical leader Perseus. Undoubtedly the Phœnicians had frequented its market and had established there their warehouses. Sardanapalus, King of Assyria, was said to have rebuilt the town, and to have died there. A mass of rubble masonry, cased in marble, was shown outside one of the gates as his tomb, and it bore a later inscription in Greek, that told how the great king had built the city in one day, and concluded with the cynical address: "Passer-by, eat. drink, laugh. All else profiteth nothing."

In the streets, in the market, all nations met, jostled, and talked in a babel of many tongues. There were beautiful straight-nosed, oval-faced Greeks, bullet-headed Romans, dark-eyed Armenians, fair-haired fresh-looking Celts from Galatia, and sallow, almond-eyed men of Turanian ancestry.

Huge convoys of goods passed through the town, silks from Persia, spices from India, metals from the Taurian mines, gangs of Parthian slaves. Not only did the manufacturers supply sack-cloth, but also skins to serve as bottles for the transport of wine, and for the covering of machines of war. *Murex* arrived from Tyre, cochineal from Armenia, and the peasants brought in saffron for the dye works. A brisk exchange of Oriental and Occidental coinage went on at the offices of the money-changers; and not a little of the vast harvests of barley produced by the alluvial plain found its way to Rome through the hands of the Jewish corn-dealers.

But Tarsus was something more than an emporium of trade. It was a centre of intellectual life.

The schools there rivalled those of Athens and Alexandria. The poet Aratus was a Cilician, though not a native of Tarsus. He had composed a poem on natural science, in the third century before our era, which Cicero translated into Latin. The fame of the Tarsian philosophers, grammarians, and orators reached Rome, and thence was drawn the stoic Athenadorus, preceptor of Octavius, and the academician Nestor.

Tarsus was moreover a focus of religious life. In it were temples to many gods, to Athene, Heracles, and Apollo, but the chief cult was that of Baal. The recent apotheosis of Augustus had led to a great explosion of religious enthusiasm; a temple had been erected to him, and for the moment his worship was the fashion.

Tarsus was "no mean city," it had its theatre, race-course, baths. Probably, like Pompeiopolis and Adona, the main street was lined with colonnades, in which the citizens walked in shade, and inhaled the sea breeze that blew inland daily an hour before noon.

The river Cydnus, clear from its cavern sources in the limestone, traversed the city, with a waft of cool air above it. Precautions had been adopted against flood by the formation of relief channels above the town; very necessary, for at the melting of the snows on the mountains, or after a cloud-break, the river became a torrent.

Turkish misrule has allowed these canals to become choked, and now ancient Tarsus is embedded in nearly 20ft. of rubble and mud brought down by freshets. The modern hovels cluster about the capitals of pillars, and stand on the crowns of buried arches.

The great plain, which it takes fourteen hours to cross, is mainly composed of the wash of the red conglomerate of the New Red sandstone, brought down by the Pyramus and the Sarus, but this is further enriched by volcanic detritus, and is overlaid in places with black mud, the result of centuries of decomposed water-weed. The plain is unhealthy, it is a hotbed of malaria and low fever; but it was more salubrious in classic times, when attention was directed to the channels of irrigation and to the drainage. Nevertheless, it was never a safe district in which to tarry after sunset, and large artificial mounds were thrown up at intervals as places of refuge for the peasants who cultivated the land, where they might spend their nights above the malarial steams.

Here almost anything grew—cereals, fruit, flowers. Mulberries and vines were cultivated; crimson clover grew rank, spreading in sheets of blood, alternating with blue rippling fields of flax. The meadows offered to the weavers of carpets patterns of harmonious colours in marvellous mixture, produced by the marigold, the poppy, and the intensely blue bugloss; fluttered over by a thousand living flowers, the butterflies as gorgeous as the petals above which they danced.

Such was the Tarsus where Paul was born about the year A.D. 4. He was of the tribe of Benjamin, a Hebrew of the Hebrews, and his parents were zealous adherents of the Pharisaic faction.

Undoubtedly there was, at this time, in Tarsus a Jewish colony rivalling those of Damascus and Antioch in size. Perhaps the Jews had been first led to establish themselves there as a place of refuge, during the wars of Pompey, Gabinius or Cassius. By what means the father of Paul acquired the right of Roman citizenship is not known. Such a right did not belong to the inhabitants of the town, and it must have been either purchased or granted as a reward for services rendered. The privilege was one greatly desired by Provincials, and was rare among the Jews. It has been conjectured that the father of the Apostle was a freedman, who had obtained his title of citizen along with his freedom. The Romans had carried away a great number of Jews after their intervention in Palestine. Cassius conveyed 30,000 from Jarichæa, and Antonius by decree gave their freedom to such of the natives of Tarsus as had fallen into captivity and had been sold away from their home. When Paul was in Jerusalem we are expressly told that there were at the time in the holy city, among many strangers, "freedmen of Cilicia," and it is possible that among these he may have been numbered. By trade he was a tent-maker, that is to say a weaver of the goats' hair cloth that was used as a covering for tents.

But a single relic in Tarsus at the present day preserves a reminiscence of the great Apostle, and that is a well. Into this a French explorer descended, and found that the water issued from an arched conduit which bore a Greek inscription, almost illegible, but in which he was able to decipher the name of Paul. It is probable enough, that after the conversion of the family their house became the centre of the young Christian community, and that in later days a church was erected on the site; and that this spring may have formed a feeder to the baptistery. But this must remain a matter of conjecture. Some day perhaps Tarsus may be excavated from the mud and pebbles that have buried it, and then possibly some evidences will be discovered of the Church here established, if not by the Apostle, then soon after his time, and that in his ancestral house.

It was a duty imposed on every Jewish father to circumcise his son, to teach him the Law, and to apprentice him to a trade. Accordingly on the eighth day Paul fulfilled the legal requirements, and he was given a double name, that of Saul, by which he was known in the family, and among his co-religionists, and that of Paul for municipal registration. The one was his religious, the other his profane name. This was by no means an unusual practice, and often that profane name was adopted which bore some resemblance in sound to the name used in the family and the synagogue, as Joseph-Jason, Hillel-Julius. The adoption of Greek names was general among those of the Diaspora, and some of the Jews who were converted are known to us by these only, as Crispus, Justus, Niger, Drusilla, Aquila and Apelles.

At five years old Paul began to read the Scriptures, at thirteen he studied them with the interpretations of the elders; at sixteen he was declared to be "subject to the Law," that is to say, capable of understanding it, and bound by its obligations. Was he, during his youth, associated with the students in the schools under the Greek dialecticians, philosophers and grammarians? It is most unlikely that he was. His parents were strict Pharisees, and the Pharisee was uncompromising in the attitude he took up towards Greek studies.

As far as might be, the orthodox Jews of the Dispersion lived apart from the Gentiles, following their own religious and national customs, walled off from them, to use St. Paul's own expression, by their pride and exclusiveness.

It was held to be a crime to contract friendship with one who was a heathen, to enter his house, and to sit at his table.

"I will buy with you, sell with you, talk with you, and so following; but I will not eat with you, drink with you, nor pray with you." Shylock did not deviate by a thread from the sentiment of the father of Paul of Tarsus.

On leaving the market or the street, the Hebrew washed his hands, to wash off the contamination of having touched what had been fingered by the uncircumcised. The Jews scattered through the cities of Asia Minor entertained for the most part the same prejudices, observed the same isolation as those in Judæa. They stood outside all the social, political and intellectual life of their time. They refused to see, to hear, to know anything that did not emanate from one of themselves, or advance their own profits. The use of wood from a Gentile forest, whether for building or for fuel, was forbidden, but could not be enforced among the Jews of the Dispersion.

The uncircumcised were excluded from all sympathy, and this estrangement grew gradually to an intensity of hatred, that drove the doctors to pronounce really atrocious judgments, as "the Israelite who kills a stranger is not put to death by the Sanhedrim, because the Gentile is not to be accounted as a neighbour," and, "if a Gentile fall into the sea, a Jew is not to pull him out; for it is written, *Thou shalt not be guilty of thy neighbour's blood*, but the Gentile is not thy neighbour."

The Synagogue decreed, "Cursed be he that shall teach Greek science to his son." Josephus assures us that those in Judæa who knew many languages were looked upon with mistrust. Jews whether at home or scattered abroad, felt, thought and acted alike. The interdict was indeed lifted from the Greek tongue, as also from traffic with strangers, and for the same reason, but all the Hellenistic Jews, to the number of three millions, who made the annual pilgrimage to Jerusalem to keep the Passover, differed from the Hebrews resident in the Holy Land in no other particular than that of language. To both alike Hebrew was a dead tongue, but the former spoke Greek and the latter Chaldee. At Alexandria, indeed, a conciliatory movement had been made. The Alexandrian Alabarc, Alexander Lysimachus, was a Jew and belonged to a sacerdotal family. He was intimate with Antonia, mother of Germanicus and Claudius, and one of his sons married Berenice, another, Tiberius Alexander, became governor of Judæa. His brother, Philo, laboured to harmonise the Mosaic law with the philosophy of Plato. But the true

Jew looked with the utmost repugnance on this attempt, and the Alexandrian school was denounced as a nest of heresy. The Septuagint version of the Scriptures was allowed currency, but all tampering with the philosophic ideas of the Greek was formally condemned.

It is unnecessary to inquire to what extent the conciliatory attempt of Philo met with approval in other colonies. Nothing leads us to suppose that St. Paul knew anything about it. Indeed, it is not probable that Philo's works were written when he was at Tarsus.

That among the Jews of the Dispersion there were many who were by no means strict in their adhesion to the Law, and above all to the traditions of the rabbis, is true enough; but Paul would be kept from associating with them by his strict father.

That he should have been in any way brought in contact with the current and eddies of thought among the Greek students is utterly improbable.

In an English University the town tradesmen do not concern themselves about the curriculum of studies in the schools, nor fall upon the examination papers with avidity. Much less likely was the Jew weaver (σκηνοποιός) at Tarsus to trouble his head about the disputes among the philosophers in the town.

That he took pains to have his son educated cannot be doubted any more than that the direction of these studies was remote from those of the students in the porches and academies.

Among the rabbis teaching was held to be of supreme importance. "Perish the sanctuary," they said, "but let the children go to school."

The first public school for young boys had been founded

at Jerusalem a century before Christ. It is not probable that there was an elementary school at Tarsus in Paul's time. He learned texts of his mother, and the interpretations from his father, but as he advanced he would be placed under instruction in the traditions, with the ruler of the synagogue.

One thing that was of supreme importance to him in after life and for the work to which he was to be called, Paul did acquire at Tarsus—the Greek language, which was spoken in his family and in the colony. He did not gain that elegance and Attic polish which is only to be obtained by acquaintance with the best models, but he acquired that facility which is procurable only by familiar usage.

The Rabbi Judah said: "If a man does not teach his son a trade, it is as if he taught him to steal." Thus every Jew had his trade, and usually it was that of his father. It is, therefore, probable that the tentcloth weaving which Paul acquired he acquired from his father; and as he worked at the loom, the old Pharisee laboured to weave as well his prejudices, interpretations, hatreds and likings into the texture of his son's mind.

It is a remarkable fact that when a man deserts the religion of his youth, the swing of the pendulum is to the opposite extreme. One who has been brought up in the straitest school of Calvinistic Presbyterianism, if he breaks away, will seek his rest in Ultramontane Catholicism, and a Romanist who rejects the creed of Pius IV., will fall into Socinianism. One again whose childhood has been restrained by the harshest bonds, when obtaining freedom does not acknowledge any restraining tie; and another who has been awarded wide liberty will seek the satisfaction of his deepest needs in the abnegation of his will and renunciation of all pleasures.

We can tolerably well measure the extent of deflexion given a mind in youth by the amount of recoil in after years.

Paul launched out against the narrowness of Judaic interpretation of duty, with a vehemence almost fury that makes one suspect that this was due to revulsion against a system which had tortured his growing mind.

From Tarsus Paul was sent to Jerusalem, to become the disciple of Gamaliel. We may judge from his own words (Acts xxii. 3) that he was still young when he made the journey; he was probably sixteen. At Jerusalem he had a married sister, and with her he almost certainly lodged.

It was his father's ambition that he should be brought up to be a rabbi, and he was therefore sent to the fountain head of instruction.

At Jerusalem, among the sticklers for the Law combined to resist the Sadducees tooth and nail, were two parties, the one a little less narrow than the other. The former was that of Hillel, the latter that of Shammai. "One day a Gentile came to Shammai, and said to him : 'I will be a convert if you can teach me the Law while standing on one foot.' Shammai for all answer struck him with his staff. The Gentile went to Hillel and put to him the same question. Hillel replied : 'Do nothing to thy neighbour that thou wouldest not he should do to thee; this is the whole Law: all the rest follows therefrom."

This may be said to be the key to Hillel's principle; but he carried his laxity somewhat far. Shammai insisted that no man should divorce his wife except in the case of adultery; but Hillel allowed a man to repudiate her if she "spoiled the roast" and proved a sorry cook.

Gamaliel was the grandson of Hillel, and followed him as a teacher. Hillel though somewhat liberal was so only in comparison with Shammai. Each concerned himself with trumpery questions, to the omission of the weightier matters of the Law. The party of Shammai held that the hands must be washed before a cup was filled with wine, for that otherwise the cup and its contents were rendered unclean by the perspiration from the fingers clinging to the vessel. But the party of Hillel insisted that this was not so, and there was a greater cause for fear lest the cup should contaminate the perspiration of the fingers. Therefore, they declared that the hands should be washed after the vessel had been filled.[1] The adherents of Shammai taught that after the hands were wiped the towel should be put on the table and not on a cushion, lest the sweat from the hands should taint the cushion, which would in turn defile whatever touched it. But Hillel and his school taught that it was a serious matter to put the dirty towel on the table, for the table might render the towel unclean, and so infect with legal impurity the perspiration, and through the perspiration, the hands wiped upon it.[2]

Another matter of dispute between the two teachers was whether the hands should be washed before using the broom to sweep the house, or after the sweeping was done.

Once more. Another matter in dispute between these schools was whether light was one or many; whether, that is, the light of the sun, and of the stars, the lightning and the flame were one in nature, or distinct.

Gamaliel, son of Simeon and grandson of Hillel, was

[1] Beracoth, f. 52.   [2] *Ibid.*

esteemed the last of the great rabbis of Israel; and it was even said that the honour of the Law ceased with his death. Before his time the teacher stood to instruct; he introduced the novelty of sitting to give his lessons. Owing to the troubles caused by Judas of Galilee, the founder of the Gaulonite sect from which sprung the Zelots, and by Theudas, as also by the spread of Christianity, Gamaliel composed a prayer for the extirpation of heresy. From the instances given of his teaching preserved in the Talmud, he seems to have been a man of a fairly liberal mind, and yet a stickler for tradition. He asserted that the evening prayer was a matter of duty not of option, and this was disputed by the Rabbi Jehoshua. "Always get an authority to quiet your doubts," he laid down; but he added, "In the matter of tithing grain do it by eye." The night after his wife died he took a bath. His disciples were greatly scandalised; they charged him with infringement of the Law. "Suffer me," said he, "I am an old man and not like others." His servant died, and he at once admitted his friends into the house to condole with him. Again his disciples were offended. "What," said they, "have you not taught us not to seek consolation when we lose our servants?" "Ah!" he replied, "my man Tabi was not like others—he was a very worthy fellow."

At the feet of this master Saul of Tarsus sat. The pupils were allowed great liberty of discussion; they might dispute the opinions enunciated by the rabbi, but then they must give a reason for so doing, based on a text. These animated debates, and the treatment of subjects often very subtle, kept interest alive and stimulated the ingenuity of the pupils.

A short example of one of these disputes, at which

possibly Paul was present, may serve to show their nature.

One day there came an Ammonite convert to the door of the school, and sought admittance. Gamaliel, who was giving instruction, at once forbade his entrance, "for," said he, "it has been commanded (Deut. xxiii. 3), *An Ammonite or Moabite shall not enter into the congregation of the Lord.*" The Rabbi Jehoshua, who was present, objected that the man could no longer be termed an Ammonite, because Sennacherib, King of Assyria, had removed the Ammonites out of their land, and that these thus removed had lost their nationality; as it was written: *I have removed the bounds of the people* (Is. x. 13). That is to say, every mark of distinction. The Ammonite had, he went on to argue, abandoned his idolatry and separated himself from his people. But Gamaliel met this objection by another text (Jeremiah xlix. 6). *Afterward I will bring again the captivity of the children of Ammon, saith the Lord.* Consequently, they are returned and still distinct. The Rabbi Jehoshua then said: "Has it not been said (Amos ix. 14), *I will bring again the captivity of my people of Israel*, yet the Israelites are not brought back; and he tacked on a few words in gloss not in the original text; *they shall return, and the Ammonites also.* Consequently, the restoration of the Ten Tribes was to precede that of Ammon.[1]

It will be seen that this is mere hair-splitting. No argument was based on broad principles; all rested on texts twisted and turned about to suit the purpose of the disputants.

St. Paul never emancipated himself from this Rabbinic

[1] Babyl. Beracoth, fol. 28.

method of reasoning.[1] Nor was the tendency to allegorical or mystical interpretation effaced.[2]

At the same time, it is worthy of remark how very little of all this remains. For a time his mind was overloaded with this teaching, but he finally rejected it.

[1] Rom. xi. 4, 8, 9, 10, 26; xii. 19; xv. 3; 1 Cor. i. 31; 2 Cor. iv. 13; Gal. iii. 10.
[2] Gal. iv. 24, 25; 1 Cor. ix. 9.

CHAPTER III

THE DEATH OF STEPHEN

A.D. 35

Paul not at Jerusalem at the time of the Baptist's preaching, or of Christ's ministry—His return to Tarsus—His qualifications—Paul's mind warped by his education—The citizenship of Paul's father qualified him to take a municipal office—Possible reaction in the mind of Paul—His quotations from the poets—The Church in Jerusalem—Authorities employed by St. Luke—James, the Lord's brother—His position—As supreme bishop—Tradition quoted by Apollonius—Why the Apostles did not separate at once—The Gospel preached first to the Jews—Probability that God designed the Gospel to be made known to the world through the Jew—Frustrated by the obduracy of the Jew—The importance of Jerusalem as a missionary centre—God seems to have two ways of working, a higher and a lower—If through man's wilfulness the higher cannot be taken, then God carries out His purpose by the lower means—Application of this theory—The Church at Jerusalem observant of the Mosaic ritual—The point of difference with the Pharisees—The appointment of Deacons—The character of Stephen's preaching—Paul now at Jerusalem—Arrest of Stephen—His so-called defence—Analysis—Its offensive character—Difference between Peter and Stephen—The Deacon's death—Paul's conversion not due to Stephen—Massacre at Samaria—Dispersion of the Brethren.

For how long time Saul remained in Jerusalem we cannot tell. If he arrived there in or about A.D. 18, he must have left before A.D. 27, which is the date of the Baptist's preaching, for he makes no allusion to it in his Epistles, and he can not have returned till after the Crucifixion, which probably took place A.D. 30, or we should have some words employed in his writings to show that he was present, and a partaker in the bloodguiltiness of those participating in that drama.

Had Paul[1] been in Jerusalem at the time of the Baptist's preaching, it is inconceivable that he should not have gone out into the wilderness to hear him, and he could hardly have heard him without being influenced by his words.

Where the dates are so uncertain, it is not possible to advance further than this.

After having sat at the feet of Gamaliel for some eight years, he returned to Tarsus, to his father's house and to the work of sack-cloth weaving. He was now a man of some consequence. In the synagogue he had a claim to be heard, as a pupil of Gamaliel. He was able to give a reason why Psalm iii. written by David when flying before Absalom precedes Psalm lvii. composed when hiding from Saul;[2] also to explain the principle on which when praying in a bath the orthodox Jew was required to kick about his heels so as to ruffle the water.[3] He could strengthen the hands of the Hillelites, who, on kindling the lamps, blessed God for the *light* not *lights* He had created.

Too much stress has been laid on the liberality of Gamaliel, as one of the causes influencing the mind of Paul. But Paul never had a liberal mind; it was essentially narrow and one-sided. He swung from one pole to the other in his convictions, but he never saw more than one horizon at a time, never allowed gradations; but of this

---

[1] I use the name Paul generally in place of Saul, as I consider that it belonged to him equally with that of Saul from the beginning, and that the transition from the Hebrew to the Gentile name in the Acts merely notes the transfer of his activities from Palestine to the Gentile world.

[2] Beracoth, f. 10.   [3] *Ibid.* f. 25.

more hereafter. Gamaliel was, indeed, more lax in his adhesion to certain moral principles and traditional usages than were others. But when a question arose relative to heresy his blood turned to phosphorus. The curse he composed to be learned by heart and used as a prayer by the believing Jew is as hateful as a mediæval ecclesiastical anathema, or as a sentence of outlawry pronounced by a Scandinavian lawman. But although in his own home as at Jerusalem, Saul was subjected to the numbing effect of Rabbinism, yet in a provincial town out of Judæa it was not possible to keep altogether isolated from the Greek world of thought and feeling, and from Roman political ideas.

As his father was a citizen and he likewise, they were not mere residents (πάροικοι) of Tarsus, but enjoyed the privileges and position of Roman citizenship. This implied "a certain attitude of friendliness towards the Imperial Government (for the new citizens in general, and the Jewish citizens in particular, were warm partisans of their protector, the new Imperial *régime*), and also of pride in a possession that ensured distinction and rank and general respect."[1]

As citizen the Jewish weaver must have been brought into constant relation with the town authorities. He was eligible to high municipal offices. Josephus speaks of Jews who became knights; that is to say, after having been clothed with functions of ædile or duumvir, had merited to receive the right to ride a horse, and take a place on the benches of the theatre and circus reserved for those of rank and distinction. Although, as Jews, the tent-maker

[1] Ramsay: "St. Paul the Traveller and the Roman Citizen," 1896, p. 31.

and his son abstained from theatrical and gladiatorial shows, yet St. Paul alludes so often to the scenes of the racecourse, that it makes it probable he took advantage of having a seat in the circus, and followed the contests with zest.[1]

In the colonnades, in the baths, Saul could not fail to catch something of the talk of the young seekers after the *Summum Bonum*. In their bright intelligent faces, in the eagerness of their words, the flush in their cheeks, as they discussed such questions as the unity of the Godhead and the end of man, there must have been an appeal to the human sympathy of the Jewish youth. And, indeed, we do know that the Hellenic Jews felt this, for they strove in a thousand ways to gain the heathen to the truth.

Whether Saul attempted to win proselytes we do not know, but it is hard to think that he did not. Intensely sincere, thoroughly convinced as he was, it was almost a necessity of his expansive youthful nature to endeavour to give to others that which he himself so prized. But if he did this, then inevitably and unconsciously the men with whom he reasoned reacted on his own mind. The result was not apparent then. It manifested itself later. It was at this time, in all likelihood, in this association, that he acquired those smatterings of the poets which he employed in his letters, quotations that no more imply acquaintance with the originals than does the use of a Shakespearian phrase necessitate an intimate knowledge of the plays of the great dramatist. So also, at this time, he may have obtained that inkling of Platonism, which appears in 1 Cor. xv., but was never properly assimilated.

A few words must be devoted to the Church in Jerusalem

---

[1] 1 Cor. ix. 24–27; Gal. v. 7; Eph. vi. 12; Phil. ii. 16; iii. 14; 1 Tim. vi. 12; 2 Tim. ii. 5; 2 Tim. iv. 7.

during the period between the Ascension and the martyrdom of St. Stephen, a period of five years, the most obscure and difficult to unravel of all those in the history of Christianity.

Our only authority for the commencement of the Christian Church is St. Luke's Acts of the Apostles. This, according to Ramsay, was composed in or near A.D. 79, consequently half a century after the events recorded. Luke had not personally seen or heard anything that he narrates up to his association with St. Paul in A.D. 52. His information was acquired at second hand. He had been at Jerusalem, but only as a visitor, never as a resident. His principal authority was apparently Philip the Evangelist. In the early part of the history St. Peter is represented as the active and leading mind; but he is not said to have been the head of the community. James, brother of Our Lord, son of Joseph by a first wife as the Eastern Church has ever held, and considerably older than Christ, was the president. He had not been one of the Twelve; he had not believed.[1] But to him Christ had appeared at His resurrection,[2] and according to the Gospel of the Hebrews—a very early version, if not the original of that of St. Matthew—it was this vision which convinced him.

This James, "the Lord's brother," stood at the head of the Church in Jerusalem. To him apply the last words of Peter, when forced to escape from the holy city.[3] To him St. Paul addressed himself when he visited Jerusalem after his journey to Athens, Corinth and Ephesus.[4] And with him, quite as much as with Peter and John, Paul laboured to effect an understanding;[5] and in the council on circum-

---

[1] John vii. 3–5.   [2] 1 Cor. xv. 7.   [3] Acts xii. 17.
[4] Acts xxi. 18.   [5] Gal. ii. 9.

cision, it was James, as president, who spoke the decisive word.[1] With this corresponds the statement of Hegesippus preserved by Eusebius, as to "James the Just," as well as a bundle of early traditions found in that Ebionite collection of works, the Clementine Homilies and Recognitions, and in the Apostolic Constitutions.

It would almost seem as though the authority of James was œcumenical, for it is difficult not to see in him the author of the Canonical Epistle, and that is addressed " to the Ten Tribes which are scattered abroad," an address to all the Churches represented allegorically as the dispersed tribes, to which Jerusalem was the spiritual capital. In the Clementine Homilies, the prefatorial letter from St. Peter to St. James is thus couched: " Peter to James, the lord and bishop of the Holy Church, under the Father of all." And that of Clement is: "To James, the lord and bishop of bishops, who rules Jerusalem, the Holy City of the Hebrews and the Churches everywhere, excellently founded by the providence of God." Although these letters are apocryphal, yet they show us clearly what was the position assigned to James in the early Church, as head bishop over all the rest.

Apollonius, at the end of the second century, relates the tradition that Our Lord Himself gave the Apostles commandment not to depart from Jerusalem for twelve years. This may be an attempt made to explain the perplexing fact that the Twelve, instead of dispersing after Pentecost, to fulfil the commission, "Go ye into all the world and preach the Gospel to every creature," remained sedentary at the heart of Jewdom.

But there is another explanation of this, without the

[1] Acts xv. 13.

supposition of a manufacture of a tradition. The command may very well have been given, and it was in accordance with what seems to have been the divine purpose that it should have been given.

The day of grace for the Jews was not over. The door of repentance was still open.[1] In his address on the day of Pentecost, Peter told them plainly that they had denied the Holy One and had slain Him, but that they did it in ignorance, and that time was still accorded them for repentance, and for the accomplishment, through them, of the promises of the establishment of the Messianic kingdom over all the earth. The promise was still to them and to their children, and to as many as should be called. "Ye," said Peter, "are the children of the prophets who foretold the death and future glorification of the Messiah—the Covenant was made with you, through Abraham—that in him and you, his seed, all the kindreds of the earth should be blessed. Therefore, repent, before the time comes for the manifestation of the Messiah and the setting up of His kingdom."[2] Again, before the Sanhedrim: "The God of our Fathers has raised up that same Jesus whom ye slew and hanged on a tree. Him hath God exalted with His right hand to be a Prince and a Saviour, for to give repentance to Israel and forgiveness of sins."[3] If the Jews would accept Jesus, acknowledge their error in crucifying Him, and hail Him as the One who was for to come, then He would return, and that shortly, and

---

[1] That those speeches of Peter given in the first part of the Acts are substantially accurate appears from their very individual character, belonging to a transitory phase that had passed away when Luke wrote, and they are quite distinct from the addresses of Stephen and Paul.
[2] Acts iii. 13–26.
[3] Acts v. 30, 31.

restore again the kingdom to Israel, with Jerusalem as the capital of the world, and the joy of the whole earth.

Knowing how patient and long-suffering is God, does it not seem probable and consistent with His mercy, that before finally abandoning the elect race, He should give the Jews a place for repentance and tears, an opportunity to atone for their great national sin of rejection?

In the second place, Jerusalem was the centre of their religion to all the Jews of the Dispersion, as well as to all their converts. In every commercial town of Asia, Egypt, North Africa, Greece, Italy—even Gaul and Spain, the Jews had their counters, and served as forerunners of the Gospel. They prepared men's minds to accept the unity of the Godhead and a revelation of moral duties. Both were to the generality of men new ideas, and such took time to be absorbed and digested. After a while, thoughtful and well-disposed heathen accepted these truths and became more or less affiliated to the synagogues. Then they became imbued with the Messianic expectations of the Hebrew race, and so the soil was prepared for the Gospel. No more effective way of announcing the glad tidings could be found than for the Twelve Witnesses to remain in Jerusalem, and proclaim—"He, the foretold Christ, is come. We are here to testify that God has raised Him from the dead. With our eyes we have seen Him, with our ears we have heard Him. He hath set a day wherein all who would be saved must repent and believe."

Such a proclamation from Jerusalem as the centre sounded to the extremities of the Roman world. Even pilgrims who scoffed returned to their synagogues north and south, east and west, and reported: "Dreamers have arisen at Jerusalem, who declare that the Christ, the Promised One, has already appeared. Him the rulers have slain, but there are twelve men who with one mouth proclaim that He is risen, has ascended into heaven, and will come again to set up His kingdom according to prophecy."

But this was not all the advantage gained. The idea of a suffering Messiah was so novel that it would take the Jew and proselyte some time to consider this doctrine, to search the Scriptures and see whether the prophets had spoken of the One who was to come as One who was to die.

Let us suppose that Mohammedanism were to undergo a transformation, that a Kalifa arose who proposed to revolutionise the Mussulman world. Would he not establish his headquarters at Mecca, whither come the caravans? Would he not by so doing adopt the most effectual means possible of propagating his doctrine throughout all nations that acknowledge the prophet? At a later period he might and would send round his emissaries, but at first he would prepare the Moslem world through the pilgrims, every hadji would become his mouthpiece.

This then would seem to have been the reason why the Twelve for twelve years remained as a constellation of witnesses in Jerusalem, preaching on one topic—the resurrection of Christ as evidence that He was and would be the Messiah, was in suffering, would be in glory. It was like whipping a pool in one spot, it sent ripples to its utmost limits. Is it not probable that, in thus acting, they acted on instructions given them by Christ during the great Forty Days after His resurrection?

The Jewish nation was given, after Pentecost, a grand opportunity of repentance and regeneration. Had the whole people come in a body to accept the Gospel, then the great work of the Christianisation of the world would have been achieved more rapidly, and the Second Coming would not have been so long delayed.

In all God's dealings, whether with nations or with men, in things spiritual and material, it would seem as though He set before Him a high and glorious scheme, which would be perfect if carried out, but that when, through man's infirmity and opposition, this fails, then He should carry out the work on a lower level, lacking the completeness and perfection of the other.

We see this even in nature. There is an ideal type to which every creature and plant develops, but if the environment be unsuitable, the material for building be inaccessible, or should the progress be obstructed by violence, then the work is accomplished, but not on the same high plane as it might have been.

Insufficient nourishment, uncongenial surroundings, accident, will stunt but not necessarily stop growth. A limb is dislocated and nature supplies a false joint, not so good as the original, but serviceable.

In our own lives we see something of the same thing. We start with keen hope and confidence of success. But we commit errors of judgment, we let slide opportunities not to be recovered, and we have to make the best of circumstances, and rectify our mistakes as far as may be. And this is also true in spiritual matters. Each man has before him the ideal of rectitude, purity, honour; but how few live up to this ideal, and carry "the white flower of a blameless life" through the gate of the grave! Life is made up of regrets over lapses, and resolves against others, and at the end the spiritual life is but, in most, a riveted piece of porcelain.

Now consider God's dealings with man.

There was at first the high ideal of man freely loving and serving God, not tasting of death, existing in unclouded happiness. Adam fell, God continues to deal with man, but on a lower plane. God led the children of Israel out of Egypt with intent to bring them at once into the Land of Promise. But owing to their rebellion this plan was deflected and they were made to wander forty years in the desert; Moses died on Pisgah, Aaron on Mount Hor, and of the rest, all but two who came out of Egypt laid their bones in the sand.

On entering the land flowing with milk and honey the ideal set before Israel was that of an elect people guided by God, ruled by God, protected by God. It was given an appropriate sanctuary in Shiloh, on a little knoll in a wide plain, an excellent place where a peaceable people might assemble, but one incapable of defence. But Israel could not rise to this ideal, live up to what God had willed for it, and its condition under the Judges was one of apostacy.

Then the theocratic government having failed, God suffered the people to pass under kings, and the sanctuary was transferred to Zion, an impregnable hill top, fortified by nature.

It would seem, as far as we can judge, to have been the purpose of God to set up the Messianic kingdom at Jerusalem. To this the prophets point. This appears to have been in the minds of the Apostles. Paul did not wholly abandon the thought. It remained in the imagination of John, and is shown us in the Apocalypse. The action of the Apostles implies as much; indeed the appointment of James was significant in this light.

THE DEATH OF STEPHEN

As of the seed of David, the representative of the royal house, he was expected to serve as a rallying point for all Israel. The genealogies in Matthew and Luke on this supposition acquire significance. They establish the kingly descent of Joseph, and therefore of James, as well as of Jesus.[1]

The Maccabees had created a kingdom, Jewish, but not of the seed royal of David. But now one of the true descent from David was placed at the head of the Church, to become the king and high-priest to the elect people of God till Messiah Himself should appear and take all power into His own hands.

And what a splendid realisation of the prophecies, what a triumph of Christ over all the world that would have been, had the Hebrew race bodily accepted Him and taken the position designed for it by God! There would have been that highly gifted people, not degraded to money grubbing and unscrupulous in its sordid greed, a source of demoralisation wherever it is, but a great fountain of enlightenment, of inspiration, ever flowing, an ever present witness to the truth; its wonderful tenacity making it a

---

[1] These genealogies have often puzzled students, and have even been adduced by some critics to show that Christ was a son of Joseph and Mary, and that the miraculous conception was a myth of later importation. This displays a curious ignorance of early conceptions of relationship. The descent was agnatic, not cognatic. The royal authority descended with the *patria potestas*. A woman on marriage passed out of her family into that of her husband, and her son was not counted as akin to the family of his mother, and inherited none of its rights. The principle *Mulier est finis familiæ* applied rigorously. Had the evangelists given Mary's descent, neither by Jewish, nor by Roman law, would the descent have been considered as anything. A right to the family inheritance did not necessarily entail blood descent, for adoption availed. Jesus, born in wedlock, inherited the rights of the family of David, for He stood under the *patria potestas* of Joseph. That was the recognised link, and *not* blood descent.

meet guardian of revelation, a whole nation become the spiritual leaders of the world.

But they were incapable of rising to the occasion. Now it is no more the Gentile accepting Christ through the Jew, but the Jew, for the sake of acres, a title, a wife, accepting Christ through the Gentile.

God's first purpose has been partially frustrated. He is working out to the great end on a lower level, and by inferior means.

And has it not been much the same in the Church? "The Church has taken Israel's place as the body in which divine influences mainly dwell, and by means of which the divine work for mankind is meant to be mainly done. And Israel's sad experience of the surrender of high ideals and the necessary working on lower ones, has been repeated in it. As completely as the ideal passed away which should have been realised at Shiloh, so completely has that high theory of the Church's position in the world been shattered which for centuries it was possible to work on, the theory to which good men passionately clung till it perished in the sixteenth century, even as Shiloh did when the deeds of the sons of Eli made the cup of its judgment overflow. The day was, when the picture might have been realised of a Church growing constantly more spiritually minded in the midst of safety and repose; of a Church gradually learning to fill all the common things of earth with heavenly life, and to consecrate them all to the service of God; of a Church contending, if forced to contend at all, only as it were upon her borders. No man who understands providence or history can hope for, or can aim at, the realising of such an ideal now. Through continued sloth and growing corruption like that which the Israel of the Judges showed, the great opportunity was lost. The time came when such acceptance of a new ideal and a lower one, was the only theory that could save the Church. Those who led the Reformation had a place to fill like that of Samuel and Saul and David. Like them, in greater or smaller measure, with greater faithfulness or less, they saw God's will and did it. But it was on a lower level than the old one that they were forced to work."[1]

We must realise what has been here laid down to thoroughly grasp the peculiar attitude of the Twelve in Jerusalem, and the beginning of that trouble which later on manifested itself conspicuously and painfully.

The first believers by no means severed their connection with the Temple and Mosaism. So long as opportunity was afforded to the Jews to repent and take their proper place in the economy of the Gospel, the Apostles could not, would not do so. They attended the religious festivals,[2] took part in the worship of the temple and synagogue; prayed at the appointed hours.[3] They observed the fasts, and imposed on themselves voluntary abstinences, and subjected themselves to vows like other pious Jews.[4] They abstained from forbidden meats and from legal pollution,[5] and circumcised their sons.[6] They were in a word, what Ananias was in the eyes of the Jews of Damascus, "a devout man according to the law,"[7] and this strictness drew on them the respect of the people.[8] The preaching of the Apostles

---

[1] Miller (W.): "The Least of all Lands." London, 1888. A thoughtful and suggestive book.
[2] Acts ii. 1; xviii. 18; xx. 6; Rom. xiv. 5.
[3] Acts ii. 46; iii. 1; v. 42; x. 9. [4] Acts x. 30; xviii. 18; xxi. 23.
[5] Acts x. 14. [6] Acts xv. 1; xvi. 3; Gal. v. 2.
[7] Acts xxii. 12. [8] Acts v. 13.

did not go beyond this: Jesus was the Messiah, suffering for the sin of men, as the prophets had foretold. Him God raised up on the third day, of which we twelve are witness, and beside us if you ask for further evidence there are some five hundred who have seen Him risen, and who are now here present to give their witness.[1] This same risen Jesus is the Christ, and He giveth you time for repentance, and then will He come and set up His glorious kingdom.

That was all. The only point in which they were at antagonism with the Pharisees was that of the Crucified being the Christ; with the Sadducees they were altogether at variance, in that the base of their preaching was the Resurrection.

The Apostles took pains to avoid any collision with the authorities. Their baptisms and breaking of bread was without ostentation. Their teaching was that the new revelation was the flower and fufilment of Mosaism, not its abrogation. Nevertheless Pharisee and Sadducee could not view this new religious phenomenon with a favourable eye. Neither could they regard the growing community as a sect of Mosaism. Paul saw what it was clearly enough; and he but reflected the opinion of Gamaliel and the rest of the Pharisees. To the Galatians he wrote: "Beyond measure I persecuted the Church of God, being more exceedingly zealous of the traditions of my fathers."[2] Never does Paul speak of that past phase in his life without showing how sharply he distinguished the Christian community from the Pharisaic party. The former is always either "the Church of God" or "the Church," and its

---

[1] 1 Cor. xv. 6. Twenty-two years later "some" of these had "fallen asleep."   [2] Gal. i. 13, 14.

adherents are "the Brethren" or "the Saints." To the Pharisees it was bitterness to be charged with having even unwittingly rejected and slain the Messiah. It was an intolerable affront to their pride. To the Sadducee the insistence of the Apostles on the Resurrection, the appeal to such a body of witnesses, was exasperating in the last degree. Not only so, but they saw in the ferment of spirits relative to the kingdom of the Messiah, and in the setting up of a scion of the royal house as head over the community, a menace to the public tranquillity.

As the Apostles at first shrank from a breach with Judaism, so did the Sanhedrim, made up of contradictory elements, part Pharisee, part Sadducee, ready to fly at each other's throats, hesitate about proceeding to violence against the Church. The Pharisees were glad to see the Apostles proclaim the Resurrection, and the Sadducees hailed Christianity as a wedge driven into the heart of Pharisaism. It was due to the mutual jealousies of those in the Sanhedrim that the Apostles were allowed to escape so easily, when brought up before the Council.[1]

But this mutual forbearance could not last long. The first verses of the sixth chapter of the Acts reveal to us the beginning of a difference of feeling from the first fraternal amity that filled the Church.

"There arose a murmuring among the Hellenistic Jews against the Hebrews, because their widows were neglected in the daily ministration." The strictly Jewish party, with its unabated intolerance and prejudices, had been favouring the poor and needy of their own native body at the expense of the others. This is probably only one

[1] Acts iv. 24; v. 41.

indication of a growing restlessness, inevitable, because none knew how long Divine Mercy would hold out its hand to the Jew, and some thought that it was high time to break with Mosaism, and launch out on a freer course.

This first dissension was appeased. Seven deacons were appointed, all bearing Greek names, consequently, all Hellenistic Jews. It is hardly likely that as yet a place in the ministry would be given to a proselyte. Of these deacons Philip went among the despised and detested Samaritans; Stephen held intercourse with the Hellenist Jews from Italy, Cyrene, Lower Egypt, Cilicia and Asia,[1] in their synagogues established in Jerusalem. His preaching was in a different tone from that adopted by the Apostles; and we cannot be far wrong in conjecturing that it was due to the aggressive character of the work of the deacons that the persecution against the Church broke out; for it is significant that no attempt was made to molest the Twelve. It was the exasperating nature of Stephen's preaching which roused the Cilician and other Hellenists to accuse him before the Sanhedrim. He was charged with speaking "blasphemous words against this holy place and the Law."[2] "We have heard him say that this Jesus of Nazareth shall destroy this place, and shall change the customs which Moses delivered to us."

Although the witnesses are said to have been false, as in the case of Christ, yet in both instances there was a basis of truth. In this instance, no doubt, Stephen had said: "Proceed as you are doing now, oppose the truth, and the Mosaic worship will be abolished." This, in fact, is what

[1] Acts vi. 9.   [2] Acts vi. 13, 14.

he stated on his trial; not indeed in so many words, but in his appeal to the history of the past as a mirror of the future.

Paul was now in Jerusalem, and a member of the Hellenist synagogue of the Cilicians. He may have been one of the accusers, and in his impetuosity have misunderstood the exact terms employed by Stephen. If not a witness, Paul would back up the accusation; he was a disciple of Gamaliel, who was then president of the Sanhedrim, and might be reckoned on to influence his old master.

Stephen was drawn before the council, and put on his defence. Having heard the charge, the High Priest would ask, "Are these things so?"

Then Stephen made his celebrated answer—defence it can hardly be called; with two words he might have cleared himself, but from the moment he stood before the council he seems to have thought of nothing else but of testifying in its presence. This speech given by St. Luke must not be taken as more than a summary of the argument employed by the deacon, as recollected in after years by Paul, and by him communicated to Luke. But the latter probably had another version of it from Philip the deacon. That it is genuine as far as it goes may be admitted; it has all the characteristics of a real speech made on such an occasion.

Of the ability of Stephen there can be no question, the speech is masterly; the temper of the speaker is hardly less disputable.

The orator imposed on himself an historic theme for his discourse, which was, in fact, the application of the parable of the vineyard and the husbandmen. The main epochs in the history of the Jewish people formed the great divisions in his discourse. The first went from Abraham to Moses. He showed Abraham, at the call of God, leaving kindred and land. So, he implied, have we, elect as was Abraham, received a summons to come out from among you idolaters to the letter of the Law, that He may make of us His peculiar people. Abraham obeyed, and was the father of the faithful. Nevertheless, his seed had to suffer affliction. So it may be now; you may afflict us who, by faith, are the true seed of Abraham, but as God delivered the seed of Abraham, so will He free us from your grip. Joseph was envied and betrayed by his brethren. Nevertheless, God was with him, and exalted him, so that his brethren were forced to cringe to him for bread. So with Christ, so with us, you have had a temporary triumph, but we shall see you stooping to us in the end, when the kingdom is set up.

The second epoch is from Moses to David. And now he proceeds to deepen the colours wherewith he paints the antagonism of the enemies of God. Moses, whom the Israelites refused, nevertheless was the chosen of God, and received the "lively oracles." But even though signs from heaven were given, attesting his mission, the Hebrews "would not obey, but thrust him from them, and in their hearts turned back again into Egypt."

The application was too obvious to be missed.

Even when the Hebrews were brought by Joshua into "the possession of the Gentiles," they were rebellious, and went after strange gods. He proceeded: Do not suppose that the possession of the tabernacle in the wilderness, or the temple in the Land of Promise, assured to the people the presence in their midst of the God whom they rejected. When Israel is unfaithful the presence is withdrawn. Now

THE DEATH OF STEPHEN

he was engaged with the third epoch. God of old had sworn to Abraham, "They shall worship in this place;" He had fulfilled His promise literally. However ungrateful the people may have been, He had been true. The temple was erected. However, that was not final. It led on to a spiritual temple. Although the Most High willed the building of the sanctuary, yet this was merely a figure of the great spiritual temple and spiritual worship that were to be for all nations. And as to the material temple, He would forsake it when His people became traitors, murderers and breakers of the Law.

The defence of Stephen had been no defence at all, but a series of wounding stabs. But this was not all. Regardless of his own safety, moved by his passionate indignation and desire to insult these doctors of the Law and rulers of the Temple, he burst forth: " Ye stiff-necked and uncircumcised in heart and ears, ye do always resist the Holy Ghost: as your fathers did, so do ye. Which of the prophets have not your fathers persecuted? and they have slain them which showed before of the coming of the Just One; of whom ye have been now the betrayers and murderers : who have received the Law by the disposition of angels, and have not kept it."

Peter, with all his impetuosity, had never dashed such outrages in the face of the elders of Israel. He had sought to win, not to exasperate. The Acts show us that Stephen was a man without self-control. He spoke truths in the most rasping manner, and couched in the most opprobrious terms.

There are two ways in which verities may be conveyed, one in the spirit of love, which was Peter's method, the other like that adopted by the ichneumon fly in depositing its eggs, by digging the ovipositor into the flesh, producing present pain and after irritation.

Gamaliel the Old, who presided at the schools, had shown marked forbearance and moderation on a former occasion, but no court with any self-respect could endure to be thus addressed. A howl of rage interrupted the testimony of Stephen.

Most readers of the Acts have supposed when it is said that the deacon's face was like that of an angel, that it wore a sort of spiritual beauty, or that a superhuman radiance enhaloed it. It is more probable that his countenance flamed with that wrath which lightened the angel, on seeing whom on Easter morning, the keepers did shake and became as dead men. When Peter had spoken, he tempered his rebuke with, "Brethren, I wot that through ignorance ye did it." No such concession was made by Stephen. The Apostle had urged to repentance, with assurance of pardon, but the deacon allowed no loophole for escape, no gleam of hope.

Among the Acts of the Martyrs at a later age, some show us the Christian confessors addressing the magistrates with the same insolence.

To certain tempers, where there is no breeding, the opportunity of saying offensive things gives positive satisfaction, rendered acute if those addressed be superiors in position and educational endowment. It was, apparently, so with Stephen. It would seem as though his conversion had been of the intellect only, and that till the vision was vouchsafed him of Jesus in the ineffable light, his heart had been untouched. Then a moral revulsion took place in his nature, and falling on his knees he prayed, in a very different temper from that in which he had addressed the Sanhedrim, "Lord, lay not this sin to their charge."

There is a significant hint in the account of his burial. It was not conducted by the believers, though they lamented his death, but by " devout men," a term specially applied to the uncircumcised proselytes. We seem to see here that Stephen had already begun to break fresh ground.

His address produced no effect on Paul except exasperation. The conversion of the latter was not due to any of Stephen's arguments, certainly not to the offensive manner in which they were thrown out.

The decree of death pronounced by the Sanhedrim could not properly be carried into effect without the sanction of the Roman procurator; but the moment was one of confusion previous to a change of governors. There had been a movement in Samaria. A set of fanatics believed that the Temple vessels were buried in Mount Gerizim, and they collected in a crowd to dig them up. Pilate, misunderstanding what this assembly was about, sent troops and massacred a great number. Thereupon the Samaritan Council appealed against him to Lucius Vitellius, Governor of Syria. Vitellius ordered Pilate to go to Rome to answer the charges made against him, and sent a friend of his, Marcellus, to govern Jerusalem during his absence.

It is not possible nicely to fix the date of the massacre, and the subsequent interference of Vitellius, but it was about this time, and if so, the Sanhedrim took the opportunity to carry out its decree and to order a persecution of the Church.

At once a good many fled for their lives as far as to Phœnicia, Cyprus and Antioch. But no steps were taken to molest the Twelve; a sharp line was drawn between those who attended the Temple services, and the hot-blooded young Hellenists who declared that God would cast off His people, and give up the Temple to destruction.

Though scattered by the persecution, they preached "unto the Jews only."[1]

[1] Acts xi. 19.

CHAPTER IV

THE CONVERSION

A.D. 35

Saul at the death of Stephen—No effect produced on him by that death—On his way to Damascus—His miraculous conversion—Three accounts of it—Apparent discrepancies—Easily to be accounted for—Result of the vision—Complete submission of Saul—The subjective side—His apostolic claim based on this vision—Apostleship not an office, but a witnessing—Attempted natural explanations of the conversion—Their failure—Paul's conversion supported by the evidence of Ananias—Paul passes from submission to a system into one of allegiance to a person—Objections made to a commission given in a vision—The similar case of Peter.

SAUL had been "consenting" to the death of Stephen. This implies that he had been made a member of the Sanhedrim, and shows that he was already a person of consequence. He was probably the junior member, charged with oversight of the execution of the decree of the council. For this reason he was present at the death of Stephen and the executioners laid their clothes at his feet.

No feeling of compunction, no inkling that Stephen was in the right and he in the wrong had entered heart or mind of Saul. He "yet breathing out threatenings and slaughter against the disciples of the Lord, went unto the High Priest, and desired of him letters to Damascus, to the synagogues, that if he found any of this way, whether they were men or women, he might bring them bound unto

Jerusalem."[1] Theophilus, son of Annas, was the High Priest. There was no likelihood of opposition from the Roman authorities in Damascus, for they always supported the jurisdiction of the Sanhedrim, even in criminal matters.

Whilst Saul was on his way to Damascus his miraculous conversion took place. Whereas to those who accompanied him the flash of light and crash that followed were an explosion of electric fire, or the fall of a meteorite, to Paul it was something much more.

Of the certainty of his conviction that he both saw and heard Christ there can be no question. It was not the flash nor the sound that converted him, but the reality of the vision and the distinctness of the voice that spake. Once before, when a voice from heaven was heard, the people said "that it thundered,"[2] and so doubtless did the guard, when they recovered from the shock.

We have three accounts of the conversion of St. Paul, and slight discrepancies exist between them, but so slight that it is puerile to make a point of the majority of them. If in one it is said that the soldiers heard no voice, or in another that they did, the reconciliation is obvious. They heard a sound, but did not distinguish articulate words. But there is one important discrepancy between the narrative of the conversion as given by St. Luke and Paul's own account before Agrippa. In the first account, and that also given by him on the stairs when addressing an excited mob, not a word is said to intimate that he then received his commission to the Gentiles. It was to Ananias that the Lord said in vision that Saul was destined by Him to work among the Gentiles. In his speech to the mob,[3] Paul distinctly intimated that he was converted on the

[1] Acts ix. 1, 2. [2] John xii. 29. [3] Acts xxii. 5-11.

way to Damascus, and that he received his commission later on considerably, in a vision at Jerusalem, in the Temple.[1] Paul as much as says that he knew nothing of the divine plan of making him an instrument for the bringing in of the Gentiles, till his visit fourteen years later. But before Agrippa and Festus he alleged that Christ, in appearing to him, said, "I have appeared unto thee for this purpose, to make thee a minister and a witness both of these things which thou hast seen, and of those things in the which I will appear unto thee; delivering thee from the people and from the Gentiles, unto whom now I send thee."[2]

The fusion of two visions into one in the address to Agrippa is comprehensible enough and excusable, if not justifiable. Paul sought to make an impression on the king's mind, and not to weary him with a long story. He sketched the history of his call and commission in bold lines and put in the colour in patches with a wet brush so that they ran together. His oratorical effort was like a coloured advertisement on a hoarding designed to arrest attention, without care about accuracy of detail, which detail was unessential at the moment.

It may be thought more likely that in speaking to a seething mob, Paul would have run the two visions together. But the mob he addressed was Jewish, and the Jews were exasperated because they thought he had introduced Gentiles into the Temple. It was therefore most apposite that he should tell them that it was in the Temple itself that he had received his commission to open the kingdom to members of other nations.

Professor Ramsay has remarked that the Oriental mind

[1] Acts xxii. 17-21. [2] Acts xxvi. 13-18.

is not historical, but artistic; it groups facts to present an effective whole, and is incapable of reproducing an event in strict chronological sequence. Nevertheless, it would have been more satisfactory had Paul been careful to be exact in his statement of the sequence of facts, and had laboured less at rhetorical effect.[1]

The vision on the way to Damascus produced complete conviction. If there had been the least mistrust in the reality of it, St. Paul never could have undertaken and carried through his great work. Of a progressive growth of opinion in his mind leading to the change there is no trace. The recollection of his conversion through the rest of his life was that of an event sudden and overwhelming, as an earthquake shock, ruining his entire past, but unlike an earthquake, constructive at the same moment. He describes the moral, spiritual convulsion in his Epistle to the Philippians as complete at once.[2] He who was once a foe was now carried in chains behind the triumphal car of Christ the Victor.[3] He had been reduced from hostility to obedience, so complete that he had no will of his own apart from that of his Master.[4] He even went beyond this. He represented himself as a mere body, inert, unless vivified by a soul, and that soul in him

---

[1] The first account of the conversion given in Acts is no doubt that which St. Paul was wont to afford when not labouring under excitement. The second, it is possible Luke may have heard during the riot at Jerusalem, and, if so, he put down what he remembered of it; if he did not hear it, then he gave what he was told that Paul had said, or what he believed he had said; and this account agrees very fairly with the first. The third, spoken in court, was probably taken down in shorthand, and we have exactly Paul's own words, and it speaks well for the scrupulous honesty of St. Luke that he records it as spoken, without correcting the inaccuracies fallen into by Paul.

[2] Phil. iii. 7–9.   [3] 2 Cor. ii. 14.
[4] 1 Cor. ix. 15–18.

was Christ. "I am crucified with Christ: nevertheless, I live; yet not I, but Christ liveth in me."[1]

Thrice he recurs in his letters to his conversion. In his Epistle to the Galatians,[2] he speaks of it as the revelation of Christ in him. He knew of Him, not by man or through man; nothing that he had seen of the Christians, nothing that he had heard from Stephen, had any effect on him, he was convinced once and for always by the action of divine grace. "It pleased God—to reveal His Son in me."[3]

In this passage Paul speaks of the subjective side of his conversion, and says nothing of the vision revealed to his eyes. But it is otherwise in his first letter to the Corinthians. In that he says: "Am I not an Apostle? Have I not *seen* Jesus Christ our Lord?"[4] And again, after mentioning the witnesses to the resurrection of Jesus Christ, he says, "Last of all He was seen of me also, as of an abortive;"[5] that is to say, not in the same order as He was seen by the rest, but by a sudden, violent parturition brought to the light of clear day.

It was on the reality of this vision that Paul based his claim to be an Apostle. An Apostle was a chosen witness, set apart to bear testimony to the reality of Christ's resurrection. It was not an office that could be communicated by imposition of hands, or delegated to another. After the fall of Judas, the Eleven chose another, "a witness with us of His resurrection."[6] True, with this went the ministry, but not of necessity. Matthias was chosen to take part in the ministry *and* apostleship.[7]

---

[1] Gal. ii. 20. [2] Gal. i. 12–16. [3] Gal. i. 16.
[4] 1 Cor. ix. 1. [5] *Ibid.* xv. 8. [6] Acts i. 22.
[7] Acts i. 25.

Some confusion exists now in people's minds as to what was meant by an *Apostle*. It is by no means unlikely that such a confusion existed in the first age of the Church. This was due to the Twelve summing up in themselves several offices. An Apostle, as we can gather from the commission of Christ, was one sent to preach the Gospel, the good tidings of salvation. But this was not how the Twelve took it, at first. They understood by it a commission to act as a body of authoritative Witnesses to the reality of the Resurrection, and therefore to the Messianic office of Christ. In the passage from the first Epistle to the Corinthians, quoted above, Paul bases his right to be regarded as an Apostle on this, that having seen Jesus since His death he was thereby qualified to be a Witness.

He appealed to the fact as to one that carried in itself all that was necessary. And it was all that was necessary if an Apostle was nothing more than a Witness to the fact that Christ lived although He had died. The Twelve were a college of Witnesses usually stationary at Jerusalem, but he was a roving Witness. Yet, in that he had seen Jesus after His death and resurrection, he considered himself to be as fully qualified as were they. It was thus, miraculously, not of men, or by men, that he was constituted an Apostle, *i.e.*, a Witness; but his Ministry he received later on, by and through men, by the imposition of hands at Antioch, and his special mission was given him by revelation in the Temple at Jerusalem. In order of time, he became an Apostle in A.D. 35, but not a minister till eleven or perhaps fourteen years later.[1]

[1] According as we compute the time from his conversion to the second visit to Jerusalem.

But he very soon found that of an Apostle something more was expected than the mere testifying to a fact. An Apostle was expected to have received a commission. And he could only speak as an ambassador of Christ and enforce obedience if he could prove his commission.

Then Paul was driven to assert that he had not only been created an Apostle or Witness by having been shown Christ risen from the dead, but also that he had been *sent*, as had the others; and to establish this he produced his vision in the Temple.

But this he could not fail to see was eminently unsatisfactory. It rested on his bare assertion; and when it was questioned, he could produce no evidence to substantiate it.

Consequently, as we shall see later, he bowed to receive manifest, public commission by the imposition of hands.[1]

The objection made to a commission received by vision was strongly felt till much later. For in the Clementine Homilies, a work emanating from the Judæo-Christian Church in the third century, this very question is raised. St. Peter is represented in contest with Simon of Giscala. The latter, like St. Paul, claimed to have received his doctrine by vision, and to this St. Peter answers that no doctrine or commission so received is to be trusted. What was derived directly from Christ by word of mouth, in the flesh, that was certain and to be relied on; but a vision was entirely untrustworthy, not only as an uncertain thing in itself, but also as being often a delusion of evil spirits.[2]

This argument brought forward by St. Peter is well

[1] Acts xiii. 3.   [2] Clem. Homil. xvii. 14–19.

reasoned and convincing. That this, which in the third
century was represented as having been objected against
Simon the Sorcerer, was raised by the Judaising party
against Paul we know did take place, and he was driven
to great straits to meet the objection. He made the
fact of his success an evidence establishing his commission.
His converts were the seal of his office. Unless he had
been sent, how was it that he had gained so many
adherents? But this was a poor and unworthy argument.
It was one that could be brought forward by the originator
of any new religion, by any heresiarch who could collect
a certain number of followers.

But to return to the conversion.

It has been explained as due to hallucination. An
electric discharge produced in him such a condition of
excitement that he fancied he saw Him against whose
servants he was waging war.

But the conversion is not to be so explained.[1]

A hallucination would not be the efficient cause of a
change of conviction, but would be produced, if produced
at all, by such a change. If Paul had been doubtful first,
and then had arrived at the assurance that he had been
pursuing a false road, and then had seen the vision, he

[1] In connection with Paul's conversion and his hearing of a voice, it
is worth noting that Columbus, after his shipwreck on the coast of Portugal, when he had swum ashore and lay sick at Belem, believing himself about to die, heard whilst half awake a voice saying to him, "God
will cause thy name to be renowned through all the world, and He will
give unto thee the keys of the door of the ocean." He relates this in
one of his letters to his Spanish Majesty, after eighteen years of waiting
and expectation, without his confidence in the heavenly prognostication
failing him. But this is not a parallel case. Columbus was already
persuaded that it was his mission to make discoveries to the West. He
was in high fever, and his feverish dreams took colour from his convictions.

would have known that, and have spoken of it as confirming his faith, not as an efficient cause of the genesis of that faith.

Besides, Paul was quite capable of distinguishing between revelations and ecstasies. When describing the latter, he speaks with hesitation, not knowing whether he were in the body or out of the body, and he shrinks from publishing what he saw in these trances, and refuses to utter the words therein heard.

But Paul's conversion was not to rest on his own statement unsupported. It was for this reason that he was struck with blindness, and was miraculously healed by Ananias, and a vision was accorded to the latter with testimony as to the apostleship of the convert. "He is a chosen vessel unto me, to bear my name before the Gentiles, and kings, and the children of Israel."

There is still another point in connection with the conversion to be considered, which makes it impossible to regard the vision as a hallucination, as some critics would have us do.

The change produced in Paul was from submission to a system to one of devotion to a person. The spring of action is conviction, and conviction is set in motion by the consent of the will. We do this or that, believe this or that, because our wills agree thereto; and they agree thereto either because this particular thing belongs to a system to which we have given our adhesion as one that satisfies the requirements of our inner being, or because we trust a person who demands of us action or belief. Paul had studied, laboured, restrained himself, in obedience to the Law, as containing that which his conscience told him was right. It was in pursuance of this conviction that he persecuted "the Way." But suddenly, in the midst of his career, a great revulsion takes place. His belief in the system crumbles to dust, and in its place arises the luminous form of the Christ, at once seizing on his affections and commanding his obedience.

What before was his glory and pride thenceforth he esteemed as dung, because of the dominating, all-pervading love and subjection to Christ, seen in vision.

We may well ask, Is it conceivable that a dream of an hysterical soul should effect this? Could a hallucination root up a weed and plant in a fruitful tree? This supposition is wilder, more impossible, than that there should have been reality in the heavenly vision. Did ever any fancy of the brain, apart from reality, inspire passionate love and complete homage—a love and a homage that lasted from youth to old age, that sustained Paul through affliction, persecution, privation, discouragement, and triumphed in his death?

Joan of Arc had her visions and voices, but they impelled her to fulfil a mission, and did not revolutionise her opinions. The parallel between her case and that of Paul seeing, hearing Christ in the Temple is complete, but not so with respect to his conversion.

There is peculiar significance in the introduction into the Acts of the Apostles of the narrative of St. Peter and Cornelius. St. Luke apparently laid great stress on this, for he not only relates Peter's vision, in the course of the narrative, but he likewise makes the Apostle repeat it himself.

The object is clear. Luke desired to show that the objection raised against Paul, when he made a new departure, applied also to Peter. Paul claimed an apostleship to the Gentiles on the plea of a vision. Peter took the bold step of baptising the uncircumcised on the ground that he had been ordered so to do in vision. Both acted in the same direction, on authority received in the same way, and an objection flung in the face of Paul recoiled on Peter as well.

CHAPTER V

ARABIA AND JERUSALEM

A.D. 35—38

Paul retires into Arabia—Arabia a term of wide application—Condition of mind of Paul after his conversion—What Paul then knew of Christ—Messianic expectations—Growth of Messianic ideas among the Jews—After the Captivity—Antiochus Epiphanes—The Book of Daniel—The Asmonæan house—Capture of Jerusalem by Pompey—Confusion of ideas relative to sin—The preaching of the Baptist—The preaching of the Apostles was Messianic—The idea of a suffering Messiah—The testimony of the Apostles to the Messiahship of Jesus—Saul returns to Antioch—Escape from it—Goes to Jerusalem—Is introduced to the Apostles by Barnabas—Learns of Christ from the Apostles—The silence of Luke relative to the spread of the Church to South and East—Did Paul then understand what his mission was to be?—Peter, in what way concerned with the founding of the Church—The law of development in things spiritual—Memory—Development of theology—Absorbance of the minds of the Apostles in Messianic expectations—The introduction of the Gentiles into the kingdom not fully expected at first—Intellectual growth—The opening of the minds of the Twelve to full knowledge.

No sooner was Paul healed of his blindness than he retired into Arabia. He had been baptised in Damascus.[1] What he had been taught we are not told. But, indeed, his mind was not ripe for receiving instruction, it was storm-tossed, clouded with a thousand problems, held in suspense and in constant agitation. What he required was repose in which to recover his mental equilibrium and clear his mind.

[1] Acts ix. 18.

ARABIA AND JERUSALEM

The term Arabia is of broad application, and not only adhered to the Peninsula, but embraced all that portion roamed over by Bedaween tribes, east of Trachonitis and Peræa, and extended to the Euphrates. It is said in Acts that Saul remained certain days with the disciples at Damascus. The writer omits all account of the time spent in Arabia, but goes on, "Straightway he preached Christ in the synagogues;" but it is not necessary to hold that this was immediately on his conversion; and the mention of Aretas as being at the time in charge of Damascus[1] makes it much more probable and chronologically possible, if we take this preaching and the persecution that followed as occurring on his return from Arabia.

We do not know what Paul did in Arabia. It is possible he may have hid himself in an Essene community. He was in just that condition of soul when such association would suit him. In the midst of the fasting, solitude, continuous prayer and occasional ecstasies of these solitaries he would think over what had taken place, hold commune with God and search the Scriptures to see what they said of Christ. His thoughts, we may be quite sure, would take one direction, the solution of the mystery of a suffering Messiah. He knew nothing of our Lord's birth, preaching, miracles, only the broad fact that He had been crucified, and that what the Apostles testified was true—He who was slain was alive again. Of the preaching of the Apostles he knew no more than that in season and out of season they insisted that Jesus was the promised Messiah, who had been slain, but who would come again in power and great glory. The only thought then occupying the minds of Christians was Messianic; the whole of the controversy with the Jews

[1] 2 Cor. xi. 32.

turned on the point whether or not Jesus was the expected deliverer.

To properly understand how important, how monopolising was the Messianic idea at this time, it will be necessary to take shortly the history of the Messianic expectations of the Jews.

From a very early period, the Hebrews were convinced that they were an elect nation, chosen from among all others by Jehovah to maintain His worship and to preserve uncorrupt the great truth of the unity of the Godhead. Alongside of this, and intensifying with the deepening of this conviction of the divine monarchy was the recognition that the nation was not acting worthily of its unique and glorious calling. The prophets, who represented the purest and noblest elements in the race, proclaimed this latter truth with vehemence, and warned the nation that unless it walked more worthily it would be chastised. According to them Jehovah employed the surrounding nations who oppressed them as scourges wherewith to correct them and bring them to a realisation of their vocation, and to a discharge of their obligations to Him.

These two convictions, acting one on the other, resulted in the production of another—that, however greatly crushed the Hebrew people might be, it was so precious in the eyes of God, and so completely assured of His protection, that its sufferings would be correctional only, and must lead to the purification of the chosen race, and to its ulterior triumph. In this belief we have all the elements of the development of the Messianic expectations of Judaism. This is the fundamental idea of a mighty trial followed by a restoration which inspired successively Hosea, Isaiah, Jeremiah, Ezekiel and the great anonymous seer of the Exile whose prophecies constitute the second part of the Book of Isaiah.

As yet all was vague; but such a hope speedily assumed definite form. In the first place, what was desired was the political exaltation of Israel, partly in order that there might be enjoyment of the fat things of the earth and the plunder of the Gentiles, partly also that the Hebrews might have the satisfaction of revenging their national wrongs on their persecutors. As to the moral elevation of the people, that was regarded as a mere means to an end; desired undoubtedly, because it would lead to triumph, but among the vulgar for that only. Prophets and wise men alone desired it for itself, and set righteousness above worldly prosperity. How and by whom the regeneration of Israel was to be effected was a matter of uncertainty. At one moment it was supposed that this would be due to the personal intervention of Jehovah, who would call to His aid all the most awful phenomena of nature; then it was believed that some member of the royal race of David would be raised up to deliver the people; and then all eyes turned to a foreign deliverer, now Cyrus, then Alexander.

On the return of the people from captivity in Babylon, they were sanguine that the great affliction was passed, the day of exaltation was dawning. They began to rebuild Jerusalem and restore the Temple, and the people, faithful and still wincing from the lash of the Babylonians, observed the Law with exactness and became happy and moderately prosperous. This was not altogether the restoration they had anticipated; there was no great political propaganda achieved, nor had they the spoil of the nations at their command, but every man could sit under his own vine and fig-tree, and though still called on to remit a small poll-tax to the Persian king, he was left pretty much to himself and was certainly not tyrannised over.

In easier circumstances, the ambition of the Jew flagged, his Messianic expectations became less keen, and the prophetic fire died out.

From being under Persian domination, the Jewish nation passed without concern and without resistance under Greek sovereignty. Governed by its High Priests, the little kingdom enjoyed practical autonomy, and it would have remained in peace but for the rival ambitions of Egypt and Syria, which disputed possession of the soil. Conquered by the Ptolemies, it rested for eighty years (B.C. 301–221) under their sceptre. This was a happy period, favourable to the propagation of Jewish religious ideas, and offering to the teeming population opportunities of expansion in the Nile basin. The Messianic idea had lost its attraction, and to those who concerned themselves with it, it was nothing more than a promise of indefinite prolongation of the present prosperity.

This tranquillity was, however, but the calm that precedes the hurricane.

The advent of Antiochus Epiphanes marks the commencement at once of a series of terrible sufferings to the Jews and of an explosion of Messianic expectations. Antiochus was resolved on the abolition of the worship of Jehovah, and the complete incorporation of the Jewish people into the Græco-Syrian system of religion, civilisation and polity.[1] With this end in view he abolished the observance of the Sabbath, forbade circumcision, and put down the Temple sacrifices. Nay, further, in December,

[1] 2 Macc. iv. 7–20.

B.C. 167, he set up a little altar on the top of the great altar before the sanctuary and offered thereon a sacrifice to Jupiter Olympius.

It was at this terrible time, when the abomination of desolation was in the holy place, that the Book of Daniel appeared in the form we have it, to revive the drooping courage of the afflicted people of God, and to assure them of an approaching delivery.[1]

In this book, which may, and probably does, contain incorporated in it an earlier document, visions and revelations were added, so explicit of the struggles between Egypt and Syria, and the existing troubles, that the majority of critics have regarded it as a composition of the year B.C. 167.

In the visions and prophecies there is an advance in Messianic expectation. There are not many allusions to a personal Messiah,[2] but new elements are introduced, as the resurrection to life and to punishment. There is a judgment, and after the judgment One like the Son of Man receives dominion and power over the universe. Previous to this, however, Messiah was to be cut off, though not for Himself.[3] He is the Prince of Princes, against whom the great persecuting king would stand up. The kingdom of the saints was to be everlasting, and to extend over all the world.

The revolt directed by Judas Maccabæus was crowned by success, and the three years and a half assigned by Daniel for the last sufferings of his people had hardly elapsed before the profaned Temple was purified and the worship of God restored, December B.C. 164. Nevertheless,

---

[1] Dan. xi. 24-29, 30, 41.   [2] Dan. ix. 25.
[3] Dan. ix. 26.

the struggle continued, and instead of the Jews obtaining dominion over all the earth, they had to make desperate battle to maintain their national existence. The victory gained by Judas over Nicanor at Adasa was followed by the disaster of Eleasa, in which the great Maccabee fell, B.C. 160. His brother Jonathan succeeded and was recognised as High Priest, and obtained peace at the price of a tribute paid to the Syrian king. Simon, the last of the Maccabæan brothers, followed. With two of his sons he was murdered in B.C. 135; and one of his sons, who had escaped, John Hyrcanus, succeeded to the government. He subdued Idumæa and Samaria, B.C. 109, destroyed the sanctuary on Mount Gerizim, and made Jerusalem the religious centre of the whole kingdom.

Now followed a series of infamous prince-pontiffs, under whom religion was outraged, and the soil of the Holy City was drenched in Jewish blood, shed in fratricidal war. To the discredited Asmonæan dynasty of pure-blooded Jewish prince-prelates succeeded that of the Idumæans.

The capture of Jerusalem by Pompey, B.C. 63, put a term to the period of Jewish independence, although still for seventy years, till the recall of Archelaus, son of Herod, it maintained an appearance of political liberty. The feeling of hatred of the stranger, joined to the tradition of the glory reserved to Israel, took at once an immense development, and it is hard to say whether the apocryphal works then produced were the expression of the feelings and beliefs of the people, or were the means of rousing and strengthening them.

The idea of a Messiah who should reign over the Jewish people, and make of them the Church of the whole world, now sprang into strong relief. That the humiliation of the elect race was due to its sins was acknowledged,[1] but the scribes had so confused the broad outlines of man's moral and religious obligations that the conception of sin was limited to transgression of some trivial regulation, omission of some ridiculous ceremony. Against such a conception of national sin the Baptist arose, and preached repentance, not a more close adhesion to niggling regulations imposed by tradition, but a reversion to the plain principles of the Divine Word—probity, sobriety, gentleness, charity.

The expectation of the Jews was that a son of David, also called a son of God, would appear and "restore again the kingdom to Israel." This Messiah was to be preceded by a forerunner, who would be the prophet Elias revived. The ideas of a judgment took sharper outline, but there was a difference of opinion as to whether it would precede the apparition of the Messiah or would succeed it. The general opinion was that the Roman domination was about to come to an end, and that Messiah's kingdom would take its place by an easy transition. "There is no difference," taught one Rabbi, "between this present age and that of the Messiah, except in this, that in the latter the pagan nations will be reduced to slavery."

The Messiah, the Christ, that is, the Anointed, as was now unanimously believed, would be a descendant of David. It was held by some that he would be born at Bethlehem;[2] but according to others that he would descend from heaven. That this expected King would be a moral reformer concerned very few; what all looked to was that he should crush the Roman power and put the Jewish nation at the head and make it impose its religion on the

---

[1] Talmud, Sanhedr., f. 97: Sabbath, f. 118.
[2] Targ. Jonathan in Zech. x. 3–4; Isa. xi. 1; Mich. v. 2.

whole world. Like Melchisedec, he was to be at once King of Jerusalem and Priest of the Most High. His kingdom was to last till the year 6000 of the world's history,[1] when would come the Judgment and the enchainment of Satan. The length of Messiah's reign was variously estimated as forty years or four hundred. An opinion was held by some that the Messiah would show himself for a while and then be withdrawn and remain hid till the time was ripe for his manifestation.

It will be seen from this summary that one element which we are accustomed to associate with the Messiah is totally absent—the idea of him as suffering and as a sacrifice for sin.

Now the whole energy of the Apostles had been directed, as far as we can judge, to convincing the Jews that this was a feature in the Messianic scheme of Redemption of Israel. In every speech, in the prayer of Peter that is recorded,[2] the dominating idea is that Christ, the Messiah, had appeared, and had been "by cruel hands" slain, and that He was risen, and now in His risen condition was withdrawn and tarrying till those who had in ignorance rejected Him would turn, repent, and prepare for His appearance, when would be fulfilled all that the prophets had said, all that the people expected. Stephen, in his defence, had gone no further. He had limited himself to the unpleasant but very true charge that the Jewish people had rejected all their prophets and great men, and that their sin had culminated in the rejection of the Christ. He had not said one word relative to a hope of His Second Coming, not allowed a chance of repentance. If Paul had

[1] Or as in the Book of Jubilees, at the close of 85 Jubilee periods.
[2] Acts iv. 24-30.

heard any of the preaching of the Apostles, which is very unlikely, he had heard no more than this.

The Apostles insisted that Christ who had been put to death in Jerusalem, was yet alive, *because they had seen Him*.

And now Paul was able to occupy the same platform, to insist on the same truth, *because he, also, had seen Him*.

At the end of three years Paul returned to Damascus, and preached in the synagogues that Jesus was the Son of God.[1]

"But all that heard him were amazed, and said, Is not this he that destroyed them which called on this name in Jerusalem, and came hither for that intent, that he might bring them bound unto the chief priests?"

After a few days the exasperation among the Jews at Damascus became so great that they appealed to the governor under Aretas, to have him arrested. Aretas had at this time been given the charge of Damascus, during the interval between the retirement of Lucius Vitellius from the proconsulship of Syria and the arrival of his successor, Petronius.

The gates were watched, but Paul escaped let down the wall in a basket, and thus got safely away,[2] and proceeded at once to Jerusalem. There he was not known to the brethren other than as one who had been implicated in the execution of Stephen, and had been foremost as a persecutor. Of his conversion they knew nothing, owing to his prompt retreat into Arabia after it, and the disturbance relative to his testifying in Damascus was of too recent occurrence to have as yet reached their ears.

[1] Acts ix. 20, 21; Gal. i. 17.   [2] 2 Cor. xi. 32, 33.

Barnabas now became Paul's sponsor, and he assured the Twelve of the reality of Saul's conversion. He had probably received letters by the hand of Paul from some brethren in Damascus recommending the neophyte to his good offices.

This introduction dissipated the suspicion with which at first Paul had been regarded, and he "was with them coming in and going out at Jerusalem." Peter he saw, and was with him in close conference for fifteen days, and he likewise saw James, "the Lord's brother," head of the Church in Jerusalem and throughout Judæa.

There was much that St. Paul had to learn from those who had been witnesses of Christ's miracles, death and resurrection, and had heard His teaching—such matters could be learned from none else. No Gospels had as yet been written. All information was oral. Such as desired to hear about Christ must come to the college of witnesses at Jerusalem.

Afterwards Paul could not have spoken so decidedly and in such detail about matters of fact in the history of our Lord's life, unless he had learned the chief incidents from those who had both seen and heard Him. At first sight undoubtedly, in reading the Epistles of Paul, one is surprised to find so few allusions to the events of the life of Jesus, so few quotations from His discourses. But this is easy of explanation. The Epistles were written late, to those who had received a preliminary instruction. And the letters presuppose this. They take for granted that those receiving them knew both what Christ did and what He taught. This course of instruction is the tradition to which St. Paul refers more than once.[1] He knew of the

---

[1] 1 Cor. xi. 2; xv. 1-9; Col. ii. 7; 2 Thess. ii. 15; Tit. i. 9.

royal descent of Christ,[1] of His poverty. In all the details of the Eucharistic institution he was fully instructed.[2] He knew how that He had been betrayed,[3] how that He had been reproached on the cross,[4] how that He had a superscription attached to the cross.[5] Of the Resurrection he knew more than is detailed in the Gospels.[6] So also there are sayings of the Lord which had been communicated to him other than are recorded by the Evangelists.[7]

It is often supposed that Paul received his knowledge of the Gospel entirely by revelation; that is to say, that he was miraculously, in vision, given the record of Christ's life and doctrine, and that he owed nothing to communication from the Apostles. But such a notion is not justified either by the words used by Paul relative to his ministerial commission, or by the facts of the case. He was at Jerusalem repeatedly. Are we to suppose that he asked no questions of the Twelve relative to Him of whom they were the authorised witnesses?

Moreover, a miraculous revelation is not conceivable when unnecessary. To hear all he needed to know about Christ, Paul had but to ask those who had both seen and heard Him. What he did obtain independently was his institution to the Apostolate, to be a witness, and that by the fact of seeing Christ; his commission he received by laying on of hands, but the field in which he was to work, that was divinely shown him.

That Paul was but a fortnight in the Holy City is not

---

[1] Rom. i. 3. [2] 1 Cor. xi. 23-26. [3] Ibid. 23.
[4] Rom. xv. 3. [5] Col. ii. 14. [6] 1 Cor. xv. 4-7.
[7] Acts xx. 35; 1 Thess. iv. 15-17.

necessarily implied by the words that he uses in Galatians; but merely that he stayed as a guest for fifteen days in Peter's house. Many indications show that although the Twelve made Jerusalem their headquarters, most of them were incessantly on the move, making periodical visits, probably to clusters of converts in Mesopotamia and Arabia. It has been well noticed that Luke is silent relating to the spread of the Church to the East and South. What interested him and entered into the scheme he set himself was to record the gradual expansion of the Church in that part of the Roman world with which he was familiar, and where he was able to obtain trustworthy material for his compilation. He did not come in contact with those who had been engaged in the diffusion of the truth in other parts than Asia Minor, Rome and Syria, and therefore, rather than stuff his pages with unsubstantiated tales, he omitted all reference to the work done in East and South. Now it is possible enough that Peter could not spare to Paul more time than a fortnight, and that then he was thrown in the society of James, the bishop.

To this period is attributed by many writers the remarkable vision in the Temple recorded in Acts xxii. 17-21, when he received for the first time his commission to go to the Gentiles, and it is thought that this vision impelled him immediately to leave. But this is in contradiction with the statement made in Acts, that his leaving Jerusalem was occasioned by a plot to kill him. "He was with the Apostles coming in and going out at Jerusalem. And he spake boldly in the name of the Lord Jesus, and disputed against the Hellenistic Jews; but they went about to kill him. Which when the brethren knew, they brought him down to Cæsarea, and sent him thence to Tarsus."[1]

He did not begin his ministry to the Gentiles till ten or eleven years after; in fact not till after his second visit to Jerusalem, and, I conceive, it was then he saw the vision and received his commission.

If this be the order of events, and it is the only order which does not involve us in difficulties, then Paul as yet had only the most uncertain ideas as to the purpose of God relative to the conversion of the Gentiles. He had heard from Ananias at Damascus what Christ had foretold to him in vision, but probably supposed that he would proceed on the lines followed by the Apostles. That, nevertheless, some thoughts of what a great door was opening entered his mind, and that he discussed them with Peter, and expressed his opinion freely, is probable enough; and it is certainly a significant fact that it was very shortly after these interviews that Peter went to Cornelius, who was uncircumcised, and merely a proselyte of the gate, and baptized him.

If Peter is to be regarded as a foundation stone of the Church of the Circumcision, in that he made the first converts from among the Hellenistic Jews, he must also be held to be a foundation stone of the Church of the Uncircumcised, for he was the first to extend the privilege of baptism to a Gentile. This he would not have done had not there been a miraculous effusion of the Holy Ghost similar to that at Pentecost, to satisfy him and others that such admission into the Church was with the divine approval.

---

[1] Acts ix. 28–30. Moreover, he would not at this time have understood such a commission. It was not for some years that his mind opened to the mystery of the call of the Gentiles.

It would seem to be a law of God that governs all creation, every form of life, physical, mental and spiritual, that it should not spring, like Athene, fully armed into existence, nor be born like the mythical calf of the Talmud at the age of three, but grow from small beginnings, "first the seed, then the ear, after that the full corn in the ear." Indeed the idea of life to us involves that of succession, and the succession is one of advance to a certain fixed point, when not counteracted by disintegrating forces. Evolution, a doctrine now so ardently embraced, is the application to the genera and species of the Law we recognise as governing individual existence. Nothing in nature reaches maturity at a bound. The mind unfolds itself leisurely as the body grows. Precocity of intellect in a child very often entails in manhood mental stagnation. It has reached ripeness before the body. The ox and the ass have been yoked together; they have not kept pace. It is the same in all things spiritual. We see that the Apostles when with Christ could not bear to receive at once all the truth He would communicate.

Time was required for the seed sown to take root downward and the plant to spring upward; for the human mind to digest and assimilate what it had imbibed before more could be given to it.

At Pentecost, an outpouring of the Spirit had been accorded to fire with zeal, inspire with courage, to bring to the Apostles' memories what had been taught them, and to guide them into all truth. Zeal, courage were immediate requisites. Guidance implies movement, progression. In a contracted human mind memory does not act as a flash of lightning illumining all things instantaneously, but travels like a search light bringing into view one object after another.

Nor does reason act differently. No man sees the full bearings of a fact at once; they appear to him by degrees, as circumstances arise to force them on his notice.

Thus was it with the Apostles. This was the manner of operation of the Divine Spirit, who is the Spirit of Life, therefore of development and adaptation to circumstances. It led them to the conviction that it was their Master's will that they should tarry in Jerusalem awhile. Why, they did not clearly discern. And as soon as the proper moment arrived, then It guided them to extend their sphere of operations, and finally wafted them to the ends of the earth.

At first all they thought of and declared was that Christ —the Christ—was come, had died and risen again. But of what theologic mysteries were involved in the Incarnation, of the depth of significance to all mankind that lay in the death of Christ, they had as yet hardly more than a perception. Of the importance of the Resurrection they saw no more at the first moment than a proof that the Jesus whom they had followed was indeed the promised Messiah.

Christian theology—that is to say, the philosophy of the facts of the Gospel—began in the most rudimentary form, but developed organically and inevitably, as events happened, as conditions arose calling for applications and solutions. The full bearing of any event is never seen all at once. It cannot be so. In a finite mind, in a series of finite minds, it is seen in a gradual unrolling, in a slow demonstration of sequences, one following on another, as effect on cause.

The Apostles at first did not see to what Christ's preaching, death, and resurrection would lead. It was under the pressure of events that their faith rose from an elementary form to a higher type. They had come to Christ by the Law and the Prophets. It was like a ladder let down from heaven that led up to God and to Christ. The idea of any contradiction between the Law and the Gospel did not occur to them, till forced on their notice. They had not had occasion to renounce the old Covenant to enter into the new; and this explains what we shall see presently, much hesitation and embarrassment when brought face to face with the tremendous revolution which was about to be accomplished.

Brought up in Judaism, the whole horizon of which was piled up with Messianic cloud figures, they did not seek to do more than show them to be gilded with the sunlight that streamed from the face of Jesus.

They accepted the whole of the eschatology of the Pharisees. They declared that they had seen and conversed with Jesus who was the expected Messiah, and they insisted that He would come again.

Apparently for some years the Twelve were ignorant of one of the great purposes of the Incarnation, the salvation of the Gentiles—at all events, in any other way than through the gate of Mosaism. This is the more remarkable because this was one of the great subjects of prophecy in the Old Testament, and it was due to that antipathy to pagans, which they had sucked in with their mothers' milk, that they were thus blind. So completely were they unprepared for this revelation, that it required a vision to St. Peter, thrice repeated,[1] before they could believe in its

---

[1] Acts x. 11. There was also the baptism of the eunuch by Philip.

possibility, and then they would not accept it as authorising more than the acceptance of one household. For eighteen years it remained a dead fact producing no after effects.

More than twenty years after the baptism of Cornelius, Paul spoke of the admission of the Gentiles as one of those things not at first made known to the Church, but as a matter of special and later revelation, and as a mystery, a puzzle to their minds. It was an "economy of the grace of God," one that even principalities in heavenly places were ignorant of, but which was revealed to them by the action of the Church.[1]

Thus we see how that the work of the Spirit was educative, evolutionary, a gradual expansion; circumstances forcing the Twelve to act in a manner they had not at first contemplated, and to formulate dogmas out of facts, from which indeed they grew naturally, but nevertheless unexpectedly.

We have not, unhappily, any record of the lives and thoughts of the other Apostles such as we have of St. Paul; but we know just enough to be sure that the same process went on in them as we shall see in the sequel was followed in Paul, though, indeed, in them it cannot have been as vigorous and rapid.

I remember, when young, and a pupil of the late Bishop of Carlisle (Goodwin) when he was a tutor at Cambridge, that he set me Euler's proof of the Binomial Theorem. I laboured at it ineffectually; it was to me as though I were striking my head against a stone wall. My tutor bade me lay it aside. A twelvemonth later I attacked it again, and now it presented to me no difficulties. My reasoning

[1] Eph. ii. 3-6.

powers had grown so as to enable me to master what previously mastered me.

This is what takes place in all minds, a gradual enlargement of scope and acquisition of power to see more than was seen yesterday.

There is but one law applicable to things spiritual as to things mental.

With the Apostles, however, there was set them no complicated problem to solve, but certain facts of which they were witnesses, the signification of which, the world-wide application of which they could not conceive at first. And no wonder. These were the articulate thoughts of the mind of God, and how could the human mind see their length and breadth and height and depth at once? What is Creation but the materialisation of the thoughts of God? And yet we are ever going further and sounding deeper, and bringing to light fresh marvels. Who can say what more may not be unfolded out of the mysteries of natural forces? And it is the same with spiritual truths. We have not yet reached the end of them. As we are able to bear it, the Spirit continuously reveals to men something rising out of those facts to which the Twelve bare witness, as facts and facts only.

CHAPTER VI

ANTIOCH

A.D. 48—49

Paul again at Tarsus—Apparently nothing done by him in his native town—The kinsmen of Paul—The Church in Antioch—The proselytes—The burning question of circumcision—The difficulty of the situation—Barnabas sent to Antioch—He goes to Tarsus to fetch Paul—The practical difficulty—The prophets are silent—Paul in an ecstasy—Paul again in Jerusalem—Hesitation of the Apostles—The line adopted by them—That suggested by Paul—The policy of Paul a new departure—The position taken up by the Apostles towards him—The vision in the Temple—Difficulties—Return to Antioch—Three stages in Church development—Importance of understanding this—Religious ecstasy—Its nature—The ecstasies of St. Theresa—Her account of them—Revelations—Tennyson's trances—Phenomena that are inexplicable and demand close investigation—Epilepsy, catalepsy, and trance—The spiritual element.

PAUL remained at Tarsus, probably with his father, for ten years. When, in his Epistle to the Galatians, he is made, in the Authorised Version, to say, " After three years I went up to Jerusalem to see Peter. . . . . Then fourteen years after I went up again to Jerusalem with Barnabas," we obtain, perhaps, a wrong impression. The words should be rendered, " In the third year I went up to Jerusalem," and the fourteen years are perhaps to be reckoned from the Conversion. If he were converted in A.D. 35, which is the date almost all critics fix, then he came to Jerusalem in A.D. 38, and he disappears from our view for ten years.

These years must have been entirely unimportant from

a missionary point of view, or we should have been given information relative to them by St. Luke. But it is a feature of this writer to describe the successes of his hero, and pass over entirely, or with few words, the failures of St. Paul. Paul founded no Church in his native city, and never once alludes to Tarsus in his letters. In his Epistle to the Galatians he mentions his having gone into Syria and Cilicia after his first interview with Peter, but is significantly silent as to what he had done there.[1] A prophet is at a disadvantage in his own city, and Paul was no exception. He worked at his trade. Whether he convinced his father and brethren is questionable. Many years later he was rescued through the instrumentality of a nephew at Jerusalem from an attempt to assassinate him, and this young man could hardly have got wind of the plot, had not his family been considered "safe" people, eager to be rid of their heretical kinsman.

However, in his Epistle to the Romans, written ten or twelve years later, he mentions his "kinsmen," Andronicus and Junia, Herodion, Lucius, Jason and Sosipater, as believers. They may have been convinced later, as they were not at Tarsus, but in Rome; it is conceivable that the fact of their believing had made Tarsus too hot for them, and they deemed it advisable to put a stretch of sea between them and their unbelieving relatives. This, however, is all conjecture. The fact remains that Luke is absolutely mute relative to any successes achieved by Paul

---

[1] This has seemed incredible to modern biographers, just as the retired life of Christ up to His ministry seemed incredible to early Christians, and both have filled in the gaps out of their imagination. Geikie devotes a chapter of thirty-four pages to a mythical evangelisation of Cilicia, to which neither Luke's narrative nor the epistles of Paul bear any witness.

in his native province. It is true that in A.D. 52 the Apostles wrote to the Churches of Syria and Cilicia, or rather "to the brethren which are of the Gentiles," in these two provinces, but this does not prove that Paul had had any hand in convincing those in Cilicia; and they who there believed were probably such as had heard of Christ at Antioch, for the province extended to within not many miles of that city.

That Paul did not in those ten years return to Judæa is certain, for he says, "I was unknown by face unto the Churches of Judæa which were in Christ; but they had heard only, that he which persecuted us in times past now preached the faith which once he destroyed, and they glorified God in me."[1]

The occasion of his reappearance was this. At Antioch, the Church had swelled in numbers, and had grown active, and with its increase in numbers and activity a great problem had come to the forefront. Were the converts from the Gentiles to be circumcised previous to baptism? Was the way into the Church to be through the porch of the Law?

Outside of Judaism was the ring of the proselytes "who feared God," men and women who attended the synagogue, refrained from idolatry and from marriages within the prohibited degrees, and from eating meat with the blood in it. But the men were not circumcised, and none were required to obey the Mosaic ceremonial Law nor observe the traditions.

Not the narrowest of the party in the Church which clung to the Law would deny instruction in the perfect way to those "who feared God," but they objected to their

[1] Gal. i. 22-24. See on all this the Chronological Introduction.

admission by baptism to full church membership and participation in the Agape and the Eucharist. The cases of Cornelius and of the eunuch had, so they argued, been exceptional.

The Church of Antioch was made up mostly of Hellenic Jews, if not entirely of such, with a huge nebulous ring of proselytes about it, men of more or less strict observance, but none circumcised. The Holy Ghost had not miraculously declared that they were to be admitted to baptism, either by an outpouring of the gift of tongues, or through the prophets. What was to be done? The outer belt was becoming so extensive as to threaten to contract and overwhelm the heart of true and complete believers, circumcised and baptized. The matter was brought before the Twelve at Jerusalem. Were the Antiochian Christians to await a revelation with regard to these neophytes, or were they to act on instructions from headquarters? "He that heareth you, heareth me," Christ had said to His Apostles, and the Antiochians were willing to obey. Let the Twelve speak out. But the Apostles were in perplexity. Such a step as to admit all proselytes was so large that they feared to take it on such a warrant as the effusion granted to Cornelius. They must have further direction from the Spirit. So they despatched Barnabas to Antioch to investigate the situation, and to report on it to them.

When he arrived, he was rejoiced at the zeal manifested by the converts, but he was not invested with authority to settle the matter, the prophets remained silent, and no flickering flames descended. He exhorted and reasoned, with the result that the outside throng became greater and the pressure on the barriers correspondingly increased.

ANTIOCH

Barnabas, in his perplexity, now thought on Paul. He was aware of his abilities, and some vague notion may have entered his head that he was set apart to solve the difficulty.

Possibly, Ananias of Damascus may have come to Antioch and have suggested that Paul should be summoned. None seem to have seen that the revelation to Peter had settled the question. The Centurion had been baptized, but we are not told that he was admitted to the Agape and to Communion.

The real problem was this. What was to be done with the "devout men"? Were they to be incorporated into the Church by baptism, and, if so, were they to be further admitted to the Agape? Here was one *crux*. A Jew might not sit down to eat with one who was uncircumcised; if the proselyte were baptized, then he would undoubtedly demand also a place at the table, where all ate in symbol of unity.

But then the Jewish members would be put in a dilemma. If they sat with them and ate, they broke the law, they became defiled. Must they go through a legal purification after every love feast? If they were obliged to do this, it was in vain for them to regard the Agape as a bond of union, it was a pledge of discord.

It must be remembered that the Church was not as yet disentangled from the Synagogue. The Christians attended the Jewish place of worship and instruction, observed the Sabbath and new moons and the ordered feasts, paid the poll-tax to the Temple, were one with the Jews to the general eye, differing from them, apparently in this only, that they superadded observance of the Lord's Day to that of the Sabbath. They attended the synagogue on the seventh day, and then adjourned to continue their pious exercises to a private habitation.

And this observance of the Sabbath as well as the Lord's Day as sacred along with it, continued after the separation of the Church from the Synagogue, for two centuries.

The presence of Christian Jews in the Synagogue raised difficulties, if it were known that they associated at table with Christian Gentiles, and were therefore subject to impurity. And the rulers had the means of enforcing their judgments and compelling conformity. For the Imperial Government accorded large powers of self-government, and the right of punishing refractory or transgressing members in any way short of life and mutilation.

The rulers of the Synagogue might be forced to expel the Believing Jew. But that would be an extreme measure, had recourse to only when others failed, as one driven out of the Synagogue could not be made to pay the Temple-toll, nor the contributions for the support of the Synagogue and the charities connected with it.

At the present day, when Christianity is organised entirely apart from Judaism, such Jews as showed Christian tendencies would be expelled the Synagogue without the smallest scruple. But it was not so at the time of which I write, when Christianity was an opinion and not a sect. Those who believed did not regard themselves as other than Jews holding the "more perfect way," as truer Jews than the Jews themselves.[1] Their religious assemblies were looked on much as strict Churchmen might regard private prayer-meetings, not as schismatical, in themselves, but as allowable peculiarities.

In another chapter I shall show how the Agape

[1] *Cf.* Rev. ii. 9.

originated; all I require here to indicate is the impossibility of a Jewish believer associating with a proselyte believer without incurring legal pollution.

In Jerusalem a *modus vivendi* had been arrived at. The antagonism against the Church was not from the side of the Pharisees, but from that of the Sadducees. In Jerusalem the difficulty relative to contact with believing Gentiles did not occur. It was, the Apostles thought, advisable to avoid or postpone a breach.

Such was the difficulty that had to be met, and Barnabas went to Seleucia, shipped over to Tarsus, and invited Paul to assist him with his counsel at Antioch. A report must be made to the Twelve, some practical solution offered; and time was aggravating the difficulty.

The two friends reached Antioch in the early part of A.D. 48. There they remained, watching the operation of the Spirit on the individual souls of the converts, and still no exterior token was given for their direction.

Some time previously—probably in A.D. 44—prophets had announced an approaching famine, and a collection was begun for the poor at Jerusalem. The famine began in A.D. 44, and probably lasted, more or less acutely, for several years.[1]

It is certainly remarkable and deserving of notice that at this moment, eminently critical, the Holy Spirit should not have spoken and shown the way in which the dispute was to be allayed. This can be explained only on the supposition that prophetic gifts were accorded in the

---

[1] It is usual to hold that Barnabas fetched Paul in A.D. 44, and that both went up to Jerusalem with the contributions in A.D. 45, and again about the question of the circumcision later. I do not see that this double journey was necessary. See as to the difficulties as to dates what has been said in the Chronological Introduction.

earliest infancy, and were now purposely withdrawn, that the Church might act on its own inherent powers. At this juncture, just before starting from Antioch, Paul fell into an ecstasy, and in this condition received a mysterious communication from on high. He wrote of this some nine years later to the Corinthians: " I knew a man in Christ, whether in the body, I cannot tell, God knoweth; such an one, caught up to the third heaven .... caught up into Paradise and heard words which it is unlawful for a man to utter."[1] In this trance Paul received instruction relative to the difficulty in which he and Barnabas and the Twelve were involved, and he was ordered to go up forthwith to Jerusalem, and communicate what had been told him to those who were the heads of the Church.[2]

Accordingly Barnabas and Paul went up to the Holy City, saw the elders, and put into their hands the sum contributed by the believers in Antioch.[3] Barnabas then visited James, Peter and John, and made his report to them; and, acting on his recommendation, Paul was called into consultation.

The account of what ensued is given by Paul in his Epistle to the Galatians. It may be thus paraphrased: "On my visit to Jerusalem, after the vision I had at Antioch, I communicated to the Apostles my view of the

---

[1] 2 Cor. xii. 2-4.   [2] Gal. ii. 1, 2.

[3] One reason why it has been supposed that there were two visits is because Paul speaks in Gal. ii. of seeing the three Apostles, whereas in Acts xi. 30, it is said that the disciples of Antioch sent the money to the elders, and it is therefore concluded that the Apostles were absent. I do not see this. The elders looked to the business. Professor Ramsay thinks that Paul and Barnabas remained some time in Jerusalem, and themselves supervised the distribution. But surely this would have been an indecent interference with the functions of the elders and deacons, and have taken off the grace of the contribution.

case, and explained to them the nature of my teaching. This was in a private consultation. I was desirous that all misunderstandings should be cleared away. I had with me Titus, a Greek, who believed, and he was required neither by me, nor by them, to be circumcised, much less was the general principle laid down that this Judaic rite was to be exacted as a necessary preliminary to full church membership. There was, however, a set of sneaking brethren peering into our proceedings and condemning them, and insisting that we should adhere to the practice hitherto pursued, which has proved to be an intolerable bondage. But not for an hour did we yield to them; either by compliance with what they demanded, or by acquiescence in their arguments. Moreover, the acknowledged leaders—be their distinction what it may—gave me no new command, but on the contrary, perceiving that I had a special vocation to the uncircumcised proselytes, just as Peter's special call seemed to be to the Jews by birth and ritual incorporation; they, I say, to wit, James and Peter and John, recognised pillars of the Church, gave to me and to Barnabas solemn assurances that they were in full accord with my view; and they decided that we should go unto the heathen, whereas they would work on, as heretofore, among the Jews."[1]

The Apostles, it is clear, were not disposed as yet, themselves, to make a new departure: it is quite possible that they may have had instructions from Christ not to finally break with the Temple and Synagogue till a sign was given them that there was to be a change in their procedure. But even if we reject this, we can allow that the Spirit had not called on them to change their course of action, and

[1] Gal. ii. 1-9.

that till He distinctly spoke they were right in remaining at Jerusalem and working from thence.

Hitherto the synagogues of the Dispersion had swept together vast numbers of pagans; some of these latter had no doubt only coquetted with Judaism, others were more or less convinced in its Monotheism, and in the cogency of its divinely given Law of the Ten Commandments. Some few, but these were very few, consented to be circumcised. Among the Syrians, Arabians, Egyptians, there was no strong prejudice against this rite; indeed, in Egypt it had been customary from time immemorial. But Romans and Greeks would not submit to it. Of these latter many learned to respect and admire the pure doctrine of Mosaism and there stopped. They were regarded as "righteous men," and were not required to do more than observe the so-called Noachian law. Such men did not visit Jerusalem, they remained in their homes. But the true Jews and the zealous and thorough proselytes, some few from the West, but plenty from East and South, came annually to Jerusalem. The amount of influence that could be exercised on these was incalculable, and could best be exerted from Jerusalem.

But also the true Jews from the West who came to the Holy City came within the range of the teaching of the Twelve, and could therefore be made by them into propagators of the truth in the West as well as the East.

At the root of the hearts of the Apostles lay the hope, not to be abandoned as yet, that all Israel might accept the truth, and the Synagogue and Temple be transformed into places of prayer and worship of God as revealed by Jesus, Jerusalem to be the centre of the Christian world, and the Temple the seat of typal worship for all races of men.

But Paul saw that the conversion of the world might be

accelerated by supplementing the system of the Twelve by another, by that of an itinerant missioner visiting every synagogue in the lands whither the Jews had been scattered, and of stimulating spiritual conversion therein. He no more thought of going directly to the nations than did the Twelve. But he did desire to visit the Jews of the Dispersion, and preach in their synagogues.

I do not suppose that the elder Apostles would at all demur to his proposal to visit the believers scattered abroad in every place where were Jewish settlements, but they might hesitate to sanction his proposal to use the synagogues in the manner suggested. This had been tried by Stephen at Jerusalem, with the result that there had been disturbance and a persecution. Was it not likely that, if Paul adopted the same method, the same results would follow? The question, in the first place, was one of prudence.

For their part they preached Christ in the porticoes of the Temple; they no longer lifted up their voices in the synagogues. They were not now invited to do so, and they did not attempt to force themselves on unwilling congregations. What Paul proposed was to take advantage of the unsuspicion and inexperience of the Hellenistic Jews abroad; and the elder Apostles doubted the expediency of such a course. The question, in the second place, was one of principle. Above all, they were desirous of avoiding the stirring up of angry passions. When once heated controversy broke out, temper would obscure reason, parties would be formed, and the chances of national submission to Christ would be cut away.

Obviously, the Apostles did not altogether trust Paul's account of his vision seen at Antioch. They thought he had unwittingly coloured it to suit his own wishes. They may have argued that for the vision to be satisfactory it should be accorded to them rather than to Paul, who was only over eager to make a new departure.

They deprecated what might precipitate a schism. So long as the Church was as a pinch of leaven in the midst of the meal of the Synagogue, it was permeating it with new life, and was transforming it. Disengage the Church from it, and it could influence individuals singly, but would be powerless to effect a national religious revolution. Then it was, that, vexed at heart because the Twelve did not respond cordially to his proposals, Paul fell into a trance, whilst praying in the Temple. He saw Christ, who said: "Make haste and get thee quickly out of Jerusalem; for they will not receive thy testimony concerning me."[1]

These words certainly intimate mistrust in the Twelve as to the fidelity to facts in Paul's statement relative to his commission received in vision.

If Paul's description before Agrippa of what he had heard at his conversion be correctly given by Luke, then it must be allowed that he possessed a faculty of giving these matters a partial aspect, and embroidering them to suit his purpose, which is calculated if not to awake suspicion, at all events to call forth reserve.

I cannot see how the elder Apostles could have acted in any other manner than they did, if possessed of ordinary intelligence and common-sense. They gave him a free hand: probably they saw that unless they gave it he would act in independence. They remained at Jerusalem and continued the work on the lines already laid. If the

[1] Acts xxii. 18.

Spirit willed that they should alter their conduct, He would reveal His will to them; He had his appointed mouthpieces, the prophets; He could address them in vision. Christ, who had specially commissioned them, would give them some sign as to how they were to act.

Were they to accept the assurance of a man of whom all they knew was that he was a weathercock in his religious opinions, and that in a matter of supreme importance? He indeed asserted that in Antioch he had been told to inform them what the will of Christ was. But they were the inspired, accredited Apostles of Christ, on whom the Spirit had visibly descended, and who had received commission and authority and instruction from Christ Himself. In common, everyday matters, no man will alter his conduct at the advice of a stranger. In courts of law there must be two or three witnesses to establish any case. In a council of war, would the assembled generals reverse their conduct of a campaign because a volunteer came in and said that he had dreamed that the war could be carried out more effectively by new means?

To return to the vision in the Temple. According to Paul's own account, Christ said to him, "Depart from Jerusalem. They will not receive thy testimony concerning me."

Then Paul informs us that he answered the Saviour: "Lord, they know that I imprisoned and beat in every synagogue them that believed on Thee; and when the blood of Thy martyr Stephen was shed, I also was standing by and consenting unto his death, and took charge of the garments of the executioners. Therefore they must be convinced of my sincerity." But Christ said to him: "Depart, for I will send thee far hence unto the

Gentiles." When Paul in his Epistle to the Galatians speaks of his apostleship being not of men, neither of his having been commissioned by men, he refers to this revelation of Jesus Christ,[1] afforded him when the Twelve were obstructive, not indeed to his working on the same lines as the Pharisee missioners, but to his insistance that on the pagans abandoning polytheism and embracing the Gospel, they should at once receive baptism and obtain a right to sit down at the Agape beside the circumcised believers.

Without further delay Paul and Barnabas returned to Antioch, taking John Mark with them.

They had brought up with them Titus, a Greek and uncircumcised, but a believer. Nothing was said by the Twelve about requiring him to be made subservient to the Law, and Paul was constrained to remain satisfied with this. But, in fact, nothing had been gained. The whole question was remitted to a further occasion. Very likely the Apostles bade Paul and Barnabas act on their own responsibility; if Paul was convinced that he had been authorised to admit the uncircumcised to baptism, let him act as directed.

There were, if I may employ the Hegelian term in this connection, certain *moments* in the progress of the Church that deserve to be noted, as there ensued friction and heat at the passage from one to the other.

The first moment or stage was this:—

The Church existed as a germ in the midst of the Synagogue, affecting it through every part. The Christians observed the customs and united in the worship of the Synagogue, very much as Irvingites now attend the

[1] Gal. i. 11, 12.

services of the Church of England. But they supplemented the Jewish worship with pious exercises of their own in private houses.

But this provoked much irritation, through the intimate association of the Christians with uncircumcised believers.

Moreover the Jews, if they chose, could make the position of the Christian members of the Synagogue quite intolerable. They could try them for every breach of traditional usage, or for heresy, and punish them by scourging, imprisoning, by all kinds of torture short of death.

Consequently there was among the Christians a tendency developed, and constantly acquiring strength, to break loose from the Synagogue.

The only restraining influence affecting the minds of the Jews was a consideration for the money of these restless believers. They did not love them personally, but they did not desire to lose their pecuniary contributions to the Temple, the Synagogue, and the support of their poor. On the other hand the Christians no doubt felt very reluctant to pay Temple, Synagogue and poor rates to a body of men who bullied and maltreated and insulted them.

The second moment or stage was this:—

The situation became so strained that at last it became intolerable, and the believers broke away from the Synagogue entirely. Paul no doubt saw that the schism must come sooner or later; and whereas the Apostles at Jerusalem strove by every means in their power to retard this stage, Paul was eager to precipitate it, and in his new foundations started his churches immediately in separation from the synagogues. We shall see presently how he effected this, and what profound exasperation he aroused in the minds of the Jews by so doing.

But if he thought that by this course he was going to steer the Church into still waters, he was vastly mistaken.

The Jewish communities were under legal protection, the synagogues were recognised by the law, and worship therein was authorised, and the rulers of the synagogues were empowered to enforce unity and order in their places of worship. But when Paul disentangled his converts from the meshes of Judaism, and planted them in communities as raw creations of his own, unattached to the synagogues as they were unaffiliated to the established paganism, these were illegal conventicles, and the members were threatened with as severe handling as were Dissenters under Stuart *régime*. They at once became members of illicit communities. Any Jew might inform against them and put the law in motion to close their meeting-houses, and imprison their pastors.

The Jews were not at all slow to grasp their opportunity, and immense annoyance was caused thereby.

A third moment or stage was attempted, as I believe, by Paul when he appealed to Cæsar, and that was to obtain the Imperial recognition of the Christian conventicles, so that they might be placed under the protection of the law, as well as the synagogues. This Paul possibly may have succeeded momentarily in obtaining from Nero, but if so it was at once withdrawn, and the Church did not enter on this stage until the reign of Constantine the Great.

With the Church in this position, enjoying protection, we have nothing to do in this volume. But to properly understand the Acts of the Apostles and the Epistles of St. Paul, we must, I conceive, clearly see the Church passing out of the first stage into the second. At Jerusalem it was in one condition, in Syria and Asia Minor in the other; and to comprehend the true significance of

Paul's appeal to Rome we must appreciate his desire to lift the Church out of the second stage into the third.

At this point we may consider briefly the very difficult question of religious ecstasy. It is a problem that can not be solved, because our knowledge of the mutual relations of soul and body is incomplete, if not wholly defective.

That in certain physical conditions the Spirit does manifest itself in very perplexing phenomena is certain, and it is also certain that intense spiritual exaltation does react on the physical system in a manner difficult to understand.

Unquestionably some persons are constitutionally incapable of ecstasy, and others most certainly have their spiritual faculties so imperfectly developed as not to be able to conceive that such a condition can actually exist. An hysterical and epileptic state may be said to conduce to it, but will not produce it, unless the soul be in a condition of spiritual tension.

In St. Theresa's autobiography, written reluctantly at the command of her director, there is a great deal relative to her experiences in rapture. She was a female counterpart of St. Paul, with the same highly strung nervous temperament, inflexible resolution, tact, and common sense. Just as St. Paul founded churches, so did the female saint found convents, and amidst persecution and obloquy very little inferior to what were encountered by the Apostle. Her record of her spiritual experiences may be entirely trusted. She is transparently honest, but of course she was quite unable to distinguish between what was physical and what was purely psychical.

Her narrative is prolix to an intolerable degree, and when she endeavours to give a definition fails, partly because incapable of defining what belonged to a sphere above ordinary experience, and therefore inexplicable by words, and partly also from lack of medical instruction as to what to observe and what discard.

"The soul," she says, "searching after God finds itself sinking into a condition of sweet and excessive delight, accompanied by a sensation of fainting, so that the breath begins to fail, as also corporeal strength, in such a manner that the hands can not be moved; the eyes are closed without our having any desire to close them; and when they are open the soul sees nothing distinctly through them. One may have a book before one, and be able to see the letters, but the faculty of reading is gone. One may hear words spoken, but the power to understand what is spoken is withdrawn. Thus the soul receives no assistance from the senses. As to attempting in such a condition to speak, it is not practicable to form the words, and even if that were done, the power to utter them is not there, because all bodily strength is gone, while that of the soul is increased. However long the time may seem in which the faculties are in suspense, it is in reality very short. Half an hour is the outside; for my part I do not think the duration of ecstasy is ever so long. Hours may be spent in prayer before this condition is reached, but when reached, it is like tasting celestial wine that produces inebriation, and the powers of body and mind are lost. But the period during which they are entirely lost is very short. There is nothing of imagination in this. In my judgment, this faculty is entirely in abeyance. On recovery from this condition one is, as it were, stupid for some hours, but little by little the faculties are brought back by God."[1]

[1] "Life of St. Theresa," c. 19. I have used the translation by Canon Dalton, Lond., 1855, without following it literally, and cutting out a vast amount of rambling matter.

It is not possible in this description to fail to recognise a cataleptic seizure.

"I should like to know how to explain the difference between the union of the soul with God and rapture, also called elevation of the soul and ecstasy. These are all different names for one and the same condition. It seems to me that in it the Lord attracts the soul just as the vapours are drawn aloft from the earth and ascend into heaven. In something in this way He transports the soul upwards and reveals to it the riches of that kingdom which He has prepared for her. In these raptures, the soul seems no longer to animate the body. The natural heat declines, and the body becomes cold, whereas the soul is possessed with great sweetness and light.[1] All power of resistance is taken from one. The soul then seems to be raised to a condition of suspension, and I seemed to understand St. Paul's words when he says that he was crucified to the world. I do not say that I felt as if I were crucified, for I was not, only the soul was lifted up between heaven and earth, and suffered acutely. The sense of God, of His infinite greatness, produces excessive pain such as sometimes takes away the senses, and it is as the agony of death itself, and yet withal is accompanied with incomparable pleasure and content. It is a sharp yet most delightful kind of martyrdom. The first token of the approach of an ecstasy produces alarm. One is afraid of dying under it. Yet when once begun, the soul would be glad to remain in this suffering state for ever, though the pain is almost unendurable. Sometimes I am pulseless,

---

[1] The passage in the original is obscure, inasmuch as St. Theresa does not distinguish between physical heat and spiritual warmth. I think the above renders her real meaning.

as my sisters inform me, and the bones (muscles?) of my arms stand out. My hands become so stiff that I cannot close them, and I feel a pain in my wrists till next day, and indeed my entire body is full of aches afterwards as though I had been dislocated."[1]

> *Thou wilt be sick with love, and yearn for Him.*
> . . . . . .
> *And thou wilt hate and loathe thyself;* . .
> . . . . *and wilt desire*
> *To slink away, and hide thee from His sight;*
> *And yet wilt have a longing aye to dwell*
> *Within the beauty of His countenance.*
> *And these two pains, so counter and so keen—*
> *The longing for Him, when thou seest Him not,*
> *The shame of self at thought of seeing Him—*
> *Will be thy veriest, sharpest purgatory.*[2]

So much for the physical conditions. As to the pain felt by St. Theresa, it is quite probable that she mixed up in her mind the anguish caused by cramp with that occasioned by spiritual sensations.

She goes on to give some account of the revelations accorded to her in this condition.

"There are, when we are in this state, certain words very distinctly formed in the soul, which, though not heard with the corporeal ears, are understood more clearly than if they were so heard. Nor can the soul avoid understanding them and concentrating her attention on them. It is useless to resist, however much we may strive. When in this world we do not wish to hear, we stop our ears or divert our attention elsewhere. But this is absolutely

---

[1] "Life of St. Theresa," c. xx.
[2] Newman: "The Dream of Gerontius," ed. 1894, p. 48.

impossible when God speaks to the soul. We are then made to listen whether we will or no."[1]

"Being one day at prayer, I saw standing near me, or to speak more properly, I felt and perceived—for I saw nothing at all, either with bodily or spiritual eyes—that Christ was close by me and heard Him speak to me. As up to this time I had been quite ignorant, and without experience in such matters, I was very frightened, and could do nothing but weep. But presently the Lord comforted me, by speaking only one word, and I found myself quieted and in great delight. It seemed to me that Christ was at my side; but the vision was not imaginary; that is to say, I saw no form, but I was perfectly conscious that He was there, on my right hand. I do not know how it was that I knew who it was, but I could not help perfectly understanding who it was. I felt and clearly understood that. I have tried to explain my experience by a comparison. If a person were blind, he might still be aware that another stood by, through his other senses. But this illustration fails; for one reason, because there is no sense of darkness. The Lord's presence is impressed on the soul by a token, clearer than the sun itself, and yet no sun or radiance is visible, only a certain light, invisible to the eye, which floods the understanding. Things that we see, we do not always see so clearly that we are not in doubt whether we have made a mistake. But in this condition there is no possibility of error or of hesitation. I admit that this is talking in language that cannot be understood except by such as have had some sort of experience in spiritual things. Our Lord plants in the soul whatever He wills it to understand, and that without

[1] "Life of St. Theresa," c. xxv.

image seen or form of words, but ecstatically revealed. Sometimes it has seemed to me that neither the powers of the mind nor the bodily senses were taken away; but this is very unusual. When the senses are lost, as is commonly the case, then all that comes to us seems to be the work of the Lord. There is no effort on our part. His communication is in us, like food conveyed into the stomach without our having eaten or knowing how it got there."[1]

"The light seen is infused and does not dazzle or weary. It is so different from that of this world, that even the brightness of the sun is dim in comparison, and though seen, yet the eyes can scarce open to behold it. Not that any actual sun or natural light is seen—it is beyond that and different in kind. It is a light that never sets, and has no night, but is always constant. Nor can any distraction divert us from it, nor any power resist it; nor, on the other hand, can any wishing to see it and striving after it enable us to attain to it."[2]

This condition of trance is familiar to medical men, but the condition of trance made use of by God for vision and revelation is another matter. If it be a state in which the soul is detached from the body in a very unusual manner, it is one susceptible to divine illumination, but not impetrating it. That entirely depends on the spiritual condition of the person who falls into trance. In certain physical states man is more amenable to spiritual impressions than in others; but it is only to such as God chooses that this condition is made the vehicle for intercommunion.

To the experiences of St. Theresa may be added those of Tennyson. In his "In Memoriam" he alludes to a sort of

[1] "Life of St. Theresa," c. xxvii. [2] *Ibid.* c. xxviii.

ecstasy into which he had fallen when musing on his
departed friend.

> *So word by word, and line by line,*
> *The dead man touch'd me from the past,*
> *And all at once it seem'd at last*
> *The living soul was flash'd on mine,*
>
> *And mine in this was wound, and whirl'd*
> *About empyreal heights of thought,*
> *And came on that which is, and caught*
> *The deep pulsations of the world,*
>
> *Æonian music measuring out*
> *The steps of Time—the shocks of Chance—*
> *The blows of Death. At length my trance*
> *Was cancell'd, stricken thro' with doubt.*
>
> *Vague words! but ah, how hard to frame*
> *In matter-moulded forms of speech,*
> *Or ev'n for intellect to reach*
> *Thro' memory that which I became.*[1]

In 1874 Tennyson wrote to a friend who had communicated to him some strange experiences he had had when recovering from the effects of anæsthetics:

"I have never had any revelations through anæsthetics, but a kind of waking trance (this for lack of a better name) I have frequently had, quite up from boyhood, when I have been all alone. This has often come upon me through repeating my own name to myself silently, till, all at once, as it were out of the intensity of the consciousness of individuality, the individuality itself seemed to dissolve and fade away into boundless being, and this not a confused

---

[1] "In Memoriam," xcv.

state, but the clearest, the surest of the surest, utterly beyond words, whose death was an almost laughable impossibility, the loss of personality (if so it were) seeming no extinction, but only the true life.

"I am ashamed of my feeble description. Have I not said the state is utterly beyond words?"[1]

Tennyson was ready to fight for the truth of this his experience.

There are two phenomena—or supposed phenomena—connected with spiritual rapture that ought to be here mentioned, as being constant in reports of such cases, yet which are not explicable by any physical laws. One is the lifting of the actual body from the ground, and the other is the illumination of the face.

It is very easy to deny the possibility of such manifestations, as contrary to known laws. One violates that of gravitation. But the evidence in favour of both is so general, that it would be advisable to hold the judgment in suspense till such phenomena or alleged phenomena have been scientifically investigated.

St. Paul certainly hints at such a corporal lifting up, when he says that during a trance he was not aware whether he were caught up bodily or not. St. Theresa says: "There comes on one in rapture such a quick and strong impetus that one feels as though being elevated between the wings of a soaring eagle. You know that you are carried away, but you know not whither. And the sense of being lifted up is so strong, that I have tried to resist, but it has cost me great pain; it seemed like struggling against an overmastering power, and left one

---

[1] Walters, J. C.: "In Tennyson Land," Lond. 1890, p. 38.

much exhausted. At other times it was impossible to resist, and then the soul was in transport, and with it the whole body was raised from the ground. This happened very seldom; but it did occur on one occasion when we were all together in the choir and I was on my knees. Once again during a sermon I felt it was coming on, and so threw myself on the ground, and the nuns came round and forcibly held me down."[1]

In the lives of all the great ecstatic saints there is mention of the same singular, not very edifying exhibition, and one might set it down to the lack of accurate observation, and proneness to exaggeration, and love of the marvellous that are common among pious Roman Catholics. But similar occurrences have been reported, in perfect good faith, outside the Roman communion. I will mention two only, of which I can guarantee the honesty of those who reported them to me. One case was this. A worthy young man, a wool-comber in Yorkshire, came to me one day in some agitation to tell me that he had just seen something that had perplexed him greatly. He had been in the church, when he saw a certain clergyman kneeling in private devotion before the altar. As he did not wish to disturb him, the young wool-comber remained quiet, when in observing him who was in prayer, to his astonishment, not unmingled with alarm, he saw him rise in kneeling position from the ground, as though drawn up. And the young man said to me: "I know it was so, because I saw the fringe of the altar-cloth continuous between him and the floor." This remained for about three minutes. The narrator knew nothing about ecstatics and the phenomena supposed to be associated with rapture.

[1] "Life of St. Theresa," c. xx.

The second case was this. There was an exceedingly holy young girl, a mill hand, dying of decline in the Yorkshire parish where I was curate. She was often in ecstasy whilst lying in her last sickness, and seemed unconscious of all around, though in spirit she was in prayer. One evening her sister came in great perturbation to the Vicarage and entreated the vicar to come up at once to the cottage, for that something strange was happening which frightened the whole family. He went there immediately and saw a very extraordinary sight. The girl was in fact in ecstasy, raised in a kneeling posture above her bed, with arms extended to heaven before her and she was touching the bed with her toes only. The position of the body was one absolutely impossible for any one to maintain naturally. Her face was in the set and radiant condition of rapture, and her lips moved, pouring forth prayer and praise. The vicar looked on thunderstruck, till with a sigh the girl sank back in her bed, unconscious that anything had been observed, that any thing strange had happened to her.

I give both these stories at second-hand, but I have not the smallest reason to doubt the good faith of those who related them to me. I am convinced that there have been others who have met with similar experiences, but who, afraid of mockery, and shrinking from disbelief, say nothing about what they have witnessed.

With respect to the second phenomenon, or alleged phenomenon, that of the illumination of the countenance, nothing shall be said here, as there is no intimation of this having attended the rapture of St. Paul, though it may be hinted at in the case of St. Stephen.

I do not, of course, assert that the elevation of the body

actually takes place, only that there is a certain amount of evidence that something of the sort does take place. What we naturally desire before admitting it, is trustworthy evidence. But it is precisely in such cases that it is not easily procurable.

It has been supposed by those who desire to find a natural explanation for everything out of common experience and apparently supernatural, that Paul was subject to cataleptic fits or to epilepsy.

In epilepsy there is foaming at the mouth, clenching of the teeth, and terrible muscular contortion. There is no evidence of any such fits coming on Paul. Catalepsy is different. In catalepsy the body becomes rigid, pulsation and breathing cease. When consciousness returns, the mind is a blank as to what took place during the fit. That trance is a form of catalepsy is possible enough; it differs from it as dreamful sleep differs from such as is dreamless. That Paul fell into rigidity of body, with loss of sensual perception and muscular control, is possible enough. In a state of perfervid prayer, the spirit may exercise such a strain on the physical system as to induce this condition. But it is not the cataleptic fit that produces the vision, but the spiritual exaltation that superinduces a temporary paralysis of the bodily powers.

Surrounded as we are at the close of the nineteenth century with an atmosphere of imposture, of theosophy and spiritualism, we are overdisposed to deny that the soul can dominate matter, as nothing of the sort falls within the range of our vulgar experience.

The holiest souls are most reticent on such matters; the blatant revelation of divine experiences comes only from the impostor. St. Theresa would never have disclosed her

experiences had she not been compelled thereto by her
superiors. It is well that we have her record, as it enables
us, in a measure, to understand the very similar condition
of the great Apostle to the Gentiles. In him we see the
same confidence as to the reality of his visions as there was
in St. Theresa. In him also we observe the same shrinking
from speaking of them. At the opening of the chapter
(2 Cor. xii.) in which he mentions them, he shows his intention of giving a record of what had been revealed to him.
But he feels uneasy at thus exposing to the public the inner
side of his life, and, in verse 5, this repugnance gains the
upper hand and abruptly arrests his pen. Instead of
glorying in his privileges, he glories in his weakness. He
never related the visions here alluded to; at the moment
when the contempt and opposition of his adversaries
impel him to do so, he halts, and lets fall the veil over
the depths of his spiritual life which for a moment he was
disposed to lift. We may remark that such revelations
came to the Apostle at all the crises of his career. In each
moment of extreme anxiety of mind, he received sudden
illumination. It was so before he went up to Jerusalem
about the matter of the uncircumcised. On leaving the
city, dissatisfied at the caution of the Twelve, again he
had a vision. It was so once more, when he was on his
way into Bithynia—he was turned about by it and sent
into Europe. On another occasion, at Ephesus, the parti-
culars of which we do not know; and when he was pros-
trated by discouragement, again he had the consolation of
hearing the voice of Christ saying to him, "My grace is
sufficient for thee." There is no class of men less understood than the mystic. As the moon has one face turned
away from earth, looking into infinity, a face we never see,

so is it with the mystic. In him there is the spiritual face—mysterious, inexplicable, but one with which we must reckon. And this it is that makes it so difficult to properly interpret the man of a constitution like Paul. We have to allow for a factor in his composition that escapes investigation.

CHAPTER VII

CYPRUS

A.D. 50

The organisation of the Church in Antioch—The prophets—The office already death-doomed—The ordination of Barnabas and Saul—Modes of election—The qualifications of Paul to be a missionary—His Judaic turn of mind—Paul's method not that of direct appeal to the heathen—For this he was unqualified—His imperfect Greek—His inability to state an argument intelligibly—His mode of preaching—His sincerity—Barnabas and Saul reach Cyprus—Cyprus full of Hebrews—At Paphos—Interview with Sergius Paulus—The Magian—The problematical conversion of the proconsul.

THE return to Antioch was followed by a revelation of the Spirit to the Church there.

Hitherto the believers at Antioch are not spoken of as constituting a Church. Now, however, this term is employed, and it indicates one immediate result of the return of Paul to the Syrian capital—a separation of the Christians from the Synagogue, that which the Twelve had especially desired to avoid. It may, however, have been forced on the Antiochian Church by the authorities of the Jewish community.

Now those who were circumcised were compelled to take a decided line, and sit down beside the uncircumcised at the Agape, or withdraw wholly from the community. And until this step had been taken, or forced on the Christian community, no organic life could take place in it. It had remained in an embryonic condition. This was a birth, a real birth, to individual existence. This is what Paul had desired. In Antioch the Church had passed into the second stage of existence, whereas in Jerusalem it still remained in the first condition.

With separation from the Synagogue began organisation, as a necessary consequence. We now hear of prophets and teachers. "Barnabas, Simeon surnamed Niger," apparently the Simon of Cyrene, father of Alexander and Rufus, who bore the cross for Christ, Lucius, also of Cyrene, and Manaen, foster-brother of Herod Antipas, and, according to the Ethiopic version of the Acts, the son of his nurse.[1]

The function of the prophets was that of guiding the infant Church in difficult circumstances, but obviously it was already death-doomed. It was provisional, and the occasion for the prophet was now at an end. In the most trying and difficult circumstances, the prophets had been absolutely useless. Their function was reduced to the indication of who were to be ordained to certain work—which indeed was sufficiently obvious without their intervention, and to prophesying famines—which every one knew by the failure of the crops must occur. Moreover, the self-arrogation of a gift of prophecy opened the door to self-deception and to wilful imposture. The primitive Church seems to have been heartily glad to be relieved of them. Under the old covenant there had been false prophets, and very speedily the like made their appearance, even in apostolic times, under the new covenant.[2]

[1] It has been suggested that Barnabas, Simeon, and Lucius were prophets, and the other two teachers, the connecting particles καί and τε indicating the distinction. But this can hardly be pressed. Barnabas heads the list as delegate of the Church at Jerusalem, Saul is placed last, and the rest are grouped between. [2] 2 Pet. ii. 1; 1 John iv. 1.

Their office seems to have been to direct the Church until it had attained to articulate thought and organic structure, when the need for it ended. And just as the seed-leaves of a plant fall off, as soon as ever it is about to advance from the preliminary stage of all, so was this office of the prophets to disappear.

When the Church at Antioch learned God's will relative to Barnabas and Saul, then a special fast was held with prayer, and the two were ordained to their work by the imposition of hands.

Nothing is said in the sacred text as to who were those who laid their hands on Barnabas and Saul, and gave them commission, and it has been concluded that this indicates a general imposition of hands by the entire congregation, as the plenitude of power was lodged in the body, and not yet concentrated in the person of the bishop. But it is more likely that the Antiochian Church followed the custom in the Synagogue, from which it had but just disengaged itself. In the latter the office of teacher was given by the laying on of hands by three rabbis, with the words, "Lo! thou art chosen; and to thee is committed power to judge." The president of the synagogue was always so ordained in the presence of the elders.

Moreover, the idea in the primitive Church seems to have been very strong that Christ was the actual head of the body and source of all authority and giver of commission. Although the Church might elect, the elected had to be submitted to Him, for Him to consecrate. "As my Father hath sent me, even so send I you," said Christ; and "Ye have not chosen me, but I have chosen you."

Acting on this precedent various methods of election were resorted to, but commission was given by one or more

CYPRUS 143

authorised thereto by Christ, and these specially so authorised were either the Apostles themselves or the prophets. In the choice of an Apostle, the Eleven had resorted to the Old Testament method of casting lots into the lap. The lot had fallen on Matthias. It is interesting to note that the word *cleric, clergy*, derives from the Greek κλῆρος signifying a lot. But at the choice of the deacons the lots were not cast, and they were chosen by vote. In the case of Barnabas and Saul, neither the lot nor the vote was had recourse to, as they were to be commissioned, not to a constituted Church but to form Churches where none existed. In the ordination of the two Apostles, probably Simon, Lucius and Manaen were the prophets who laid their hands on them.

The terms used by the Spirit in the revelation are remarkable. Instead of declaring that Christ had already chosen and set apart Barnabas and Saul, He instructed the Church to do this. "Do ye set them apart," was the command, "Do ye ordain them to the work for which I have called them." This, in itself, indicates that the day of extraordinary spiritual manifestations was at an end, and that the organic body was to act on its innate life by its proper members. The Holy Ghost had been given in such manifest mode as to impress all with the miraculousness of the intervention in the infancy only of the Church. This was now to cease. The Church was to develop her own divinely conferred, indwelling powers.

And now, before we see Paul start on his first missionary journey, we may pause to inquire what were his qualifications for the work, what was the Gospel he was about to preach, and to whom he purposed addressing himself. His early training under Gamaliel had not only made him thoroughly acquainted with Holy Scripture, it had also given to him subtlety of reasoning, and it had furnished him with an entire body of doctrine. It was from the Old Testament that he derived the primary and fundamental notions of his system: the ideas of God, of revelation, of justice, and of sanctity.

In nothing did he differ from the Twelve with respect to views relative to the Messianic kingdom, and in expectation of his living to see the return of Christ;[1] as already insisted on, the Messianic appearance as looked for by the Apostles differed from that expected by the Pharisees only in this, that they held that Jesus was the promised One who would return.

Paul was consequently admirably adapted to address the Hellenistic Jews in their synagogues. They would understand his appeals to Scripture, his phraseology would be comprehensible, and much of his doctrine that with which they were familiar. The proselytes, moreover, would understand what they had read in the Septuagint translation, and were to a certain extent indoctrinated with Jewish ideas.

But when Paul undertook to address those who were pagans, then the case was wholly different. He had not a soil prepared beforehand in which to sow the seed of life. He could not appeal to Scripture, nor use the familiar arguments that told in an address to the synagogue. Many of his theological expressions would be totally unintelligible to such as had not been given a previous schooling in their significance.

We form an altogether erroneous idea, if we suppose Paul going on his journeys preaching to the pagans. He

[1] 1 Thess. iv. 15, 17.

did nothing of the sort, except on rare occasions which are noted. Everywhere he went to the synagogues, and when the Jews refused to hear, then he drew off as many of the proselytes as he could entice from the synagogues. It was not possible for him in the brief visits he paid in each centre to convince and instruct heathens. He did not attempt it; he worked upon those already prepared.

If the Epistles written by him to the Churches be carefully considered, it will be seen that they are addressed to such as are saturated with Mosaism, in a way inconceivable unless they had been steeped in the teaching of the Synagogue. They presuppose not this only, but such a clinging to habits of mind and ceremonial usages as would be impossible in raw converts.

Moreover, Paul was not qualified to succeed as a preacher to the heathen. He could speak Greek passably, but his pronunciation, and his Hebraistic turns, his occasional lapses into bad grammar, were such as to subject him to ridicule among the highly cultured and such as were accustomed to listen to the orators in the Forum and the Porch. Those who heard him, from among the cultured, shrugged their shoulders, and said, "His bodily presence is weak, and his speech contemptible."[1] In his writings he was guilty of many solecisms. He confounded the tenses, putting the pluperfect for the præterite, the præterite for the present, the infinitive for the imperative; now one case is employed in place of another, then the substantive is taken in place of the adjective; now he makes an irregular use of the particles that serve to tie together the parts of his discourse, taking them in their Hebrew signification, making such confusion in his sense that the

[1] 2 Cor. x. 10.

antecedent seems to be the consequent, and conclusions take the place of premisses. He rambles from his point in an argument, is easily led away from his thread of reasoning upon a side issue, and it is sometimes very difficult to understand his drift.[1] Now if this is so in a letter that has been carefully revised, what must it have been in his extempore discourse?

So hard to be followed is his reasoning in his Epistles that for nearly two thousand years students have laboured on them to try to discover the line of argument pursued, and it may fairly be said that it is only in the last half century with our extended knowledge that we are in a position at last to unravel his meaning.

Happily, in addressing the heathen, the necessity of the case forced him to simplicity. We have given us in Acts three discourses, one at Antioch in Pisidia,[2] one at Lystra,[3] and one at Athens.[4] The first of these was addressed to the Jews, the other two to the pagans. Moreover, he has left us a summary of his apostolic preaching in the First Epistle to the Corinthians: "I declare unto you the gospel which I preached . . . . For I delivered unto you first of all, how that Christ died for our sins, *according to the Scriptures*; and that he was buried, and that he rose again the third day *according to the Scriptures*; and that he was seen of Cephas, then of the Twelve," &c.[5] It is apparent from this and similar passages, that he recited the events of the Passion and of the Resurrection, and argued from a scriptural basis that this was as foretold. Take away

---

[1] Sabatier, "L'Apôtre Paul," 1896, p. 150; Renan, "St. Paul," 1893, p. 231; Farrar, "Life and Work of St. Paul," excursus ii.
[2] Acts xiii. 16-41; 46-47.　　[3] Acts xiv. 15-17.
[4] Acts xvii. 22-31.　　[5] 1 Cor. xv. 1-9.

the scriptural argument as inappropriate for heathens, and his preaching consisted, when addressing the Gentiles, in a series of assertions of facts. To the Jews, all turned on textual evidence, and so Paul is spoken of by the author of the Acts as disputing in the synagogue of Thessalonica from a scriptural starting-point.

But in speaking to such as knew not the prophets he was forced to adopt another method. And in the Epistle to the Romans we see what his line of reasoning was. He insisted on the Gentiles having lost the knowledge of God originally given to man; and, losing that, their moral conscience became clouded. Nevertheless conscience still spoke spasmodically, and did not leave the heathen in repose.[1] Such was his groundwork. The address at Lystra is very brief, it goes no further than to insist on the testimony of the moral and religious conscience of mankind to the unity and goodness of God. That at Athens was more carefully thought out and is preserved at greater length. We shall have something to say about it later on.

But with Paul, what constituted his strength and enabled him to convince minds was his thorough sincerity, and this sincerity gave to him an eloquence that carried away his hearers, and made them overlook his inaccuracies in grammar and colonial dialect. However poor in style, incorrect in phraseology, and inconsequent in argument, his speech like his own frail body, "an earthen vessel," seemed to be rent by the force of the soul within; as in the case of the broken pitchers of Gibeon, the sherds were forgotten in the flash of the light that blazed through their interstices. His eloquence may be conjectured from his Epistles, written in the heat of controversy. It is like

[1] Rom. i. 18–32; ii. 15.

a torrent that digs out its own bed, and overthrows all barriers. Unfinished sentences, daring admissions, rabbinic subtleties, half thought out arguments, biting sneers, violent apostrophes, original ideas, all are whirled along on the waves, jostling each other, the significance of each lost in the irresistibility of the current which hurries them down.

The discourses given us in Acts are but faded and dried-up specimens, as much like the original as the plants in a herbarium resemble the same when living and blooming on the mountain side or in the hedge-row.

Yet, as already intimated, Paul rarely addressed the heathen; never if he could help it. His congregations were those of the wholly, or half-converted to Judaism in the synagogues. When he had formed a separate community out of these, then he placed over them men of Greek, or, at all events, non-Jewish, origin, more capable than himself of converting those who were weary of the monstrosities of pagan worship and the emptiness and inconclusiveness of classic philosophies.

When he got off the familiar ground of Old Testament prophecies, and where he could not quote texts, when he was not battling against Judaistic tendencies in his converts, he was helplessly at sea.

Early in March A.D. 46, Barnabas and Saul, taking John Mark with them, sailed from Seleucia for Cyprus, and, the wind being favourable, they shortly reached the island, and disembarked at Salamis. Barnabas was a native of Cyprus, and doubtless he had suggested to Paul the advisability of commencing operations there. It almost seems as though a sort of agreement had been come to with the Twelve that Barnabas and Paul should try their method at a distance, and then return and report on it whether it answered or not, whether the Divine Spirit manifestly favoured their mode of procedure. Paul and Barnabas did not attempt to convince the pagans on reaching Cyprus. They went at once and solely to the Jews and their satellites, the "believing men" in the synagogue. This we are plainly told. They attempted "to preach the Word of God in the synagogues of the Jews only."[1]

The thought of direct missionary work among the pagans never occurred to them. That could not be undertaken in a flying visit. A flower will often remain furled for days till a sunbeam touches it, when instantly it will expand. This was all Paul sought, either in Cyprus or elsewhere, in his after journeys—to touch with conviction those whose hearts were like a closed blossom. But he never sought to dig the ground, sow the seed, or tarry till ripe, where there was no preparation.[2] The Law, as he afterwards said, was a pedagogue leading to Christ; and so he used the Synagogue as an academy in which he might give to those instructed in the prophecies the announcement of their fulfilment in Christ.

Cyprus swarmed with Hebrews, who were sufficiently numerous to be a menace. They monopolised the trade, and they held the pleasure-loving natives in their grip as usurers. Cypriots and Jews lived in simmering hate. Fifty years later, in an outburst of fanatical detestation, the Jews rose and massacred, so it is said, 240,000 of the natives.

Barnabas and Paul went through the island, halting at every town on their way where there were a *ghetto* and a synagogue. That they met with no success is implied by

[1] Acts xiii. 5.
[2] Rom. xv. 20 and 2 Cor. x. 13–16 may be objected, but they do not apply. In these passages he refers to his working on ground already occupied by other Apostles, not ground prepared by the Synagogue.

the manner in which Luke hurries over the narrative to give an account of a meeting between Paul and a sorcerer before the governor of the island.

On reaching Paphos in the west, the two Apostles received an order from the proconsul to show themselves to him at New Paphos, where was his residence. This proconsul was Sergius Paulus. Pliny, about a quarter of a century later, mentions one of this name as an authority in natural history, and the same still later is commended by Galen.

Among those who formed the retinue of the governor was a magian impostor named Bar-Jesus, or Elymas—the same word as that used now for the Ulemas, doctors of the law among the Mohammadans.

Elymas occupied a position of some importance in the house of the proconsul. It was customary at the time for every noble and wealthy family to maintain a philosopher, who acted as friend, comforter, and guide, holding a sort of chaplaincy in the house, combined with a tutorship of the sons. Inquiring minds turned towards the East, and astrologers and charlatans of all sorts flocked from Chaldæa. It would appear from the presence of Elymas in the household of Sergius Paulus that this was the case here. If this proconsul be the searcher into natural science praised by Galen and referred to by Pliny, then we can quite understand that there should be in his retinue a man who professed a knowledge of the stars.

"The magian represented in his single personality both the modern fortune-teller and the modern man of science, and he had a religious as well as a merely superstitious aspect to the outer world. No strict line could then be drawn between lawful, honourable scrutinising of the secret powers of nature and illicit attempts to pry into them for selfish ends; between science and magic, chemistry and alchemy, between astronomy and astrology. The two sides of investigation passed by hardly perceptible degrees into one another."[1]

Paul most certainly addressed the proconsul on the truths he believed. We may take his speech at Athens as the type of those he would employ on such occasions. He could not fall back on Scripture, for Sergius Paulus knew it not, and he could not claim the great poets as thinkers —as later did Clement of Alexandria—because he himself was acquainted with them only by such snatches of their lines as had passed into common usage. But just as at Athens he seized on a local object illustrative of the religious bewilderment of the Greek mind on which to hang his discourse, so doubtless would he do now. He would point to the vileness of the cult of Venus in the isle—there in that Paphian temple on the height, white against the gentian-blue sky—and from this show that it must be false, odious in the sight of God, who was, as the conscience of man proclaimed, of purer eyes than to behold iniquity. That the magian rudely endeavoured to interrupt him is likely. He is represented as "seeking to turn away the deputy from the faith," and "pervert the right ways of the Lord." The Bezan revision of the text says that he did so "because the proconsul was listening with much pleasure to Paul." The Apostle at last, irritated at the interference of the man, turned on him, and, fixing his eyes steadily on him, exclaimed, "O full of all subtilty and all mischief, thou child of the devil, thou enemy of all righteousness, wilt thou not cease to pervert the right ways of the Lord?

[1] Ramsay: "St. Paul," p. 78.

And now, behold, the hand of the Lord is upon thee, and thou shalt be blind, not seeing the sun for a season."

Immediately a mist and a darkness fell on the magician, and he was seen groping his way, to find a hand that would lead him forth.[1]

Sergius Paulus, we are told, "believed, being astonished at the doctrine of the Lord."

We are not told that he was baptized, nor that any of his house believed. He expressed courteous acquiescence in what Paul had said. It agreed with his own views. It deepened his disgust for the obscenities of the worship of the Paphian Aphrodite, but it went no further. We hear no more of this proconsul, either at Rome or elsewhere, and Christian history and legend are equally silent concerning him. It has been often said that Paul now assumed that name in compliment to his first Gentile convert. But it is far more probable that Paul was his name from the beginning, by which he was known among Greeks and Romans. Up to this point Saul had been among Hebrews, and therefore bore the Hebrew name only; but when he left Palestine, and came among Hellenic Jews, the author of the Acts drops the Hebrew name and for the rest of his narrative employs that by which he was commonly known out of the Holy Land.

That so far the labours of Paul had been without result may be concluded, not only from the silence of Luke relative to any conversions in the synagogues, but from the way in which he makes the most of the incident at Paphos.

From this time the relative positions of Paul and Barnabas are altered. Hitherto the latter had taken the lead; now he fell into the second place.

[1] Acts xiii. 7-11.

CHAPTER VIII

GALATIA

A.D. 50—51

Paul and Barnabas in Pamphylia—Desertion of Mark—Probable cause—The scheme of Paul—The thorn in the flesh—Probably low fever—Professor Ramsay's account of it—The character of central Asia Minor—Plan of Paul to stud the trade route from the East with missionary stations—Ethnology and religion of Anatolia—Original stock—Primitive condition of Polyandry—Inheritance through the mothers—The political organisation of the people—The religion—Papas or Men—The goddess Leto—Sabazios—"The Divine Life"—Mystery plays—The demoralising nature of the Anatolian religion—Feeling of the cultured towards the dominant superstition—The attraction of Judaism—Its repellent side—The Anatolian cult of the dead—Judaism impotent to meet the craving for knowledge as to the life after death—Reasons inducing the Anatolians to accept the Gospel—The Greek element in Asia Minor—The important part played by the Greek in the diffusion of the Gospel—Dean Church on the Greek—The Gaul in Asia Minor—Paul never penetrated into Galatia proper—The Jews in Asia Minor—Paul in Pisidian Antioch—Paul's sermon in the synagogue—Disturbance and expulsion of Paul—Iconium—Paul and Thecla—The Acts of St. Thecla—*Mulieres subintroductæ*—Paul driven from Iconium—Lystra—Derbe—Perga—Return to Antioch in Syria.

From Paphos Paul sailed with Barnabas and John Mark for Asia Minor, and landed in the port of Perga in Pamphylia. And here at once a rupture took place with Mark. The occasion is not told us. The desertion by Mark rankled in the mind of Paul for years.

Various explanations have been offered, but it is most probable that the withdrawal of Mark was due to a

difference of opinion connected with the direction in which
Paul proposed to go. Mark had doubtless supposed that
the two Apostles would go on with the work in Pamphylia
that they had attempted in Cyprus. They would be
among a population of the same race, same culture. But
Paul had resolved to begin operations in Galatia, among
the proselytes from a people of entirely different blood,
language, and character, thinly scattered over a high
tableland, walled off from the sea and from civilisation by
ranges of mountains.

Perhaps Paul may not have plainly told his intentions to
his companions before starting. Perhaps dissatisfaction at
the miserable or no results of the Cyprus campaign had so
worked in him, that when he reached Asia Minor he
resolved to go to a people as opposite in every description
as he could find to those he had failed to reach in Cyprus.
Barnabas, always self-diffident and yielding, raised no
objections. But it was other with John Mark; and Paul
was not a man who could endure to have his will crossed.

The situation was much as if Messrs. Moody and Sankey
had landed in Liverpool with the object of evangelising
England, and one of them had proposed to begin with
Cumberland. Why did Paul at the outset commence work
in the most sparsely peopled district in Anatolia, and among
almost the most backward in civilisation therein?

From Jerusalem the Twelve sent out wave after wave of
converts, and the ripples ran to the limits of the world.
Here was the Apostle to the Gentiles starting operations
where apparently the effect would be reduced to a minimum.
The determination of St. Paul has seemed so astonishing
that apologists have sought in various ways to account for
it. Professor Ramsay supposes that the Apostle caught

malarial fever in Perga, and went to the hills as a health-resort. But the tableland of Phrygian and Lycaonian Galatia is the most malarial, unhealthy region he could have selected, far worse than the rocky sea-coast of Pamphylia.

"In summer nine-tenths of it is an arid waste, bearing salicornia, wormwood, and similar plants, and broken up by great marshes and wide patches of salt, while in the winter season inundations cover the whole distance from Koniah (Iconium) on the west, to Tyana on the east, so that sometimes the whole district is like an inland sea, and perfectly impassable. To this is owing the extreme unhealthiness of Lycaonia, for the rivers and streams which descend from the many mountain ranges bordering the plain, have no visible outlet; and, as summer advances, and the inundations begin to disappear, a deadly malaria is generated from the half-dry surface of the marshes."[1] "Only the winds from south and north are healthy; all others blow across marshes, and therefore come laden with malaria. This, combined with the great dampness of the place from the plenteous supply of water, and the sudden and extreme changes of temperature between day and night, cause deadly dysenteries and fevers. Severe congestive fevers, *cold* fevers (or pernicious fevers, as they are called in Alexandria) are common and very fatal."[2]

Professor Ramsay shows good reason for the opinion that the "Thorn in the Flesh," of which St. Paul complained, and which is first noticed in connection with the Galatian mission, was malarial fever. He says:—

"In some constitutions malarial fever tends to recur in very distressing and prostrating paroxysms, whenever one's

[1] Davis: "Life in Asiatic Turkey," 1879, p. 237.   [2] *Ibid.* p. 241.

energies are taxed for a great effort. Such an attack is for the time absolutely incapacitating: the sufferer can only lie and feel himself a shaking and helpless weakling, when he ought to be at work. He feels a contempt and loathing for self, and believes that others feel equal contempt and loathing. In every paroxysm, and they might recur daily, Paul (in the publicity of Oriental life) would lie exposed to the pity or the contempt of strangers. If he were first seen in a Galatian village, or house, lying in the mud on the shady side of a wall for two hours shaking like an aspen leaf, the gratitude that he expresses to the Galatians, because they 'did not despise nor reject his infirmity,' was natural and deserved. Fresh light is thrown on this subject by an observation of Mr. Hogarth, my companion in many journeys. In publishing a series of inscriptions recording examples of punishment inflicted by the god on those who had approached the sanctuary in impurity, he suggests that malarial fever was often the penalty sent by the god. The paroxysms, recurring suddenly with overpowering strength, and then passing off, seemed due to the direct visitation of God. This gives a striking effect to Paul's words in Gal. iv. 14, 'You did not despise nor reject my physical infirmity, but received me as an angel of God': though the Galatians might have turned him away from their door as a person accursed and afflicted by God, they received him as God's messenger. A strong corroboration is found in the phrase, 'a stake in the flesh,' which Paul uses about his malady (2 Cor. xii. 7). That is a peculiar headache which accompanies the paroxysms. Within my experience several persons innocent of Pauline theorising, have described it as 'like a red-hot bar thrust through the forehead.' As soon as fever connected itself with Paul in my mind, the 'stake in the flesh' impressed me as a strikingly illustrative metaphor, and the oldest tradition on the subject, quoted by Tertullian and others, explains 'the stake in the flesh' as headache."[1]

It is surely improbable that John Mark should have deserted Paul at Perga because the latter was ill. He must have quitted him on account of a difference of opinion, probably as to the course to be pursued in the prosecution of the mission. Moreover, it is vastly more likely that Paul was attacked by fever on the swampy Galatian plain than on the breezy sea-coast.

No intimation is given us that Paul went to Galatia because he had received a divine command to do so. Had there been a revelation, we cannot suppose that Mark would have been disobedient to the heavenly vision. It is admissible to conjecture that Mark failed to appreciate the principle on which Paul had resolved to labour, and that he considered the plateau of central Anatolia as a very unsuitable field for operations. But it seems to me that Paul had already formed a plan on which to work, that was perhaps not fixed in detail, but existed as a general conception.

In the many years he had lived at Tarsus, he had perceived that the main artery of life connecting the East and the West ran through Southern Asia Minor. From the Ægean and its busy commercial cities, it struck up the valley of the Mæander and Lycus to Apamæa. There it branched, the upper road passed under the northern spurs of the range, now called Sultan Dagh, and pursued its course

---

[1] Ramsay: "St. Paul," p. 96. Professor Ramsay prefers to translate σκόλοψ by *stake*. In Homer undoubtedly the word has this meaning, but by later writers it is used for a prickle or thorn.

over the vast salt plains of the Axylon to Cæsarea of Cappadocia, and so to the Euphrates. The southern road reached Pisidian Antioch, then ran to Iconium, and so by the Cilician Gates to Tarsus. But there was an alternative route; the southern road again branched before reaching Iconium, and by Lystra and Derbe led through the Taurus to the sea at Trachæan Seleucia, and so along the coast to Tarsus and through the Syrian Gates to Syrian Antioch, or else by sea across the Cilician Gulf to Syrian Seleucia.

Paul considered that his most suitable plan would be to thread mission stations along the great trade route between Syria and Rome. We know that when at Pisidian Antioch he desired to go down the Lycus valley to the coast, but was prevented by the Spirit; and we know that afterwards he did effect his object of dotting churches along the road, at Derbe, Lystra, Pisidian Antioch, Colossæ, Laodicæa, Ephesus, and Corinth. So also he dotted them along the Egnatian Road. This seems to me to have been in accordance with a definite plan. Each station would not only serve to evangelise the neighbourhood, but might be calculated on doing something to influence the swarms of travellers who passed along the highway, and might be made the vehicles for conveying the seeds of the truth to the ends of the earth.

The scene of Paul's labours for some time, nearly two years, was the Thibet of Asia Minor, an elevated table-land partly of chalk, partly of red sandstone, vast and monotonous, strewn with salt lakes and marshes. It lies high, from three to five thousand feet above the sea, and the contrasts in temperature are extreme. The winter is long and bitter, the summer short and burning. In early spring it is a field of waving flowers, the air is sweet with thyme, rosemary and lavender; but when the sun becomes strong all is burnt up, except along the watercourses, where poplars grow, in which sing innumerable nightingales. This vast plain extends to the horizon, with a faint blue haze hanging over it, caused by evaporation from the lakes and swamps, and out of this start boldly the conical volcanoes of Kara Dagh, the Black Mountain, and Hassan Dagh shooting into two pyramidal summits, capped with snow. Far away the plain is bounded by ridges ever wreathed in glaciers. In places small cones of eruptive scoria mark volcanic vents, but there are now no active volcanoes in Anatolia. The whole plateau has been heaved up by the internal fires between the cold lips of the limestone and conglomerate and granite ridges that run along the north and south, and rise rapidly out of the Mediterranean on one side and the Euxine on the other.

"This elevated region is as the bridge connecting Europe and Asia. Across this bridge the religion, art and civilisation of the East found their way into Greece; and the civilisation of Greece, under the guidance of Alexander the Macedonian, passed back again across the same bridge to conquer the East and revolutionise Asia as far as the heart of India."[1] If this fact be well appreciated, we shall see the wisdom of the Apostle in laying hold of the bridge in the name of Jesus Christ.

Now let us pass to another point of perhaps greater importance than the geographical position of Paul's first settlements, and that is the peculiar disposition of the inhabitants of Anatolia at the moment that the Apostle came among them.

For the understanding of this, a few pages must be

[1] Ramsay: "The Historical Geography of Asia Minor," 1890, p. 23.

devoted to the ethnology and religion and social condition of the Anatolians.

At some period vastly remote, Asia Minor received its population from the East. To what stock it belonged, Semitic or Turanian, cannot be stated with confidence. They were a nomad race, and this fixed their social institutions for a considerable time. A migratory race takes with it few women, and the result is that these women become common property. It was so with the Picts of North Britain, it was so with the natives of the South Pacific Isles. The toilsome migration over wintry plains, or the long sea voyage in canoes necessitated the reduction of the number of women to, at the outside, one to ten men, and when the wanderers settled, each woman belonged thenceforth to ten men at least. Actually, the few females were the common property of all the men.

When established in settlements, then a certain form of organisation took place; property in land and in habitations was acquired, but as polyandry still existed, all right of inheritance devolved through the woman; and an institution which was morally degrading to the female, socially elevated her, as being the sole channel through whom real property could be acquired.

As the race became more cultured, probably by its own spontaneous advance in moral and social organisation, perhaps also through contact with the Greeks, the family became articulate, and each man had his own wife and home, and could recognise his own children.

The political organisation of the people kept pace with its social development. A number of villages were united, like the old German *gau*, with as centre a *hieron*, a temple endowed with lands, served by a fixed body of priests and priestesses resident in a sacred village near the temple. The worship throughout Anatolia was much the same, but with local variations, and the deities were also the same under different names. When the Greeks arrived, and settled in the land, they gave to these deities names that identified them with some of the Hellenic Olympus, and settled down to worship them in the fashion of the natives.

Above all was the great god, Men or Papas, but vaguely apprehended, whom the Greeks at once labelled Zeus. Then came the mighty goddess, variously called Leto, Cybele, Artemis or Demeter. Through fraud she became by the great god a mother and brought forth a divine son, variously called Sabazios, Sozon, now identified with Helios, as the giver of light, then with Æsculapius, as the source of health, with Poseidon, the earthshaker, who produced the seismic shocks, with Dionysus, as the giver of the vine, and with Heracles, as the conqueror over the powers of destruction.

But this son is none other than the father in a new form, with the same characteristics and the same nature, and consequently the one was often confused with the other.

There was a further myth, that the mother gave birth to a daughter Kora or Persephone, who in turn became a mother and bore Sabazios, by the same father.

From the Greek colonists who settled in cities in the midst of the native race, the Anatolians obtained no religious ideas whatever; instead they infected their conquerors.

"Let us now look at the character of the Anatolian religion," writes Professor Ramsay. "Its essence lies in the adoration of the life of nature—that life subject apparently to death, yet never dying but reproducing itself in new forms. The annihilation of death through the power of self-reproduction was the object of an enthusiastic worship, characterised by remarkable self-abandonment and immersion in the Divine, by a mixture of obscene symbolism and sublime truth, by negation of the moral distinctions and family ties that exist in a more developed society, but do not exist in the free life of nature."[1]

In an earlier condition of social organisation, every male and every female was doubtless required at certain periods to serve in the temple, the men by cultivating the lands belonging to it, the women by reverting to the condition of polyandry. But as the population advanced in numbers and civilisation, this was perhaps no longer exacted; but any woman at any time might vow herself for a month or more to the "divine life," and then return to her home with a reputation, from a religious point of view, unsoiled.

Not only so, but every disease, accident, loss was attributed to the wrath of the gods, and was to be atoned for by a vow of service in the temple. A husband or wife might thus devote him or herself, or so devote a child or a servant. Nor was this all. The religious ceremonial in the temples at certain festivals consisted in the solemn performance in mystery play of the deception of the goddess and of the birth of the son-god.

Such a condition of religion was at once an anachronism, and a repulsive anachronism. It was the consecration of the early condition of life out of which the race had emerged; it must have been felt as intolerable by the nobler spirits among the men, and as a horror and infamy by the women instinctively modest.

[1] "Cities and Bishoprics of Phrygia," 1895. p. 87.

The Greek colonists could give the Anatolians nothing better. The Roman emperors introduced, indeed, the worship of Augustus, and of the genius of Rome, but this was as a political cult, a bond of union through the empire among the many races and nations it combined, and had no religious effect on the mind and morals.

The condition of feeling in Anatolia may be in a measure understood by comparison with that now existing in France. There, educated Frenchmen and intelligent Frenchwomen regard the established Romanism with contempt and dislike —with contempt because of its puerile superstitions, its Lourdes and La Salette miracles; with dislike because of its clericalism and meddlesomeness in the affairs of a family. But the Roman Catholic religion tends to purity and sanctity, whereas the Anatolian religion was grossly demoralising. We must therefore add to the Frenchman's contempt for superstition, and dislike of priestly interference, the super-added sense of contamination introduced into every household. We shall not be far wrong in concluding that there was, at the time when Paul was in Asia Minor, a desire to be rid of the established religion, and to have it replaced by another that met and fostered the best instincts of humanity. This it is which accounts for the wide circle of proselytes, more or less attached, that engirdled every synagogue. In the Jewish religion these men and women of Galatia and Phrygia found a God of purer eyes than to behold iniquity, and a divinely promulgated moral law.

But Judaism had its repellent side; it was purely national. No man could be thoroughly identified with it in its hopes who was not of the seed of Abraham, and submission to circumcision did not wholly ingraft him into the sacred stock.

Mosaism was a negative system; a denial of the plurality of gods and a condemnation of certain acts. It gave no positive assurances of a future life to the individual. It prophesied solely the coming exaltation of the race.

There was another cause predisposing the Anatolians to embrace Christianity.

Like the Dolmen builders of Europe and India, and the Chinese, the original inhabitants of Asia Minor were deeply, intensely imbued with the conviction of there being a life after death, and a consequent reverence for the dead, who, on passing into the higher life of spirit, became entitled to a certain amount of worship. The structure and maintenance of tombs with them was of the highest importance, and was a sacred duty. The expectation of a better life after death robbed the grave of all its terrors.

The Greek, on subjugating the native population, contributed nothing towards the elucidation of the mystery of the life beyond the grave; on the contrary, he troubled the established, ingrained conviction. He introduced, if not scepticism, at all events a doubt, and the Anatolian felt himself carried off his feet where he thought he stood on firm rock.

The Jew could not offer him much comfort. The Old Testament Scriptures are singularly barren of promises to be construed to the benefit of the individual. It was only through the Gospel that life and immortality were brought to light. We can therefore understand how the preaching of the Resurrection exactly met a craving in the Anatolian mind, and blew away the clouds of doubt which had begun to darken his sky.

There must have been some strong reason or reasons that induced the natives of Asia Minor to accept the Gospel with such enthusiasm, and caused it to run like wildfire throughout the peninsula and lay such hold of the people that even in Pliny's day the temples were deserted, and for three centuries Anatolia became the religious focus of Christianity.

And I believe that the causes of this ready, enthusiastic reception of the Gospel are to be found in the revulsion of the moral sense of the people against the predominant religion, and in the Gospel providing their ancient inrooted conviction of an after life with a new security.

But we must not think of Asia Minor as occupied by a purely Oriental race. That race was overlaid and altered by the Greek colonists, who had established Hellenic cities with Greek municipal government in every district, and who had made Greek to be the language of civilisation and of literature. The Græcism was, however, superficial, a veneer, and nothing more.

In Greece itself the Greek had become degenerate. He retained his cleverness, but had lost the power of using his natural gifts to any useful end. The Roman conquerors wondered at his ability and despised him for his levity. He was a wayward, witty, graceful child, and had no manliness in him and no power of political organisation. But in Asia Minor the Greek had acquired a new vigour, and, with an infusion of Anatolian native blood, gave promise of a future. The Greek was the civilising element of the original races of Asia Minor, and to the Greek these races largely owed their moral uprising, and therewith the faculty to appreciate and receive Christianity.

In thinking of Paul's mission to Anatolia, we must not lay too much stress on the non-Aryan element in the population.

The Gospel was sent to the Jew, and then to the Greek; and only after the Greek and through the Greek to the Latin races. If the first converts were Jews, the next were Greeks or Hellenised Asiatics. Look through the catacombs of Rome, and on all sides you see the inscriptions in Greek, those in Latin being the more modern.

After Paul passes away, we see the figure of St. John at Ephesus giving to the Greek Church the rudiments of its philosophy of Christianity and its ecclesiastical form. The Epistles to the Churches are addressed to Greek Churches only. The Greek apologists and fathers occupy the scene, and only in the third century make room for African writers. Considering what the Greek race was—decaying; what its character—false, frivolous, flexible, and tortuous— one might have thought that Paul and John would have done better to have addressed themselves to the Romans. But in that we should err. The Greek is with us to the present day, an indestructible race; and where shall we look for the modern representative of the Roman? Not certainly in Italy. The race, as a race, is gone from the face of the earth.

"It was the Greeks," says Dean Church, "a people imbued with Greek ideas, who first welcomed Christianity. It was in their language that it first spoke to the world, and its first home was in Greek households and in Greek cities. It was in a Greek atmosphere that the divine stranger from the East, in many respects so widely different from all the Greeks were accustomed to, first grew up to strength and shape; first showed its power of assimilating and reconciling; first showed what it was to be in human society. Its earliest nurselings were Greeks; Greeks first took in the meaning and measure of its amazing and eventful announcements; Greek sympathies first awoke and vibrated to its appeals; Greek obedience, Greek courage, Greek suffering first illustrated its new lessons. Had it not first gained over Greek mind and Greek belief, it is hard to see how it would have made its further way. And to that first welcome the Greek race has been profoundly and unalterably faithful. They have passed through centuries for the most part of adverse fortune. They have been in some respects the most ill-treated race in the world. To us in the West, at least, their Christian life seems to have stopped in its growth at an early period; and, compared with the energy and fruitfulness of the religious principle in those to whom they passed it on, their Christianity disappoints, perhaps repels us. But to their first faith—as it grew up, substantially the same, in Greek society . . . . they still cling."[1]

In nature there is nothing preserved to which there is not a destiny allotted. That which has fulfilled its function decays and passes away; but that which is continued in a state of suspended animation has a future predestined to it. So may it be also for the Greek nation and the Greek Church. They may have their mission in the future, as may have the Jewish nation.

There is one element of the amalgam of races in Asia Minor of which so far nothing has been said, and that is the Celtic. In B.C. 279, a great migration of Gauls had taken place from Europe across the Bosphorus. They had wandered over Asia Minor, plundering, subduing, devastating. But in B.C. 240 they had been defeated by Attalus I., and forced to settle down in the mountains. In Northern Galatia they maintained their customs, language,

[1] "The Influence of Christianity on National Character," 1873, p. 14.

and tribal and clan organisation; but as they hired themselves as mercenaries, they gradually learned the use of the Greek language. They were obliged at last to submit to Rome, having been conquered by Manlius B.C. 187. From that time they became faithful in their allegiance. Augustus converted their land into a province, with Ancyra as the capital, and into it were incorporated portions of Lycaonia and Phrygia.

But we cannot think that the infusion of Gaulish blood was strong in that portion of the province—its extreme south—traversed by Paul.

Some writers have been pleased to detect in the peculiar faults of the Galatians, as revealed by the epistle of Paul, characteristic Celtic failings; but this is far-fetched, and the attempt was made when the range of Paul's travels was extended into Galatia proper. Now it is pretty well established that he never went further into the province than Iconium; that he confined his labours to a strip of land about 140 miles long and not twenty wide.

In Phrygian and Lycaonian Galatia there were probably very few Gauls—not enough to temper in any way the native character. The Celtic element may therefore be left out of consideration.

The high table-land nourished great flocks of goats and sheep, the former a sacred animal to the Anatolian, and its flesh consecrated to the gods. The mountains possessed veins of silver, lead, and tin, and in the wash from the granite peaks was found gold. Moreover, near Derbe, the mountains yielded a marble, white and crystalline as refined sugar, much in request by sculptors. The towns in Central Asia Minor were few and far between, nor were they wealthy. The Jews, who went only where money abounded, did not form large communities in these towns, and they do not seem to have obtained a firm foothold in Lycaonia till after it had been subjected by the Romans. They enjoyed great liberty; they were free to exercise their religion unmolested. Certain public charges that weighed on the natives they were able to evade, on the plea that they were against their principles. The Roman government favoured them as useful allies in the event of any trouble arising with the indigenes, and they gradually monopolised the trade in wool and in the metals from the mines of Taurus.

Antioch in Pisidia was a colony, enjoying Italic rights. It was governed by its own elected officers. Here it was that Paul began his ministry, and he began it in the synagogue. His address there delivered has happily been preserved by St. Luke. It is interesting as following the historic lines inaugurated by Stephen, but it is characteristically different. The deacon gathered together what he could out of the history of the nation wherewith to affront his hearers; Paul, on the other hand, sought in their past instances of Divine mercy and guidance to Christ. Although he shows them the guilt of the rulers in condemning Christ, yet he finds an excuse; it was "because they knew Him not." In this discourse, moreover, we have the first intimation of his future theory of the Promise pitted against the Law.

The sermon consists of three parts. In the first (Acts xiii. 16-23), Paul narrates the history of the elect people up to David. With David he stops, for it was of the seed of David that the Messiah was to come.

In the second part of the discourse (verses 24-37) Paul shows how that the promises are fulfilled in Christ Jesus.

Then, in the third part (verses 38-41), is the application. Nothing is said of atonement and justification, for as yet Paul had not worked these ideas out. But the whole discourse, of which we have but a faded copy in the text, is admirably conceived from beginning to end.

The envy and alarm of the Jews at seeing Paul draw away their proselytes and attract others from among the heathens, devout men and women whom they had themselves expected to make use of, caused a disturbance in the town, and Paul and Barnabas left. "They shook off the dust of their feet against them, and came unto Iconium."

There also they entered the synagogue and spoke to the Jews and believing natives. The result was precisely the same as at Antioch, and for precisely the same reason.

Here it was that Paul converted Thecla, a young and beautiful girl, whose "Acts" form so great a hagiographical curiosity. As they have come down to us, they are not in their original form, but have undergone amplification. But that the core is a very early document has been vindicated by scholars, who are prepared to acknowledge that they substantially narrate a genuine incident in this part of St. Paul's ministry.

Although Tertullian seeks to invalidate the authority of the "Acts" by pointing out that the priest who had written them out of devotion to St. Paul was degraded from his office for so doing, yet it does not appear that this priest had invented the story, but that he had furbished it up with apocryphal details.

The document as we have it belongs to the latter part of the second century, and is an incrustation about the earlier Acts written much about the same time as those by St. Luke of the journeys of St. Paul.

The substratum is this. At Iconium, a virgin of the

name of Thecla, whilst in her room at the window, heard Paul preach, was stirred to the heart, and when he was imprisoned, bribed the gaoler with her bracelets and a silver mirror to admit her, and was found in the morning sitting at the feet of the Apostle, listening to his instructions. When her mother and others attempted to draw her away, she clung to Paul "in a manner that excited among the spectators suspicions devoid of all foundation"— in a word, that he had bewitched her with philtres. Paul was expelled the town and concealed himself in an old tomb. When nearly famished, he sent two disciples into the city for food; they found Thecla wandering about, and brought her to Paul. She resolved to cut her hair, dress as a boy and follow him. He objected, but she was so resolved that at length he yielded, and she attended him wherever he went, till at Antioch she was arrested and exposed in the arena, but escaped mainly through the interest taken in her by Tryphæna, queen mother of Polemon, King of Pontus, a distant cousin of Claudius, who was residing in Antioch. Then, dressed as a boy, laden with presents, she went after Paul to Myra in Lycia. There can be no doubt now entertained that there is a very strong basis of fact in this story.[1]

[1] Professor Ramsay points out and establishes that, 1. The Acts of Paul and Thecla go back ultimately to a document of the first century; 2. That this original document mentioned facts of history and antiquities which had probably passed quite out of knowledge before the end of the first century; 3. That this document, not being protected by canonical character, was subjected to alterations, due partly to change of views in the Church, partly to the growth of the Thecla legend. He shows that the original document must have been composed on the spot in Phrygian Galatia, and that Queen Tryphæna is an historical person living at the time indicated, yet known only through coins and inscriptions; also that the description of the change in Thecla's dress would, as described, be unintelligible after the first century.—Ramsay: "The Church in the Roman Empire," 1895, cap. xvi.

The fame of Thecla was great in the early Church, and some of her proceedings, such as baptizing, not meeting approval, the story was altered to suit changed ecclesiastical views. It was further expanded by having interminable speeches and absurd miracles intruded into it.

But if the story be in the main true, how is it that St. Luke passes it over without a word? There must have been a reason, and the reason in all likelihood was that profane and flippant persons might comment on it as did the mother and others when they found the girl in the prison of Paul.

There is one feature which comes out very distinctly in the "Acts of Paul and Thecla," that she was not a young person who would be denied having her own way.[1]

It may have been injudicious on the part of Paul to take the girl with him. He pointedly told her it would be so, but she forced herself on him, and would not be sent back. He saw no other way of delivering her from pagan surroundings and an unbelieving husband, and allowed her to accompany him till he was able to place her under the care of a respectable matron. It is difficult not to see an allusion to this incident in Paul's first Epistle to the

---

[1] According to tradition St. Thecla spent the rest of her days in a cave near Seleucia in Cilicia, and here the Emperor Zeno built a basilica over her grotto and grave. But it is remarkable that at Rome, close to the cemetery of Lucina, in which St. Paul was laid after his martyrdom, is the early catacomb of St. Thecla, with a subterranean church or basilica. In this have been found pagan tombs, one of the date of Claudius. But the tombs, so far as can be judged from the rare remains of inscriptions that are attributable to Christians, belong to the third century. Is it possible that Thecla followed Paul to Rome and suffered there? And that the Oriental reverence for the grotto at Seleucia is due to her having resided, and not died there?—See *Römische Quartal Schrift*, vol. iii. p. 343, 1889, in which is an account of the exploration of this catacomb in 1889.

Corinthians.¹ The story had reached Corinth and was commented on there unfavourably; and Paul thereupon entered on a discussion as to the difference between a female companion and a wife.

We know that actually the usage of a presbyter maintaining a *Mulier subintroducta* was tolerably general somewhat later. Indeed, in the middle of the third century the usage had to be forbidden. The intimate association of a priest with a young female, who passed to the world under the name of a virgin, called forth the re-iterated and strong condemnation of Jerome, Gregory Nazianzen, and Chrysostom. The Council of Nicæa finally, by canon, stopped the practice.²

As Héféle says: "In the first ages of the Church, some Christians, clerical and lay, contracted spiritual alliances with unmarried women. They lived together, it is true, but their connection was purely spiritual, and they encouraged each other in the practice of Christian virtues."³

St. Paul addresses himself to this custom, in writing to the Corinthians, and his words may be thus paraphrased: "There is a difference between a wife and a female companion. It is much better to be attended by the latter, and to live in platonic affection, because then the time of the woman is not taken up with domestic affairs. But if one so living finds that his affection is ripening into love, by all means let him marry her. There is no harm in his so doing. Yet the former is, to my mind, the condition, under present circumstances, most to be recommended."

[1] 1 Cor. vii. 34-40; compare 1 Cor. ix. 5. [2] Can. iii.
[3] Héféle: "Hist. des Conciles," i. 370.

The passage reveals a condition so opposed to our nineteenth century notions of propriety, that commentators have laboured to torture it into meaning something quite unobjectionable to modern feeling.[1]

When we find an usage fully established at the end of the second and in the third centuries, we may be quite sure that its roots are to be sought in the first.

Men of exalted enthusiasm and simplicity of heart are liable to do acts of indiscretion, from which it is difficult for men of the world to extricate them. But during the first and second centuries, it is quite certain that such a practice did not so much cause scandal as provoke admiration. Moreover, in the case of Paul, what was a paramount consideration was the salvation of Thecla. It was but an early example of incidents that have occurred ever since, wherever there is proselytism, as in the "little Mortara" case, and one much more recent in which "General" Booth was concerned.

From Iconium the Apostles were driven as they had been from Antioch, and they betook themselves to Lystra, where at first they were regarded as gods and so honoured, and then, with the versatility of unreason, cast out and stoned.

From Lystra, accordingly, they departed to Derbe, where apparently they tarried a considerable time, till the excitement at Lystra and Iconium had abated, when they returned over the same ground, confirming the little knots of believers in each town, and giving to each community an organic life by ordaining presbyters to each.

After having thus settled the Churches in Derbe, Lystra, Iconium, and Antioch, they recrossed the boundary range

---

[1] See, for instance, Geikie: "Life and Epistles of St. Paul," ii. 160–1. The attempt is grotesque.

of the Taurus, and descended to the sea coast and preached the word in Perga, no doubt, as was Paul's invariable rule, in the synagogue, detaching from it the "hearers" and forming of them an independent church. From Perga, Paul and Barnabas sailed for Seleucia, and on landing there, at once made their way to Antioch.

CHAPTER IX

THE COUNCIL AT JERUSALEM

A.D. 52

The question of circumcision reaches a crisis—The proselytes' objection to circumcision—The difficulty of the Rule of Meats—And of the Law of Purifications—Laxity of practice—The delegates from Jerusalem—Their function—Illustration—In the synagogues of the Dispersion were no trained scribes—Consequently little of the Rigorist feeling—Paul's method of preaching—Uses the synagogue as a means—The result was that he carried away from it nearly all the proselytes—This the real cause of offence—Condition of affairs in Jerusalem—Impossibility of dissociating the Church from the Law—Excommunication—Sayings of Jesus Christ relative to the Law—Some Rigorists visit Antioch—Peter dissociates himself from the proselytes—Is reproved by Paul—The great practical difficulty of the case—The matter referred to the Apostles—What Paul asked for—Arrival at Jerusalem—The case of the Rigorists—Its strength—The council—The decision pronounced by James—The encyclical epistle—Constitution of such a council—The decision not a compromise.

It was well that Paul and Barnabas had returned to Antioch. The difficulties about the admission of the proselytes had reached a crisis. A determination as to whether they should be received into complete communion could no longer be delayed, and a decision could not be reached without their presence. The question was one of much more difficulty, and involved more issues than is generally supposed.

To understand the difficulty we must consider what was the temper of mind of the Jews of the Diaspora, and what

THE COUNCIL AT JERUSALEM

was the relation in which the believers stood to Mosaism in Jerusalem. Among the Jews of the Dispersion, the Rigorist sect, which at Jerusalem was represented by the Pharisees, was in the minority. Hebrews living in Greek cities and in Rome were insensibly affected by their surroundings. They were cut off from association with the heathen by circumcision, by the Rule of Meats, and by that of Purifications. They could not attend the public baths, nor exercise in the gymnasia, without becoming the objects of galling pleasantries, and that disinclination for water which seems to affect the Jew when he has not acquired our Gentile habits, is due largely to this shrinking from being seen naked. Instead of looking on circumcision with pride, as a pledge of covenant, the Jew learned to blush at it, if he ventured into the baths. As the neophytes could not, and would not do without their baths, they positively, stubbornly refused to submit to circumcision.

The Rule of Meats presented another difficulty. Unless the ghetto was sufficiently large to maintain its own butcher, it was plunged in difficulties; and even if it had its own flesher, the Jew dealer in meat was sufficiently alive to the fact that there was no competition to regulate his charges accordingly. It was intolerably irksome for the Hebrew to have to institute a series of minute inquiries before each meal, as to whether all the blood had been run out of the beef, and the fowls had been decapitated not strangled; whether inquiries had been made at the shambles as to whence proceeded the meat; and whether the butcher's word could be trusted that none of it had come from a sacrifice. The Hebrews of the Dispersion were obliged in a thousand cases to shut their eyes, and ask no questions for conscience sake.

The Law of Purifications was equally harassing. If carried out to the letter, it required the Jew to be washing himself all day long, to scrub off every contaminating touch of man or thing. It interfered with social intercourse. No Jew could offer to a Greek or Roman the least hospitality, and he was wholly precluded from acceptance of any offered to him. Most serious of all—it stood in the way of effecting many a good bargain.

Consequently much laxity of practice prevailed. In every community of Jews there was a kernel of Rigorists, but the bulk of the Hellenistic Jews managed to slip one shoulder from under the yoke. They argued that the regulations made for a nomad people, necessary to maintain them in health, were inapplicable and unnecessary to those engaged in commerce, and living in well-drained towns provided with baths and shambles. They recognised that the grandeur of the nation, and the excellence of their religion, did not derive from a series of petty observances, but consisted in the recognition of the monarchy of Jehovah and the possession of a moral code. They saw that it was precisely these two elements which were the lode-stones attracting the wise and noble from paganism to the Synagogue, whereas the ceremonial restrictions alienated and disgusted them.

But this liberality of opinion and practice was not allowed to pass unnoticed. Delegates, apostles of Judaism, went forth "travelling over sea and land," visiting the several synagogues, with authority to investigate into these matters, to rebuke, exhort, and, if need be, excommunicate. There is happily an illustration at hand, given us by Josephus. At this very time, Jazates, King of Adiabene, had been convinced of the truth of monotheism by a Jewish merchant named Ananias. This man advised the king to disregard circumcision as an empty ceremony, and as likely to damage his authority over his subjects. But one of the emissaries of the orthodox Jews at Jerusalem arrived in Adiabene, and vehemently opposed Ananias; he so worked on the mind of the king as finally to induce him to submit to circumcision.

The broad views of the liberal party naturally inclined them to accept the Gospel, and all the heathens who had been drawn to Judaism by its pure faith and moral law, embraced with enthusiasm a doctrine which dispensed with the vexatious requirements of the Rabbis. The preaching of Paul drove a wedge into the heart of Judaism, dismembering it, detaching from the Pharisees all the best in Israel, and the entire body of proselytes. There was another cause tending in the same direction. In the communities of the Diaspora, there were no colleges of Scribes, as at Jerusalem. In the synagogues any one might address the congregation who had a gift of speech, or had acquired respect on account of age, wealth, or piety. No ordination was required, as in Palestine, no proof of knowledge—nothing save that the preacher should be over thirteen years, and not exhibit himself in rags.[1] Usually those called upon to speak were the "men of leisure," well-to-do merchants and money-lenders, who had little time for study, and did not concern themselves about the hair-splitting debates of the rabbis. When the Sabbath was over they returned to their counters just as naturally as the rich merchants of Cairo, affiliated to the dancing dervishes, after the accomplishment of their teetotum exercise, lay aside their white veils and resume business in the bazaars. Such doctors had

[1] "Mishna Megilla," iv. 6.

their heads occupied with something more profitable than the subtilties of the rabbis. They laid hold of the invectives of the prophets and the Messianic promises. Their preaching was limited to the great and simple verities of religion and morality just suited to a people to whom was impracticable the rigid observance of the Law possible only in Jerusalem.

Indifference to the minutiæ of the Law led to forgetfulness, to contempt. The Jews of the Dispersion, or the majority of them, limited their obedience to the observance of the Sabbath, of circumcision, of the great festivals, and to the restrictions on marriage, and abstention from idol sacrifices.

We do not find that the Jews in Lycaonia and Phrygia were offended at Paul for insisting on the spirit of the Law being regarded and not the letter. That which exasperated them was the manner in which he alienated the Gentile converts from them. This meant the diversion of their subscriptions. More than that. Through the proselytes, the Jewish merchants and traders were able to draw a good deal of business into their hands, and they resented Paul's action as depriving them of a great commercial advantage. And there was this additional aggravation, that Paul had used their pulpits, their synagogues, for the purpose of depriving them of their clients.

We can see that they were sent to be unconscious John the Baptists, and to make straight the way; but this *they* could not see, and wholly failed to relish. Suppose that for half a century the Wesleyans in Fiji had been labouring to convert the natives, and had drawn away thousands from fetishism, and that some Jesuits arrived on the island without credentials, but professing to have received their education at Richmond Methodist College, at the feet of some eminent Wesleyan; and on the strength of this obtained the use of the pulpits, which was graciously accorded them, and seized on the opportunity to declare that Wesleyanism was heresy, and that there was no salvation save in obedience to the Pope. Would the Wesleyans like it? especially if they found themselves suddenly deserted?

This was in fact the mode of operation everywhere adopted by Paul. He nowhere addressed himself directly to the Gentiles, made no attempt to gather to him the heathen. He went always, at once, to the synagogues, and employed them for his purpose. I shall have more to say concerning this later. Suffice it here to indicate that it was his system of carrying on his missionary work.

At Damascus he had initiated it. "Straightway he preached Christ in the synagogues."[1] In Crete, on his first missionary voyage, he and Barnabas, who acquiesced, "preached the Word in the synagogues of the Jews."[2] At Antioch, he "went into the synagogue on the Sabbath day, and sat down"; and when the rulers incautiously said, "Ye men and brethren, if ye have any word of exhortation for the people, say on"; then he seized on the occasion to harangue on what lay near his heart.[3] Driven thence, he and Barnabas proceeded to Iconium where "They went both together into the synagogue of the Jews, and so spake that a great multitude, both of the Jews and also of the Greeks, believed."[4] Expelled from Iconium the Apostles went to Lystra and Derbe, where almost certainly they pursued the same tactics.

[1] Acts ix. 20.
[2] Ibid. xiii. 5.
[3] Ibid. xiii. 14, 15, 16.
[4] Ibid. xiv. 1.

On the second journey it was the same. At Philippi there was, indeed, no synagogue, only a proseuche, and only women attended it, so Paul met with no difficulty, but at Thessalonica "where was a synagogue of the Jews, Paul, as his manner was, went in unto them, and three Sabbath days reasoned with them out of the Scriptures."[1] Expulsion was the inevitable result. At Berœa it was probably the same; at Corinth it was undoubtedly so;[2] and so also at Ephesus,[3] where he was treated with really astonishing forbearance.

From his own point of view, Paul acted rightly. The synagogue, as Paul viewed it, was not the private property of the Jews, to be used as a vehicle for making proselytes who might become customers and bring them in much gain. It was the House of God, and he, as coming from God, had a just right to use it.

Moreover it was God's will that the Gospel should first of all be offered to the Jews, and that then, and then only, when they had rejected it, was it to be presented to the Gentiles. He was accordingly bound by his commission to go to the Jew, and go to him where he was to be found, in the synagogue.

And if the congregation had been composed of Hebrews only, they would have listened with equanimity; even if they refused to accept his message, they would have dismissed him with courtesy. But the congregation was mixed. To such a number of Jews there were so many, perhaps double the number, of Greek and Syrian "hearers." And when Paul shook off the dust of his feet against the incredulous Jews, he carried off with him all, or nearly all,

---

[1] Acts xvii. 2. [2] *Ibid.* xviii. 4.
[3] *Ibid.* xix. 8.

THE COUNCIL AT JERUSALEM 183

their converts. It was a secession of over half the congregation, and that of their best customers.

From his own point of view Paul was justified, but it is obvious that from that occupied by the Jews, staring with blank countenances at the empty places, and feeling at once in their pockets that they had come to suffer financially from Paul's preaching, a sense of resentment inevitably resulted, and that they should use every means in their power to rid themselves of Paul is not to be wondered at.

In Jerusalem the Church remained as though fixed in a vice. Many of the priests had joined, and in the Church made their influence felt.

Even if the Apostles had wished to have it otherwise, they could not so have it. In Judæa the synagogues, in Jerusalem the Sanhedrim, exercised tremendous powers of compulsion, allowed them by the Roman State, which was glad that they should administer their own affairs without troubling the proconsular court with matters that in no way interested the Roman governor or concerned the State. The Law had its stronghold and guarantee of its continuance in the existence of the Jewish polity. So long as the Temple stood, and the Jewish communities were accorded powers of self-government, it was absolutely impossible for the Church to manifest independent life.

The ceremonial law was also the civil law, and the Jew could no more live in disregard of the former than could any man in England live in daily violation of the common and criminal laws of the land. The condition was much that in which the Spaniards were during the worst period of the Inquisition, but with this aggravation, that every synagogue was an inquisitorial court, and every Jew was required to be a delator. None could disregard the ceremonial law, not even the Sadducees, who despised it and made mock of it. All alike were held in its iron meshes. Neglect was visited by expulsion from the Synagogue. There were three degrees of excommunication. For a first offence a delinquent was cast out for thirty days. If at the end of that time he was still contumacious, he was pronounced "devoted to God," corresponding to the Roman "sacer"—*i.e.*, doomed to death—and a court of ten then pronounced a solemn malediction and final sentence. He was either strangled or stoned to death. Properly the Jews might not execute those whom they had sentenced, but were required to hand them over to the proconsul; but that they did so in certain cases appears from the case of the woman taken in adultery, and from the martyrdom of Stephen. But even if unable to carry out their own sentence they could make life impossible, for the excommunicated was denied food and drink and shelter. No Jew might speak to or touch him, and to live he must escape from the land.

Consequently it was not left to the option of believers in Judæa whether they would observe the Law or not. To do so was a necessity. And in this necessity James, Peter, and John recognised the hand of God, requiring them to continue in the fullest sense Israelites, only distinguished from the Pharisees in the one point of believing that Messiah had already come, but willingly conforming in all other respects to the existing order.[1]

---

[1] This was obvious to the heathen at a later date, that Celsus said: "It is folly for Jews and Christians to strive with each other. It is like fighting over the emperor's beard. There is nothing of importance in their controversy; both believe that the Divine Spirit foretold the coming of a Redeemer, and the question between them is solely this— Has He or has He not come?"—"Orig. Cont. Celsum," iii. 1.

THE COUNCIL AT JERUSALEM 185

Men are never divinely commanded to do impossibilities, and it was an impossibility to act in any other way in Jerusalem. That the Apostles saw in this the finger of God indicating His will, the course they were to adopt, and the great end designed, the national conversion of the race, is certain. They superadded to the services of the Temple and Synagogue that of the Eucharist celebrated in private houses. They did nothing else. The time was not come for independent articulate life. If it were God's will that such life should begin, He would make it possible.

James knew how that the Lord had said that He came not to destroy the Law, but to fulfil it. "Till heaven and earth pass, one jot or one tittle shall in no wise pass from the Law till all be fulfilled. Whosoever shall break one of these least commandments, and shall teach men so, he shall be called the least in the kingdom of heaven."

The sticklers would have it that the Saviour had thrown the mantle of his sanction over the glosses of the Scribes. "I say unto you, that except your righteousness shall exceed the righteousness of the Scribes and Pharisees, ye shall in no case enter into the kingdom of heaven." To them the term righteousness signified minute ceremonial observance, and they held that the saying of Christ exacted a still closer obedience to the traditions of the rabbis than that of Scribes and Pharisees. These latter, said Christ, "sit in Moses' seat. All, therefore, whatsoever they bid you observe, that observe and do."

Tidings of the freedom assumed by Paul and Barnabas at Antioch reached Jerusalem. Certain of the narrow faction thereupon went to the city on the Orontes to observe their conduct, and counteract the tendency of their teaching. "Certain men came down from Judæa, and taught the brethren, that except ye be circumcised, after the manner of Moses, ye cannot be saved."[1] "False brethren, unawares brought in, who came in privily to spy out our liberty."[2]

They gave out that James, the head of the Church, was in accord with them.

Peter was, as it chanced, in Antioch at the time,[3] and he at first yielded to these new comers, misled by their false representations of being sent by James, whose opinion he considered himself bound to respect. The situation was, in fact, extremely perplexing. In Judæa and Samaria, as already shown, observance of the Law, with its system of *taboo* and purification was enforced in such a manner that neither James nor Peter could withdraw from it; and by living in strict observance, considered it a matter of duty to do so—as ordered by God. But Peter's mind was much opened by his vision at Cæsarea, and when he came to Antioch he was ready enough to accept the new condition of things which was possible out of Judæa, but not possible in it.

In fact, the Church was simultaneously existing in Jewry in one, and that the lowest and most inarticulate, protoplasmic form, and out of Jewry, at Antioch at all events, in the second stage, wherein traces of a vertebral column and

---

[1] Acts xv. 1. [2] Gal. ii. 4.
[3] There is considerable difficulty in settling the sequence of events mentioned in Acts and Galatians. I have at this point followed that proposed by Professor Ramsay. The usual arrangement leads to inextricable difficulties. It is alleged that the rebuke administered to Peter was after the council at Jerusalem. It is incredible that he who had taken part in the council, and signed the encyclical, should directly after violate the conciliatory judgment there given. It has been supposed that there were two visits to Antioch, and that twice the same difficulty arose. The arrangement followed solves all perplexities.

THE COUNCIL AT JERUSALEM 187

differentiation of members were beginning to manifest themselves. Now it was very hard for an elder Apostle to see that the march forward was to begin at the wing and not from the centre, that development of organic life was to show at the margin and not at the core of the Christian community. Yet Peter accepted the fact as he found it.

When, however, delegates from Jerusalem arrived at Antioch and demurred to this, and pointed out that James, the divinely constituted viceroy of the new kingdom of David, observed the law of purification, and did not eat with the uncircumcised, at once Peter, with his natural self-diffidence, which was mixed up with much impulsiveness, swung about and submitted to what he believed to be the opinion of James, as in duty bound to the vicegerent of Christ.

Even Barnabas, a timid, gentle man, began to waver. But Paul at once faced Peter, and said to him, "Why compellest thou the Gentiles to conform to Jewish ceremonial when thou, a Jew, hast been consorting with and eating with them?"

That is to say, he pointed out to Peter that his conduct was not that of a man acting on principle, and was that of a feeble follower of expediency. Peter at once saw the force of what Paul said, and yielded.

To quite understand the circumstances, we must take a look at the development in organisation that had already taken place in the Antiochian Church.

At first the believers had attended the synagogue on the Sabbath, and at the conclusion of the service, at the same hour as that of the evening sacrifice in the Temple, ensued a feast, in which the Jews did honour to the day as to a departing king. This feast was held in the synagogue, and was the δεῖπνον, or *prandium* of the Romans.

When discord broke out in the synagogues, the Jew believers were forced to absent themselves from this meal, as men rendered polluted by their association with the uncircumcised Christians; and then the Agape was instituted in Christian houses, early in the afternoon, at 3 P.M. in the place of the δεῖπνον in the synagogue. But some of the stricter of the Jewish believers remained in communion with the Synagogue and continued to eat of the Sabbath feast there, whereas the rest of the believers, those unqualified through uncircumcision or legal impurity, ate the Agape at the same time in a Christian household.

This was an unsatisfactory condition of affairs, and was eminently subversive of unity, or rather it brought the want of agreement between the parties to open day. Peter on arriving at Antioch had partaken of the Agape, but when the delegates from Jerusalem arrived and pointed out that he was splitting from the Synagogue, after purification he went back into communion with the latter, ate of the Sabbatical feast, and reconformed to the mode of life practised at Jerusalem.

This was not a condition of affairs that was tolerable. In Jerusalem and throughout Judæa the Church had one mode of existence, embryonic. In Antioch and wherever new communities of believers were founded or founded themselves, there was sure to arise the same discordance of practice and the same antagonism of opinion. Some of the believers would eat in the synagogue and abstain from the Agape, and others unite in the Agape and walk out of the synagogue the moment the bread and wine were

THE COUNCIL AT JERUSALEM 189

produced for the sabbatical feast. Those remaining in the synagogue would look on those leaving as schismatics, and those leaving for their own feast would despise such as partook in the synagogue as obfuscated by rabbinic error. Unity could not be made a mark of the Church, charity and brotherly love could not exist till this condition of affairs was changed.

Probably at Peter's suggestion, the question was referred to an assembly at Jerusalem, under the presidency of James. Peter, though himself convinced, had no authority to pronounce judgment in the matter. James acted as head of the Church, occupying the same position therein as did the High Priest to Mosaism.

Paul was quite willing to have the matter so settled. He saw that the quarrel would break out anew unless the Apostles pronounced decidedly in one way or the other. His own work would be hampered incessantly by men professing themselves to be emissaries of the Mother Church, the source of jurisdiction, and the standard of the truth.

But he did not feel that the time was come when he could ask for all he wanted.

What he would have liked, no doubt, would have been the entire ripping away of the Church from the Synagogue. This Cæsarean operation he performed wherever he went in Galatia and Syria. But he could not require this of the Apostles at Jerusalem, for such a dissociation was impossible of attainment there.

Nor did he wish it to take place at Jerusalem; so long as at the centre of Jewdom the Pharisaic party was tolerant of the Church—indeed, looked on it with something akin to favour, as observant of the Law—it opened access to all the synagogues of the Dispersion. A rupture at headquarters would close them all to him, and frustrate his favourite scheme.

Besides, it is by no means improbable that he agreed with the elder Apostles in believing that a conversion *en masse* might take place at Jerusalem, and that therefore a condition of affairs that was intolerable elsewhere might be allowed to continue at the religious capital of the Jewish world.

All, therefore, that he sought was the recognition of the emancipation of the Gentile converts from the law of ceremonies—above all, from circumcision, which was the one difficulty that was predominant standing in the way of the heathen and of the proselytes accepting Christ.

The Jewish converts might go on as before, attending the synagogue, partaking of the Sabbatical feast, withdrawing from the Christian Agape; he would not concern himself with them—he left them to Peter. But he did demand liberty for the converts from among the nations, and he foresaw that in time, the restriction of circumcision having been removed, the influx would be so great that the Jews would be swamped and the neophytes would be able to dictate their own terms to them, in place of being admitted, as hitherto, on sufferance. To Jerusalem, then, as the court of final appeal, Paul, Barnabas, and Peter, as also the false brethren, went up.

"And when they were come to Jerusalem, they were received of the Church and of the Apostles and Elders, and they rehearsed all things that God had done with them. But there rose up certain of the sect of the Pharisees, which believed, saying, It is needful to circumcise the Gentile believers, and to charge them to keep the law of Moses. And the Apostles and Elders were gathered together to consider this matter."

We cannot follow exactly the phases of the dispute; but if we look at the matter debated from the side of those who urged the observance of the whole legal system, we can see that they had a very strong case. I shall have occasion to speak of it again when we come to Paul's polemical epistles; suffice it here to indicate the main outline of their argument.

They pointed out that the Law was given by God, and that nothing was said of its transitory nature; that God was immutable, and that therefore the Law partook of His immutability. Nay, further, there were passages of Scripture that declared the Old Covenant to be everlasting, and its obligations to be perpetually binding.[1]

They went on to say that Christ Himself had observed the Law. He had been circumcised, and that it was the duty of every follower of Christ to conform to His example in all things.

Next they appealed to His words, to His solemn and reiterated asseveration that He had *not* come to abrogate the Law, but to fulfil it; that is to say, to obey it in every nicest particular. How could they be justified in repealing the paramount institution of the Law when He had declared that not a jot or tittle should be abrogated? Where, when, had He pronounced that the Mosaic revelation of the will of God was set aside? Had He done so after His

[1] Julian the Apostate, in his book against Christianity, urged this. "If the Christians accepted the Pentateuch, why did they disregard its provisions? And why ignore its declarations of being eternally binding?"—"Cyril c. Julianum," ix. The texts to which he refers are Deut. iv. 2; vi. 17; xxvii. 26; &c.

resurrection? Had the Spirit done so by revelation? No—so far from that, the prophets had been mute, touching this matter. Till a miraculous interposition assured them that the Law which God gave and declared to be eternal, was to be done away with, and superseded by another, they were in duty bound to go on as hitherto.

The case could hardly have been stronger.

Everything was in favour of the Judaisers except the force of circumstances. God speaks by the irresistible pressure of events as well as through signs and wonders. His finger can be seen pointing the way as door after door opens and fresh horizons manifest themselves.

When the Twelve and the Elders were gathered together to decide in this matter, there sounded no voice from heaven, there gleamed no miraculous flames, there was heard no rushing wind; but the Apostles had been provided with common-sense and the indwelling Spirit to direct them aright, and with authority to decide in such questions, when given the power to bind and loose.

The first to speak was Peter. His address has been preserved to us by St. Luke, and on its face bears the impress of genuineness.

The words of Paul spoken to him at Antioch had eaten into his heart, and he reproduced them substantially in his speech. "Why tempt ye God, to put a yoke upon the neck of the disciples which neither our fathers nor we were able to bear?"

When Peter had ceased, then Paul and Barnabas gave an account of their work, and a highly coloured picture of their success in Central Anatolia. They showed how that the Gentiles were crying out for reception into the Church, how that they showed tokens of sincerity, and that the presence of the Spirit was manifest in those baptized yet uncircumcised.

Then James, as president, gave judgment. "Simeon hath declared how at the first God took care to gather from among the Gentiles a people for His name. And to this agree the words of the prophets; as it is written, I will build again the tabernacle of David, that the residue of men may seek the Lord, and all the nations upon whom my name is called, saith the Lord, who revealeth these things continuously from the beginning of time."

We can see through these words into the very mind of James. He held inflexibly to the belief that it was to be through the Jews that all nations were to be brought to God, that the Davidic kingdom was about to be re-instituted, and that Jerusalem, with Christ reigning therein, would become the axle about which the whole world would revolve.

Then James concluded: "Wherefore my sentence is that we trouble not them which from among the Gentiles turn to God, but send instructions to them to abstain from the pollutions of idols, and from fornication, and from what is strangled, and from the use of blood as food. For," he added, "Moses from ancient generations hath in every city a congregation of Jews in which he is preached and read every Sabbath day." The council at once decided to issue an encyclical to this effect:—

"The Apostles and Elders and Brethren unto the brethren which are of the nations in Antioch and Syria and Cilicia, greeting. Forasmuch as we have heard that certain which went out from us have troubled you with words, subverting your souls; to whom we gave no commandment; it seemed good unto us, having come to one accord, to choose out men and send them unto you with our beloved Barnabas and Paul,[1] men that have hazarded their lives for the name of our Lord Jesus Christ. We have sent therefore Judas and Silas, who themselves also shall tell you the same things by word of mouth. For it seemed good to the Holy Spirit, and to us, to lay upon you no greater burden than these necessary things—that ye abstain from things sacrificed to idols, and from blood, and from things strangled, and from fornication;[2] from which if ye keep yourselves, ye shall do well."

For a proper understanding of this gathering at Jerusalem, we must lay aside our modern ideas of a question being put to the vote, and the chairman delivering judgment according as the "Ayes" or "Noes" have it. This was foreign to the practice in both Roman and Jewish courts and assemblies. There was a president, with assessors or advisers, who recommended what they held to be the proper judgment, but could not impose their opinion on the president. Practically he took the sense of the meeting, and did not oppose it, but he was under no constraint so to do. Peter on this occasion gave his opinion as an

---

[1] Observe that natural touch. In Galatia it was Paul and Barnabas, but the Church in Jerusalem knew them as Barnabas and Paul, Barnabas being the senior in dignity or calling.

[2] Baur suggests, and Professor Ramsay accepts, as the explanation, "Marriage within forbidden degrees," but surely this is a prohibition against one of the great temptations of Syrian idolatry. In the "Clementine Homilies" we have the rule insisted on twice; vii. 4: "Abstain from the table of devils, nor taste flesh of beasts that have died, nor blood; and purify yourselves from all pollution." vii. 8: "Abstain from the table of devils, that is from food offered to idols, from animals that have been suffocated, and from blood, and live no more impurely."

assessor, and it weighed with James, but it was with James that the decision lay.

All commentators unite in considering the decision of the council as a compromise, and some go so far as to treat it as a cowardly postponement of a vital question.

I think this is a mistake. Paul got all he wanted: he did not ask for the Jewish believers to be forbidden to partake of the Sabbatical meal in the synagogue; he did not hope that at once the rift would be healed. All he asked for was that he might have a free hand with his proselytes. He knew—for he had put his finger on their pulses—that they detested circumcision, and would never submit to it; and that, with this bugbear removed, they would come like an avalanche, and bury Jewdom under it. If it were God's will that the Jewish nation should be converted altogether, this would not be affected by his work, which was outside that.

The elder Apostles also saw that an advantage would be gained in the same contingency, for in every city there would be the synagogue converted into a Judæo-Christian church, to be a nucleus for the neighbourhood; just as Jerusalem would be the nucleus of the whole world. Every synagogue would be the cathedral, so to speak, of a wide district, giving the type of worship, regulating the order, and sending out its ministers. And, above all, the spring of all jurisdiction would be Jerusalem, with Christ enthroned in the seat of David, enlightening, ruling, instructing, disciplining the entire kingdom of mankind through His officials, the Jewish race.

Neither Paul nor James thought that the decision gave a party advantage. It was a judgment which was exactly what was necessary; temporary, doubtless — all such judgments must be temporary—till it was made certain whether the Jews would accept the place to which they were called, or refuse it.[1]

[1] Considerable doubt exists as to whether on this visit to Jerusalem Paul took Titus with him. To do so would have been to exasperate feelings before the Council met, and would have been as injudicious as it would have been in bad taste. This has appeared so obvious to some commentators that they have supposed the reference in Gal. ii. 1, to apply to a former period, perhaps even to a later. I can hardly believe that one so ready to consider prejudice, and so eager to avoid causing unuecessary irritation, should have wilfully provoked offence, and have committed, moreover, such a tactical blunder.

CHAPTER X

THE SECOND JOURNEY—GALATIA

SUMMER, A.D. 52

Return of Paul and Barnabas to Antioch, attended by Judas and Silas—The latter becomes a companion of Paul—Quarrel between Paul and Barnabas—Barnabas in Cyprus—Disappearance of Peter—His epistle from Babylon—Where was Babylon?—Did Peter found the Church in Rome?—Legends—Semo Sancus—Peter cannot have been in Rome prior to the date A.D. 63—Difficulty in thinking that his having founded the Roman Church is a matter of importance—Silence of Scripture—The real supremacy in the hands of James—Paul in Cilicia—Again in Galatia—Timothy—His character suitable to Paul—Why Timothy was circumcised—Paul's intention to visit Bithynia frustrated—Arrives at Troas—Makes the acquaintance of Luke—Remedies for low fever and epilepsy—Luke converted.

THE assembly ended, to the satisfaction of all save the extremists, Paul and Barnabas departed for Antioch, accompanied by Judas Barsabas and Silvanus or Silas, deputies from the Apostles at Jerusalem to Antioch, to inform the Church there of the decision of the council at Jerusalem and to present the letter. Arrived in Antioch, these deputies executed their commission, and then Judas prepared to return. Not so Silas, who had completely fallen under the fascination of Paul's commanding character. He was a Hebrew by birth, apparently, but a Roman citizen, like Paul, and this Roman side of him rendered him one who might be useful to Paul in his further travels and mission work.

The great difficulty at Antioch settled, Paul resolved to return into Asia Minor and revisit the communities he had founded in Phrygian Galatia. He communicated his intention to Barnabas, who consented to accompany him, and proposed to take with them his kinsman John Mark.

To this Paul objected. He harboured something very much like personal resentment against the man who had ventured to differ from him in opinion three or four years before; and he had already made up his mind to take Silas as his companion, one who had no will of his own apart from that of his leader.

Barnabas was offended, and resented this slight cast on his relative, and the contention (St. Luke uses a strong expression—the paroxysm[1]) was so great that the two Apostles saw it was no longer possible for them to work together, and they separated never to meet again.

Years after, when Paul was a prisoner at Rome, this same Mark came to him along with Timothy, and the aged Apostle then, maybe, regretted his earlier violence, and corrected his hasty judgment. "He is profitable," said he then, "to me for the ministry."

Barnabas drops out of the sacred record. He is thought to have gone to his native island, Cyprus, and there to have organised the Church and ended his days. A late tradition says that when, long after, his sarcophagus was opened, he was found therein with a copy of the Gospel of St. Matthew on his breast, which it was thought he had transcribed with his own hand. An epistle was attributed to him, and by most of the fathers regarded as genuine, though not taken into the canon. But modern criticism unanimously puts it down to an Alexandrine forger. It

---

[1] Acts xv. 39.

could not have been written by a Levite, blundering as it does about matters concerning the Temple worship; and the ideas belong purely to the school that grew out of Philo's Judæo-Platonism. Mark attached himself to Peter.

It is interesting to observe that, in the Egyptian Church he founded and organised, circumcision as well as baptism was instituted. In the Abyssinian Church, an offshoot of that in Egypt, circumcision is still practised, as among the Copts to this day. But neither Copt nor Abyssinian regards circumcision as sacramental; he treats it as of no other value than a following of the example of Christ.

A more remarkable disappearance from the Acts than that of Barnabas is that of Peter. After he had given the right hand of fellowship to Paul, he steps into the background and into obscurity. It is advisable at this point to treat briefly of his relation to Paul, and his position in the Church. With him, as already shown, the Church had received its initiatory impulse, both at Jerusalem and at Cæsarea. After that Paul rises above the horizon, he is eclipsed. Two epistles written by him to the Churches of Pontus, Galatia, Cappadocia, Asia, and Bithynia remain, written from Babylon; where this Babylon was is a matter of conjecture. Had it been of vital importance, some word would have been dropped to explain its whereabouts.

At the Babylon in Mesopotamia was a large colony of the Jews. Indeed, by no means all those which had been in captivity there returned to the Land of Promise. They flourished there, in trades and in merchandise, and had no inclination to shut up their shops and return to ploughing and land-dressing. Consequently the colony in Mesopotamia remained large and important.

It is probable that, as Peter regarded himself as Apostle

to the Circumcision, he may have devoted himself to the evangelisation of the Mesopotamian Hebrews.

But there was another Babylon in Egypt near Memphis, and this was esteemed the mother whence the Mesopotamian colonists swarmed at a remote period. As Mark was the companion of St. Peter, and Mark was the evangelist of Egypt, it is conceivable that he may have gone there with Peter, and that it was thence that Cephas wrote his letter.

But there is another claimant—Rome. The Papacy, in its eagerness to show that it rests on Peter, insists that the Babylon of the epistle is Rome. It may be so. The author of the Apocalypse used the same euphemism. But then, if so, the epistle must have been written at a late period. Without entering into criticism here, it is sufficient to say that, to any one endowed with the critical faculty, it is plain that the First Epistle can only have been written about A.D. 80. It is either falsely attributed to the Apostle Peter or he lived on to a much later date than is generally supposed, and, instead of suffering in the persecution of Nero, A.D. 64,[1] died in that of Domitian.

That St. Peter was martyred at Rome may be fairly allowed; the evidence in favour of his tomb being there is tolerably good. And if he was buried there, he probably had something to do with the Church there, or, rather, with the Jewish believers there. But, then, this must have been late, after the Church had been founded and established in Rome by St. Paul.

This may have been after the death of Paul in the Neronian persecution, whereas he himself did not suffer till the Flavian period.

[1] The question of the date of 1 Peter has been investigated by Professor Ramsay in "The Church in the Roman Empire."

From the Epistles of St. Paul we learn nothing about Peter save the interesting fact that he always travelled about with his wife.

Dionysius, who was Bishop of Corinth *circa* A.D. 170, says that Peter was there, but this is probably due to a misunderstanding of Paul's words (1 Cor. i. 12).

Irenæus states that Peter and Paul preached together at Rome, and founded the church there. Tertullian alludes to Peter's death at Rome, and Caius the Priest refers to the trophies of the Apostles, meaning their tombs, near the city, and adds that these two established the Roman Church. These are the *only* early testimonies. All later statements are worthless. There is reason to suspect that the tradition rests on a misapprehension. In Acts we read that the Apostle silenced Simon Magus at Samaria, and prophesied against him. It was supposed that Simon must have practised his magical arts elsewhere, and a wonderful series of romances was produced purporting to show Simon flying from Peter who pursued him from town to town, disputing with him, till at last they came to Rome, where a final dispute arose. Simon attempted to fly, and like Dædalus fell, but not because his waxen wings melted, but because Peter prayed that his attempt might be frustrated. The people, exasperated at the death of the sorcerer, who had bewitched them, rose against Peter, denounced him to the prætor of the city, and he was executed on the cross. The romance was invented for the purpose of using the dialogue as a vehicle for argument against Gnosticism; and is heretical, as Peter is made an exponent of Ebionitism.

Now there was an old Sabine deity Semo Sancus—some statues of him are now in the Vatican—and Justin Martyr

(A.D. 167) actually supposed that this Semo Sancus was none other than Simon the Sorcerer, deified by the Roman people.

Justin puts the coming of Peter to Rome as occurring in the reign of Claudius. Modern Roman writers assume that he went there after his escape from prison in A.D. 44, and that he returned to Jerusalem when Claudius expelled the Jews from Rome in A.D. 49, and so was able to be present at the council. But this first coming of Peter to Rome in the reign of Claudius must be regarded as entirely against evidence. The Epistles which Paul wrote from the city show that no Apostle had been there before, or was there along with him. They contain no allusion whatever to Peter. On the contrary, Paul expressly says that he strives to build on no other man's foundation. In Paul's Epistle to the Romans no salutation is sent to Peter, no allusion is made to his work among them. The character of the letter is certainly not that of one Apostle meddling with a Church under the direction of another.

These considerations certainly disprove the supposition that Peter was at Rome either in the reign of Claudius or before the writing of the Epistle to the Romans. If Peter ever was there, it was after A.D. 63.

From a religious point of view there is another consideration relative to this matter that deserves attention. It is contended by the Roman Church, that its right to supremacy over all churches is due to the fact that it was founded by St. Peter, to whom the words were spoken "On this Rock will I build my Church," and to the grant of the keys of the kingdom of heaven. Supposing that the Rock in question was intended to be Peter, and supposing that the gift of supremacy was made to him, then, surely divine providence would have supplied such evidence that Peter did organise and establish the Church at Rome as would be indisputable.

Is it conceivable, if it be necessary to recognise the Roman See as the head See over Christendom, and the source of jurisdiction, that Holy Scripture should, as it were, studiously avoid telling us that Peter went to Rome at all and had a part in the founding of that Church? Is it conceivable, on the Roman supposition, that Scripture should represent Peter as set aside to make way for Paul, and then that we should be allowed no other glimpse of him than as retired, probably with his good wife, to Babylon, and not furnish us with any hint as to where that Babylon was, nay, rather go out of the way to make obscurity around the place of his retreat?

We can account for the tradition of his having had a hand in the conversion of certain in Rome without supposing that he went there. Every year numbers of Jews and proselytes from Rome came to Jerusalem, and after the issue of the edict of Claudius expelling the former, doubtless many Jews did arrive there. When in Jerusalem, Peter very probably instructed them in the truth, and so may have established a loose claim to be regarded as the founder of Christianity in Rome.

It is surely significant enough that in speaking of Paul's coming to the capital of the world, St. Luke never alludes by half a word to Peter, never intimates that the Church there had an apostolic founder. Is it conceivable, had Peter been in Rome, and his work there in establishing a primatial See been regarded as an important fact, that Luke should have said nothing about it?

Surely had Peter's visit to Rome and work there been of consequence to the Church, and to the salvation of mankind, divine providence would not have left such a matter to repose on conjecture and evidence hardly worth quotation.

One word in Holy Scripture to establish the link between Peter and Rome would have sufficed, but that one word is withheld. The withholding that word is significant. We can show from Scripture that Peter was at Jerusalem, that he worked at Antioch, that he was at some place—Babylon that may be in Mesopotamia, or in Egypt or Rome—but we cannot be sure that in Rome he ever was. The holding back of this one piece of evidence by the Divine Spirit, absolutely breaks down the pretensions of the Papal See to represent the authority and supremacy of Peter.[1] What is certainly remarkable is the position given to James as head over the Church, and that at a time when, as all ecclesiastical critics are agreed, the episcopal office was undeveloped, and that moreover in the most nebulous Church of all, that of Jerusalem. This I conceive can only be explained on the grounds of his being of the royal race of David, and the position accorded him as viceroy till the Messiah should appear.

From Antioch, Paul, attended by Silas, crossed the ridge that divided the Syrian plain from the Province of Cilicia, and descended into the plain—the delta of the Pyramos and Saros, and across its wide tract, waving with flowers, saw the gleaming limestone temples of his native Tarsus.

Although there were Churches in Cilicia, Paul does not

---

[1] We may go further. Holy Scripture pointedly shows us James exercising pontifical rights, and not Peter, and Peter set to rights by an Apostle of an inferior order, Paul.

seem to have had anything to do with their foundation, or Luke would certainly have said so. What had become of the old weaving establishment? Was his father still alive? With what eye did his kinsfolk regard Paul? Whose was now the old house, and had the factory gone into other hands? Paul's father had been in comfortable circumstances, and had been able to give his son what we should call a university education. But now we find Paul very poor, and obliged to work at his trade wherever he halted, so as to maintain himself. Supplies from home for some reason or another were cut off.

From Tarsus Paul and his companion threaded a defile of the Taurus to the Cilician Gates, a natural portal in the rocks that was closed at night against bandits. The road was defended by stations of soldiers at intervals. It mounted continuously, till at length it reached the elevated plain, with its salty marshes, damp chill atmosphere, and fevers—where Paul had worked and shivered and been encouraged on his first visit.

First he came to Derbe, where he was cordially received, then, having exhorted the brethren, he went on to Lystra, some thirty-five miles north-west.

At Lystra, previously, he had converted an old Jewish lady named Lois and her daughter Eunice, who, with the laxity into which many Hellenic Jews had fallen, had contracted marriage with a Gentile and a heathen. Eunice had a son, Timothy, and the two women had taken vast pains to educate the boy in the knowledge of the Books of Moses and the Prophets.[1] Undoubtedly they followed the manner of the liberal school in leaning on the moral and

---

[1] 2 Tim. iii. 15.

theological teachings of Scripture, and in passing over slightly the Mosaic ritual and purificatory legislation. On his first visit, Paul had baptized Timothy, although uncircumcised.

Timothy was now grown to man's estate, he was well spoken of in Lystra and Iconium, and Paul decided on associating him with himself in his labours. The young man was enthusiastically devoted to his father in the faith, and was not a man of such independence of character that Paul might fear any contrariety of opinion from him. Timothy was ready to follow with blind docility, as Paul wrote of him after, "As a son with the father, he hath served with me in the Gospel."[1] But the young man was not of a robust constitution;[2] inclined to be lachrymose;[3] evidently a tender-hearted, gentle, sensitive person, whose bringing up by two women, and whose delicate health, made him wanting in initiative.

This was precisely the sort of person Paul liked to have about him; one who would obey without questioning and follow without murmur. It is a general characteristic with men of immense personality that they cannot endure contradiction, and surround themselves with creatures of moderate abilities and pliant tempers, and alienate those with as strong wills and as able heads as themselves. It was so with Cromwell, Napoleon, Bismarck. Paul was the same. He could make followers, but not substitutes. He had now with him two humble admirers and faithful servants, Silvanus and Timothy.

Paul now took a step that has surprised some critics, who have accused him of inconsistency—he had Timothy

[1] Phil. ii. 22.   [2] 1 Tim. v. 23.   [3] 2 Tim. i. 4.

THE SECOND JOURNEY—GALATIA 207

circumcised. They cannot understand why he should have refused to allow Titus to do that which he allowed in the case of Timothy.

But the explanation is simple. Timothy was half a Jew, Titus wholly Greek. But more than that. Paul was now entering on a fresh missionary field, and purposed working, as heretofore, in the synagogues. But the uncircumcision of Timothy would not only so irritate the Jews against him as to cause them to refuse him a hearing, but might be the occasion of their denying him speech in the synagogues. If he had Timothy circumcised, it was to facilitate his work among the Jews, or rather the proselytes through the Jews.

From Lystra Paul went to Iconium, and thence to Phrygian Antioch, under the great range of the Sultan Dagh. He was now on the confines of the province of Asia, and it was his intention to preach along the great road that followed the Lycus, at Apamæa, Colossæ, Laodicæa; and then, entering the valley of the Mæander, to harangue in the synagogue of Tralles and, with a divergence, at Ephesus.

But he was arrested by a command from above. He was "forbidden by the Holy Ghost to preach the word in [the province of] Asia."[1]

Accordingly he changed his course, and crossing the mountains to the north, made his way towards Bithynia.

He and his companions had probably reached Kotiaion, aiming at Nicæa and Nicomedia, when again he was mysteriously arrested. "The Spirit suffered them not" to go on.

Then, instead of taking the north road, the little party

[1] Acts xvi. 6.

turned sharply round to the west, and passing through Mysia came to Troas.

Here it was that Paul made a fresh disciple, and secured not only a companion, but an historian of his work, Luke the physician, afterwards evangelist.

Perhaps Paul, suffering from a relapse of his fever, consulted Luke as a medical man, and took advantage of the occasion to convert him and withdraw him from his business.

What the remedies would be that Luke would employ we may gather from Pliny. Against fever and against shivers he would recommend the burning of incense in the hollow of a canine tooth of a crocodile, and an application of crocodile fat.[1] For the headache attending malaria he would prescribe the rust from door-hinges dissolved in vinegar, the touch of an elephant's trunk, or the rope with which a man has been hung.[2]

If, however, Paul consulted the physician relative to epileptic fits, from which it is not certain that he suffered, then the infallible recipe was the sloughed skins of newts.[3]

It may be that Luke had become conscious that the medical science of his day was mere quackery, and was glad to cast it from him. He was, it is thought, a native of Philippi, in Macedonia, and after his conversion he spoke to Paul of the field that was open there. The Apostle listened, and then dreamt that he saw a Macedonian appear to him, extending his arms and praying, "Come over and help us."[4]

It is significant of a new chapter being opened in the history of Paul's work that it was prefaced by three super-

---

[1] Plin.: "Hist. Nat." xxviii. 8.   [2] *Ibid.* c. 4.
[3] Appuleius: "Disc. on Magic."   [4] Acts xvi. 9.

natural tokens—two warnings not to take the road which Paul had purposed taking, and then a distinct intimation as to the way in which he was to go.

Luke was a proselyte and uncircumcised,[1] of a gentle and enthusiastic character, and, like Timothy, seems to have been expressly adapted to be Paul's companion.[2]

[1] Col. iv. 14, 15.   [2] Phil. ii. 20.

CHAPTER XI

THE SECOND JOURNEY—MACEDONIA

A.D. 52

Paul crosses to Macedonia—Philippi—Position of woman in Macedonia—No synagogue at Philippi—Only female worshippers—Lydia—Supposed marriage of Paul—The pythoness—Silenced by Paul—Disturbance—Paul and Silas in prison—The *Robur*—The earthquake—Paul's release—Leaves Philippi—Thessalonica—Preaches the Second Coming—This expected to be immediate—Portents—Renewal of disturbances—Their real cause.

FROM Troas by ship, Paul, with his companions, crossed the head of the Ægean Sea, by the island of Samothrace, to Neapolis, the port of Philippi, and at once made their way to this town. Amphipolis had been the chief city of the division to which both belonged, but Philippi was fast outstripping it in prosperity, and the two places stood to each other much in the relation of Minneapolis and St. Paul in the State of Minnesota at the present day.

A low range divides Philippi from the port of Neapolis. Paul and his companions crossed this and saw before them the fertile plain, with white marble crags rising into lofty mountains to the north, curving round this plain, much as the heights enclosed that at the edge of which stood Tarsus. But the situation of Philippi was other than that of Paul's native city. It was built on a ridge, and was dominated by its acropolis and by its agora and temples. Down the side flowed the city to the level ground, where the military highway traversed it, and where were the taverns, hostelries, and warehouses.

The soil about Philippi was ever moist with oozing springs, and willows, poplars, mulberries formed a belt of green about its white buildings. In the lower part of the town, moreover, the miners congregated from their gold-washing diggings—rough, roystering fellows—and gangs of slaves, driven by a steward (*ergastularius*), who searched them after leaving work, and the day's toil ended, locked them up for the night in the *ergastulum*, where they herded till, with the break of dawn, they were roused to renewed drudgery. So abundant was the gold in the granite rubble that it was believed it grew as fast as collected, just as grass sprang up in the fields after it was mown.

Octavius had recognised the importance of the situation when he won the battle of Philippi, and as soon as he was master of the empire he planted there a colony and granted it the *Jus Italicum*. The old soldiers settled there, relics of the army of Antony, natives of Italy, brought to the frontiers of Macedon and Thrace their probity, gravity of manner, and frankness of speech. Along with their native characteristics they brought their rustic tutelary deities. Sylvanus was accorded a temple and a college. But there were also shrines of Minerva, Diana, Mercury, and Hercules; the Syrian Men, the Moon-god, had also a sanctuary, and the oriental Sabazius was there honoured and his mysteries frequented. The gross worship of licentious native deities, so universal in Asia Minor, was supplanted here by purer rites, and in the temples were chanted those orphic hymns which attracted the admiration of the early Christians, hymns that extolled the unity of the Godhead, the immortality of the soul, and exalted the heart to the pursuit of true virtue. Descent in Macedonia was by the spindle; the woman was the true head of the family. The wife, the mother occupied there a higher place than even the Roman matron. She enjoyed right of property, and public monuments were erected in her honour. That the Philippians were a pious people and very cosmopolitan in their devotions is attested by the sculptures on the marble rocks, which bear the statues of gods and goddesses or are scooped out in niches to receive them, and are scored over with inscriptions in their honour.

When Paul arrived in Philippi he was disappointed to find there no *ghetto*, and that the very few Jews settled there had no synagogue. Nevertheless there were some "devout men" and more pious women who had been attracted to Judaism, and these met by the river side in a *proseuche*, an enclosure, a yard, or a garden, on the Sabbath, for prayer.

The Via Egnatia, the main thoroughfare to the east, ran through Philippi. The gold-dust from its mines was conveyed by Amphipolis, the old capital, to Thessalonica, and thence across the peninsula to Dyrrachium, where it was shipped for Brundusium. The points between which the line of vessels ran were this Dyrrachium and Egnatia, that gave its name to the road.

There is but one stream, the Gangas, in the Philippian plain that enters it from a deep gorge. It passes to the west of Philippi, and loses itself in a marsh.

Paul and his three companions walked along the paved highway between the tombs of wealthy and noble citizens, till they came out among gardens near the river, where bloomed the centifoil rose, which was indigenous to the Pangæan mountains behind the town.

On reaching the place of prayer, Paul was a little discouraged to find the attendance almost wholly made up of women. But among these was one of consequence, a Lydian of Thyatira. She was a dealer in dyed cloth, especially in that which was purple, a costly commodity and a luxury of the wealthy. She was probably a widow, as her husband is not named, but with the independence of the country, she kept her shop and managed the business.

Although his audience was entirely composed of women, Paul did not disdain to speak to them and expose the Way of the Lord. The heart of the woman Lydia was opened "and she attended unto the things which were spoken of Paul."[1]

We need not suppose that she was baptized the same day. Paul certainly tarried some time in Philippi. But baptized she was, and she invited Paul and his companions to lodge in her house. She did more than invite, "she constrained us," says St. Luke.

Paul had been very particular not to be a charge to the believers in the cities where he went. He was perhaps unreasonably touchy on this point, but here he could not refuse. The stronger will of the well-to-do, peremptory, and hospitable woman prevailed.

And now if we may trust certain indications, Paul's course of missionary expeditions was nearly brought to an end, and his sphere of labour limited to Macedonia.

There are reasons to surmise that Lydia's religious ardour got mellowed with personal affection; and that she and Paul were either married at Philippi or would have been so but for untoward circumstances. The reasons for this conjecture are, that from her and the Philippians alone he

[1] Acts xvi. 14.

condescended to receive remittances of money; that in his Epistle to the Philippians he does not name her in his salutations, but he does send a special message to his " true yoke-fellow" to "help those women which laboured with me in the Gospel."[1] That Paul was married is attested by several early writers. Ignatius in his Epistle to the Philadelphians says "Peter and Paul, and the rest of the Apostles, were married men." Clement of Alexandria and Eusebius both understand the "true yoke-fellow" in the sense of "trusty wife." Nor does the passage in the first Epistle to the Corinthians exclude this. There Paul says that it was in his power, had he willed it, to "lead about a believing wife, as well as other Apostles."[2] This does not imply that he had none, but that he was not of so uxorious a nature as Peter, who could go nowhere without his good woman at his side.

Another passage which seems to militate against the idea of his being married is 1 Cor. vii. 7, 8. He is advising husband and wife to separate for a period "lest Satan tempt you for your incontinency," in order that this period may be devoted to prayer and fasting. Then he adds, "For I would that all men were even as I myself. . . . . I say, therefore, to the unmarried and widows, it is good for them if they abide even as I." In the first place he seems to hint that the married would be better if they, although married, lived apart from their wives, wholly devoted to asceticism; and in the second, that the unmarried and widows should remain disengaged from earthly affection. It is, however, more probable that Paul did not marry Lydia, but maintained an affectionate remembrance of her.

[1] Phil. v. 3.   [2] 1 Cor. ix. 5.

THE SECOND JOURNEY—MACEDONIA 215

With the "true yoke-fellow" who was to look after the women in Philippi, Paul mentions other females there, Euodias and Syntyche. Five or six years later some men had joined this Philippian Church, Epaphroditus, "my brother and companion in labour and fellow-soldier," but from this it would appear that he was an importation not a convert there. Clement was another "whose name was in the book of life."[1]

But at the outset there appear to have been only women, unless Lydia induced the freed man who attended to her business, kept her books and counted the bales, to accept the Gospel.

If the widow and Paul were married, which is doubtful, they must have been an incongruous pair, she, thriving—and like all Jewesses when youth is past, stout; he, frail, pallid, short of stature, with bandy legs, a long nose, and head already inclining to baldness.[2]

In vision Paul had seen a man of Macedonia inviting him over; so far he had found only women. But Lydia could influence her household—the slaves under her actual control and her needy hangers-on. Some of these, doubtless, were sincere, others suffered themselves to be baptized out of complaisance to their mistress, and with a politic eye to future favours.

The situation of Paul at Philippi was not one of the most dignified, with a train of female admirers hanging on his lips, and under the more or less despotic control of the

---

[1] Phil. v. 3-4.
[2] The personal description is from the Acts of St. Paul and Thecla; and the anonymous author of the dialogue "Philopatris" (A.D. 363), relying on tradition, makes Kritias say of St. Paul: "I met with a bald-headed, long-nosed Galilean, who . . . . had been up into the third heaven."

rich shopkeeper, Lydia. He was delivered from it by a very peculiar circumstance, and the Church of Philippi was given a chance of growth independent of his presence.

As Paul went to the oratory through the lower town, he daily passed where a slave-girl was shown off, who was possessed by a python—that is to say, she was hysterical, half crazy, and had a gift of ventriloquism. She was managed by a company, which shared the profits of her divination; and these were considerable. The gold miners were credulous, and wished for advice where to find nuggets, or to have the thief pointed out who had robbed them of their store. Mothers whose sons were about to cross the Ægean, anxiously inquired what would be the weather, and asked if their sons would return in health; merchants desired news of their convoys, even citizens standing for election, sought to know beforehand what were their chances of being chosen to the magistracy.

Where there is a demand, there is always a supply; the age was superstitious, and there were always men and women ready to make money out of the credulous.

The girl was not a conscious impostor, but an hysterical subject.

Very probably she was one of the Bachanals employed about the oracle of Dionysos in the hills among the Satroe, but purchased as a speculation by a company of Philippians who utilised her for profit. Dionysos was undoubtedly the prophet-god of the Thracians.[1]

We shall not be far wrong in regarding her as an hysterical person, possessed with low cunning and inordinate vanity. Such creatures exist to the present day, and to attract a little attention are capable of committing any folly.

---

[1] ὁ μάντις Θρῇξι, Eurip.: *Hec.* 1267.

THE SECOND JOURNEY—MACEDONIA 217

As Paul and his companions went to prayer, this girl worried them by shouting after them, "These men are the servants of the Most High God, which show unto us the way of salvation." It is improbable that she had listened to any of Paul's teaching, directly from his lips, but she may have heard people talking about him, and what he had said. Her words did not mean to those who heard her what they imply to us. "The Most High God" was a common pagan expression, applied to various deities in their pantheon, and "the way of salvation" in her mouth meant no more than good luck on voyages, escape from robbers and pirates, from shipwreck and from disease; in mining, it signified the finding of nuggets. She perhaps may have meant no more than to invite Paul and his companions to unite with her in the working of the concern, and derive a revenue from the sale of amulets, and the performance of incantations. That was to be their department, and hers the discovery of secrets and the foretelling of the future. They would have played into each other's hands and driven a flourishing business.

That something of the kind was in her head would seem to be implied by the anger of St. Paul. A victim to hysteria and delusions would be a subject for pity, not wrath; but anything like conscious fraud, and an invitation to participate in it, roused his indignation.

Paul turned at last on her, after this annoyance had been of long continuance, and said to the spirit, "I command thee in the name of Jesus Christ to come out of her."

At once all her powers failed her. The rebuke, the manifest superiority of the Apostle quelled her. "She was utterly disconcerted, and lost her faith in herself, and with it her power. Along with her power, her hold on the superstitions of the populace disappeared; and people ceased to come to her to have their fortunes read, to get help in finding things they had lost, and so on."[1]

In all hysterical delusions a peremptory and threatening address is the only means of dissipating them; to humour them is to encourage their growth and mastery over the patient.

The company that had shares in this girl was very indignant; the source of their gains was dried up. The dupes, the populace, were also angry, and a tumult arose. A mob swept off Paul and Silas to the Agora, and clamoured for the magistrates to hear the case, and punish the two Jews who were upsetting the populace with their novel teachings. The owners of the girl did not sue the Apostles for an indemnification of their loss; they were sufficiently shrewd to seize on an accusation much more likely to be promptly dealt with. The crime of proselytism to an unauthorised religion was a serious one; in the case of a patrician it entailed deportation, in that of one of the lower classes it was capital.[2]

The magistrates in such a colonial town as Philippi were citizens, rich merchants, landowners, proprietors of the mines, and were elected by their fellow citizens. They were timorous, dreading to offend their townsfolk, and terribly afraid of being called to order by the central authority of the province, still more so of being appealed against to Rome.

In the clamour that was raised, Paul's voice, asserting

---

[1] Ramsay: "St. Paul," p. 216.
[2] Jul. Paulus, Sentent. v. 21; Servius, Ad. Virg. Æneid, viii. 187; Dion Cassius, vii. 36.

the citizenship of himself and Silvanus, was not listened to, perhaps not heard, and all these fussy, frightened magistrates thought of was how best to pacify the mob and send it home quietly. They at once ordered Paul and his companion to be scourged and then thrown into prison. They did not even go through the legal form of calling the prisoners *rei*, and then of hearing evidence for and against them.

The Apostles were accordingly taken to the prison-house, and thrust into the *Robur* or *Lignum*. Here were the stocks, so contrived that the legs could be distended to such an extent as to almost dislocate the hips. They had in them as many as five holes.[1]

Outside the *Robur* was a court. No light entered the prison save through the door when open, and the stench in the place was one of its worst discomforts, as it communicated with the sewer.

During the night, whilst the Apostles were singing hymns, an earthquake shook the prison; the doors flew open, and the chains which were stapled into the walls fell down.

The gaoler, who was responsible for the prisoners, in alarm came from his house, and seeing the doors open, thought that the captives had taken advantage of the opportunity and had escaped. They could easily hide in the mountains, or, by hastening to Neapolis, get away in a sailing or rowing boat. The first impulse of the gaoler was to kill himself. Paul and Silas within, in the dark

---

[1] A representation of the stocks has been found at Pompeii. Le Blant: "Revue Archéologique," 1889, p. 149. The *Robur* was the place in which the executions took place. It was pitch dark. Festus uses the expression "a place into which a set of malefactors is precipitated which had already been imprisoned in strongholds."

prison chamber, saw him without, guessed his intention, and called to assure him that they were there. Then he cried out for a light and came in, brought them into his house, and washed their wounds and set food before them.

Paul then preached to him the Word of God, and he and his whole house believed.

By next morning the prætors had come to the conclusion that they had done a very stupid thing, and had laid themselves open to a grave charge. No doubt that Lydia and her friends had represented the matter to them, and had insisted on the citizenship of Paul and Silvanus. Accordingly these magistrates, who knew as little of the law as many an English justice of peace, were frightened, and sent to the prison to have Paul and his companion set free.

But it did not suit Paul's plans to be smuggled out of the gaol in that way. He saw clearly enough that he and Silas could not remain in Philippi, but he had made up his mind to leave his companions Luke and Timothy behind, and also to revisit the town himself as soon as possible. It was advisable, therefore, to let the magistrates feel what they had done, and give them a good wholesome lesson not to meddle unnecessarily and illegally.

Paul said: "They have beaten us openly, untried, being Roman citizens [and the *Lex Porcia* forbids the beating of citizens]; they have cast us into the *Robur*, have put us in the stocks; and now do they thrust us out privily? Nay verily; but let them come themselves and fetch us out."

To this these Philippian Dogberries were obliged to submit.

As it was no longer possible for Paul and Silas to remain

THE SECOND JOURNEY—MACEDONIA 221

in Philippi, they departed along the Egnatian road, but left Luke and Timothy behind to get the little Church into something like shape, and to give the converts some rudimentary teaching.

It was, to Paul, perhaps unfortunate that he was obliged to go on without Luke, but as he was resolved to continue on the same course, addressing the synagogues and, through the Jews, working upon his proselytes and such as were being influenced by them, it did not so greatly matter.

Had Luke been with him he might possibly have tarried at Amphipolis and Apollonia, both important places; but as there was no *ghetto* in either, he was without a foothold, and knew not how to address the Gentiles.

He and Silas pushed on to Thessalonica, where was a large Jewish settlement with a synagogue.

Thessalonica was at that period almost as important a centre as is Saloniki now. In all Greece, Corinth only excepted, there was not so excellent a harbour; sheltered by the Chalcedonic peninsula from winds, the water in it was glassy as oil, and there was good anchorage. But Thessalonica was not merely a great port and a station on the highway; it had its hot baths, and was therefore in resort by the infirm, and it was, above all, a busy manufacturing town, much like Tarsus, where the loom rattled all day; a great quantity of cloth was made, of bright dyed wool and of coarse goats'-hair.

Paul was in a place where he could earn his livelihood, and he took up his quarters with a Jew named Jason, probably a dealer in woollen and goats'-hair stuffs. There he worked at his loom both night and day,[1] so as to be

---
[1] 1 Thess. ii. 9; 2 Thess. iii. 8.

chargeable to none. On the Sabbath days he visited the synagogue. His subject-matter is summed up in one verse by St. Luke. He argued that the prophecies declared that the Messiah should suffer; then he showed that Christ Jesus had suffered and risen again, and then he went on to declare that the expectations of Israel would be accomplished on the second coming of Christ, which would shortly take place.

He reasoned with great gentleness and patience, trying to instruct and lead those who heard him, just as a mother or a nurse trains a babe.[1] And what he said was well received, not as the word of men, but as the word of God.[2]

About this time men's minds were in a ferment of alarm and expectation. The feeble brain of Claudius was becoming weak to imbecility, and he was completely dominated by his wife and niece, the younger Agrippina, and by the palace eunuchs. The Rome of Augustus and Tiberius was sinking into an abyss of impotence and infamy, and sinister presages were noted. The earthquake that had occurred at Philippi had been felt in many other places.[3] There had been a general failure of the crops. Birds of ill omen were seen to perch on the Capitol. Perhaps at this time Paul was particularly impressive in his declaration that the end of all things was at hand. Later, when he wrote his Epistles to the Thessalonians, the prodigies had been more marked, and the consequent excitement greater. Lightning had struck the military ensigns, a swarm of bees had settled upon the cupola of the Capitol, and a pig farrowed with the talons of a hawk.[4] A comet was seen; the Arch

[1] 1 Thess. ii. 7.
[2] Ibid. ii. 13.
[3] Tacit. Ann. xii. 43.
[4] Ibid. xii. 64.

THE SECOND JOURNEY—MACEDONIA 223

of Drusus was struck. Then Paul wrote, accentuating the fears and expectations of his converts, "We which are alive and remain unto the coming of the Lord shall not prevent them which are asleep. For the Lord Himself shall descend from heaven with a shout, with the voice of the archangel, and with the trump of God; and the dead in Christ shall rise first. Then we which are alive and remain shall be caught up together with them in the clouds."[1] The second Epistle to the same Church is full of these prognostications, but somewhat apologetic, because the great Day had not arrived quite when he had led the Thessalonians to expect.

That in his apocalyptic prophecies Paul had let slip some expressions relative to the Messiah coming to rule all nations, and be King above the princes of the earth, is shown by the commotion caused, and the charges made against Paul and Silas, that they did contrary to the decrees of Cæsar, and proclaimed the advent of another King, one Jesus.

The Jews which believed not were the movers in this disturbance, and the cause is not far to seek. Of the devout proselytes, "a great multitude" clave to the Apostles, "and of the chief women not a few." These commercial Jews, as elsewhere, were most unwilling to have their hold over the believing Greeks relaxed, lest it should interfere with their profits.

Josephus tells us how that a wily Jew in Rome persuaded a noble lady, Fulvia, to send rich gifts to the Temple, and to entrust them to him to take for her, and how that he sold the goods and pocketed the money.

There is no reason for supposing the Thessalonican Jews

[1] 1 Thess. iv. 15-17.

guilty of any such roguery, but they, no doubt, liked to carry up abundant gifts to Jerusalem as the donations of " our converts," and they little relished the idea of this stream being dried up.

The result was that Paul and Silas were expelled from Berœa.

CHAPTER XII

THE SECOND JOURNEY—ATHENS

A.D. 52

Paul leaves Berœa—Arrived in the Piræus—The Macedonian mission —Luke and Timothy left in Macedonia—A new scene—Incapacity of Paul to appreciate the art or philosophy of Greece—Indifference to Nature—Paul's entry into Athens—The Agora—The Acropolis— The Areopagus—Paul drawn before the Areopagus—His address— Mistakes at the outset—The unknown gods—The rest of the address —Misconceived by the hearers—Two converts only—What Christianity owes to Greek philosophy—Second mistake—The speech a failure—Character of his hearers—The cross on the Areopagus.

FROM Berœa, Paul was again obliged to escape, being sent away by the brethren, and he went by sea to the Piræus, the port of Athens. The mission to Macedonia had given him great hopes. He liked the people, their frankness, and especially the independence of the women, and their amenability to his preaching. He wrote to the Thessalonians that they were his hope, his joy, his crown ; and he used the same expression relative to the Philippians.[1] From among them he drew some of his truest friends and companions, Secundus, who was with him in his last journey, and Aristarchus, who followed him to Rome, and shared his prison.[2] Nowhere, neither in Syria nor in Galatia, had he found hearts so open to conviction, so generous in disposition, and so resolute in their adhesion to

[1] 1 Thess. ii. 19; Phil. iv. 1.
[2] Acts xx. 4; Col. iv. 10; Philem. 24.

the truth. These Macedonians were the Yorkshiremen of Greece.

At Thessalonica, Paul had been rejoined by Timothy, but when he left Berœa, he did not take either him or Silas with him, but left them behind to organise his work, establish in the faith those whom he had convinced, and they were to come on to him later to Athens, and advise him what prospect there was of his return to Macedonia. His heart was warm towards the good zealous people of Thessalonica and Philippi. He was eager " once and again" to return to them, but either the attitude of the magistrates at Philippi or his reluctance to bring trouble on Jason at Thessalonica, who had stood security for him, prevented his revisiting these places for some years.

He went to Athens, not because called by the Spirit, but as a mere waiting-place, till he could go back to the scene of his late successes.

At Athens he was in a new scene, among new surroundings, yet in a place where there was a Jewish colony. At Tarsus, indeed, there had been famous schools, that turned out men of ability, but as a university it stood to Athens much in the relation of Durham to Oxford. At Tarsus, Paul had been entirely outside the circle of studies, and his mind was untrained by the great men of Greek philosophy. He was willing enough now to be " all things to all men," but he was incapable of being a philosopher among philosophers. An attempt to lecture to the Athenians would be as great a blunder as a man standing up in the theatre of Oxford to discuss Roman literature, when he made false quantities in his first quotation, and revealed the fact that all he knew of the writers was through magazine articles.

Paul was as incapable of appreciating the art treasures of Athens as he was of giving proper value to its philosophy. He looked not even with indifference at the glorious statuary, the work of Phidias, Agoracritus of Samos, and Alcamenes, or the bronzes of Praxiteles. To Paul these were idols, and idols only. He had no more notion of these sculptors straining after the ideal of beauty than he had of the philosophers striving after the ideal of truth. That these men had used their God-given faculties to do the best they could, that did not come within the compass of his perception. These incomparable achievements of art, instead of filling him with admiration, made him angry: "His spirit was stirred in him, when he saw the city full of idols." We are told he disputed in the synagogue with the Jews, and with the "devout persons," *i.e.*, the proselytes, and in the market daily with those that met with him.

It is interesting to note the gaps there were in Paul's mental and perspective powers. As he had no appreciation of art, so had he none for Nature. Whereas the Divine Master incessantly appealed to the teachings of creation, to bird and flower, to the harvest field, the fig tree and the vine, Paul passed all by as though he did not see them. He did indeed once allude to the stars, and once to the growth of the seed, but so defective was his observation, that when he came to speak of the grafting which must have gone on under his eyes repeatedly, he blundered egregiously, and spoke of the wild olive as grafted on to the cultivated tree, and becoming good thereby, and founded an argument upon this extraordinary misstatement.

So, he was ignorant of Greek history, and out of sympathy with the noble struggles of the past. As Dean Farrar admits, "he might stroll into the Stoa Pœcile, and there peer at the paintings, still bright and fresh, of Homeric councils of which he probably knew nothing, and of those Athenian battles about which, not even excepting Marathon, there is no evidence that he felt any interest."

He must in Athens have been as much out of harmony with the whole tenour of thought and feeling of the Greek as were two Essex artisans with whom I once went through the British Museum. Nothing interested them, nothing awoke admiration, or inquiry, and their verdict on leaving was, "They must have been blokes who made all those things, and they were blokes who took the trouble to collect them, and blokes and only blokes those who go to look at them."

The entire system of training under Gamaliel had been stunting to the finer qualities of the mind. As Dean Farrar again says, " Nothing in the Talmud is more amazing than the total absence of the geographic, chronological, and historic spirit. A genuine Jew of that Pharisaic class in the midst of which St. Paul had been trained, cared more for some pedantically minute *halacha*, about the threads in a *tsitsith*, than for all the pagan history in the world."

Athens was at the time no longer a great focus of liberty and democracy, but it was a museum and a sanctuary. The worship of the Olympian deities had been given a halo and eternal youth through the genius of the sculptors and architects.

On his landing in the Piræus,[1] Paul saw temples, statues on all sides, altars erected to foreign gods, even to

---

[1] Some have supposed that he landed at the port of Phalerus, but this is not a harbour into which any but a flat-bottomed boat could enter.

such as were unknown by name, with a sort of generous hospitality, a readiness in this great sanctuary of religion to welcome all strange deities from Syria, Asia, and Egypt. As he paced up the long walk from the Piræus to Athens, he observed the tombstones, on which the fleeting soul was figured as a butterfly, or the extinction of life was symbolised by an inverted torch; where Hermes Psychopompos was represented conveying away the little darlings from the outstretched arms of their parents, or the wife from the distracted husband.

On entering Athens, his eyes fell on the statues of the tutelary deities of the city, standing by the gate, Athene and Poseidon. Not far off was the Temple of Demeter adorned by the masterpieces of Praxiteles. Following the first street he reached the Agora. This had been originally, like the Forum of Rome, an open space between the hills of the Acropolis, the Areopagus, the Pnyx, and the Museum height. It lay at the foot of the upper town, and was the market-place of primitive Athens; but it had been encroached upon by buildings, and it now formed the most busy quarter of the city, and was crowded with as many statues as there were living men who moved in it. There Paul might have seen the image of a Jew in pontifical habits, the High Priest Hyrcanus, friend of the Athenians; and a little beyond the statue of a Jewish princess, the beautiful and dissolute Berenice, before whom a few years later he would plead in chains. Above the Agora towered the Acropolis, with its marble piles, the Parthenon, the Erectheion, and the Propylæa.

Under the shadow of trees planted on the Agora by Cimon, stood the white statues of Solon, Conon, Demosthenes, Theseus, and Heracles. In the centre of the square rose the altar of the twelve great deities. The hill of the Pnyx was consecrated to Zeus, the theatre to Dionysos; the prison was a temple of Cybele, the senate-house contained an altar to Hestia, and statues of Zeus and Apollo. Traditional gods and goddesses did not suffice the Athenians, they imported Serapis from Egypt. They deified and adored abstract virtues, also vices; pity, modesty, fame, persuasion, religion, but likewise impudence.

The platform of the Acropolis was crowded with objects of priceless value, in marble, bronze, ivory, even gold. The Herè formed out of the spoil of Marathon was twenty-five feet high, and stood on a pedestal of twenty feet. There were to be seen Theseus fighting with the Minotaur, Heracles strangling serpents, Aphrodite rising out of the waves, Apollo bending his bow. Pausanias, who visited Athens nearly a century after St. Paul, and who has left us a record of what he saw, declares that there was more statuary in Athens than in all the rest of Greece, and he adds that nowhere were people more enthusiastic in their religion. A sort of superstitious intoxication laid hold of all minds, and although the philosophers scoffed, and the comic playwrights ridiculed, the hold of the traditional religion on the people was indestructible.

After a while the accredited lecturers in the University heard that there was a Jew who did not confine himself to haranguing his fellows from Palestine, but who had the audacity to speak in public to Greeks and strangers.

"Certain powers were vested in the Council of Areopagus to appoint or invite lecturers at Athens and to exercise some general control over the lecturers, in the interests of public order and morality. There is an almost complete lack of evidence what were the advantages and the legal

THE SECOND JOURNEY—ATHENS 231

rights of a lecturer thus appointed, and to what extent or in what way a strange teacher could find freedom to lecture in Athens. There existed something in the way of privileges vested in the recognised lecturers. . . . . The scene described in Acts xvii. 18-34 seems to prove that the recognised lecturers could take a strange lecturer before the Areopagus and require him to give an account of his teaching and pass a test as to its character."[1]

Some of the Stoic and Epicurean philosophers said of Paul, "What would this rag-and-patch man say?"[2] Others said, " He is apparently introducing certain foreign divinities."

The tribunal was held on Mars' Hill, a red conglomerate outcrop on which, according to fable, the gods assembled to judge Ares. The court sat in the open air, on benches cut in the rock; at the foot of the nodule was the sanctuary of the Furies. Usually, trials were there held at night, so that the judges might hear, not see, the accused; and the accuser stood on a block dedicated to Implacability. But this was no criminal trial, and would not therefore be heard in the night.

Outside the ring of the seats of the judges and assessors was the *corona*, the dense circle of the populace always present on such an occasion, as in the Forum at Rome, as in the National Assembly during the Revolution at Paris; and here, as in Rome and Paris, the orator talked rather to the people outside than to those within, as an actor may

[1] Ramsay: "St. Paul," p. 246.
[2] Spermologos, a word of Attic slang, meaning in the first place a bird that picks up among the offal in the streets, then a rag and bone man, and lastly one who gets hold of scraps of learning and uses them ignorantly. Ramsay translates "a bounder."

strut and rant to the galleries for the sake of the cheap applause.

St. Paul had now such an audience as he had never before had a chance of addressing, and that he made a great effort to succeed cannot be doubted. If he failed, it was due partly to his inability to understand the minds of those to whom he spoke, mainly to their indifference to truth. " Ye men of Athens [it was *ad populum*], I observe that you are more than others respectful of what is divine. For as I was going through your city and surveying the monuments of your worship, I found also an altar with the inscription, 'To the unknown God.' That divine nature, then, which you worship, not knowing what it is, that is it which I declare unto you."

Unable, as with Jews and proselytes, to appeal to Scripture, he went direct to this inscription. And here, unhappily, he made his first blunder. He had misread, and wholly misconceived, the dedication.

When the Vikings sailed to harry a foreign coast, they put the heads of dragons or other monsters as figureheads to their vessels, with the object of scaring away the *landvætir*, the deities of the country they proposed invading, and so leaving it unprotected. When they came peacefully, they shipped their figureheads.

The Greeks had as childish notions, which took a somewhat different form. Our ships now have figureheads and names connected with these heads. These figures and names replace the saints or gods under whose protection vessels were anciently put, whose *ikons* or statues were placed on the poops and received daily worship.

When strange vessels from foreign lands came into the ports of Athens, the Greeks received the gods who were supposed to travel along with the ships under their protection, and accorded them worship, lest these deities should be offended and retaliate for neglect by inflicting pestilence, earthquake, or fire on the port or town. The altars erected in the Phaleron and the Piræus were greetings to these "unknown travelling gods."[1] In like manner, when the Greeks besieged a city they set up altars and invited to them the gods and goddesses, known and unknown, of the beleaguered city, that they might leave the besieged and come over to the besiegers. Paul, then, it would seem, had misread the text and misconceived the drift. Steeped in Jewish ideas, he thought that the inscription was an appeal of the human soul away from polytheism to the one unknown and supreme Deity. Not a Greek had such a thought. Consequently the opening of his address fell flat. He was moving in one plane of ideas, to which the minds of his audience had not reached.

There is, however, a chance that he may have actually seen an altar to the Nameless God that was erected after Epimenides had purified the city. The occasion was this: A pestilence raged in Athens B.C. 560, and the citizens sent to Crete to invite Epimenides to their city to expel the plague. He came and ordered a sheep, half black, half white, to be procured, and an altar to be erected on the spot where the sheep lay down. This was done, and the plague ceased. As the Athenians did not know who the god was who had afflicted them, and who had been appeased, this altar was nameless.

[1] " Inscriptio aræ non erat ut Paulus asseruit : *Ignoto Deo*, sed ita : *Diis Asiæ et Europæ, Diis ignotis et peregrinis :* verum quia Paulus non pluribus indigebat diis ignotis, sed uno tantum Deo ignoto, singulari verbo usus est."—St. Jerome, in Tit. i. 12.

Even if Paul had seen this altar, and referred to it, his application was without point, for no Greek would consider this god who had plagued them capriciously as a supreme deity above the Olympian divinities, but rather as some mischievous demon.

Paul proceeded: "The God that made the world and all things therein, He, the Lord of heaven and earth, dwelleth not in temples made with hands, and is not served by human hands as needing anything, since He Himself giveth to all life and breath. And He made of one nature every race of men to dwell on all the face of the earth, and fixed determinate limits of time and place for their habitation, that they should seek the God, if haply they might feel after Him and find Him, although indeed He is not distant from any one of us, for in Him we live and move and have our being, as certain also of your poets have said, 'For we are also His offspring.' Being thus the offspring of God, we ought not to think that the divine nature is like unto gold or silver or stone, graven by art and device of man."

Thus far, what Paul said was not anything with which the philosophers following Plato could disagree. His quotation, given somewhat vaguely, was from Aratus, a Cilician poet, and therefore a compatriot; but something of the same sort is also found in a hymn of Cleanthes to Zeus, which he was not likely to know.

Paul had been asked to give an account of his doctrine, and he therefore went on to what was special in his teaching.

"Now the times of ignorance God overlooked, but at present He chargeth all men everywhere to repent, inasmuch as He hath set a day on which He will judge the world in righteousness, in the person of the Man whom He hath ordained for this office. And that Man is Jesus Christ whom I preach. If you desire a guarantee, you have it in this—that this same Jesus, after He had declared the will of God, died, and was raised from the dead."

The speech, of which this is but a summary, was well-reasoned, masterly, and admirably conceived. Nearly all the points of his doctrine were in it. God is One, God is good, God is immaterial, God is to be worshipped in spirit, God is just and He will judge the world, and judge it by One whom He has set apart for the purpose, and that all may know who this One is, in Him God hath wrought a miracle in raising Him from the dead. The only vital point omitted was forgiveness of sins through the name of Jesus Christ, but to that he was certainly coming when interrupted. He had already warned the people who heard him that God required repentance. How to repent and obtain pardon and restoration would have followed had not a howl of derision risen at the mention of resurrection from the dead.

To the Greek death was associated with cremation, the reduction of the body to a handful of ashes. Without staying to think whether resurrection could be a less startling phenomenon in a case of carnal interment, the populace broke into jeers, interrupted the hearing, and the tribunal declared it had heard sufficient. A few who had listened sided with Paul, and asked to hear more. But these exceptions must not lead us to doubt that this first apparition of Christianity among the enlightened classes of Athens, excited nothing but surprise and contempt. It was no doubt the recollection of this reception which, a few years later, induced Paul to exclaim in a tone of disappointment, if not of irritation, "It is written, I will destroy the wisdom of the wise, and will bring to nothing the understanding of the understanding ones. Where is the wise? Where is the grammarian? Where is the disputer of this world? Hath not God made foolish the wisdom of this world? For after that in the wisdom of God, the world by wisdom knew not God, it pleased God by the foolishness of preaching to save them that believe."[1] In a few years, the doctrine of the Logos, of which Paul was probably ignorant, or if he knew it, despised it— this doctrine, enunciated by Plato, would be the foundation of Christian philosophy laid by the author of the fourth gospel, developed and applied by Augustine; long after, the teachings of Aristotle would become the basis of the learning of the Christian schoolmen. It would be out of Athenian philosophy, not dry Rabbinism, that Christian apologists would seek their weapons wherewith to combat paganism.

Paul was stepping off a reef into deep water when from addressing Jews he spoke to Greeks, and the summary given by Luke of his speech shows the flexibility of his mind, and his desire to come into touch with the Greek intellect. But this was not possible for him with his defective education. That he was pleased with his attempt is certain, or Luke could not have embodied it in his narrative. Paul had no companions with him at the time to recollect it. He must have written it out and sent it to Luke.

He made a second and a serious error in attempting to embody his entire scheme in one speech. It was unneces-

[1] 1 Cor. i. 17-22.

sary, and was the occasion of his expulsion from Athens. All that was requisite was for him to have argued against idolatry, to have insisted on the unity and justice of the Godhead; then he might have gone on to say that God would not leave Himself without witness, and that He had sent His Son, Jesus Christ, into the world to reveal to man what was His will. So much his audience could have digested. The Epicureans would have been disgusted, but not so the Stoics.

But he tried to bring in too much, his entire system, and to introduce mysteries his audience was totally unprepared to receive.

How little the Greeks comprehended his words about the resurrection (*Anastasis*), or were likely to comprehend them, is shown by the early Greek fathers, who would certainly understand the pagan mind, when they explain that those who heard Paul supposed he was preaching about a male and female pair of deities, Jesus and Anastasis.

That may have been the case, and the outcry may have been raised against him as a bringer-in of new gods. This was much like the charge brought against Socrates. It was against Roman law. A man might worship what god he would in private, but not invite publicly to unauthorised devotions.

There can be no disguising the fact that this defence of St. Paul was a failure, and he himself felt that it was so. He left Athens precipitately. He wrote no epistle to the Athenians, never mentioned the Church or the converts there in either of his letters to the Corinthians, and on his next voyage he avoided Athens.

Nevertheless the address was not absolutely resultless.

Dionysius the Areopagite—one would like to know whether an archon or the mere keeper and cleaner of the court —and a woman of doubtful character[1] were convinced. A few men professed a willingness to hear more, but nothing further is told us of Paul attempting to address an audience in Athens, and their languid desire to hear more subsided in a day or two.

Yet the cause of Paul's want of success lay not so much in his deficiencies as in the defect in seriousness and sincerity in his hearers.

"The pedagogue," says Renan, "is the least convertible of men; for he has a religion of his own, and that is his routine, his belief in his old authors, and his taste is for literary exercises. That quite contents him and extinguishes in his heart every other desire."[2]

Athens in its decline had become an arena for logistic contests. It was a place of lecturers, theorisers, schoolmasters, who without seriousness threw out their systems like soap bubbles. These Greeks of Athens had acquired a habit of listening with one ear to the talkers who harangued in succession, as wavelet follows wavelet lapping the sand, and each effaces the ripple mark left by the wavelet preceding it. Ours is the novel-reading age. The

---

[1] Professor Ramsay says: "It was impossible in Athenian society for a woman of respectable position and family to have any opportunity of hearing Paul; and the name Damaris (probably a vulgarism for *damalis*, a heifer) suggests a foreign woman, perhaps one of the class of educated *Hetairai*, who might very well be in his audience." But it is quite as likely that the woman was a Jewess or Syrian, and that her name was Tamar, which was Græcised into Damaris. Anyhow it is not easy to conceive of a reputable woman being with the crowd listening to the defence of the Apostle. A Greek woman could not have done this.

[2] Renan: "Vie de St. Paul," p. 199.

romance with us takes the place of the disputes in the schools. What serious work, written with purpose, produces a lasting effect on the devourers of light literature ? What leading article, however powerful, is not effaced in its effect on mind and conscience by those read immediately after in other journals, or forgotten in the interest of those on the day succeeding ?

The mental and moral quality of the Greeks was already in decadence. In Paul's age Athens had in it no men of commanding ability; and as the philosophers degenerated into pedants, the professors of equitation and pugilism rose into importance. In another century a range of busts of the hairdressers and costumiers who frizzed and depiled and dressed the young student fops would be erected about the agora in the place of philosophers and historians and poets.[1]

The Greeks were a people of high artistic culture, but of no depth of character. Among the Galatian Phrygians Paul had found enthusiasm, but fickleness; among the Macedonians an almost Teutonic strength of purpose; but here was but a degenerate and *blasé* race, out of which all power of rejuvenescence was gone; a noble race in appearance, brilliant in parts, refined in taste, but in heart deceitful, selfish, shifty, vain. A butterfly nature was in the people, loving sunshine, sipping honey, without a thought of the grave, and solicitude as to what was beyond it.

Could Paul have thought, could these shallow sciolists have conceived it possible, that the badly expressed words in which he professed his convictions would outlast and overmaster all their cobweb-spinning, and that in a few

[1] Now in the museum of the Archæological Society at Athens.

years, deep into the rock where Paul stood and received their jeers, the cross would be cut, that cross which was to the Greeks foolishness, and that churches to Christ would be reared out of the ruins of their temples, and all their festivals forgotten in the supreme joy of the annual commemoration of the Anastasis?

CHAPTER XIII

THE SECOND JOURNEY—CORINTH

A.D. 53

Paul goes to Corinth—The city of Corinth—The character of its population—Paul lodges with Aquila and Priscilla—He preaches in the synagogue—Reminiscences of the failure at Athens—Quarrels with the heads of the synagogue—Irritating behaviour—Converts—The moral character of his converts—Discouragement—Violent language towards the Jews—An uproar—Gallio—Paul is charged before him with high treason—He is discharged—Sosthenes maltreated as an informer—Renan on Paul before Gallio—Organisation of the Macedonian Churches—Unorganised condition of the Corinthian Church—Development a law of God—Early Christianity amorphous—Development of doctrine—And of Church organisation—The Agape at Corinth—Moral mischief arising out of it—Impossibility of restoring a developed Church to its primitive condition—Arrested developments.

FROM Athens Paul went precipitately to Corinth. It was like going from Cambridge to Newmarket; but it was more than Newmarket, it was Chicago and Newmarket in one, a great mercantile centre, and a place for jockeys[1] and athletes; it was more, it was a Paris also, the seat of every description of profligacy. The East sent thither its licentiousness, Rome its brutality. Corinth was that one town in Greece that was least Greek. It swarmed with settlers of every nationality; its streets were noisy all night with drunken men. Jew pedlars,

[1] Chariot drivers, not riders.

Levant sailors, gangs of slaves, prostitutes, wrestlers, and racing men—such was the population of Corinth.

The old Greek city had been destroyed by Mummius, B.C. 146, and left a heap of ashes. It had remained desolate till Julius Cæsar sent thither a colony from Italy, composed for the most part of freed men.

The position was not one to be neglected. Situated in the furrow between the Saronic Bay and the Gulf of Corinth, it was as Xenophon termed it, " The gate of the Peloponnesus." It was, moreover, a halfway house between Italy and the East, and it was dominated by the Acropolis, two thousand feet above the sea, garrisoned by four hundred soldiers and fifty dogs.

Ships from Italy reached the port of Lechæum, and on rollers were drawn by oxen along a straight and even road, five miles long, to Diolcus, where they were again floated to continue their voyage to the East. Or, if the vessels were too large, then their lading was transferred to packhorses, tumbrils, and the backs of porters, to be carried across the isthmus and re-shipped at the other port.

Necessarily Corinth was full of sailors drifting east or west and of soldiers on their way to Syria and Asia Minor, or returning to Italy.

The little Roman colony planted by Cæsar was soon engulfed in the floods of strangers who came to Corinth scenting gain. Some of the old Greeks returned, but too few and too poor to constitute an aristocracy. In such a town, power, position, were in the hands of the rich merchants, the contractors, and jobbers.

On the Acrocorinth was the temple of Venus Pandemos, served by a thousand beautiful priestesses, all courtesans. But indeed the whole town was a pandemonium, in which the vilest orgies were perpetrated with utter shamelessness.

There, and there only in Greece, were to be seen the butcheries of the gladiatorial shows and the fights with beasts.

Every third year were held the Isthmian games, by the temple of Poseidon, near the town; and for some time previous the streets were resonant with the twanging of strings, the twittering of pipes and the screaming of singers running up and down the chromatic scales. Athletes went into training and wrestled and leaped and threw quoits, women even stripped to contend for prizes in the circus. Beasts for the amphitheatre were landed from Africa and Asia, and attended by crowds of boys from the landing-place to their caveæ. The knowing ones watched the horses being trained and made books for the coming races. In the squares, in the midst of a ring, mountebanks exhibited, like that man described by Appuleius, who swallowed the head of a pike and made a little boy twirl on tiptoe at the other end of the shaft. For a while the whole place went mad with excitement, and every restraint of order and decency was cast aside. It was a Barthlemy Fair carried to a pitch incredible to a Northern mind.

On reaching Corinth, Paul took up his abode with Aquila and Priscilla, he a Jew of Pontus, who had been settled in Rome, but had left it on account of the edict of Claudius against the Jews. By trade Aquila was a tent-maker, and as he was already a Christian, he and his wife gladly welcomed the Apostle. They do not seem to have been disposed to settle permanently in Corinth, for we meet with them later at Ephesus; then they returned to Corinth, and finally passed into Asia. Evidently at the time this worthy couple was not well off, and Paul suffered from want, till relieved by money sent him by his converts in Macedonia.

As soon as Paul was in lodgings, he went on the Sabbath to the synagogue, as a large Jewish settlement was at Corinth, "and he reasoned in the synagogue every Sabbath, and persuaded the Jews and the Greek proselytes."[1] He was now on familiar ground, he could go over his old arguments, quote the same much-used prophecies, confident of the same success that had followed elsewhere. He had done with the method ventured on to the Greeks of Athens. "Brethren, when I came to you, I came not with excellency of speech or of wisdom [as I did at Athens], but declared to you the testimony of God. . . . . My speech and my preaching was not with enticing words of man's wisdom, but in demonstration of the Spirit and of power; that your faith should not stand in the wisdom of men, but in the power of God. Howbeit we speak wisdom among them that are perfect, yet not the wisdom of this world, nor of the princes of this world, that come to nought."[2] The first Epistle to the Corinthians was not written till two or three years later, and yet it is clear that the recollection of the dismal failure at Athens still rankled in his heart. The epistle abounds in thrusts and gibes at secular, wisdom.[3] Presently Timothy and Silas arrived from Macedonia, and then Paul took a bolder line. Hitherto, so as not to be burdensome on his hosts, he had worked for his living, and had but the Sabbath day in which to address the Jews, and then only when suffered by the rulers of the synagogue.[4] But on the receipt of money from Thessalonica and Philippi, he was at greater liberty, and gave himself up wholly to preaching, "testifying to the Jews that Jesus was the Christ."

[1] Acts xviii. 4.
[2] 1 Cor. ii. 1-6.
[3] 1 Cor. i. 17-28; ii. 1-8, 12-16; iv. 10.
[4] 2 Cor. xi. 9.

The heads of the *ghetto* at Corinth, rich merchants and money-lenders, now began to stir themselves, and he found himself excluded from the synagogue. Thereupon he pursued a course vastly aggravating.

"He shook his raiment and said to them, Your blood be upon your own heads: I am clean: from henceforth I will go unto the Gentiles. And he departed thence, and entered into a certain man's house, named Titius Justus, a godfearing proselyte, whose house joined hard to the synagogue; but Crispus, the chief ruler of the synagogue, believed in the Lord with all his house; and many of the people of Corinth used to hear and believe and receive baptism."[1]

As Professor Ramsay says, "It must be acknowledged that Paul had not a very conciliatory way with the Jews when he became angry. The shaking out of his garments was undoubtedly a very exasperating gesture, and the occupying of a meeting-house next door to the synagogue, with the former *archisynagogos* as a prominent officer, was more than human nature could stand."[2]

Paul certainly at Corinth met with considerable success, so that he was induced to remain there eighteen months. In addition to Aquila and Priscilla, there was Erastus, the treasurer, apparently the only man of consequence whom he gained; Crispus, the elder in the synagogue; and Caius, baptized by St. Paul with his own hands, as were Stephanas and his family, he who received Paul into his house on the second visit of the Apostle to Corinth. There were others, probably descendants of the legionaries of Cæsar, Quartus, and Tertius, and freed men, Achaicus and Fortunatus. All the rest belonged to the lowest class,

[1] Acts xviii. 6–8.   [2] Ramsay: "St. Paul," p. 256.

poor and humble, many of them slaves,[1] sick and infirm persons as well,[2] "not many wise men after the flesh, not many mighty, not many noble,"[3] an euphemism for none at all.

Women joined him in numbers, always inclined to cling to and find refuge in a religion of purity. One, Chloe, had a large household, and slaves who were sent with messages to and fro between Corinth and Ephesus;[4] another, Phœbe, had the honour of carrying the Apostle's letter to the Romans hidden in the folds of her *himation*. Mary also, Tryphena and Tryphosa, and Persis "the well-beloved," may have been Corinthian converts who returned to Rome when the edict of Claudius had become a dead letter.[5]

But in his single-minded enthusiasm and readiness to accept any one who professed conviction, Paul seems to have admitted some of the very scum of the city—"fornicators, adulterers, effeminate, those guilty of unnatural crimes, thieves, extortioners, drunkards, revilers,"[6]—to discover afterwards that he had been too precipitate.

Notwithstanding his success, he had failures of heart; perhaps the hostility of the Jews caused him to fear, or he may have doubted whether all this rabble of professing Christians, with their ugly past and hardly abated passions, steeped in dissolute habits, could be got into shape, and would not in the end bring discredit on the cause. "I was with you," he wrote, "in weakness, and in fear, and in much trembling."[7] At one time his discouragement became so great that he thought of leaving the place. "Then spake the Lord to Paul in the night by a vision,

---

[1] 1 Cor. vii. 21 ; xii. 13.   [2] 1 Cor. xi. 30.
[3] 1 Cor. i. 26.   [4] 1 Cor. i. 11.
[5] Rom. xvi. 6, 12.   [6] 1 Cor. vi. 9-11.   [7] 1 Cor. ii. 3.

Be not afraid, but speak, and hold not thy peace; for I am with thee, and no man shall set on thee, to hurt thee: for I have much people in this city."[1]

But it was against the Jews that he turned the flame of his resentment. When Seneca called the Israelite a rascally race, and Tacitus reproached the Jews as the enemies of humanity, these heathens did not express themselves with greater harshness than did Paul against those of his own flesh and country. From Corinth he wrote his First Epistle to the Thessalonians; the second had already been sent, written from Berœa. The First Epistle was composed when his blood was boiling against the Jews of Corinth. "They have killed the Lord Jesus," he wrote, "and their own prophets, and have cast us out [of the synagogue]; and they please not God, and are perverse with all men, forbidding us to speak to the Gentiles that they might be saved, to fill up their sins alway; for the wrath is come upon them to the uttermost."[2] Both epistles breathe the expectation of the immediate coming of Christ.

At length the Jews caused an uproar. The province of Achaia was under a proconsul who resided at Corinth. This was Marcus Annæus Novatus Gallio, brother of Seneca, and uncle of Lucan, the poet. He had been adopted by the rhetorician Junius Gallio, and had assumed his name. He was regarded as one of the most able men of his time, as well versed in literature as in the natural sciences; he was a man of exquisite courtesy of manner, nobility of mind, and he was much beloved in the literary circle to which he and his brother belonged.

As at Thessalonica, so here at Corinth, the Jews, led by Sosthenes, the new ruler of the synagogue, charged Paul

[1] Acts xviii. 9-10. [2] 1 Thess. ii. 14-16.

with high treason, with having spoken of the approaching death of the Emperor, and the coming of Jesus as King. At this time, in Rome, Furius Scribonianus was sentenced to exile for having consulted the magicians as to how much longer Claudius was likely to reign, and the Senate issued an edict ordering all soothsayers to be expelled from Italy. But Gallio must have instituted inquiries and discovered the true character of the opposition against Paul, and when the accusation was heard, the case against him resolved itself into a question of the law, whereupon Gallio contemptuously dismissed it as one out of his department. It was a matter for the Jews to settle among themselves.

No sooner was the court cleared than some Greek roughs fell upon Sosthenes and beat him. They hated the Jews and were glad of an excuse for maltreating one of them. And the excuse was there. The charge of high treason was one peculiarly obnoxious, and a delator was looked upon as a public enemy. Gallio took no notice of this piece of lynch law; probably he was glad that the mob had taken the occasion of expressing its objection to this sort of delation. A charge of high treason dismissed by a magistrate subjected him to the risk of himself being accused of lack of zeal for the Imperial safety and honour.

There is a fine passage in Renan's "Life of St. Paul" relative to the Apostle before the judgment-seat of the Roman procurator that merits not merely quoting, but well considering.

"How often are clever men lacking in foresight! Here, face to face, were two, one certainly foremost among the ablest men of his day, and gifted with a very active intelligence; the other, a man of the strongest and most original character of the time. They passed each other without coming in contact. One of the causes why men of the world commit most of their faults is a superficial dislike inspired in them by under-educated or under-bred individuals. Manners are a mere outside form, and those who do not affect them have sometimes good reason on their side. The man of society, with his frivolous disdain for what is not up to the mark, almost invariably passes by the man who is about to give shape and impress to the future without even seeing him. They are not men of the same world, and the common error of all 'in society' is to think that no other world exists of any account except their own."[1]

St. Paul now resolved to leave Corinth. He had remained there longer than was usual with him, and from Corinth he was in communication with the Macedonian Churches. To the latter some sort of organisation was given; Luke was at Philippi, Timothy had been left for a while at Thessalonica, and Paul could write of "bishops and deacons" in the Macedonian Churches. But he seems to have done nothing to articulate and shape the Corinthian community. He mentions neither presbyters there nor president. He advises "subjection" towards the household of Stephanas and all such as assisted in the work and labour of the Church.

Something must have been done, but not much. There were, indeed, prophets whose prophecies had not as yet been put to the test, those who spake with tongues, making unintelligible noises; some had more or less the word of wisdom, others a certain amount of knowledge, others again made great profession of their faith. But there does not seem as yet to have been any organised life. The Church of Corinth was in a sort of jelly-fish condition, without

[1] "Vie de St. Paul," p. 224.

differentiation of members and distribution of offices. It is the law of God, imposed on life in every manifestation, vital, mental, or spiritual, that there shall be advance from the protoplasmic to the highly articulate. Every living organism passes out of the *larva* condition into that of *pupa*, out of a state without structure into radiate or vertebrate life.

It was the same, it could not fail to be the same, with Christianity. As I have said in the Preface, there are two kinds of organisation, that which is vital, and that which is mechanical; the former derives from God, the latter from man. Man puts together the parts of a machine that he has schemed, and until every wheel and connection is in place, and the force is applied, the whole thing is motionless; moreover, in the machine itself there is no progress, only deterioration through friction and decay.

But with those creatures which God calls into existence it is altogether different. They are none of them put together of already contrived pieces, but are existences having in themselves the faculty of development up to a pre-ordained type. Americans can turn out artificial eggs, but not such as can hatch into birds. In an early condition of life the members are not developed, nor are their functions determined.

We find on the watercress of the brook a transparent lump, like a piece of jelly. It is the amœba. It has no parts; it absorbs food through its pores, but it has no particular stomach, nor any brain. It has no eyes and no feet. It assimilates its food in the lump that thinks in a rudimentary fashion, and moves to suitable positions by means of the gelatinous mass that is at once head, stomach, hand, foot, and mouth.

It was so, though not in so extreme a fashion, with early Christianity. It was, if we may employ the expression, in its grub condition. It is supposed by some that every after-expansion must be a violation of God's will because it did not exist at the outstart. But in the child the teeth are a development, and a natural one. So are intellect and a rational soul; so are the wings of the butterfly; so is the transformation from yelk and albumen into the articulate animate bird; so is the plant from the seed, the planet from the nebulous mass without form.

Where there is life, God's great gift to the world, there must there be growth and articulation. " First the blade, then the ear, after that the full corn in the ear." It is inevitable. For a body to be at a standstill is for it to be deathstruck.

Compare the last Gospel with the first. St. Matthew's is a bare record of the *verba* and *facta* of Christ. St. John's passes over historic facts to plunge into theology. It is cast in a totally different mould. In the first years, when the recollection of the incidents of Our Lord's ministry, death, and resurrection were fresh in the minds of the Apostles, they laid stress on them. It was to these that they were appointed to act as witnesses.

But after a while, when these facts were accepted and became the foundation of belief, then out of them naturally and inevitably sprang up Christian dogma. Men ceased to ask, Did these things take place? and inquired instead, What do these things mean?

We may take an example of growth of ideas from the Messianic expectations of the first believers. They were firmly convinced that Christ would shortly return, so shortly that they doubted the advantage of preaching a general resurrection of the dead, as they expected that all would be alive at the second coming. But when year passed after year, and the sign of the Son of Man did not appear in heaven, then, and only then, did they begin to understand the doctrine of the Resurrection and to see that Christ was the firstfruits of a mighty harvest-field.

So with Church organisation. It was inchoate. After the Ascension, the Apostles met in an upper room, but they attended the daily Temple worship, and this connection with the Temple continued as long as the latter lasted. It could not be other in Jerusalem, and it was only when the Temple was destroyed that God revealed the new direction to be taken.

So also with the ministry. It was in abeyance. The Apostles could not set up a rival priesthood to that of Aaron, and direction was spasmodic and vague through the prophets. In the *Didache*, a work of the first century, we get a glimpse of the primitive Church in Judæa in its initiatory stage, just escaping from its swaddling clothes. In it we see the first budding out of a hierarchy, bishops and deacons appear, but on the same level with prophets and teachers, and their several functions not neatly distinguished.

Appuleius, in his Apology, quotes an unknown poet, who says:

I hate precocious wisdom in young boys.

That is because it is unnatural; mental and physical growth to be wholesome and lovely should keep pace. So in a community divinely given life. It grows like a child, it reasons as a child, it uses its limbs like a child, it will employ its left hand as readily as the right, and its toes as freely as fingers, but none well. As the community becomes strong and manly, it becomes intelligent, and it employs its every part for a particular purpose.

The worship of the early Church in like manner was inchoate. I have already pointed out how that at Antioch the Agape grew out of circumstances, the Christian love-feast was the counterpart then of the synagogue feast of farewell to the Sabbath, at the close of the sabbatical worship. But it had a different meaning at Jerusalem, it was there a commemoration of the Last Supper.

The Agape was carried on till midnight, with hymns and exhortations, the utterance of prophecies; and when midnight was passed and the hymn of midnight sung,[1] then ensued the celebration of the Eucharist. Such was the order at Troas, as appears in the account in Acts.[2]

But it was inevitable that these gatherings, lasting from the *cœna* at 3 P.M. till just before daybreak on the following morning, should give umbrage to the heathen. Pagan husbands very strongly, very naturally, and perhaps rightly, objected to their wives absenting themselves for so long and at night, and returning in the early hours of the ensuing morning, their breath smelling of wine. Even if nothing objectionable took place at these nocturnal, promiscuous gatherings, still they did not bear the appearance of being respectable. No wonder that the heathen thought badly of the assemblies. Nor were they wholly unjustified, for grave scandals did occur.

[1] " It was at midnight that thou didst perform thy most mighty works.
  At the beginning of the midnight watch, this night, didst thou give to thine elect the victory.
  It was at midnight that thou didst speak in dream to the King of Gerar."
And so on with a series of memorials.
[2] Acts xx. 7–11.

This was inevitable. So slight is the film that separates religious fervour from sensual passion, that the former when allowed its freedom roars readily into a blaze of licentiousness.

It is this which makes revivalism of every description so dangerous. The spiritual element in man is most beautiful and pure, like those placid tarns, crystal clear and icy cold, that sleep in the vents of ancient volcanoes. But we never know but that a throb, a shock, may at any moment convert them into boiling geysers or raging craters.

The otherwise inexplicable strictness with which the Church from the third century insisted on fasting Communion can only be understood as due to the shudder and recoil at the orgies which had taken place under the old system at the love feasts.

When Paul left Corinth he left the community of believers there almost wholly unorganised, to develop itself, healthily and naturally, as he trusted, through the indwelling life.

It was unfortunate that it was so, for afterwards he was constrained to write to this Corinthian community and remind it of the fable of the Body and its Members. It was, however, a body only, without limbs, one projection serving indiscriminately for this or that purpose. The condition was, in fact, very little above that of the basest forms of physical existence. "If the whole body were an eye," Paul wrote, "where were the hearing? If the whole were hearing, where were the smelling? .... If they were all one member, where were the the body?"[1]

The attempt has often been made to reduce theology,

[1] 1 Cor. xii. 17.

public worship, church organisation, to primitive pulp. But although out of such vitalised matter order springs in sequential growth, you cannot throw back an already differentiated body into an amorphous condition without detriment to its vitality.

By pulling off the wings of a butterfly, plucking out its antennæ, shearing its legs to stumps, the insect may be reduced to something more or less like the caterpillar out of which it sprang, but at the expense of everything that makes life beautiful and precious.

And so also, under the blow-pipe, it is possible to reduce the diamond to its constituents, destroy its translucency and its iridescent facets; but the result is the attainment of something absolutely worthless.

Reformation is a different process altogether, and not to be mistaken for mutilation, unless ruthlessly carried out. The latter is an excision of organic parts; the former, a removal of supergrowths that impede vital action.

Paul was somewhat disposed to over-estimate the virtues of those who followed him, as he was to disparage and decry those who could not accept his leadership. So confident was he in the vigour of his new foundation, because of the gush and unction of his converts, that he left this strange congeries of questionable characters to shape itself haphazard into a Church. Such confidence was sadly misplaced.

There are in nature such phenomena as arrested developments. In Christianity it is not otherwise. In the Ebionite Church of Palestine, on the one side, and the Marcionite communities of Greece and Asia, on the other, we have two such examples. The first shows us a Judaising Church, stunted in its growth, and with consequent doctrinal aberrations and constitutional malformation. In the Marcionite sects we have, on the other hand, Churches very much like that at Corinth when the presence of the Apostle was withdrawn. Marcion was himself a moral man, but some of the sects professing the same belief were grossly licentious.

In his entire conviction that the seed of the Word of God had in it the germ of life, Paul sowed it in Corinth, and trusted it to spring up a beautiful and fruit-bearing plant. But he forgot one important truth, that a germ of life will only act healthfully upon wholesome material. On that which is not so it serves as a ferment, and a process of cleansing is gone through, which brings the scum to the top and develops noxious and unsavoury gases.

Later on we shall see more of this. At present no signs of mischief appeared. The accumulation of street-sweepings was too newly raked together to manifest its nature in the short period during which Paul was at Corinth— eighteen months from first to last.

No missionary nowadays would admit a convert to full Christian privileges till he had his sincerity tested. Paul does not seem to have allowed of gradations in goodness, and when these worn-out sensualists accepted the Gospel, being in quest of a new sensation, or under the depression caused by temporary disgust at their past, he took them into the Church, just as they were, and, more astonishing still, left them to themselves. His overflowing charity and single-minded faith were destined to bitter disillusionment.

CHAPTER XIV

THE LAW AND THE GOSPEL

A.D. 55—58

Paul resolves to visit Jerusalem—The vow of the Nazarite—Goes to Ephesus—Arrival in Jerusalem—Coolly received—Reason of this—Reports of disorders provoked by him—The Apostles desire peace—Their method successful—The question of circumcision again arises—The difficulties of the converts—The disciplinary difficulty—The difficulty of principle—How Paul endeavoured to meet these—How he might have answered objections but did not—He establishes a distinction between the Promise and the Law—The Roman process of adoption—He argues that the Law was given to convince the Jew of sin—This argument opposed by fact—How the Gnostics laid hold on this doctrine—Inspiration does not affect arguments—The world not turned or led by argument.

PAUL now deemed it advisable to visit Jerusalem again. He took on him the vow of a Nazarite: for what reason we are not told.

Perhaps he had learned that his conduct had been misrepresented to the Apostles, and he may have been aware that a feeling of estrangement and misunderstanding might grow acute unless he made a personal explanation. Then, to furnish himself with an excuse and to cut off occasion for his friends to attempt to dissuade him, he adopted this method, which made his departure irrevocable.

By the vow he was obliged to abstain from wine during thirty days, and then to shave his head. The Nazir who had not arrived in Jerusalem before the expiration of the month kept his hair that had been cut off till he reached the Holy City. When there, after seven days spent in purification, he had his head shaved again, and threw both crops of hair into the flames of the sacrifice.

The month of the Nazarite came to an end at the moment when Paul was ready to sail. He bade farewell to the brethren at Corinth, and submitted his head to a barber at Cenchræa.[1]

That his proceeding in the matter of the vow is inconsistent with the strong line adopted by him towards the Law and the traditions of the Rabbis can hardly be disputed.

But he acted to allay suspicion roused against him. Aquila and Priscilla accompanied him as far as Ephesus. Their business had not prospered in Corinth. Ephesus, long famous as a place of manufacture of tents and goats'-hair fabrics, seemed more likely to afford them occupation; and the departure of the Apostle from Corinth determined them to leave along with him.

At Ephesus Paul separated from these attached companions, but the vessel tarried sufficiently long in the port for him to visit the synagogue and say a few words there.

Thence he sailed for Cæsarea, where he disembarked, and whence he pursued his way to Jerusalem.

It is not difficult to see from the reserve with which Luke deals with this visit, not even mentioning the name of Jerusalem, that his hero was not received there with effusive cordiality. At the same time we may be mistaken if we attribute this to a divergence of views as to doctrine between him and Peter, James, and the rest.

At this point almost all writers of the Life of St. Paul pause to administer a lecture to the Apostles for their

[1] Acts xviii. 18.

THE LAW AND THE GOSPEL 259

narrowness and shortsightedness in not recognising the incomparable superiority of Paul, and in not submitting themselves unreservedly to his dictation.

Here is the way in which that mouther of common opinion, Dean Farrar, scolds: " Had James, and the circle of which he was the centre, only understood how vast for the future of Christianity would be the issues of his perilous and toilsome journeys, had they but seen how insignificant, compared with the labours of St. Paul, would be the part which they themselves were playing in furthering the universality of the Church of Christ, with what affection and admiration would they have welcomed him!"

This is begging the whole question. How can we say that the work of the Apostles at Jerusalem was not as great, if not indeed greater, in its result than that of Paul? They sat at the centre, forming as it were a powerful battery sending out shock after shock to the limits of the civilised world. But their method was not so striking in story as the comet-like whirls of Paul. They strewed the seed over every tidal wave that rolled to Jerusalem at every feast, and then retreated to the ends of the earth, whereas he darted about dropping grains here and there. He has had his story told by an admirer whom he furnished with biographical details; not so they. But in the realm of grace it is not always such as are most advertised who have achieved the greatest things for God, but the silent and hidden workers whose labours have been unrecorded.

We can understand the coolness with which Paul was received without supposing that this was due to difference of doctrine.

The incessant influx of Jews and proselytes from all quarters, rising to a veritable spring-tide at the Passover, brought them acquainted with Paul's mode of initiating his missions in the several towns he visited. This would be represented to them in adverse colours heightened by resentment. The Jews from Galatia and Macedonia would complain that his process was little better than that of conveying into his own basket all the fish other men had caught. They would also, with great truth, affirm that the result of his proceedings was to produce a riot and to stir up angry feelings. The Apostles remembered that they had had experience of this sort of thing with Stephen; and they were almost certain to call for an explanation from Paul.

I do not see that we need assume a doctrinal difference, of which there is so little trace in the Acts and the Epistles.

Inevitably his conduct with its results would reach their ears, and as inevitably would they entertain doubts as to whether he was justified in adopting and pursuing his method. Having still at heart the design of making of the Jewish nation, with its ramifications throughout the world, the missionary power whereby the nations were to be brought to Christ, at least of giving to it the opportunity of becoming so, the Apostles may have thought that Paul was unnecessarily interfering with and running counter to their design.

There is a chapter in Renan's "Life of St. Paul" headed "Propagation sourde du Christianisme," and others beside him have been led to remark on the singular and apparently inexplicable manner in which Christianity radiated everywhere without any Paul or Barnabas rushing about founding churches. But this was entirely due to the plan adopted by the Apostles from the first. It was extra-

THE LAW AND THE GOSPEL

ordinarily successful, and so long as it succeeded they considered themselves justified in pursuing it. But some of the Twelve had already departed to plant centres elsewhere, and those still in Jerusalem could not object to a method of diffusion of the Truth that was obviously of advantage. They desired, as sincerely as did Paul, that the nations should be brought within the one fold, but they saw in the peculiar position of the Jewish race, in its dispersion and in the influence it everywhere gained over the minds of the well disposed—in this they saw a providential means of enlightening the entire world, and they were extremely reluctant to make of the Jews enemies to the Gospel instead of evangelists.

I think, therefore, that the coolness felt towards Paul is explicable without having recourse to the theory of doctrinal antagonism proposed by Baur. The Tübingen school have assumed that a split occurred between Peter and James on one side and Paul on the other, and that this is thinly veiled in the Epistles and disguised in the Acts. This latter work they pretend was written with intent to falsify facts, so as to represent the Apostolic Church as harmonious, whereas it was torn by furious faction.

Without such a violent assumption, we can understand that there should exist a slight uneasiness relative to Paul's conduct in starting a mission, of which uneasiness indeed traces remain; as also that there might be impatience on his part relative to the long-suffering exhibited by the elder Apostles towards the Jews.

There were questions rising to the surface that provoked differences of opinion and of conduct in facing them, but none calculated to produce lasting estrangement.

The new wine in the old bottles was working, and was rending the sides and oozing forth. The Gospel and the Law could not unite without chemical action and the development of a corresponding heat, but when the combination was effected the heat would subside.

The first manifestation of heat was over the question of circumcision. Was it obligatory as a preliminary to baptism, or was it not? This the Apostles had decided by virtue of their authority to bind and loose. But, inevitably, the question started up again in connection with the Agape. Were the uncircumcised to be admitted to the Lord's table?

There can be no dispute as to the fact of there having been a Judaising party in the Church. But that which I venture to dispute is that James and Peter were moving springs in it.

They may have foreseen, they probably did foresee, that at some future time a rupture would ensue between Church and Synagogue, but the privilege offered to Jewdom was so great, and the advantage to the Church of a national conversion so incalculable, that they were unwilling to precipitate it. They were disposed in small matters to concede to Jewish prejudice; but it was precisely as to what were small matters and which were matters of principle that difference of opinion might arise.

It is admitted by the Tübingen school that there is no evidence of real antagonism of opinion to be traced in the Epistles of James and Peter, and therefore these letters are scornfully rejected as fabrications composed to give a false appearance of unity where discord actually prevailed.

The question could not fail to be ventilated in every Church composed of Jew and Gentile converts, to what extent the Law was repealed; whether, indeed, it was at all repealed.

It was a question that would start up in every mind and trouble every conscience.

So prepossessed are we against the Judaisers, so easy do we feel under the solution of the problem arrived at eventually, that we have come to regard the Judaic faction as impracticable and bigoted, and to suppose that what is obvious now to every National School child was as clear to the early believers.

In the Middle Ages there was a controversy that caused infinite trouble, excited furious partisanship, and which lasted for over half a century. It concerned investiture. The Emperor claimed the right to invest a prelate with his office by the giving of staff and ring, and the Pope resisted this as a sacrilegious encroachment by the temporal power. All at once, after fifty years of conflict and the shedding of much blood, it suddenly occurred to each party that there was right on both sides. All the Sovereign demanded was the power to confer temporal jurisdiction over the See, and he made no claim whatever to the giving of spiritual authority. A reconciliation followed at once. The entire struggle had been due to misconception.

So now the strife about the position of the Law was one due to misconception. Directly this was perceived the waves sank.

The difficulty in the mind of the Judaisers was very real and very justifiable. They asked but one thing—to be given a convincing reason why they should neglect certain commands that had been imposed by God.

Paul was of an excitable nature, irritable under opposition, and incapacitated by his rabbinic education for thinking clearly, so that he was unable to furnish the reason which would at once have set men's minds at ease and cooled down all the heat.

He no more saw the strength and sincerity of the opposition, and that it was based on a real right, than did Gregory VII. when he launched excommunication against Henry IV.

The line that Paul might have taken seems to us so obvious that we are surprised it never occurred to him. We will come to that later.

Let us now see what the difficulties were that perplexed the converts.

I. *The Disciplinary Difficulty*.

This has been already touched on. But in order that the reader may be able to understand that the objections raised by the Judaisers were not captious, and that they really sprang out of conscientious scruples, it is as well to recapitulate shortly what has been said before.

The Jew believer was put in a dilemma by his association at the Agape and Eucharist with the Gentile convert. If he ate with him then he became ceremonially unclean, and must undergo purification that was irksome to himself and implied a slight on the Christianity of the Gentile brother. It did more than that. It introduced an element of discord; in practice it denied the unity of the members of the one body.

There were two ways of getting over the difficulty. One was boldly to proclaim the abolition of circumcision, and forbid the Jewish converts from purifying themselves after communion with their uncircumcised brethren. The other was to make the acceptance of circumcision a qualification for communion.

Paul would have undoubtedly declared for the first alternative. But there were others who would answer: You may be right in principle, but is not this a case in which charity recommends a compromise?

Practically, the whole thing resolved itself into this shape. Was the Church to be made up of communicants only, or might it consist of communicants and an outer body of baptized believers?

We, at the present day, have no hesitation in saying that the latter is preferable to the Elizabethan summary system of enforcing communion on every English adult under pain of imprisonment and confiscation of goods.

As the Apostles at Jerusalem, perhaps acting by divine guidance, did all in their power to maintain amicable relations with the Pharisees, was it not advisable, for a time at all events, to reserve to the circumcised the right to sit down at the Agape? Let the others, the baptized, occupy the same position in the Church as did the " righteous men " in the Synagogue. The acceptance of circumcision needed not to be enforced as a matter of principle as, in itself, conveying grace, but as a charitable concession. By submitting thereto such neophytes as were sincere would give the best possible evidence of their being in love and tenderness of heart to others, and would deserve the blessing specially pronounced on the peacemakers.

They would further have the satisfaction of knowing that they were acting in accord with the feelings of the Apostles in Jerusalem who desired to prevent broils and to stave off a schism.

I do not pretend that we have this argument textually produced, but I do think that such a line is one which must have been adopted. It is one which the party would be forced to employ. But the disciplinary difficulty overlay another of more serious nature. It was but the foam cresting the wave and not the wave itself.

At bottom lay a principle, and this it was which gave real gravity to the opposition.

II.—*The difficulty relative to principle.*

The much abused and misunderstood Judaising faction argued as follows:

1. God gave the law in a peculiarly solemn and manifest manner, on Mount Sinai in the sight of all the people.
2. He then said nothing to imply that its nature was provisional, and that it was to be, in time, repealed.
3. God in His nature is eternal and immutable. What He promises He fulfils. What He reveals partakes of His eternity and immutability.

A. *Therefore:* There is a *primâ facie* improbability that the Law should be abrogated.

Again:

1. Christ, when on earth, did not abolish the Law. On the contrary, He emphatically declared that He had come to fulfil, that is to obey, it, and *not* to destroy it. He had declared that not a jot or tittle of the Law was to pass away.
2. Christ, the Way, the Truth, and the Life, who is set before man as an example whom they should follow, observed the Law when He lived on earth. He was circumcised on the eighth day. He attended in the synagogues. He worshipped in the Temple. He observed the feasts.
3. Moses ascended into the Mount, and received the

Law, and came down with radiant face. Christ went up into the Mount and was transfigured. But He brought down no new law. He was transfigured between Moses and Elias, in token of ratification of the Law and sanction of the prophets.

B. *Therefore*, we conclude from the Lord's acts and words that He did not abrogate the Law.

But again, it may be urged, that although He did not do so, yet He purposed that it should be swept aside, and that this was to be done by His Apostles to whom He committed "all power in heaven and in earth," when He breathed on them, and conferred commission and authority.

But :—

1. The Spirit conferred on the Church has not pronounced openly and solemnly and unmistakably that the Law is repealed.
2. The Spirit speaks through the prophets, an order ordained to serve as channels of communication and direction. They have been mute.
3. The Apostles were specially instituted by Christ, received the plenitude of His power, and in the Great Forty Days between His resurrection and ascension were fully instructed by Him in all things concerning His kingdom, the Church. They also have remained silent.

C. *Therefore*, we conclude from the silence of the Spirit and of the authorised expounders of Christ's will that the Law was not to be abrogated by the Church.

From this, later, the opponents of St. Paul went on to disputing his apostolic character. But this personal opposition we will consider in another chapter.

What we have put into incisive form was a question that arose independent of him—that sprang up in Rome, where he had not set foot, as well as in Antioch and Galatia, where he had made his influence felt. It was a question that flashed out wherever the Law and Gospel met, as when steel and flint are struck together.

How the Apostles at Jerusalem answered the questions put to them we do not know. But such questions arose inevitably, and arose out of the consciences of sincere men. Indeed their sincerity would have been very doubtful, or their intelligences altogether stunted, unless they had asked them.

Now let us see what should have been Paul's response.

He might have dissipated the trouble agitating the Churches and racking men's consciences, in a very few words.

He might have said this: The Moral Law is of universal application.

God has given to all animals instinct whereby they fulfil the law of their destiny.

But man has not such a clear and controlling instinct; consequently he must have been given an exterior law at the time when he was created.

Such is the Law which was reimposed on Sinai. It was no new law, it was old as man.

Man as a creature, and a rational creature, has duties that he owes to his Maker. Him he must reverence, worship, and obey. The fact of his existence, and of his having an intelligence whereby he knows that he owes his existence to God, necessitates a first Table of Commandments, relative to his duties to God.

But man is also a social being, and his happiness and

progress in civilisation necessitate a second Table of Commandments, regulating his duties to his fellow men.

Admit that man is an intelligent creature of God, and made to live in community with his brethren, then the imposition of a law ruling his relations to his Creator and to his fellows becomes a logical necessity.

It was through forgetfulness of this law that idolatry and its associated evils arose on one side, and violence and licentiousness on the other.

But the law of rites and ceremonies stands on another footing altogether. It is not of universal obligation, for it is not required by any necessity of man's nature.

It was given to one nation only, and that for special reasons, (a) to preserve it as a guardian and witness in the world to the truth; and (β) as leading up to and finding its interpretation in Christ.

So soon as He came to dispense the knowledge of the truth to all the world, then the function of the Jewish nation was at an end. And so soon as the ceremonial law had led up to that which it foreshadowed, its office was also at an end.[1] It had accomplished its purpose and expires.

To understand the perplexities of men's minds at the time of the promulgation of the Gospel, we must put ourselves back mentally into that period. So only do they present themselves to us, but it is far easier to see the cause of these distresses and questionings than it is, with our experience, to understand the difficulty in reaching often very simple solutions.

It is instructive to see how Paul, confronted with these problems, strove to find his way out of them.

[1] This Paul did see. Col. ii. 17.

Instinctively Paul perceived that the ceremonial law, the law of purification and of initiation into covenant, was an anachronism, that it never was designed to be of universal application, and that to insist on or recommend it to the neophytes from among the Gentiles would wreck the Church as she left port. But how to disengage this ceremonial law from the moral law, how to disallow the first and establish the second he did not know. He beat about for arguments, and caught at the most inconclusive, because he failed to perceive the very simple and elementary reason for distinguishing them that lay under his eyes.

But is it not so in all men's perplexities, not religious only, but social and political as well, that to escape from the labyrinth, he lays hold of every thread but the clue of Ariadne; that in trying to make his way out of the wood of errors, he takes every path except that which conducts directly into the clear?

Let us now see how Paul endeavoured to meet the difficulty that arose as to the overlapping or mutually destructive elements of Law and Gospel.

1. He attempted to establish a distinction between the Promise and the Law.

The Promise was made to Abraham, whilst he was in uncircumcision. The Law was given later to his descendants by natural blood relationship. Now there are two modes of filiation: there is the descent by generation from father to son, and there is a spiritual filiation.

He referred to the custom of adoption so common in Roman society. A man took another into his family, and by making him a partaker of the family cult, the worship of the ancestral *Lares*, he became legally and to every intent a son. The person to be adopted was emancipated by his natural father, who surrendered all natural rights over him, and the adoption created the legal relation of father and son, just as if the adopted son were born of the blood of the adopted father in lawful marriage. The adopted child assumed the name of his adoptive father. For instance, P. Cornelius Scipio Æmilianus was the son of L. Æmilius Paullus, but he was adopted by P. Cornelius Scipio, whose name he accordingly assumed, retaining only a trace of his natural descent in the Æmilianus. The real bond in the Roman family was participation in the ancestral worship of the household gods. Naturally a son united in this, but another man taken into the family and associated in this cult became a son as truly as the other.

This is the idea that was in Paul's mind when he worked out his scheme of spiritual descent from Abraham. The Jew was Abraham's child by nature, the believer his child by partaking in the ancestral cult, that is to say, by the *nexus* of faith.

Now as the Promise of Christ was given to Abraham in uncircumcision, his cult became that of Christ and the means—faith. All those, out of every nation, who partake in the same cult, by the same means, faith, become the sons of Abraham, by adoption indeed, but adoption is as real a relationship as that of blood.

The argument, if only Paul had drawn it out more clearly, would have been very telling at the time. To us, who do not understand the Roman principle of family worship constituting a spiritual but very real and legal tie, the argument is unintelligible and pointless.

Moreover, Paul tangled up his argument with rabbinic subtleties relative to re-marriage after the death of the first husband[1] and to mystic ideas concerning Agar and Sarah, Mount Sinai and Jerusalem,[2] which could weigh only with rabbinic scholars.

By this line of argument he laboured to show that as the Law was imposed on the natural descendants of Abraham at a later period, it could not bind the spiritual descendants.

The argument laboured under two disadvantages.

> 1. It presupposed that the Roman law of adoption, and relationship through observance of the family cult of the *Lar pater*, applied to Abraham and to all mankind. In a word, it elevated this Roman law into one of divine institution.
>
> 2. The only moral law under which Abraham lived was that of Nature; at least, we know of no other. Consequently his children by adoption, by spiritual generation, have no other moral obligation than instinctive, natural law. For instance, any son of Abraham by faith might live in polygamy, like his father, the patriarch.

The second was a moral objection. The first vitiated the entire argument till Paul had succeeded in establishing the divine institution of adoption.

II.—A second method introduced a dangerous principle. Paul urged that the Law was ordained by God to bring man to a consciousness of sin. At first he had upheld that the Law was given as a barrier to prevent the Jew from falling into such corruption of life as existed among the heathen. But he threw away this explanation of the function of the Law and declared that it was an ordinance given by God, not to retain man from sin, but to convince

[1] Rom. vii. 4–6. [2] Gal. iv. 22–26.

him that he was sinful, and powerless to avoid sin. Regulations were multiplied to increase transgression, and torture man with a sense of his impotence. The Law, he said, is holy, just and good,[1] but it is powerless to do good. It has but one object, the multiplication of sin.[2] It holds man fast, like a jailer, in the bondage of sin. The Law shows man what God's righteousness is, but does not help him to attain it. It is like a flash of lightning flaring in his eyes, not to show him the way, but to convince him that he is lost. Its function is to carry sin to its highest maturity. In this sense it is " the power of sin."[3]

Till the Law came there was no consciousness of sin, and where no consciousness is, there no sin exists.

Unhappily for this theory, it was completely falsified by facts.

According to Paul, the Gentile having no Law, must be unwrung by a sense of transgression, whereas the Jew set in a thicket of prickles must be wincing and crying out in agony for escape. But practically just the opposite was the case. The Jew, to whom the Law had been given to cultivate in him an acute sense of sin, was lapped in self-satisfaction, and had no feeling of transgression, no desire for a Saviour.

On the other hand, the Gentile, outside the Law, who, according to Paul's theory ought to be incapable of the sense of contrition, cried out in agony of mind for redemption.

The Law had acted precisely, according to Paul, as it was not predestined to act. It had hardened the Jew; and where there was no Law there men were ripe for the Gospel.

[1] Rom. vii. 12.   [2] Rom. v. 20; vii. 7-11; Gal. iii. 19.
[3] 1 Cor. xv. 56.

But there was something so repulsive in his view of God creating a law for the sake of torturing man, that one cannot be surprised that it led to consequences he had never anticipated.

Be it so, said the later Gnostics. The Law is sin. It produced sin in the world, where, without the Law, there would have been no sin,[1] as sin has no positive existence, but is found only where there is consciousness of transgression. Does not this imply, said these Gnostics, that God is the author of sin? Consequently the Giver of the Law is a malignant deity. And then because they held that the Creator of the world was evil, since matter is evil, they added that it was He, the God of the World, the Demiurge, who was also the Giver of the Law, and that He was in constant antagonism with the supreme and good God, the Father of spirits.

Paul did not originate Gnosticism. It existed as a philosophic and theologic system before he was born, but when this Magian religion took into it Judaic and Christian elements, its teachers laid hold of the handle thus incautiously offered them by Paul.

What he meant is obvious enough, that the Law was given so as to ripen in the minds of the Jews that sense of need, that broken and contrite heart without which man would not value the message of salvation. If that were its sole purpose, it had failed, and the failure was due to man's perversity.

"When we consider," says Baur, "the position which the Apostle assigns to the Law, and the terms he uses to describe its distinctive character, we see that the law is here degraded from its absolute value, and reduced to the

[1] Rom. iii. 20; vii. 7–9.

rank in a subordinate stage. Thus we can easily understand how Gnostics of the most pronounced Antinomianism appealed to our Apostle's authority."[1]

We hold that Paul was divinely inspired for the work he undertook, and that his writings were also inspired. But inspiration does not affect arguments, nor transform a man's intellectual capacities. What the Apostle received from God, that he communicated; and in his communications was directed aright. But when he attempted to establish doctrines by reasonings, there he went astray. He left the platform of inspiration to use those natural faculties he possessed, and those deformed by rabbinic education. Had he been put through a course of Euclid as a boy he would have argued in a very different manner, and not so as to be unintelligible or inconclusive.

Inspiration did not prevent him from bungling in the matter of grafting of an olive-tree, and from producing a bad argument through want of observing a very simple process in arboriculture. I do not see why we are to assume that his arguments elsewhere are any better. Besides, in argument a man steps on to ground that can be disputed by any other who has a mind wherewith to reason. The appeal is to reason, and reason answers the challenge. Inspiration is revelation of facts or guidance in the promulgation of doctrine, or direction in the governance of Christ's kingdom. Paul was inspired doctrinally and was perfectly right in his struggle with the Judaisers, divinely urged to resist every attempt to restrict the Church, but the Spirit did not furnish him with reasons.

The cause which he advocated has been victorious, but not through his arguments. The Apostle himself, with his

[1] "Life and Work of St. Paul," ii. 203.

burning zeal, his inflexible resolution, his transparent sincerity, his intense sympathy, and his overmastering conviction in his mission, was better than all his reasons.

How often do we find that it is not the man with broad ideas and tolerant mind who becomes the leader of men, and who makes his mark in history. Those who have achieved the greatest things have been men whose ideas have been reduced to one, and that one has been filed to a point, who, having a door before them, beat at it, and never desist, though it be planked with oak and studded with iron, till with bleeding hands and broken knees, they have beaten it down.

How often do we see that it is not the sound argument that convinces the world, and turns it about in its course, but the invincible cogency of the truth propounded. Men do not weigh the argument that recommends it, or weigh it and find it wanting, yet accept the truth itself because it appeals to their inner sense, to a sort of divine faculty of discrimination between right and wrong, truth and falsehood, and because they see in the sway of the world and the bending of opinion the hand of God requiring its acceptance, and approving its truth.

CHAPTER XV

THE GOSPEL AND THE NATURAL LAW

The change in opinion taking place in the legal mind in Rome—The Civil Law and the Natural Law—How the *Jus Gentium* came into existence—The edict of the Prætor—Paul must have known of the two codes—The advantages of the Natural Law—Paul seeks to make of the Gospel the *Jus Gentium* of the Church—The Gospel not then written—The appeal to the spirit not the letter—The Gospel is the Natural Law restated—The simultaneous appearance of Christianity and of the revolution in judicial estimate of the Law of Nations—How Rome was saved from petrifaction—The origin of Equity in England—The revolution in Roman jurisprudence assisted the spread of the Gospel—And the Gospel supplied the *Jus Gentium* with a sure basis.

THERE is yet another point, in connection with the Law and the Gospel, and St. Paul's attitude towards them, that deserves consideration.

Having spent so many years in Asia Minor, Syria, Macedonia, and Greece, and having moreover been more than once before the courts, he must have been fully aware that in Roman jurisprudence there were two codes, the *Jus Civile*, based on the Twelve Tables, explained and applied by the *Responsa Prudentium* or answers of the learned, which code applied only to Roman citizens, and also the *Jus Gentium*, a code based on what was presumed to be natural law, and which answers to our equity, which code was of general application to all aliens out of every race who came to live under Roman domination.

It was presumed that at the basis of all law lay first principles of justice, common to all mankind, and finding expression in the laws of all nations. At first, indeed, this *Jus Gentium* was a mere makeshift, looked upon contemptuously by the Roman citizen, but in process of time it ceased to be so regarded, and assumed a very much higher position, as an imperfectly developed model to which all law ought, as far as possible, to conform. It came to be regarded by the Roman lawyers as the lost primordial code of Nature imposed by the Creator on man, and, annually, the Prætor Peregrinus on entering office issued his edict, which superseded as much as possible the Civil Law, by affirming the institutions of the great natural law of equity; a law of universal application, and of superior grandeur to the once so esteemed *Jus Civile*; for the latter was based on engraved plates, by whom engraved none knew, whereas the law of equity was inscribed by the finger of God on the consciences of all mankind.

This *Jus Gentium* was annually recited and reimposed with amplifications to suit fresh circumstances by edict of the Prætor Peregrinus, and it did not pretend to be other than a summary of natural law so far as could be gathered out of the consent of mankind and those principles of justice which lie in every heart.

It was not till the reign of Hadrian that the Prætor's proclamation was stopped. It had been enlarged every year, and it obtained the name of the Perpetual Edict, that is, of the unbroken or continuous law. Its texture was unsystematic, and it was felt at last that it would be well to give it a final and logical shape.

It seems to me that St. Paul was conscious of the complete revolution in opinion which was in process in the

THE GOSPEL AND THE NATURAL LAW 279

Roman world relative to the respective values of the *Jus Civile* and the *Jus Gentium*, and that he saw striking analogies between the former and the Mosaic code, and between the latter and the Gospel.

The civil law rested on the engraved Twelve Tables, so did the Mosaic Law on the code promulgated by God from Sinai. There was an authoritative text in both cases. But the text in neither instance answered new conditions of life, consequently it had to be expanded, twisted and turned about so as to fit new requirements. This was done in Rome by the " Answers of the Learned " diligently collected and formed into books ; and among the Jews by the Mishna and Gemara of the Rabbis.

The *Jus Gentium* was designed at first to apply merely to aliens to the commonwealth of Rome, the highly valued *Jus Civile* being applicable to the citizens alone.

Now, owing to various anomalies, the Roman citizens were seeking relief from the civil code by applying to have their cases tried by the natural law of equity.

Paul saw that the Jew was under the trammels of his old code, and was endeavouring to force the alien to pass under it, and become equally subject to its intolerable provisions. In their narrowness the Jews were in fact going against the stream of opinion in the civilised world without.

He was desirous, accordingly, of making of the Gospel a counterpart to the *Jus Gentium* of the Roman State.

Christ had reasserted the primeval principles of right; the Gospel was a prætorian edict of perpetual and universal obligation, and Paul and the rest of the Apostles were its interpreters.

The Gospel was not the promulgation of a new code,

"A new commandment give I unto you," said Christ, "that ye love one another,"[1] yet this was not actually, only relatively, new; it derived from the first institution of man, of one blood, and was new only because forgotten by the Jews. When the Pharisees came to Christ asking, "Is it lawful for a man to put away his wife for every cause?" He replied by a return to first principles: "Have ye not read, that He which made them at the beginning, made them male and female, and said, 'For this cause shall a man leave father and mother, and shall cleave to his wife; and they twain shall be one flesh?' What, therefore, God hath joined together, let not man put asunder. They say unto him, 'Why did Moses then command to give a writing of divorcement, and to put her away?' He saith unto them, 'Moses, because of the hardness of your hearts, suffered you to put away your wives; but from the beginning it was not so.'"[2]

Here we have a distinct assertion of the natural law as the basis of conduct, superior to the text. The revelation of Jesus Christ is the clearing away of all the obscurities that had darkened and confused the first revelation. He it was who, having made man, gave him life, "and the life was the light of men. The light shineth in darkness; and the darkness comprehended it not."[3]

Men's hearts were clouded and they no longer saw the truth. He came to give to them the power to understand and embrace it, but the truth, the light, was the law of man's nature, first imposed on him when he was created.

This must be understood, that the Gospel was the reassertion of the fundamental laws necessary for man's well-being and progress, laws that had been forgotten and almost

---

[1] John xiii. 12.   [2] Matt. xix. 3–8.   [3] John i. 4, 5.

THE GOSPEL AND THE NATURAL LAW 281

wholly lost, but laws after which the Roman jurists were groping.

There was as yet no written code. The Gospel had not been committed to paper; but the Twelve knew what Christ had actually spoken, and Paul himself, by revelation, knew what the will of God was, and from the beginning had been, relative to man's conduct.

Thus Paul set the proselytes in the Church beside the Judæo-Christians, as subject only to the *Jus Gentium* of the Gospel, and in no way under the *Jus Civile* of Moses, and he afforded to the Jews an escape from the Mosaic Law by placing themselves under the natural law as reaffirmed by Christ.

He could not appeal to a written code, the Gospel being at the time traditional only, so he fell back like the Roman jurisconsults on the natural law "written not with ink, but with the Spirit of the living God; not in tables of stone, but in fleshy tables of the heart."[1] This latter code is contrasted with the former as being the more glorious,[2] it is a spiritual code and not textual, is based on broad natural principles reasserted by Christ.

The same idea pervades a passage in the second chapter of the Epistle to the Romans.

A certain number of commentators express surprise at the amount of elementary moral instruction given in the Epistles of Saints Paul, James, Peter, John, and Jude, as unnecessary and puerile; but they fail to grasp the new position. There was no moral code extant, the Gospel of the sayings of Christ had not been committed to writing, therefore they were obliged to write their sentences on all kinds of moral matters, to be the "Responsa Prudentium"

---

[1] 2 Cor. iii. 3.   [2] *Ibid.* 6–8.

of the Christian Church, useful indeed after the Gospel had been written by the evangelists and was in circulation, but indispensable before that. In fact, before the Gospel appeared every apostolic letter was a prætorian edict, but after that it furnished a *mishna* or sentence of the wise in comment on the text.

I do not think that hitherto sufficient weight has been laid on the simultaneous appearance of Christianity with the revolution in opinion as to the basis of law, if, indeed, the two have been at all considered in relation to one another. To understand this, I must be allowed to make a somewhat lengthy quotation from Sir Henry Maine's "Ancient Law."

"A barbarous society, practising a body of customs, is exposed to some especial dangers which may be absolutely fatal to its progress in civilisation. The usages which a particular community is found to have adopted in its infancy and in its primitive seats, are generally those which are on the whole best suited to promote its physical and moral well-being; and, if they are retained in their integrity until new social wants have taught new practices, the upward march of society is almost certain. But unhappily there is a law of development which ever threatens to operate upon unwritten usage. The customs are of course obeyed by multitudes who are incapable of understanding the true ground of their expediency, and who are therefore left inevitably to invent superstitious reasons for their permanence. A process then commences which may be shortly described by saying that usage which is reasonable generates usage which is unreasonable. Prohibitions and ordinances, originally confined, for good reasons, to a single description of acts, are made to apply to all acts of the same class, because a man menaced with the anger of the gods for doing one thing, feels a natural terror in doing any other thing which is remotely like it. After one kind of food has been interdicted for sanitary reasons, the prohibition is extended to all food resembling it; though the resemblance occasionally depends on analogies the most fanciful. So again, a wise provision for ensuring general cleanliness dictates in time long routines of ceremonial ablution; and that division into classes which at a particular crisis of social history is necessary for the maintenance of the national existence degenerates into the most disastrous and blighting of all human institutions—caste. Ethnology shows us that the Romans and the Hindoos sprang from the same original stock, and there is indeed a striking resemblance between what appear to have been their original customs. Even now, Hindoo jurisprudence has a substratum of forethought and sound judgment; but irrational imitation has engrafted in it an immense apparatus of cruel absurdities."[1]

A code of laws, especially when claiming divine sanction, may become the most paralysing of all strait-waistcoats. So also may stereotyped traditional usage. And most of the nations and races of the world are so arrested in their intellectual, social, and political development.

So would the Romans have been stunted, even as the Hindoo or the Chinese, had they adhered to the Twelve Tables, erected them into a code beyond which it was impossible to advance, to which it was necessary to recur for every prohibition and authorisation.

Happily they were preserved from this fate, almost by accident. For various reasons strangers came to Rome,

[1] Maine: "Ancient Law," 1885, p. 19.

from many parts, and increased to such numbers that they might have forced the Romans to admit them to citizenship, unless the Romans themselves had formed courts in which to settle their quarrels, and try their criminals. Thus arose the *Jus Gentium*, looked upon at first with supreme contempt. Gradually, however, it attracted more and even more attention as the principle of equity on which the law was based that governed the decisions of the magistrate in these courts became better understood, and the Stoics had drawn attention to natural simplicity as the source of all virtue. Little by little, but very surely, the excellence of a natural code over one purely artificial came to be recognised, and the jurisconsults came to conceive of it as a primordial law imposed on all men, to which all codes ought to be accommodated, and of which the textual codes were more or less perverse distortions. They did not regard this natural law as abrogating civil laws, but as correcting their deficiencies. The conception was very valuable, as it held up before the mental vision an ideal type of law as the rule of absolute equity, and it inspired the hope of indefinite approximation to it; and as this conception grew in strength so did respect for texts decline. It was the appeal of intelligent man to the spirit away from the letter; the Roman jurisconsult was as fully aware as was Paul that the letter might kill whereas the spirit would give life.

The Jew, as Paul saw clearly enough, was bound hand and foot to the text of his Law. If Christianity was to be thus trammelled, it never could become a religion for the world, nor one of progress. This, indeed, he did not see, but he felt it, by a sort of feminine instinct, and what he felt, that he was convinced was right, and he did everything in his power to obtain the emancipation of the believer from the text.

We shall, perhaps, understand the situation best by comparison with the condition as it was in England, and the manner whereby it was found necessary to escape from "the letter that killeth." In England strict law was found by experience, in a good number of instances, to sanction intolerable injustice. Accordingly an appeal was made for relief from the courts to the King's conscience. He handed over the custody of his conscience to the Chancellor, and thus arose the system of Equity, devised to correct the abuses of justice caused by strict law.

In the United States the Constitution is practically unalterable. It was drawn up in a condition of life quite unlike that which now exists; and the work of a legal adviser in the States is largely that of devising expedients for turning the corners of statutes that block progress, and which unless turned would paralyse business.

It is the same in the older States. The laws were drawn up by the Puritans, and are severe and intolerable. Some of these so-called Blue laws, if put in force, would become occasions of monstrous tyranny. For instance, in Massachusetts it is penal to kiss in public, and actually, quite recently, this law was put in force against a man for kissing his wife in Boston, when bidding her farewell on his way to England.

The revolution in the Roman judicial ideas and that in the Christian Church synchronised and ran in parallel lines. In each it was the recurrence to natural law, to first principles, to the spirit, against what was artificial, antiquated and textual.

Stoic philosophy immensely assisted the efforts of the

jurisconsults to effect the revolution in the estimate of law. The Stoics pleaded for a return to nature, to its simplicity of life, and to equilibrium. They taught the unity of mankind, and when once it was admitted that all men were by nature equal, then a natural law became recognised as of supreme obligation. Then the Prætor in framing his edict strove to approximate its jurisprudence to the original type from which all law had devolved, and in its devolution had become adulterated. And his aim was to revive, as far as was possible, those institutions by which man had been governed when in a primitive state.

Such being the condition of men's minds, it will be seen that everything was ripe for Christianity which revealed these first principles of morality and equity which the legists sought tentatively, and which when found they were unable to base on any authority. These first principles Christianity not only revealed, but revealed them as imposed by the Creator on His creatures, and therefore of universal application and obligation.

CHAPTER XVI

THE THIRD JOURNEY—EPHESUS

A.D. 55—56

Paul on the Third Journey goes over same ground—The Galatian Churches—Goes to Ephesus—Ephesus described—The Temple of Diana—Importance of Ephesus as a missionary centre—Renan on cosmopolitan towns—Reaction against the local cult—The Magians—Their doctrine—The Jews of Ephesus—Colossæ—Laodicæa—Hierapolis—Aquila and Priscilla—Difficulty of finding work—Disinterested conduct of Paul—Opposition breaks out—Paul separates from the Synagogue—The sons of Sceva—Supposed miracles.

AFTER Paul had saluted the Church (in Jerusalem) he went down to Antioch. And after he had spent some time there, he departed and went over the country of Galatia and Phrygia in order, strengthening all the disciples.[1]

It will be seen that Paul followed the same route as on his second journey, and that, though he passed through Tarsus, there is complete silence observed as to there being any believers in it, or of Paul attempting to speak in the synagogue of his native city.

He visited the faithful in Derbe, Lystra and Iconium, and was disappointed to meet with less cordiality than he had expected and had a right to demand.

Paul had been at Jerusalem for the Passover, then, after a visit to Antioch of a few months, his travels through

[1] Acts xviii. 22, 23.

Cilicia and Lycaonia occupied at least two, and he arrived at Ephesus about the time of the grape gathering, before the snows had begun to fall on the passes of the mountains.

During his visit to the Galatian Churches he probably planned the collection for the poor at Jerusalem, which was made universal throughout the new Churches during the ensuing three years, and this was, as before, done in agreement with the Apostles at Jerusalem, before they parted. To Ephesus Paul went by the direct route that crossed the united waters of the Hippourios, Senaros and Glaucus and reached Ephesus on the north of the Messogis range. He avoided the great highway leading through many important towns, Apamæa, Colossæ, Laodicæa and Tralles.

He probably had resolved to begin mission work at the westernmost city of the Province, with a view to further work eastwards, in the direction of Apamæa. Ephesus occupied the most beautiful valley in Ionia. The Cayster, issuing from a gorge to the east, twisted serpentine through the plain feeding lagoons in which swam myriads of swans. To the west gleamed the dark blue of the Ægean studded with gleaming isles. On all other sides bold mountain ridges enclosed the basin in which the city lay.

The port was becoming silted up through some misdirected engineering efforts to improve it, but was still in use. It communicated with the sea by a canal. On the land side stood a temple to Apollo, the Theatre, the Agora, and the Forum. Above this towered Mount Coressus, out of the side of which was scooped the amphitheatre. The walls of the city enclosed all these buildings, and ran, like those of Genoa, up the mountain crest, defended at intervals by towers.

THE THIRD JOURNEY—EPHESUS

The great temple of Diana stood behind the hill Coressus and outside the city gates. For a furlong around it was sanctuary for malefactors, enclosed like old Whitefriars within walls. Above the temple at the rear shot up Mount Solmissus, now called Aia Solouk (Agios Theologos) after St. John the Divine who was there buried.

The temple was one of the seven wonders of the world. After its destruction by Erostratus, who set fire to it so that his name might be remembered, it was rebuilt by coutributions from all Asia, the women even despoiling themselves of their jewels to furnish the means of its reconstruction. The divinity there adored was the Black Madonna of Anatolia, a wooden image of Cybele, rather than of Artemis, the bust covered with breasts distilling milk, but with the lower portion swathed in bandages decorated with every sort of animal form, and inscribed with magical formulæ. A fine, perhaps idealised representation of this goddess is in the Vatican museum. It was found near Tivoli.

The temple was served by emasculated priests and troops of priestesses.

An opulent town such as was Ephesus inevitably attracted to it large numbers of Jews. The extravagance of the Oriental worship of the goddess, the grovelling superstition of the vulgar, could not fail to revolt sober minds, and thus throw them under the influence of Jewish missionaries and Chaldean magicians.

The entire district, which swarmed with towns, was full of Jewish settlements, and everywhere their religious influence made itself felt. The general observance of the Sabbath shows this, more so even the coins of Apamæa, struck in the reigns of Severus and Macrinus, bearing on the reverse the Ark with the dove and olive-branch, and NOE inscribed on the roof.

Paul plainly discerned the immense importance of Ephesus as a missionary centre. None of the cities in which he had laboured presented such advantages. Antioch, Thessalonica, and Corinth had been admirably situated for his purpose, on account of the current of travellers incessantly passing through them, but none of them had the value of Ephesus. Upper Syria was but a strip of cultivated land between the desert and the sea; it formed the fringe of the empire, and seventeen towns only sent their delegates to the great festivals that took place in the capital. Thessalonica was a bustling seaport, but behind it was mountainous Macedonia, a province of no great extent. Thessaly was thinly populated, without great towns; Epirus half desert, "nothing remaining there but villages and barns."[1] Corinth was a place recovering from its ruins, without an established order of burgesses, occupied by a rabble of adventurers and of rogues from all quarters of the globe, and the Peloponnesus was devastated. "In all Greece," Plutarch said, not long after, "there could not be found three thousand fighting men."[2]

With Ephesus it was otherwise. The province of Asia was populous, rich, and flourishing. In it were five hundred towns, all thriving on commerce and manufacture, and in every one of these was a community of Jews. In Laodicæa alone there were eleven thousand adult males of this nation.

"We have had occasion frequently to remark," says M. Renan, "that Christianity found its strongest *raisons d'être* in the cosmopolitan towns multiplied by the Roman

[1] Strabo, ix, v., 15.   [2] "De Defect. Oraculor.," viii.

THE THIRD JOURNEY—EPHESUS

Empire—towns outside all nationalities, strange to all love of country, in which all races, all religions, jostled one another. Ephesus was, like Alexandria, Antioch, and Corinth, the type of one of such cities. One can see the like to-day in the great Levantine towns. What strikes the traveller when he traverses the labyrinths of pestilential bazaars, of narrow and dirty lanes, of temporary structures, not intended to last, is the complete absence of all that is noble, of public or municipal spirit.

"In these ant-heaps of men, baseness and good qualities, indolence and activity, impudence and amiability, meet together. Everything is there except that which constitutes an old local aristocracy, grand traditions cherished in common. Along with all this is found much good-fellowship, endless tittle-tattle, plenty of frivolity. Every one concerns himself about the affairs of his neighbour. The population is swayed by the vain curiosity of empty heads, greedy after news. All seek to follow the fashion, but are without the capacity to start fashion.

"Christianity was the fruit of the sort of fermentation which takes place in such localities, where man, freed from the prejudices of birth and race, easily assumes a cosmopolitan and humanitarian way of viewing all things, in a manner impossible to the peasant, the burgess, and the noble or feudal citizen. Like modern socialism, like all new ideas, Christianity germinated in what is called the corruption of great cities. That corruption, in fact, is often nothing other than a fuller and freer life, a great awakening of the mightiest forces of humanity."

Again, wherever paganism ran riot, and assumed its most monstrous forms, there a reaction from it was most certain to ensue. On this Paul could calculate.

Already the reaction had begun, but, being undirected, it had taken a wrong direction, and such as despised the black doll in the temple, and turned away their faces in disgust as the half-drunken troops of priests and priestesses went by capering, howling, scourging their backs—such had sought in necromancy what they could not find in the traditional heathenism. The Chaldee theology, with its doctrine of emanations, seemed to the troubled religious mind to offer a solution to the enigma of the universe, to supply a principle for the conduct of life. Swarms of magi wandered through the empire at the time when confidence in the traditional religion was shaken, and they formed the dominant priesthood over the minds of the educated classes.

They taught that there was one supreme God from whom at one time spiritual existences had been evolved which had lost their way in the world of matter, but which were gradually yet surely returning to their first estate in the *pleroma*, the fulness of the Godhead, and which approached that consummation more and more as they disengaged themselves from the matter that adhered to and dragged them down.

The magi, who professed to have largely emancipated themselves from the dominion of the grosser nature, claimed thereby to have acquired a great control over the spiritual powers. Such was their doctrine. Their practice was one of unmixed chicanery. They pretended to evoke spirits and to consult them, to control storms, to expel diseases, to stay earthquakes. They composed talismans, and determined what days were lucky and what unlucky for contracting marriage or starting on a journey. They consulted the stars and described horoscopes. They threw themselves into transports, and in them saw visions and foretold the future.

Ephesus seems to have been infested with these adventurers, preying on the religious needs of the cultured; but, indeed, every Greek city was full of them.

There were Jews in Ephesus ready to get money by the same unworthy means. The sons of one Sceva, a Hebrew, made it their trade to charm and cast out devils[1]—that is to say, to profess to work cures by quackery.

The Roman province of Asia which was now to have Christian teaching introduced into it, was not limited to the basins of the Cayster, the Mæander, the Lycus, and the Hermus. It comprehended Mysia as far as Mount Olympus, Lydia, Caria, and a portion of Phrygia.

Personally, Paul founded the Church in Ephesus alone, but thence, and through his energy and urgency, the Word was conveyed to other portions of the province. The seven churches addressed in the Apocalypse more or less directly owed to him their origin.

Three cities became celebrated in the history of the Church, lying in the direct course between Pisidian Antioch, and Ephesus, thus forming a chain of pearls that extended from Cilicia to the Ægean sea. These Churches were those of Colossæ, Laodicæa, and Hierapolis. The Epistle of Paul to the first of these has rendered its name familiar; it was, however, the least considerable of all at this period. Strabo speaks of Colossæ as a small town. Its importance was in the past. Xenophon had seen it "populous and flourishing." Planted at the roots of the Cadmus, closing one of the passes inland, its situation was not unfavourable, but it suffered from proximity to the

[1] Acts xix. 13-16.

more thriving Laodicæa, some eight miles further down, and nearer the Mæander.

The river Lycus passed through a suburb of the town, and plunged into a chasm which it traversed, boiling and thundering after a storm in the mountains. Above the town stood the *hieron*, the ancient religious centre of the district, and the focus of much demoralisation to the neighbourhood. In later times it was seized on by the Christians, purified, and dedicated to the Archangel Michael.

Hierapolis, on the right bank of the Lycus, faced Laodicæa, and the snowy crest and peak of Cadmus. It was an ancient *hieron* with its sacred priestly town, and the religious centre of that district, whereas Laodicæa was the political centre of Seleucid foundation. It was planted on a mountain ledge, 300 feet above the valley, at a point where numerous hot springs, gushing forth charged with calcareous matter, deposited stalactites wherever they fell over the rocks and spread sheets of travertine on the terraces and in the plain. To the present day mill-wheels on the Lycus have periodically to be cleared of the stony envelope which the water leaves about them. The stages of the limestone mountain are heavy with wreaths of lace and folds of drapery, with long white ropes, and have glittering pillars leaning against them, all of stalagmitic deposit. The whole lit up by a glorious sun flashing down out of a gentian-blue sky makes of Hierapolis a marvel of nature.

The place was in much repute for its thermal waters, and was largely visited by invalids. There may still be read among the ruined walls: " Hail to thee, fairest land of mighty Asia, city of gold, holy city (Hierapolis), nymph divine, nought can surpass the springs that are the cause of thy fame."

The meadows between Hierapolis and Laodicæa, watered by the Lycus, were rich with herbage and spangled with flowers. The latter town was an industrial centre, and the seat of administration of the province. There large fortunes were made. The water of the thermal springs was esteemed specially good for setting the purple and crimson dyes, and the black cloth of Laodicæa had a world-wide reputation. The citizens, filled with pride and love for their beautiful city, vied with each other in adorning it with stately buildings. When the Romans occupied Ionia, an old Phrygian city, Cybira, was selected as the capital of the district, but the proconsuls speedily recognised that Laodicæa was the true metropolis, and they made of it the seat of their administration and the political centre of the twenty-five cities that constituted the diocese of Cybira.

There were other and important cities that could be reached and influenced from Ephesus, Miletus, Smyrna, Sardis; Philadelphia and Tralles were smaller, but not insignificant. Even Pergamos was not beyond reach of Paul's preaching; and from Pergamos the sound of the Gospel would extend to Thyatira, the native place of Lydia.

At Ephesus Paul was at once received by his old friends Aquila and Priscilla. The former was a Jew and freedman, his wife probably a Roman, and on that account in St. Luke's record, her name usually preceded that of her husband. Paul remained in Ephesus from the autumn of 55 to May 58, working for his living, and barely earning it. Towards the end of his residence there he wrote: "Even unto this present hour we both hunger and thirst, and are naked, and are buffeted, and have no certain dwelling-place; and labour, working with our own hands."[1]

He made it his boast not to receive any payment or contributions from his converts, excepting only from Lydia and her friends in Philippi. That he was in such poverty must have been due to his being a bad workman; so only can this wretchedness be explained in a busy manufacturing district. Frail in health, suffering from "the splinter in his flesh," the intermittent low fever that continued to wear and depress him, with shaking hand, enfeebled sight, it could not be otherwise. When he says that he had no certain lodging, this seems to imply that he had to be continually leaving the masters who employed him.

But, beside physical infirmity, he had other interferences with his work. The whole time he was at Ephesus, it was one of mental activity and of worry, because the Judaisers were at Corinth and in Galatia undermining his authority, and his brain was incessantly engaged in seeking for arguments wherewith to combat them.

At a later time he reminded the Elders of Ephesus that he had not been in any way chargeable to them. "I have coveted no man's silver, or gold, or apparel. Yea, ye yourselves know, that these hands have ministered unto my necessities, and to them that were with me."[2]

This disinterested conduct Paul felt was needful in a grasping, avaricious community, where the Jews especially made gold their one object, with utter unscrupulousness as to the means whereby it was acquired.

Into the synagogue at Ephesus he could enter and speak by invitation. He had received a welcome on his former visit, and, perhaps, in consequence of his interview with

[1] Cor. iv. 11, 12.   [2] Acts xx. 33, 34.

the Apostles at Jerusalem, he maintained almost amicable relations with the Jews at first. " He went into the synagogue, and spake boldly for the space of three months, disputing and persuading the things concerning the kingdom of God."[1]

But this could not last long. The usual opposition was roused. There were gainsayers. "I have fought with beasts at Ephesus," was the way in which he expressed the violence with which he was met in his disputes. All did not accept his teaching, and such " spake evil of that way before the multitude." At the end of the three months, Paul adopted the same course as that pursued by him elsewhere. " He departed from them, and separated the disciples," and hired the school of Tyrannus after lecture hours, *i.e.*, the fifth hour (11 A.M.), as a meeting-house in which he could freely discourse to such Jews as cared to hear more, and such pagans as were attracted by his teaching.

"And this continued by the space of two years; so that all they which dwelt in (the province of) Asia heard the word of the Lord Jesus, both Jews and Greeks."[2] The sons of the Jew, Sceva, who exorcised, met with a rebuff that greatly disconnected them, and for a moment diverted popular superstition to Paul. A maniac whom they endeavoured to cure, fell on them and beat them, tore off their clothes, and yelled out that they were good for nought beside Paul and the Jesus he preached. This created a great sensation, and many of those who had professed to believe, and yet had preserved their magical books and charms, were by this induced to destroy all this costly rubbish. But the general run of the people are not to be

[1] Acts xix. 8.   [2] *Ibid.* xix. 10.

drawn at once from their superstitions, and for a moment losing faith in the amulets supplied from the temple, and the charms distributed by the Chaldees, they snatched at kerchiefs and loin-cloths that had been used by Paul, in the belief that they were endowed with miraculous powers. We are not told that Paul himself countenanced such proceedings, but that in certain cases they were believed to be efficacious.

On the summit of Mount Coressus stands a ruined tower, from which the whole site of Ephesus may be seen, the silted-up port, the crumbling walls of theatre and stadium, the platform of the temple, the foundations of the gymnasium where Paul taught.

On the north-east side of this height is the Cave of the Seven Sleepers, who, so it was said, retired into it in the reign of Decius, when paganism was predominant, and Christianity was persecuted, and who awoke three centuries later to find paganism a thing of the past, and Christ triumphant: a picturesque legend that expresses well the wonder that possessed the ancient world to see how that by " the foolishness of preaching " the Cross, the world had been subdued, the counsel of princes brought down, and the wisdom of the wise made of none effect.

CHAPTER XVII

THE PERIOD OF CONFLICT

Contest with the Judaisers—The causes of the Judaic reaction—1. The double condition of the Church at the same time—2. The persecution to which the Church was exposed when separated from the Synagogue—3. The argument of safety—4. The recoil of the Anatolians from *anomia*—Visitors from Jerusalem—The new form of attack—Paul's apostleship questioned—The Epistle to the Galatians —How Paul defended his apostolic position—How he defended his doctrine—How he safeguarded morality—His failure in this portion of his defence—The practical working of his *anomia*—The Church in Corinth—Paul's Epistles to the Corinthians—The first Epistle—He sends Timothy to Corinth—A suppressed letter—A change of opinion in Corinth—Paul goes to Philippi—The second Epistle—The character of the first—Factions in the Church—The new form of opposition—The character of the second Epistle—A crisis in the condition of Paul—Change of opinion relative to the second Advent.

THE years at Ephesus were spent by Paul, not only in spreading the Word through the province of Asia, but in contest with the so-called Judaising faction which threatened his influence over the Churches he had founded, and which also manifested its strength in such as had received the seed through James, Peter, and John.

The same tendencies were manifest in Rome as in Galatia and Achaia, and which even stirred the converts in Macedonia.

The cause of this reactionary movement has already been indicated; but it would be more correct to speak of the Judaising reaction as the result of several causes.

Although I have already spoken of the principal of these, I will next sum them up, that the reader may be able to clearly understand how inevitable this movement was, and how certain it was to break out; and that whether or not there had been a Paul in the field.

1. This agitation and friction were due, in the first place, to the Church being in two conditions simultaneously—at Jerusalem in embryonic state, at Antioch and Rome, in Galatia and Achaia, in a more developed state. And these differences of condition were consequent on circumstances. At Jerusalem it was not, as already shown, possible for the believers to organise themselves into a religious community apart from Judaism. Whether they liked it or not, conform to the Law they must, or they would be scourged, outlawed, and constrained to leave Judæa. The Christian element, doctrine, and discipline, organisation, and ritual, was in a condition of suspense; it had not been precipitated because it could not be so.

But among the Diaspora it was otherwise. There the believers had been ejected from the Synagogue, and had formed conventicles of their own, in which they had their own teachers and rulers, their independent worship, and from these more or less of the Judaic element was being cleared out as so much lumber.

The attitude of the Apostles at Jerusalem was something like that of Erasmus towards Romanism. They hoped to infuse the Jewish Church with the spirit of the Gospel, and transform it. But in the provinces the rupture was accomplished, and once accomplished organisation began to take place in the independent communities.

Now in these Churches among the Gentiles, inevitably there must have been two tendencies, one towards a thorough emancipation from Mosaism, the other a conservative one, which prompted the retention of as much as possible of the usages of the Law. Such is human nature. In every collection of men, in a Parish Council, on a School Board, everywhere, some will be for new experiments, and others will cling to precedent.

Undoubtedly Paul had brought the friction to flaming point, but the friction and flame were inevitable without him.

Again, whatever visitors came from Judæa to the provinces were certain to be startled at the independence of the Churches there, and to contrast it with the amorphous condition of the Church in Jerusalem, and to compare unfavourably the manner in which the Churches of the Dispersion dispensed with Mosaic forms with the respect shown for them at the centre of Christianity.

2. But this was not all. As already indicated, the secession or expulsion of the believers from the synagogues had touched the most sensitive part in a Jew's system—his pocket.

The Jews, as has been said before, found that their proselytes brought into them a good deal of business. These converts dealt with them in the bazaar, introduced their friends to their shops, gave orders for foreign merchandise through them, and if in need of a loan, applied to them for it.

Now the result of the split was that the Jews of the synagogue lost their clients, and their profits fell off considerably. There were two ways open to them: either to set the laws in motion against the Christians, or to attempt to effect a reconciliation.

The new believers were, by their schism, exposed to great

danger. According to Paul's own account, one powerful inducement to his converts to seek to come to terms with the Synagogue was their desire to avert persecution.[1] For, as St. Jerome observes, all the circumcised if they became Christians were treated by the Jews as heathen, while the uncircumcised Christians were equally persecuted by Jew and heathen.[2] Roman law protected the Synagogue, but no new organisation could be formed for religious or social purposes that was not exposed to being forcibly suppressed and its members severely handled. This was a very present and a very great difficulty, that met Paul at every turn. Now when both parties in a quarrel see that there is a good deal to be gained by reconciliation, and nothing by estrangement, a great step is taken towards reunion.

The Jews of the Synagogue made the first advance. They argued somehow thus: "Let us sink our differences. We are all going one way, looking to one end; have one hope—in the coming of the Messiah."

Their object was to recover their connection with the proselytes. It was a business speculation, nothing more.

On the other hand, the proselytes had twinges of conscience. They knew that they owed a great deal to the Synagogue, and thought that they had shown something like ingratitude to their first teachers. But added to this was the great protection from persecution, the security they would assure, by returning under the wing of the Synagogue.

3. Next came an argument that told with the timorous. The Jews and Judaising Christians did not demand submission to circumcision as necessary to salvation, but as a concession to prejudice, and to give security to converts.

[1] Gal. vi. 12, 13.   [2] Hieron. in Gal. ii. 10.

They said: "Do not decry the ceremony. It was divinely ordered. It is always best, where there is any doubt, to be on the safe side. We do not enforce it, and do you allow it. We want nothing beyond this."

4. But the reaction in the Churches of Galatia was due mainly to the alarm taken at the character of Paul's teaching.

The Anatolian proselytes had been attracted to Mosaism by the Law. They clung to the two tables written with the finger of God, as their sole protection against general demoralisation, and their only security to enable them to make moral and social progress. As has already been represented, Anatolian religion was essentially licentious. Originally every woman was common property. The condition was not one of organised polyandry, but of promiscuity; and when this became intolerable, and could no longer be enforced, then it was counselled, not commanded. Every woman was encouraged to dedicate herself either for all her life or for a certain specified time to the "divine life," that is to say to become a harlot. When a sickness occurred in a family, or a murrain among cattle, or a blight came on the harvest, it was at once concluded that the Great Mother was wroth, and was only to be propitiated by a vow to the temple service. And the greater repugnance a woman felt to undergo it, the greater was the merit of the sacrifice.

In this horrible condition of affairs, where every temple sent its rill of poison into every household, the necessity for a divine law forbidding such evil became imperious, and only a divine law could be set up in opposition to the pretended divine encouragement of promiscuous intercourse.

When Paul spoke in Anatolia of the Law being done away with, the Galatian converts were stupefied with dismay. They thought that he was robbing them of that one safeguard for the purity of their families which had been provided by the Synagogue. It produced, inevitably, a recoil that led to extravagance. Rather than sacrifice the moral law they were willing, eager to embrace the ceremonial law. When reactionaries came from Judæa, they found the Galatian believers in a condition of moral panic. It was not they who stirred up the converts to mistrust; the mistrust was already there and fermenting. They but showed the Galatians how to get back on to a firm moral basis.

No code had been promulgated by Paul in the place of the Two Tables. He had denounced the Law in those vague terms that may mean anything or nothing. He had made no distinction between the moral and the ceremonial law.

We who have the Gospels before us, and who know by heart the Sermon on the Mount, can hardly realise the condition of dismay in which the Galatian converts were. The teaching of Jesus Christ had been put much in the background, that the facts of His death and resurrection might be given prominence. None of the Gospels had been written at this time. What Our Lord had taught was known only by hearsay.

If, then, the Law was to be regarded as abrogated, then man was thrown back on the law of Nature, and the insufficiency of this was a matter of experience.

Let us suppose that in 1792 the National Convention had abolished all existing weights and measures without instituting any new standards.

Into what confusion would men's minds have been thrown! How utterly disorganised would have been all business throughout France! How impossible would have been all trade beyond her frontiers!

Into much such a state of mind were the Galatians cast by the tirades of Paul against the Law.

Let us suppose a case such as might occur in any household in Phrygian Galatia. In a family where the father and mother believed, a child is stricken with fever. In an agony of mind, and in hopes of saving the child, the mother lapses into superstition, and cries out that the child is stricken by the goddess, and can only be saved by a vow to the "divine life." The husband interferes. Then retorts the wife: "It was well enough before, when you said God spake from Sinai, and engraved the command on tables of stone, 'Thou shalt not commit adultery.' But now this new preacher has declared that this Law does not apply to all men, it was imposed on Jews alone. I am not sure which and what is right; but I know that through the goddess many a stricken child has been restored by the mother vowing to her." What would the husband answer? All effective reply was taken away from him.

Such then, I conceive it, was the condition of minds in Galatia, when Paul heard of it. It had been aggravated by the arrival of certain believers from Jerusalem, who were able to represent the condition of the Church there as something very different from that in the Churches of the Dispersion, or rather of the proselytes captured from the Jews of the Dispersion.

No doubt whatever that these visitors would take advantage of the trouble of mind in which they found the Galatians to recommend submission to the whole Law;

and no doubt also they could not resist the temptation of representing themselves as armed with authority from James, whereas all that they could really show was letters recommending them to the hospitality of the believers in Christ, everywhere.

It was under such a condition of affairs in Galatia that Paul wrote his epistle to the Churches there, of his founding.

But now, for the first time, the arguments employed against him assumed a personal complexion. It was inevitable that his claim to be an Apostle should be called in question. His believers did no more than was their duty in asking for some guarantee that his commission was not self-assumed.

The attack took this shape.

It was said : " The Apostles at Jerusalem, we know, received their authority from Jesus Christ. They had been His disciples during His ministry. They received instruction from His mouth. He breathed on them and gave them commission to establish His kingdom, and to preach His Gospel. God has confirmed their mission by signs and wonders.

" But you, Saul of Tarsus, who were in Cilicia at the time when Jesus taught and suffered and rose from the dead, you arrived in Jerusalem after the miraculous outpouring of the Holy Ghost at Pentecost. Yet you set up to be an Apostle and to have authority. Your preaching to us seems to be opposed, diametrically, in the matter of this Law, to that of Him whose Apostle you claim to be. How do you account for this?

" We do not deny that you have seen Christ in a vision. We do not deny that you are acting under commission from Him; but we are bidden to try every spirit, and we ask for some better evidence than your bare, unsupported word.

"You profess to have received your consecration in the Temple, by vision. You must excuse us if we remark that your conduct on that occasion was not such as we should have supposed to be right. No sooner did you see the Lord in trance, and hear His words, than you ran away from Jerusalem direct to Antioch. We are sorry to appear captious, but in our opinion the right thing to have done would have been to have at once gone to James, Peter and John, and subjected your mission to scrutiny. We do not deny that you have been sent, but we can hardly put you on the same level as the Twelve, and we are justified in asking for your credentials. We know that false prophets and false apostles will arise. Already in Samaria one has appeared, called Simon, giving himself out to be some Great One; every ambassador brings some token of his commission. We are bound in conscience to ask for yours."

Such was the position assumed by the Judaisers, with regard to Paul's apostleship.

In the second place they pressed the argument already detailed, that it was contrary to what they held to be consistent with the nature of God, to give a law with certain formalities, which was to be set aside without a manifest revelation that it should be abrogated, and that its function was temporary only.

Thirdly, they pointed out that the repeal of the Law left man without moral restraint. How was morality to be safeguarded if the Law were abolished?

The entire Epistle to the Galatians is occupied in

answering these three objections. If it has a more formal character and structural completeness than the rest, it is due to the fact of the opposition to Paul having been neatly formulated.

It is divided into three parts to meet the threefold attack. The first part is compressed into chapters I. and II., the second occupies chapters III. and IV., and the third part is comprised in chapters V. and VI.

I. Paul asserts a co-equal authority with the Twelve, and this on three grounds.

Firstly: Because his miraculous conversion proves it, and with that conversion came his vocation to the apostleship.

Secondly: His apostolic office was acknowledged at Jerusalem by Peter, James and John, who gave him the right hand of fellowship and allotted to him his special sphere among the uncircumcised.

Thirdly: He showed that when Peter stepped out of his province, then he, Paul, interfered to set him right, and that Peter recognised his authority and submitted to his correction.

The answer that his conversion was miraculous was beside the mark. It constituted him an apostle only in the limited sense of a witness to the fact that He who had died was alive again, and so, as witness, he had a right to go everywhere and testify that Jesus was alive and in heaven. But it established no more than this, and that his conversion was miraculous nobody who knew his previous history was inclined to doubt. But his commission still rested on his bare assertion, unsupported. Yet he made a point when he showed that Peter, James, and John had recognised his apostolic and authoritative position, and that Peter had even bowed before his superiority.

At a later period he seems to have become aware that some better evidence was necessary than his own assertion, and then he brought forward the success of his work as evidence that it received divine approbation; and if divine approval covered his work, then it implied that he who had worked so successfully did so by commission.[1]

II. Next as to his doctrine.

He was encountered by this proposition. "We are the children of Abraham. Salvation is promised to the elect race. In token of election God gave the seal of circumcision. If then we are to become the elect of God, we must accept the seal."

To this Paul replied: "The promise was made to Abraham when in uncircumcision. There are two kinds of descent, that which is carnal and that which is spiritual. The Promise belongs to the latter, the Law to the former."

Then he applies this. You Galatians, being uncircumcised, received the Gospel and believed. Therefore you belong to the spiritual filiation. But the Law was something superadded, parenthetical, provisional. It served a purpose, and that purpose accomplished, it passed away into limbo.

III. Paul now passed to the safeguarding of the moral law.

"True," said he, "you have passed out of bondage into liberty. But what is this condition of liberty? It is one of freedom from the works of the flesh. The moment you follow the flesh you lapse out of the Gospel and fall under the Law once more. To live a life of faith, and to continue in sin, is a logical impossibility. The spiritual life is one

[1] 1 Cor. ix. 2.

of emancipation from sin, but you are only living that spiritual life when in a sinless condition."

His failure in this portion of the argument is abject.

He, himself, in his exaltation, in his fever to do his Master's work, frail in health and almost bloodless, was not a prey to fervid passions. But it was otherwise with his converts, and this he was soon to learn from Corinth, where the lusty disciples were plunging into fornication and incest, under the eyes of the Elders, not only unreproved, but encouraged in their disorders, as showing how glorious was the liberty of the Gospel, which had no moral law.

"Ye are puffed up," he was constrained to write, when one of his converts was living in incest with his own father's wife. That such an one should be refused admission to the Lord's table had not occurred to any of these Corinthian saints.

Paul's theory that the believers were elevated by their faith into a spiritual atmosphere unruffled by passion was utopian and impracticable. And this is what he had now to learn. He was afforded a practical exemplification of the working of his lawless Gospel, in the body of his Corinthian Church.

Very soon after Paul's arrival in Ephesus, he heard rumours that all was not going on sweetly in Corinth. He then wrote a letter that has been lost; and in this he forbade the Christians associating with persons of debauched life.[1]

It is supposed that one page of this lost epistle remains, and has become attached to the Second Epistle.[2]

To this letter the Corinthians replied.[3] They explained

[1] 1 Cor. v. 9.   [2] 2 Cor. vi. 14–vii. 1.   [3] 1 Cor. vii. 1.

that it was not possible for them to dissociate themselves wholly from such as led bad lives.

They next proceeded to put to him a series of questions relative to celibacy, marriage, the eating of meats offered to idols, and to certain manifestations, rather extraordinary than edifying, that had taken place after the Agape among their more excitable members.

It would seem that Greek scepticism in relation to the resurrection of the dead had invaded their Church. The resurrection of Jesus Christ was not denied, but the converts could not quite overcome their difficulties in believing that all those who had died and been buried and burned should be restored as before. Others, expecting the immediate advent of Christ, doubted whether a general resurrection would be required, and contented themselves with baptizing for dead relatives and friends, so as to make the advantages retrospective.[1]

Apollos, who had been at Corinth, arrived at Ephesus about this time, and he also gave a bad account of the Church because of its rivalries and quarrels.

The letter of the Church of Corinth was brought to the Apostle by some servants of Chloe. He at once answered it. He administered to the Church a sharp reprimand for its moral laxity, and then proceeded to answer the questions put to him. This letter is the First Epistle that has come down to us, but is actually the second written to the Corinthians by him.

As to the incestuous Corinthian, Paul pronounced his death sentence, hoping and expecting that, as God had struck down Ananias and Sapphira, when excommunicated by St. Peter, He would in like manner suddenly slay the

[1] 1 Cor. xv. 29.

man whom he delivered over to Satan for the destruction of the flesh.

This letter Paul sent by the hand of Timothy.

But as Timothy was young, Paul was not sure how he would be received, and he announced that he himself would shortly personally visit the Church.

Soon after, perhaps, on receiving a letter from Timothy painting the critical condition of affairs, Paul hastened to Corinth, and was received not merely with coldness but with insult. Some one member of the congregation affronted him so publicly and so gallingly,[1] that he returned precipitately to Ephesus, a prey to shame and anger. From Ephesus he wrote a third letter, very violent, and no sooner had he despatched it, than he regretted the strength of the terms employed, stinging with all the sarcasm of which he was master, and he sent Titus to follow it up, and smooth down the ruffle in the tempers of those who had received this letter. We have not got this Epistle. It was rigidly suppressed. The Corinthian Church did not relish the exposure it made of its condition, and the Apostle had no reason to be proud of it. Nevertheless it answered its purpose. A milder reprimand would under the circumstances have failed in its purpose; but this knotted lash made the Corinthians wince and set about an amendment.[2]

Titus used his persuasive eloquence, and a turn took place in the versatile minds of the Corinthians. The majority of the Church in an assembly condemned the man who had insulted Paul, and decided to send excuses and

[1] 2 Cor. ii. 5, vii. 12; x. 7-11. This is by some supposed to be the incestuous person, but it can hardly be so. See Sabatier, " L'Apôtre Paul," 1896, pp. 169-171.

[2] 2 Cor. vii. 8-11.

expressions of regret by Titus, and at the same time to give to Paul assurances of unalterable affection.

In the mean time, the Apostle, in a fever of impatience to know the result, had left Ephesus and hurried to Macedonia, to meet Titus, who was returning that way. There he encountered him, and at once, from Philippi, where he was probably staying with Lydia, he wrote a fourth letter which is the Second Epistle that has reached us.

This is one supposition. But there is another, more commonly held. It is generally thought that the man mentioned in the Second Epistle [1] to whom he extends forgiveness is this same man over whom he had pronounced a death sentence. If so—then we must admit that Paul's sentence had failed, had proved a *brutum fulmen*. But he recovered from this and made the best of the circumstances, assuring the Corinthians that if the man still lived, it was because he had himself withdrawn the sentence.[2] This may be so. But I am inclined to consider the two persons as entirely distinct.

If we examine the First Epistle, we find that it lacks organic connection and unity. But then, as it rose out of peculiar circumstances, and consisted of a categorical reply to questions proposed, that had no natural connection between them, this was inevitable. In it the party spirit of the Corinthians is mentioned and condemned. It sprang out of the inherent character of the people who lived upon the excitement of the race-course, and formed factions, green, blue, red, and white. This propensity they imported into religion. One faction was of Paul, another of Apollos, another of Cephas, and another of Christ; and it is by no means improbable that among these feather-headed

[1] 2 Cor. ii. 5-11.   [2] *Ibid.* ii. 10, 16.

Corinthians they attributed to each his colour. The factions in the Church had no more polemical and serious character than those in the race-course. There is no indication that there was any difference in doctrine in the parties. They formed parties for party sake. But much took place before the Second (fourth) Epistle was despatched. By that time a real controversy had broken out; it was the same as that which disturbed the Galatians. It is by no means improbable that the minority that had been overridden reasserted itself, and, looking about for a good excuse to renew the struggle, and to gain an accession of members and force, had laid hold of the question of circumcision.

They could calculate on the adhesion of the Jewish converts. But the controversy now assumed a different shape. It was put in this form: Paul pretends that the Law and the Mosaic priesthood are abolished, and he sets himself up as above Moses, and the ministry he establishes as higher in dignity than the Aaronic priesthood. Is he justified in this?

The Second Epistle is divided into two parts. In the first he addresses the favourable and docile majority, which accepted his opinions without question, and bowed meekly beneath his lash. He pours over them effusive expressions of his gratitude and tender affection. And he furnishes an illustration by which the Second Covenant can be compared with the First.

Moses on Sinai received the first promises and covenant, and his face shone, but he was obliged to veil his face to conceal the dazzling glory from men unable to bear the light. But the veil is somehow transferred from the face of Moses to the hearts of the Jews, where it lies till the

Jew is converted, when the veil falls away and he sees no longer Moses but Christ. It is a clumsy illustration. But there is more hinted at. Moses on Sinai was radiant, and his radiance was hidden by a veil; but he—Paul—had been caught up not to a mountain top but into the third heaven, and he also wore a veil—the veil of humiliations and distresses. The Corinthian opponents objected to this veil. It was so because the veil was on their hearts and they could not perceive the superlative glory of Paul's countenance shining, like that of Moses, with reflected light.[1]

The first portion of this Epistle is addressed to those who followed him without inquiry and dispute. The second exhibits the Apostle turning sharply round to pour out galling satire against such as questioned his ministry.

A twelvemonth or more, probably eighteen months, elapsed between the writing of the First and of the Second Epistle.

The period intervening had been one of great mental anguish to Paul. He wrote of his trouble, of his having been oppressed out of measure, beyond his strength, insomuch that he despaired even of life. But he said, this had taught him not to trust in himself but in God, "who delivered us from so great a death, and doth deliver, in whom we trust that He will yet deliver us."[2]

What this trouble was we are not told. It would seem to have been a great spiritual crisis, for it is associated with inner travail of the soul; but it would seem to have been a sickness of the body as well, perhaps brought on, certainly aggravated by his condition of mind.

"Blessed be God, who comforteth us in all our

[1] 2 Cor. iii. 1, 6–18; iv. 3–12; xi. 18–33; xii. 1–12.
[2] 2 Cor. i. 8–10.

tribulation, that we may be able to comfort them which are in any trouble, by the comfort wherewith we ourselves are comforted of God." And he associates those to whom he writes with the trouble that had nearly brought him to death. "Our hope of you is stedfast, knowing that as ye are partakers of the sufferings, so shall ye be also of the consolation."[1]

We can hardly fail to understand that this sickness was brought about by worry over the scandals caused by the Corinthian Church, and the repudiation of his authority, which had driven him back to Ephesus.

He took both to heart intensely. His excitable character, his impatience, his intolerance of opposition were wrought to fever point; and the manner in which some of his arguments were torn to tatters before his face, and his inability to supply anything sounder, convinced as he was of the soundness of his theories, but incapable of proving them, must have terribly discouraged him. His model Churches either stank in the nostrils of the not over nice pagans, through their immoralities, or backed out of antinomism into Judaic observance.

Hitherto he had confidently anticipated the immediate coming of the Lord Jesus, and to seeing Him in the clouds, without tasting death. In some of his tangles he had trusted that this would arrive as a happy solution of his perplexities.

But now he was disappointed, and gave up this hope.

He had started on his apostolic career sanguine of success, confident that he had but to set a match among the stubble to produce an universal conflagration. He had been impatient of the slow methods adopted by the elder

[1] 2 Cor. i. 3-7.

Apostles. He had indeed met with considerable success, and as he had no knowledge of geography, he supposed the world was very small, and that he could overrun and convert the whole of it in a very few years. But he was disappointed. He could not make his scheme of salvation intelligible. It was misunderstood, or rather his conception of evangelic freedom was misinterpreted, and his doctrine had been made a handle for " working all uncleanness with greediness." His churches, which were to astonish the world and confound that at Jerusalem, were wavering in faith, torn by jealousies, sullied by immoralities, hotbeds of strife, of insolence and of scandal. In every one of them a party arose that mistrusted him, even openly defied him. His reasonings convinced nobody, and he was himself conscious at last how poor and ineffective they were. Even his death sentences—if we take the man in the Second Epistle to the Corinthians to be one with him in the First—were not ratified by God. Then in his discouragement, he yearned for death, to be away from his failures, rid of his disappointments, and to be with Christ.

CHAPTER XVIII

ST. PAUL'S MODE OF ARGUMENT

The training of St. Paul to be considered when reviewing his arguments—Different systems of reasoning—Inspiration different in degree and its limits—Inspiration did not make Paul reason according to the rules of Western logicians—His method Oriental—Examples—He bases his demonstrations on texts—Arbitrarily taken and sometimes inappropriate—The antithesis of faith and works—No real antithesis—A dialectic blunder—Faith in its two stages—Customary law—Christian ethics in process of development—Paul's disadvantage in discussion.

In considering one of St. Paul's arguments, we are bound to take his training into account. We have no right to suppose that one who had no acquaintance with the methods of the classic thinkers should be able to frame his arguments according to the laws they imposed. Of reasoning in such a manner as would convince an intelligent Greek and Roman, Paul was probably incapable. His method was that which passed muster in a rabbinic school; but that was precisely one that a Western intellect could not appreciate. It would seem illogical, artificial and far-fetched. It took centuries of contact with European minds to produce a Spinoza.

The masters of Saul of Tarsus were not Plato and Aristotle, but a set of quibblers who proved whatever they listed by the most arbitrary use of texts torn from their settings, in total disregard of the circumstances which called them forth and of the purpose for which indited. To attempt to fit the arguments of St. Paul to the logical forms which we are accustomed to regard as legitimate is to attempt too much and to invite failure.

Divine illumination was with Paul to inspire him as a teacher, but not for the purpose of dis-Orientalising his mind. He was inspired to instruct, not to argue. He was shown his course, but was not furnished with reasons why he should pursue it.

A great deal of the difficulty felt by some thinkers in accepting the writings of the Old and New Testaments as inspired, arises from a misapprehension as to the nature and limits and purpose of inspiration. Inspiration is of two degrees. In its lower degree it assists the natural faculties to attain to some truth or make some discovery which may and will render mankind happier and better. It stimulates the natural powers to their highest point of exercise. It is that spark falling sometimes on a genius, often on one very far from such, which causes an act or provokes an invention which is helpful to mankind. Such was the discovery of bronze, that of iron, that of the use of grain, the manufacture of pottery, down to that of the Röntgen ray. Each of these advances is made when God sees fit, and then the faculty or the occasion for the invention is given. But so also are ideas inspired, as that of the brothers Grimm to collect the Folk tales which were to be the joy of innocent children; such the creation of an original melody, the conception of something beautiful in art. This flash of inspiration never falls on the brute beast, only on man, because in man alone is the faculty of progress.

I take, then, inspiration in its first significance to be

that illumination given by God to man in his various stages of culture which enables a man to do something, to impose a law, to discover something, which will be for the material, intellectual, and social advantage of the human race.

But man is a complex being, and he has his spiritual nature and religious cravings. In the second place, inspiration is the illumination of man in matters concerning his spiritual nature. Such illumination differs from the other in this, that the first kind merely leads man to do or discover something by means naturally provided; but in the latter case, the illumination gives to man what he can by no means discover for himself. It is, in a word, a revelation. No man by searching can find out God, no amount of speculation can reach certainty as to the future life, and as to what is God's will that men should follow; that may be guessed and disputed over, but cannot be known unless revealed.

We have no right to limit this highest form of revelation to the Jewish nation, or to the Apostles of Jesus.

There have been prophets and inspired teachers among all the leading peoples of the world, men in whom the intuition of God as the Creator, all holy, all loving, everlasting, has come home with such conviction as to make of them apostles of the truth. And as certainly as there have been these illumined souls with their revelation, so certain is it that this revelation they have preached has been beyond the comprehension of all who have received it, and that it has become corrupted and degraded by vulgar minds and heavy souls.

Take an instance in Hinduism. The ancient hymns of the race show that there were men among them who had conceived the thought of a deity, the spring and sustainer of all life, to be worshipped by purity of heart and innocence of life, by tender charity and self-abnegation. But the general Indian mind was unable to soar so high, and its pantheistic creed became polytheism and idolatry, with rites of the vilest sensuality and worst cruelty.

Inspiration as to the nature of God and the end of man is something more than a supernatural elevation of the moral and spiritual faculties, it is a communication from God. Such inspiration flashes everywhere and is not confined to any race or degree of civilisation, but it presupposes a receptivity without which it fails to enlighten. I suppose that there are few men not in the whirl of business, or tangle of social frippery, that have not their moments of elevation into commune with God, when sudden visions of truth, not to be accounted for by any apparent causes, burst upon the mind; their moments when God is present and very real to them in a manner quite unutterable by words. Such are divine inspirations, gleams from the ever-acting Spirit of God that lighteth every man that cometh into the world.

But though all men are susceptible to such revelations it is not true that all men receive them in the same degree. God gives as He sees fit, and for a certain purpose; and as men are ripe to take at least one step forward in correspondence with the revelation.

Christianity is the fullest and most complete revelation ever made, but it is not the only one ever given. The Jew was not the sole recipient in the old world of God's communications. He spake in time past to all men, in every race, under every clime, in each cultural stage. If we find, as we do find, in every religion grand flashes of the truth, it is due to such inspirations; and if we find elements of evil, low and degrading superstitions and bloody rites, that is due to the inability of man, in his then condition, to receive the truth. Paul saw this of the heathen. He said: "God *hath* showed it unto them; for the invisible things of Him from the creation of the world are clearly seen, being understood by the things that are made, even His eternal power and Godhead; so then they . . . when they knew God, glorified Him not as God, neither were thankful; but . . . changed the glory of the uncorruptible God into an image made like to corruptible man."[1]

The human soul is constituted to receive divine illumination, and everywhere is touched by it, but does not everywhere respond to it. The Light was ever in the world, but the world knew Him not.[2]

The truths which the mind of man craves to know are those relative to the nature of God, to His purpose with regard to man, and the law of man's being, and the destiny of the creature.

Man may speculate on these matters, but can attain thereon nothing more than probabilities. Certainty can only be acquired by revelation of God, and the revelation of these verities is inspiration.

Inspiration such as this was given to the Apostles. By it they were divinely instructed as to the nature of God, His scheme of salvation for man, and the purpose for which man was made; and how, therefore, by fulfilling that purpose as a rule of life, man may attain to the perfection of his being—*i.e.*, to happiness. In the epistles of Paul, we see him laying down great principles, doctrinal and ethical. In so doing he was acting as the oracle of God.

[1] Rom. i. 19-23. [2] John i. 10.

But the moment he stepped outside the ray of light, he dropped back into darkness. Illumination was not given to him to make him know physical laws, nor political economy, nor to solve mathematical problems. We must not, then, be surprised and shocked to find him bungle in dialectics, for when he entered into controversy he was in the natural sphere, and outside of that illumined by the divine light. I do not consider that we are justified in supposing that inspiration, even in its highest manifestation, came to an end in the apostolic age. We are expressly told that the Spirit was to be ever with the Church to guide into all truth, and the Spirit is life; where the life is, there is the faculty of discrimination, election, and determination.

From what has been said, it will be seen that we are almost bound to discriminate between Paul as an inspired Apostle and as a disputant. The grace of God did not give him a handsome and stately person, nor relieve him of ague. Why should we assume that it rectified congenital blemishes and educational distortions?

When Paul attempted controversy, it was with such arms as he had been furnished with in the rabbinic schools, and he used such demonstrations as were calculated to be accepted by those similarly trained.

But when compared with the reasoning methods in vogue in Greece, it was like contending with flint weapons against steel.

His Hellenic proselytes were certainly able to draw a distinction between Paul as an inspired Apostle and Paul as a dialectician, and when they saw him floundering in dispute, they looked on with wonder and compassion as they did when he was in the throes of malarial fever.

These latter attacks were never wholly understood, and were regarded by them as a sort of possession; indeed, Paul himself had some such opinion of them,[1] and his arguments were to the Greeks so marvellous and incomprehensible that they were disposed to regard them also with the superstitious respect that they paid to epilepsy.

To many persons skilled in music, Gregorian melody is crude and strange. That is not because Gregorian music is unscientific, but because it belongs to different *modes* from that only mode in which modern music is composed.

So with the ratiocination of St. Paul. It is different in kind from anything to which we are accustomed. It belongs to another system of dialectics from that of the Academy. It was calculated to the requirements of a rabbinic brain, and followed the rules of argument adopted in the schools of interpretation of the Law. It was quite beyond the compass of a classic intellect.

To understand Paul's method of demonstration, it is idle to look to classic precedent; we must go to the Talmud, and see there how the masters and contemporaries of Paul wrangled and drew conclusions.

An example or two of his method will suffice. In the Epistle to the Romans, Paul endeavours to prove that the believer is no longer subject to the Mosaic Law. He argues thus:

1. A woman is subject to her husband so long as he is alive.

2. When he is dead, then her time of subjection terminates.

3. When she remarries, then she falls under subjection to her new husband.

[1] 2 Cor. xii. 7.

Then he applies this:—

1. The Church was subject to the Mosaic Law.
2. The Mosaic Law is dead. Therefore she is released from obedience.
3. She is now the bride of Christ. Consequently she is under His domination.

This is a neat and suitable illustration, but it is no proof; for it assumes the very point in dispute—the cessation of the life and authority in the Law.

What Paul probably wanted to state was this—that the Church was under Christ as its head up to the Crucifixion, but that Christ represented the Law, and His death on the cross was therefore the death of the Law; but He rose, and so became the new Husband of the Church, with a new domination.

If this were his meaning, he did not know how to bring it out distinctly; and had he developed it, what a poor, strained, extravagant argument it would have been!

Another curious piece of reasoning is in the Epistle to the Galatians.

Paul is seeking to show the freedom of the believer under the Gospel, and to contrast it with the bondage of the Jew under the Law.

He attempts the demonstration thus:—

"It is written: Abraham had two sons, the one by a bondwoman, the other by a freewoman."

At the outstart, we see the quality of this argument. It is purely textual and rabbinic.

1. He of the bondwoman was carnal, but he of the freewoman was by promise—*i.e.*, spiritual.
2. This represents the two covenants; the Mosaic is figured by Ishmael, the Christian by Isaac.

That the generation and birth of Isaac was as truly carnal as that of Ishmael, Paul leaves out of sight.

Then he draws out this equation :—

Ishmael, issuing from Agar = the Law proceeding from Mount Sinai. Why so, we are not told.

Isaac, the child of promise = the Gospel.

Ishmael, moreover = Jerusalem.

Isaac, on the other hand = spiritual Jerusalem.

And then he pronounces for the supremacy of the latter and the rejection of the former, by the text: "Cast out the bondwoman and her son." That is to say, because God ordered the rejection of Ishmael, therefore He pronounced the death doom of the Law.

"*So then*"—this is Paul's conclusion—"we are not children of the bondwoman, but of the free."

The argument, if it deserves such a name, is fantastic, and is vitiated by the facts of the case, for the father of the Jew was actually Isaac. It was of him that the Law came, and not from the descendants of Ishmael. On the other hand, Ishmael, as parent of a portion of Gentiledom, might very well have been stretched to represent the whole of it.

This is the sort of demonstration that was common in the Jewish schools, and perfectly legitimate there.

In the Epistle to the Galatians, Paul bases an argument on the use of the singular *seed* in place of *seeds* in the plural, to show that the promise made to Abraham was limited to one person, Christ. The reasoning turns on the number of the noun, and is rabbinic in its character. The word "seed" in Greek and in Hebrew is a collective noun, like "crowd," and in the original the plural could not have been employed, as that would have signified "crops of grain," whereas the word *seed* in the singular has a recognised significance, meaning "posterity." The error is grammatical, and is a mere quibble possible only to one who had been trained in a school that made quibbles the basis of demonstration.[1]

In the Epistle to the Ephesians, when quoting Psalm lxviii. 18, because the original would not serve his purpose, Paul altered it to suit.[2] "Wherefore he saith, 'When He ascended up on high, He led captivity captive, and *gave gifts unto men.*'" On this text he shows that Christ is the giver of grace to men; and he proceeds to enumerate the gifts conferred in accordance with the prophecy. But David had said nothing of the kind; he had described Jehovah as a victorious monarch returning from battle, and ascending to Zion, receiving on His triumphal march the homage and oblations of all men, even of His enemies.

If the reader will look back to p. 56, he will see that in the rabbinic schools, when a text did not exactly suit, it was deemed allowable to alter it to answer the purpose of the disputant.

Paul is thoroughly Oriental in his indifference to the welfare and sufferings of the brute creation. This comes out in the passage (1 Cor. ix. 9, 10): "It is written in the law of Moses, Thou shalt not muzzle the mouth of the ox that treadeth out the corn. Doth God take care for oxen? Or saith He it altogether for our sakes? For our sakes, no doubt, this is written." He imputes to the Almighty the same insensibility to pity and care for the dumb beast that he possessed. We may safely assert that he absolutely reversed the purport of the command, which was given because the Great Father of All *does* care for the oxen,

[1] Gal. iii. 16.   [2] Eph. iv. 8.

just as Paul's divine Master said that He cared for every sparrow,[1] and for the ravens.[2]

Dr. Geikie says of the condition of beasts in Palestine: "Each animal had its galls and raw places; no horse used to harness in Palestine is without them, for there is no law against cruelty to animals, and no pity in the native heart towards dumb creatures to supply its place."[3]

So incredible to Paul did it seem that there should be any compassion for a poor beast in its Creator, that he puts such an idea aside as undeserving of consideration, and says "no doubt" the command was given only with a view to the well-being of preachers of the Gospel in the far off future, for—it is a *reductio ad absurdum*, "Doth God care for oxen?"

That Paul should have based his arguments on texts is evidence of the bent of his mind, and the arbitrary manner in which he uses these texts, in total disregard of their original purport, is proof that he thought only after the habit acquired in the rabbinic schools; out of that thraldom he never escaped. It did not for a moment occur to one of the exponents of the Law to ask whether the passage on which he built up a superstructure would bear the weight imposed on it, whether the signification forced upon it was at all justified by the context, and whether it did not apply to a totally different condition of affairs and train of thought.

No man was a more thorough-going literalist than Paul. With him the letter was everything; the spirit that had indited it did not concern him. It could not do so. Such a method was beyond the range of Jewish ideas.

[1] Matt. x. 29. [2] Luke xii. 24.
[3] "The Holy Land and the Bible," 1887, vol. i. p. 82.

But he went even further than this. Although trained to read Hebrew, he did not trouble himself to compare the Septuagint text, a wholly unauthorised translation, with the original; and if the former served his purpose, even although a mistranslation, he freely used it. For instance, in the third chapter of the Epistle to the Galatians and nineteenth verse, he quotes a passage from the Septuagint, for which there is no warrant in the Hebrew text, and he uses it to insinuate therefrom the inferiority of the Law, because it was not directly delivered by God, but came through the instrumentality of angels, to a mediator, Moses, whereas the Gospel came by direct revelation. At a somewhat later period this furnished an argument to the Ebionites that the Law had suffered corruption in transit, by interpolation effected by the angels and by men.

As an instance of the manner in which Paul builds upon texts gathered together in random fashion, we may refer to his attempt to show that all mankind was accounted guilty before God, because it was written: "There is none righteous, no, not one; there is none that understandeth, there is none that seeks after God. They are all gone out of the way, they are together become unprofitable. There is none that doeth good, no, not one. Their throat is an open sepulchre; with their tongues they have used deceit; the poison of asps is under their lips; whose mouth is full of cursing and bitterness; their feet are swift to shed blood; destruction and misery are in their ways; and the way of peace have they not known. There is no fear of God before their eyes."[1]

This, which purports to be one solid quotation, is in fact a conglomerate, made up of Psalm xiv. 1-3 (Septua-

[1] Rom. iii. 10-18.

gint version); liii. 3; cxl. 3; x. 7; Isaiah lix. 7, 8; Psalm xxxvi. 1.

In the first passage in this congeries David is expressing his own opinion relative to the men of his time, so far as his limited knowledge went. That is to say, he supposed that because there were bad Jews, and the Philistines were bad, that all the population of the unknown world were at the moment no better. Nor does the text refer to all time, but only to that when David indited this psalm, some one thousand one hundred years before Paul made his quotation. Does it follow because our British ancestors dyed themselves with woad that we are blue?

The quotation from Psalm cxl. is most inappropriate. This is the context:—

" Deliver me, O Lord, from the evil man; preserve me from the violent man; which imagine mischiefs in their heart; they have sharpened their tongues like a serpent; adders' poison is under their lips."

The quotation has nothing whatever to do with the general guiltiness of mankind in the sight of God, in all time and everywhere. It describes the personal enemies of David, and gives expression to his feelings toward them at a particular moment of trouble. It is the same with the quotation from Psalm xxxvi. It proves nothing. In it is a description of the wicked man, as a type, and there is not a word to imply that all mankind came under the designation.

That all the sons of Adam, Jew and Gentile, were guilty before God, that is true enough, and no man can honestly look into his own heart and not see therein the writing of condemnation. But the mode in which Paul set to work to establish this truth in characteristically Jewish.

ST. PAUL'S MODE OF ARGUMENT

Biographers and commentators have been quite incapable of bringing themselves to contemplate Paul's reasoning from the only point of view from which (knowing what we do of his inherited qualities of mind, and of the system of education he underwent) we are justified in considering it.

Dean Farrar says: " It would take a long time to read all that has been written about them (Paul's ideas as developed in the Epistle to the Romans) in interminable pages of dreary exegesis, drearier metaphysics, and dreariest controversy. Traducianist and Pelagian, Calvinist and Armenian, Sublapsarian and Supralapsarian, Solifidian and Gospeller, Legalist and Antinomian, Methodist and Baptist, have wrangled over them for centuries, and strewn the field of polemical theology with the scattered and cumbering *débris* of technicalities and anathemas."

But, it may well be asked, how could this have been possible, had Paul written so clearly as to be generally intelligible, had his argument been such as could be followed by Occidental minds, and had his propositions not been contradictory according to the canons of logic of general acceptation?

Theologians have failed to see this, and those occupying opposed camps have each read into St. Paul's words what it appeared to them he ought to have said, or that he must have said, and in his ambiguities have found material for conflicting doctrines.

Take, for instance, his famous antithesis of faith and works, over which theologic war has raged for nearly two thousand years.

Paul opposes obedience to the Law, which he calls works, to belief in God through Christ, which he designates faith.

But the opposition is purely fallacious. It is a statement of antithesis where no logical antithesis exists, for it is an opposition propounded between a motive for conduct, and conduct itself. Let us for a moment consider the Jew seeking justification by works; that is how Paul puts it. The works are done in obedience to the revealed will of God, together with certain acts not directly revealed, but supposed to be consonant with revelation, as arising in a new condition of life for which no regulations were formerly made when the Law was imposed.

Why did the Jew obey? Why was he so scrupulous to conform his whole life to the Law? Solely because he believed in God, believed in His revelation. No men ever led such a life of faith as did the Jews. It was through faith that they received the Law; through faith that they clung to its every word and letter; through faith they rested in the promises of the Messiah. In faith they studied the Scriptures, in faith they offered the sacrifices, in faith submitted to the minutest discipline of the Law. By faith they resisted to blood against Antiochus, and fell as martyrs under the Asmonæan dynasty. By faith they stood out against the Sadducean compromise with the world power. This was readily enough recognised by the author of the Epistle to the Hebrews, in his magnificent description of faith. When he sought for examples of living, heroic, self-sacrificing faith, he went to those who held to the Law as the commandment of God. The faith of the Jew showed itself in obedience. That obedience was rooted and grounded in faith, and in nothing else.

There was a moment, a transitory moment, in the history of the Jews, when the faith of the Israelite was of a somewhat different character. It was that moment when Moses descended from the Mount, having received the revelation of the will of God. Then, Israel was required to believe in Moses, as the mediator of the Covenant. Nothing more was required for that moment but to accept the messenger of the Covenant. But directly the messenger announced the Law, then, instantly, the obligation to obey began. Thenceforth, a living faith showed itself in obedience. Obedience sprang out of it as the lily out of the bulb, its necessary product. Only if faith became dead did obedience wither.

Paul did not understand this. He overlooked the principle, and saw only the consequence, obedience and that frittered away in observance of minute ordinances—an error of judgment and direction, not a fundamental defect in principle.

On the other hand was the New Covenant. The moment in the history of Christianity was precisely the same as that at which in Jewish history Moses appeared in the plain at the foot of Sinai. People were called on from every nation to believe in the Messenger. Let them accept Christ as the Mediator of the New Covenant. That was all that was required for the moment.

As yet no Gospels had been composed. There was no code, no text, nothing but traditional sayings of Christ passed from mouth to mouth, many genuine, some apocryphal.

Christian faith consisted in acceptance of Christ as the Messiah, the Messenger of the New Testament—what message He brought, what law He imposed—that was uncertain. Till the new code was promulgated nothing more was required than faith in the person and mission of Jesus Christ.

Paul seized on this transitory and initial act of faith in the promulgator, which was evinced of old by the Israelites, and was now required of Christians, and held it up as something diametrically opposed to a manifestation of that faith which accepted the law promulgated. In a word, he contrasted the initiation of life with the manifestation of life at its fullest development.

There was a period in the history of all nations before law was codified; then it was oral and reposed on custom.

The Church was so young that custom in her was only in process of formation. To be true in word and just in act, to be temperate, and chaste, these were customs the Christians were acquiring, and they were taught to acquire them as being consonant with the teaching of Christ in whom they believed.

How uncertain the primitive Christians were as to the customs they must observe is seen by the instance of the Corinthian, who supposed he was at liberty under the Gospel to commit incest with his stepmother.

Paul saw the Jew obeying a code, and he represented him as under bondage, whereas the Christian, at the moment, had no code at all; his law was in process of evolution. But no sooner did a Christian know his duty, learn the will of God, than he stepped into precisely the same position as the Jew. His law would not be niggling and ceremonial, but it would be law all the same, and he would be every whit as much under obligation to obey, if he had a living faith, as was the Jew. The Jew was justified by faith when he submitted to the ordinances of purification because he believed the minister of God, and the Christian was required by his faith to accept the new law as it reached him in driblets, because he believed in Christ, the new Minister of God.

There was confusion of ideas in Paul's mind. A man is justified in drawing a comparison between an acorn and a walnut, but not between an acorn and a walnut tree; or between two pieces of mechanism, but not between the steam loom and the fire which heats the boiler.

Possibly this will be made more comprehensible when stated in tabular form.

| The Christian believes. | The Jew believes. |
| Therefore he obeys. | Therefore he obeys. |

Paul established an opposition between the first term on one side, and the second term on the other; and left out of sight that in the first it is a cause, and in the second it is an effect. It is because it has seemed impossible that the Apostle should have argued so badly, that the antinomian sects that have looked to him as their authority, have attempted to rectify the antithesis, and have replaced his by the following, which is a genuine one:

| The Jew's faith produces obedience to God's commands. | The Christian's faith emancipates him from all restraints and requirements. |

That is to say, the Jew who believes must live in accordance with God's revealed will; but the Christian is at liberty, so long as he has blatant self-assurance, to indulge in all licence with impunity, because the Law no longer binds.

But although such an antithesis is logically sound, yet it is impossible to maintain it as having ever been entertained by Paul; for had he done so—of what use would be all his moral counsels and ethic directions? A thousand passages in his writings show that such a conception of Christian faith was far from his mind. Orthodox theologians have therefore had no difficulty in proving this. But then, however much they may disguise the fact, it is at the expense of Paul's logic.

That initiatory stage in faith, which reposes in the Messenger before the message is received, is necessary in every man; but then it is only the initiation into the Christian life, and that is a life of faith, and of faith working by love, fulfilling God's will, so far as that will is known.

What Paul really desired was to deflect the faith of the Jew from Moses and make it pass through Christ to Jehovah instead of through the ancient lawgiver.

He saw the Jew with a sort of blind faith doing many absurd things, and lading himself with an intolerable burden of ordinances, and he overlooked the reason which was the mainspring of the Jew's conduct, and so totally misrepresented it.

What man in his senses supposes that had Paul descended into the arena to try a fall with a professional wrestler, he would not have been tripped up at the first grip? We do not suppose that he would be miraculously empowered to throw an athlete. Why then are we to expect that in the contest of dialectics, he should be a master, in spite of his limited intellectual capacities, and his miserable education?

In considering him as a controversialist we are bound to take into consideration the terrible disadvantages under which he laboured, and to estimate him, not beside Plato and Aristotle, but beside Hillel and Gamaliel, and we must never look to find him fighting with the weapons which his hands were unaccustomed to hold.

CHAPTER XIX

THE RIOT AT EPHESUS

MAY, A.D. 57

Recapitulation—The First and Second Epistles to the Corinthians—The month of Artemis—Falling off in pilgrims—And in the sale of shrines—Demetrius the silversmith—Riot—The Asiarchs—The Jews in danger—The chancellor allays the disturbance—Paul escapes into Macedonia.

PAUL, as already stated, had sent the First Epistle to the Corinthians from Ephesus. It had gone by the hands of Stephanas, Fortunatus, and Achaicus.

He had endeavoured to induce Apollos to accompany them, but the Alexandrian doctor had seen quite enough of these "saints" of Achaia to decline a second visit.[1] Accordingly Paul sent Timothy, who was to make a circuit by Macedonia. The Apostle himself at first intended to go to Corinth and thence proceed to Macedonia, then return to Achaia, whence he would embark for Palestine with the contributions for the poor of Jerusalem.[2]

As has been said in a preceding chapter, he probably did go there,[3] and was publicly insulted.[4]

He hastened to Macedonia, whence he wrote again. Titus was with him, and he commissioned him to take the letter to the Corinthians.[5]

---

[1] 1 Cor. xvi. 12.   [2] 2 Cor. i. 16.
[3] 2 Cor. xii. 14; xiii. 1, 2.   [4] 2 Cor. ii. 5-11; vii. 12
[5] Professor Ramsay's arrangement is different. He does not sup-

Paul now returned to Ephesus, where he intended to remain till he had collected all the contributions of the Churches, and then to sail for Palestine.

The month of May arrived, dedicated at Ephesus to the Great Goddess, as in Roman Catholic countries it is to Mary.

Ephesus was the Lourdes of Asia Minor, and in the flowery sweet month of Artemisia it was crowded with pilgrims. Many came out of devotion, some for amusement. Not only were the religious sacrifices and processions abundant and splendid, but the theatres, the race-courses, and the amphitheatre, afforded spectacles.

Some year or two before, Paul had written to the Corinthians that a great door was open to him at Ephesus, but that there were many adversaries; and now the storm rose and broke, but it was from an unexpected quarter.

The Temple of Artemis at Ephesus found business for numerous artizans, and a large trade was carried on in little temples or shrines with the goddess represented in it, made of terra-cotta, of marble, and of silver. Some of these were offered in the temple by such as had been miraculously cured by the goddess, like the hearts, &c., that are now hung up round a miraculous Madonna. Others were carried away by the suppliants, like the tokens of mediæval pilgrims, and the medals still sold for the purpose at Romanist shrines; or like the "Remembrances of Scarborough," "of Ventnor," &c., bought and taken home by holiday-makers at English watering-places. During

pose that Paul went into Macedonia till driven away from Ephesus. Moreover, he puts the riot at Ephesus as occurring in January. But it is much more likely to have taken place at the great festival of the year, when disappointment at the falling off in numbers of pilgrims and the diminution in demand for shrines made itself felt.

the last two years the sale of these "*objets de piété*" had very sensibly declined. And in the month of May, 56, there was so poor a demand for these articles in the stalls outside the temple, so little money was turned over, that the craftsmen were in dismay.

Demetrius, master of the guild of silversmiths, took the initiative in organising a riot. He called together the guilds and addressed them: "Sirs, ye know that by this craft we have our wealth. Moreover, ye see and hear that, not only at Ephesus, but almost throughout all the province of Asia, this Paul hath persuaded and turned away much people, saying that they are no gods which are made with hands. Thus, not only is our business in danger of being ruined, but also a risk is run of the temple of the great goddess Diana being despised and her magnificence destroyed, whom all Asia and the world worshippeth."

This appeal to cupidity and superstition succeeded. The artizans, in a fury, swept through the streets roaring out, " Great goddess of Ephesus ! "

They surrounded the house where Paul lodged, but either the Apostle was absent or was too closely concealed for them to find him. Anyhow, he escaped; and the mob laid hold of two of his disciples, Gaius and Aristarchus, and rushed away with them to the theatre.

In the towns of the Roman Empire the theatres were the usual places for the meeting of assemblies. The orators could stand on the stage, and the audience crowded the benches and the pit. The theatre of Ephesus, cut out of the rock of Mount Coressus, would accommodate 25,000 spectators. From the upper town on the height, from the porticoes, and the market-places near the theatre, a crowd collected, and, not knowing what the cause of the commotion was, some cried one thing and some another.

Paul, knowing the danger that menaced his brethren, was eager to take his place in the theatre and obtain their release; but his friends held him back, and by main force retained him out of danger. Some of the Asiarchs also, whose respect Paul had won, sent a message to him on no account to venture into the theatre.

The Asiarchs were the official high-priests of the cult of Augustus. They presided at the games celebrated in the cities, and had to defray most of the cost out of their own pockets. The office was honourable, but costly, like that of high sheriff in an English county. Although there was only one Asiarch at a time, annually appointed, yet the ex-Asiarchs bore the title in courtesy. Clearly these official presidents were men of a liberal and enlightened mind, who despised the vulgar superstition, just as, perhaps, some mayor of Lourdes may conduct a procession of officials to the Grotto, in his sash, whilst laughing in his sleeve at the whole concern.

The riot, however, grew in force, and the crowd became more dense. Some of those who shouted called out that the Jews were at the bottom of the mischief, and so they were. It was they who had drawn proselytes about them, away from idolatry; but Paul had converted a snowball into an avalanche.

The Israelites, in great alarm lest the mob should burst into their dwelling-houses, or ransack their shops, put forth a spokesman Alexander—probably the coppersmith alluded to afterwards by Paul—to turn the brunt of the resentment of the rioters against the Christians.

Alexander, thrusting, elbowing his way through the

THE RIOT AT EPHESUS

crowd, scrambled on to the stage, signed with his hand that he desired to be heard, and gained an audience. But no sooner did the mob recognise that he was a Jew than their howls broke out again: "Great Artemis of Ephesus!"

At last, when they had yelled themselves hoarse, a lull ensued, and the magistrates seized their opportunity to send forward the chief municipal officer, the Chancellor, who kept the town archives and was treasurer for the wealth of the Temple of Artemis. He came out from behind the side-scenes, and, stepping to the front of the stage, ordered silence. The people at once obeyed, and he addressed them: "Ye men of Ephesus, what man is there that knoweth not how that the city of the Ephesians is temple-keeper of the great goddess Artemis, and of the image that fell down out of heaven? Seeing, then, that these things are incontestable, ye ought to be quiet and do nothing rashly. For ye have brought hither these men, which are neither temple-robbers nor blasphemers of your goddess. If Demetrius and his fellow-craftsmen have any complaint to lodge against any one, the sessions are going on, and there are proconsuls; let them settle the matter between them at law. But if you are making any further inquisition about any other matter, it shall be discussed in the regular monthly meeting of the assembly. For I give you this warning, such a turbulent piece of proceeding renders us liable to a charge of sedition, since we are wholly unable to give any rational explanation of this mass meeting."

This douche of cold common-sense sufficed. The rabble dispersed, and Paul was smuggled out of Ephesus and sent off to Macedonia.

Professor Ramsay says: "The more closely we are able to test the story in Acts, the more vivid and true to the situation and surroundings does it prove to be, and the more justified are we in pressing closely every inference from the little details that occur in it."[1]

[1] "The Church in the Roman Empire," 1895, p. 173.

CHAPTER XX

THE EPISTLE TO THE ROMANS

A.D. 56—57

Paul's visit to Macedonia—The mission to Illyricum—The origin of the Church in Rome—Condition of the Church there—In an unorganised state—No hostility to Paul—First symptoms of party strife—The Epistle to the Romans—Its tenour—Paul's scheme—The divisions of the Epistle—Adoption by faith—The moral difficulty—Never met by him—The Jew supplanted by the Gentile—Confusion in the conclusion of the Epistle—No evidence in Paul's Epistles to show that the Gospel had made any impression on the well-to-do classes —The burning questions of the ensuing centuries—Untouched by him—The question of family rites—The question of official rites— The question of education—The question of the classic literature— The question of military service—Two schools formed, Opportunists and Irreconcilables—These questions not raised at the time when Paul wrote—His converts were of no social position.

FROM Ephesus, Paul probably escaped in a small coasting vessel to Macedonia. It is quite possible that the visit to Troas mentioned in the second Epistle to the Corinthians took place then, in which case this epistle was not written till after his arrival in Philippi subsequent to the riot. But I have assumed that it was written on a previous hasty visit. It is, of course, very difficult, with the scanty notices we have, to come to a conclusion relative to the exact date of this letter. In Macedonia Paul was among friends, and he used his stay there during the summer in confirming the Churches and in spreading the Gospel as far to Illyricum. He does not seem to have gone there himself, but to have sent missioners there along the Egnatian way. Part of Illyricum was in the province of Macedonia, and part in that of Dalmatia. As, later on, Titus is spoken of as in Dalmatia [1] it is probable that he was then—in A.D. 62—superintending the Churches, the beginnings of which date from this summer of 56.

Paul himself, after a stay in Philippi and Thessalonica went through Hellas, that is to say the Greek portion of the Macedonian province. He spent the three winter months of December 56, and January and February 57, in Corinth.

It was during this time that Paul wrote his Epistle to the Romans.

To understand this letter we must glance at the beginning of the Church in the Imperial City.

In Rome there had been for long a large Jewish colony. Yearly some had made their way to Jerusalem, bearing the Temple offering, and yearly Jews from Jerusalem had come on business, private or public, to the capital of the Empire.

Even as early as the great Pentecost when the Spirit had descended on the Church, there had been proselytes of Rome in the Holy City; and not only did the Jews come frequently to the centre of their nation and faith, but so also did such as believed and had become neophytes. Such had heard the preaching of the Apostles, and many believed.

The result was a great commotion among the Jews at Rome, so great that the Emperor Claudius interfered and ordered the banishment of all Jews out of Rome and Italy. This was about the year 52. In consequence Priscilla and

---

[1] 2 Tim. iv. 10.

Aquila had gone to Corinth, where Paul made their acquaintance and learned from them the condition of Christianity in Rome.

The edict of Claudius was imperfectly executed, or fell into abeyance, and the Jews rapidly returned or emerged from their hiding-places, resumed their business and refilled their synagogues. But the rupture between Christians and Jews was aggravated, and probably just as at the Reformation in a German town, some churches were taken possession of by the Lutherans, whilst others were retained by the Catholics, so was it in Rome now, some synagogues fell into the power of that party which believed the Messiah *had* come, but would return, whilst others remained under the control of such as looked to His coming and disputed the first advent. Such congregations consisted of a nucleus of Jews, with an outer ring of circumcised proselytes and a further margin of uncircumcised hangers-on.

No Apostle had been among them, but it is very possible that Peter, in Jerusalem, may have paid special attention to these Roman pilgrims. That Peter had done more than this, that he had even sent them properly authorised teachers, and had ordained elders for them, can not be allowed. Paul's epistle excludes such a possibility. He built on no other man's foundation.

The Church at Rome consisted of a body very much like the amorphous body in Jerusalem. It formed a party in the Synagogue rather than a Church. The Gentile converts had all been thoroughly Judaised in mind by having been grounded in the Scriptures, supplemented probably by the apocryphal Sibylline Oracles, and had all come to expect a Messiah.

Consequently, when Paul wrote his Epistle to the

believers in Rome, it is couched in such a form, and contains such ideas, as are suitable only to those saturated through and through with Judaism. The Church was composite, but its Gentile element had ceased to think and feel as Gentiles, or Paul was incapable of addressing them in any other way.

But although thus steeped in Judaism, it was not Judaising. It was far less inclined to stickle at ceremonial according to the Law than other Churches, probably because the Jews of Rome had been more lax and liberal in opinion than those elsewhere.

A disturbance there had been in 52, over the question whether Messiah had or had not come, and whether, if He had, Christ had been that Messiah, but the Jews had received a salutary caution from Claudius not to make their quarrels public, and they were indisposed to incur a fresh edict of banishment.

In the Epistle to the Romans we see no trace of that personal feeling in Paul which is so conspicuous in his addresses to the Galatians and Corinthians.

He does not write to the Church as being in any way hostile to him.[1] He expresses his longing to visit a community in such good repute, and to preach the Gospel among the believers in Rome.[2]

He gives to the members all the gracious appellations, which he lavished usually on only his most docile adherents. They are "called to be saints," "called in Jesus Christ." He desires to be with them that he may confer on them some spiritual largess, probably the grace of an apostolic ministry, which they were without, and which was the first element of vertebrate life.

[1] Rom. i. 6–8.   [2] *Ibid.* i. 15.

In the whole course of the Epistle, he writes as though there were no ill-feeling whatever among the Romano-Jewish believers against him. He labours to instruct, not to refute. Those whom he rebukes are the heathen converts who boast of their privileges as exalting them above the Jews;[1] but also the Jews who hug themselves in their hereditary privileges, and do not live after the Spirit.[2]

It is apparent from this that the progressive and stationary parties were about to take shape in this Roman community, though, so far, they had not become active and embittered against each other. As yet the great question of the abrogation of the Law had not been thrown as the apple of discord into their midst.

Possibly the Jewish and pagan converts in the capital of the world knew very little of Paul and of his system, but had they felt keenly on any of these matters which stirred the other Churches, he could not have written to them in the terms he employed: "I beseech you, brethren, that ye strive together with me in your prayers to God for me; that I may be delivered from them that do not believe in Judea, and that my service, which I have for Jerusalem, may be accepted of the saints; that I may come unto you with joy by the will of God, and may with you be refreshed."[3]

Since Paul had written his Epistle to the Galatians he had reconsidered the arguments he had used in it; some he strengthened, some he laid aside. In the Epistle to the Romans we have his matured thought, and as it was not written when he was in a condition of great excitement, was probably revised before despatch. The Epistle is

[1] Rom. xi. 17-24.   [2] *Ibid.* ii. 17-23.   [3] *Ibid.* xv. 30-32.

divided into three parts; the first contains his scheme of salvation, the second is his justification of his method of provoking a schism, and carrying off the converts from the Synagogue, and the third is an attempt to safeguard morality.

His scheme is summed up in this: "The power of God unto salvation, to every one that believeth; first to the Jew, then also to the Greek. Therein is the righteousness of God revealed from faith to faith, so that the just may live by faith. But the wrath of God is revealed against all unrighteousness."[1] The Apostle was unable to think clearly, and consequently could not express what he felt in intelligible form.

1. (Chaps. i. 18–iii. 31). Paul shows two things, (*a*) that Paganism plunged man in misery and utter corruption, without giving him any means of escape. Consequently man is driven under Paganism to despair, and in the darkness and wreckage of all morality cries out for grace and light—light to show him the truth, grace to help him to attain to righteousness. (*b*) That the Jew is shown by the Law the way of righteousness, but that he is unable to follow it, being destitute of grace. In his pride he despises the Pagan, yet is in himself no better off. Although he may observe the Law outwardly in the letter, yet he sins against its spirit. He also can do no other than despair, unless he turns to the Gospel and appeals for grace to help him. Paul then takes up his old argument (chap. iv.) employed in the Epistle to the Galatians, that God made promises, and that trust in the promises, that is to say, faith, admits into a new covenant, *i.e.*, into adoption into the family of God. Abraham and David believed

[1] Rom. i. 16, 17.

God, and thereby were justified, that is to say, were brought into spiritual sonship. So also any men, out of every nation, who believe, pass by this method into the spiritual family.

Then he goes on to show (chap. v.) that the carnal life of obedience to the Law was barren, but that the spiritual life under the Gospel is not sterile; it consists of a development of energy productive of good fruit. The condition under the Law was negative, that under the Gospel is positive; the former consisted in abstention from evil, the latter in active fulfilment of righteousness.

2. Paul was next brought face to face with that crucial objection which met him at every turn, and which made him writhe and twist to escape, but ever ineffectually. If, it was contended, the Law was set aside as no longer of cogency, then how was common morality to be saved? This he attempted to meet (chaps. vi., vii., viii.).

The answer—any Sunday-school scholar could answer nowadays—never occurred to the Apostle, at all events at this period. That answer would be given by the writer of the Epistle to the Hebrews—that the moral law given from Sinai was not, and never could be, repealed. That which was transitory was what led up to and found its interpretation in Christ.

The Epistle to the Hebrews is too able a tract, too closely reasoned, and too lucid to have been written by Paul, unless furnished with the ideas and the argument by a man of superior intellectual discipline, perhaps Apollos.

In the place of this very simple argument, which could be at once laid hold of, and which would have immediately commended itself to the mind, he contrived a wonderful theory. By baptism man passes from death to life, and as sin is a mere creation of the Law, by becoming a child of God through faith, man is wholly emancipated from the Law.

He has emerged into a new life; and so long as he is living the spiritual life, which is holy, he is flying in an upper element, but the moment he sins, his wings lose their buoyant power and he drops back into the region of the Law. The Christian is, in fact, a sort of flying fish, now skimming above the waves of sin, then plunging through the waves, dipped in the bitter waters of the Law; that is to say, he passes his life, now in Life and then in Death, as Paul termed it, at alternate moments.

The theory was as impossible as it was illogical. Sin having nothing but a negative existence in one place, he has no right to speak of it as a positive force in another, as reigning in the mortal body, and exercising dominion over the saints.

That the objection to this system of Paul was not groundless the whole of the history of Christianity has shown. A hideous shadow of antinomianism has dogged it throughout all time. It was manifest in the immoral sects of the apostolic period; nay, it broke out as a plague in Paul's own cherished Church of Corinth, it lingered on through the Middle Ages, it burst into febrile heat at the Reformation among the Anabaptists of Münster and the Adamites and other obscene sects: and all these appealed to the *argument* of Paul and away from his *injunctions*.

Paul had made no provision against self-deception. Nothing was more certain than that some who had begun in the Spirit would come to puff themselves up with spiritual pride, consider themselves in a state of justification, above all need for self-control, above all law, hardened into self-righteousness, and rendered incapable of feeling compunction for sin, however gross, into which they might lapse, become, in a word, dead to all sense of sin.

So long as there is a law of divine authority to regulate the life, whereby to measure the conduct every day—the rule of God's commandments—so long no man can go far wrong without knowing it. But take that rule away and he is deprived of every test.

Paul had no intention to throw open the flood-gates to immorality, and to make of the Gospel a licence to sin. He laboured again and again by his exhortations and moral injunctions to show that he demanded of his converts a godly and decent life. But the law of God and the sentiments of an Apostle of questioned authority were of very different cogency, and human nature is ever prone to find an excuse for getting the shoulder from under the yoke.

I remember whilst I was at Cambridge that the University architect pronounced the tower of St. Mary's to be in a dangerous condition, the foundations giving way, and cracks appearing in the walls. The University Syndicate met and ordered the cracks to be papered over.

Paul seemed, by his argument, to be withdrawing the foundations of the divine Law from under the Church, and then to be plastering over the cracks that gaped with exhortations to good living and avoidance of this and that form of evil.

He did not intend to do what the objectors supposed he was doing, and the rest of the Apostles took good care to ram the foundation blocks more firmly than ever into their places and to bed them in concrete.

3. Paul next addressed himself to another point. He had the foresight to perceive that the Jewish element in the Church was destined to dwindle to nothing, and that the Gentile element would predominate and finally entirely fill the Church. And that this already menaced was seen by others, and it made them, if Jews, very uneasy. Paul undertook to relieve them of their alarm. The Jews said: How can this condition of affairs be according to God's will when He made a perpetual covenant with Abraham? Paul answered (ix. 6-29): It is not for you to ask such a question. God is free to do as He likes with His creatures. Nothing constrains Him to act this way or that.

Nevertheless (ix. 30–x. 21) God is not capricious nor unjust. He did promise, but the Jew has rejected the offer made to him. The salvation of the world by Jesus Christ must be effected, and the means of effecting it has been offered to the Jew. As he declines the office allotted to him he is set aside, and his setting aside is due to himself alone.

He proceeds (xi. 1-28). Nevertheless, God is true. He does not utterly cast away His people. Let them return, at any time, and take up the work they have refused, and God will employ them again and restore them to their own place as the first among the nations of the earth.

This argument is very well put, and admirably worked out.

Paul now turns to moral exhortations and advice to act in all things with charity. The conclusion of the Epistle shows such confusion and dislocation of subjects, that the latter portion of the Epistle has caused great perplexity to commentators who are prepossessed with the idea of logical thought in the head of the writer.

THE EPISTLE TO THE ROMANS

Baur raised great doubts as to the authenticity of chaps. xv. and xvi., and the manuscripts of the Epistle are in disagreement. As we have it the letter has four, even five, conclusions: xiv. 23 is, perhaps, a conclusion; xv. 33 is certainly one. But then we find another in xvi. 20; another again in xvi. 24; and the actual conclusion xvi. 25-27. According to Renan, several copies of the letter had been made and sent abroad, each with its own termination; one to the Church of Ephesus, to which was appended the conclusion xvi. 1-20. As Paul was pleased with his production, and considered his arguments as having some force, he would send copies of the treatise to other Churches beside that of Rome. When, however, the Epistle was taken into the canon then all these several endings were united.

This is possible enough, but it is also quite consistent with the manner of Paul to finish off his Epistle in his own impulsive and hasty manner, and then add codicil after codicil as omissions occurred to him.

None were able to write with more beauty as well as sincerity about the strictness of life that was expected of the Christian, to express with greater force the obligation of charity and the purifying nature of a living faith. Probably no one made much sense out of his tangled arguments; and his Epistles awoke admiration and acquired respect from the moral exhortations alone, and it was due to these that his writings found acceptance and recognition in the canon.

If we search St. Paul's epistles for indications that his preaching had penetrated, even to a small degree, into heathen households of the middle and upper classes, we shall be disappointed. Those questions which must inevitably catch fire so soon as the Gospel passed the threshold and presented itself before men invested with civic and political offices and duties are left untouched.

It is certainly true that Paul advises husbands, wives, and children, as also slaves, how to conduct themselves toward one another, but he barely glances at those complex questions of conflicting obligations that did spring into life and trouble men's minds a very few years later.

He addresses believing wives mated to unbelieving husbands, but without entering into such detail as might guide them in domestic perplexities, and doubtless many of these believing women were, like Eunice, Jewesses. He writes concerning meats offered to idols, but this was a matter of debate among the Jews, and inherited from them by the Christians. He exhorts to absolute submission to magistrates, but gives no directions how Christian officials are to comport themselves. He requires children to be obedient to those set over them, but gives no hint as to the great education question, which speedily became a most difficult and perplexing one.

We will glance—we can do no more—at some of these problems set the believers from the middle and upper classes.

During the centuries in which the ancient paganism had maintained an undisputed and undisturbed hold on the world, it had entered into and tinctured every portion of domestic, civic, military, commercial, and political life.

Religion had hitherto been national, the expression of national unity and national feeling.

In every state, in every city, religion had been the bond that bound men together; and to withdraw from the established cult was to be irreligious, and this was but another word for being unpatriotic.

Foreign religions were tolerated because the Romans regarded the gods of Greece, of Gaul, of the Germans and Syrians, of the Anatolians and the Egyptians, as the divinities presiding over these peoples, whom it was impolitic to offend. Jehovah was viewed in no other light than as the local divinity ruling the Jews. The Romans firmly believed that Rome was great and sovereign because of her piety to the gods. "It is because they have attracted to them the gods of the universe," said Cæcilius to Octavius, "that the Romans have become masters of the world."[1] Neglect of the obligations of the State religion drew down disaster on the armies of Rome.

But Christianity was not a national religion at all; it was universal and exclusive. One who refused homage to the gods of Rome, and to swear by the divinity of Cæsar, was looked upon as disloyal. Religion was, above all, a political expression.

It is obvious that the diffusion of the new faith must provoke great heartburnings, and profoundly embarrass its professors coming out of paganism, if they were members of a constituted household and had a civic position. It was a nice and delicate matter to unravel social and political duties from those which were religious.

A vagabond rabble made up of drifting material—freedmen, hucksters, half-breeds, day-labourers—might do pretty much what they liked; the State concerned itself little if at all about them and their attendance at sacrifices. But it was otherwise with settled citizens.

The family bond was religious. The cult of the divine

[1] Min. Felix, *Octav*. vii. 6.

ancestor was the domestic tie, and not necessarily community in blood. And a common devotion tied the families together into the *gens* or clan, in which each head of a household maintained his position by performing a stated sacrifice on a particular day.

To touch the domestic religion, to refuse honour to the family hearth, was to paralyse the principle of cohesion by which the family and the community were tied together.

There was not an act of family life that was not associated with religion, with sacrifices. No visitor entered the house without saluting the presiding deity. At every meal the *Penates* were invoked, and a portion of the meal was set aside for their altars. No cup was drained till a libation had been poured to their honour.

No event of domestic life was unconnected with a sacrifice: a birth, the assumption of the manly toga, a marriage, and a funeral. There were numerous festivals when the doors were garlanded, the images were burnished and decorated, and day and night lamps were kept alight before them.

What conduct was to be observed by a believing wife, child, slave, in the midst of such a network of pagan observance?

No householder, no man who was a citizen, could emancipate himself entirely from the ritual acts that preceded and closed every municipal function. The magistrate, the petty official, the soldier, the sailor, the surveyor, the clerk, could not withdraw from the ceremonies connected with their offices, especially such as were in honour of the prince, without proclaiming themselves disaffected.

The State religion consisted of rites to which very little

significance was attached, like the saluting the colours or bowing to the throne nowadays, and the title of *Divus* attributed to the Emperor was as unmeaning as that of " Your Worship " given to a Lord Mayor or a magistrate on the bench, and the Romans could not understand how the Christians scrupled to conform to what were to them hollow formalities. They were regarded as perverse, if not deranged. Even clement and tolerant governors, such as Pliny the younger, lost patience, and dealt with them as unreasonable and wrong-headed.

What were the Christians to do?

In the household and forum, what was to be their attitude? It was impossible to withdraw entirely from association with the heathen. Were they in their daily intercourse to make a misery of family life—by protests at every moment, at every meal, by disregard of domestic rites, by refusing participation in family festivals? Was the believing wife to extinguish the sacred fire and knock the heads off the idols? Was the soldier to refuse respect to the Eagles? Was the clerk to throw up his calling? the senator to desert the comitia? the magistrate to vacate his chair? Must the merchantman refuse to import frankincense, and the shipmaster to alter the title of his vessel when under the protection of a heathen deity? Was the farmer to refuse to deliver cattle in the market if aware that they were bought for sacrifice? And the quarryman to throw away his tools because the block he was cutting was destined for a temple? Were sculptors, painters, metal-workers, to abandon their trades and throw up their means of livelihood because pagan imagery was ordered of them?

What was to be done about the education of the

children? Could they be sent to school where they were taught to read the poets whose every line savoured of heathen mythology? Were the youths to sacrifice the advantages of a polite education because the philosophers and rhetoricians knew not God?

No sooner did Christianity find admission into a family in easy circumstances than this difficulty had to be resolved. The education in the schools was anti-Christian, in so far that it laid hold of the young minds and ardent imaginations, filled them with pagan pictures, and gave them their direction. The consequences were serious. The child, to whom, as St. Augustine said, the wine of error had been poured forth, learned to love it all his days. Those who had read Plato and Homer, Cicero and Virgil, could not forget them. As St. Jerome cried out: "Will you have us cast out of our memories what we acquired as children? I can swear that I have read no profane authors since I left school; but I read them then. Must I drink the waters of Lethe and recollect nothing?"[1]

In what way was all the splendour of intellectual achievement of the past to be regarded? Were all the writings of the poets, the philosophers, the orators, to be burnt or placed under ban? St. Paul did indeed write, "Beware lest any man spoil you through philosophy," and coupled it with "vain deceit."[2] But he warned against what he imperfectly understood; and St. Augustine later said: "To pretend that one must fly philosophy is to command one not to love wisdom";[3] and when Julian the Apostate forbade Christians to use the schools of philosophy and dialectics, St. Gregory Nazianzen retorted: "What! is there no other Hellene but thyself?" He felt

[1] *Adv. Rufinum*, i. 50. [2] Col. ii. 8. [3] *De Ordine*, i. 32.

that the literature of the past was the common heritage of the Greek race.

And the entire Roman world was saturated with literary culture; it had lived long in an atmosphere of intellectual activity, and had ripened into high civilisation. To every well-bred and well-to-do man the classic authors were so familiar that they formed an integral portion of his mental life, and it was not possible for him to eliminate this, nor did he wish to do so. Unless he were narrow as a wire, he recognised that he was a nobler, more liberal-minded man through his acquaintance with them. The Greek, the Roman had no relish to see his sons brought up in barbarian ignorance.

When St. Ambrose wrote a treatise for the clergy of the Catholic Church, he took as his model the *De Officiis* of Cicero. When St. Augustine was in retirement at Cassisiacum, in the morning after prayer, he lectured on Virgil. St. Clement wrote his "Patchwork" to show that the poets, philosophers, scientists of old wrote as the Spirit of Truth taught them, and that they fell short of perfection only in this, that the knowledge of Christ did not co-ordinate and give direction to their energies. St. Jerome excused his employment of heathen literature by a quotation from Deuteronomy, which allowed a Jew to take to him a heathen woman if he first cut her hair and pared her nails; and St. Augustine assumed that the spoliation of the Egyptians by the Jews warranted Christians in appropriating all the best things of classic antiquity.

There was another question full of difficulty that speedily came to the fore.

Singularly enough, the army was a seed-bed of Christianity. It was long since the armies of Rome had been made up of Latin citizens. The soldiery was recruited from the conquered races. In the reign of Tiberius a Gaul had said of the Roman army: "In it there is nothing worth aught save that which is foreign."[1]

It was probably due to this fact that so many Christians were to be found among the military; they were drawn from districts where the Church had already obtained a strong foothold.

Tertullian condemned the bearing of arms by a believer, and he gave two reasons for this. Christ had bidden Peter put up his sword into the sheath; and in war a believer might be required to fight a brother in Christ who was among the barbarians. Tertullian repudiated everything like patriotism and loyalty to Rome. "We," said he, "have our republic; it is the entire world." He wrote a treatise on the matter, so important and harassing had the question become.

Some soldiers, full of zeal, laid down their arms at the feet of their officers, and declared that their faith forbade them to fight. They were at once put to death. Even after Constantine, St. Martin, who was a centurion, presented himself before the Emperor on the eve of a battle, and said: "I am a soldier of Christ; I am not allowed to draw the sword."

But St. Augustine, with his healthy common sense, said that if the empire was to be maintained, and Roman civilisation was not to become a prey to the barbarians, the consciences of the soldiers must be reassured. He quoted Christ as bidding them do violence to none and rest content with their pay. He never bade them lay

[1] Tacit. *Ann.* iii. 40.

down their arms and turn traitors to their country and prince. This remained the doctrine of the Church, and in A.D. 314, shortly after the victory of Constantine, a council at Arles pronounced anathema against those who refused to serve in the army.

But this judgment was arrived at only after much Christian blood had been shed through refusal of soldiers to fight, because they conceived it to be against their conscience.

How much misery of mind, what tortures of doubt, would have been obviated had St. Paul spoken on the duties of those placed where they were dragged in opposite directions, in apparent conflict of allegiance and obligation!

It may be said that no sooner was Christianity the religion of men and women of settled position than two schools arose—one narrow, remorselessly logical, opposed to compromise, and the other ready to make some concessions to social and civil usage. In a word the dispute raged— Were believers to be opportunists or irreconcilables? Was Christianity to leaven society or to withdraw out of it?

The question occupied men and women in the falling Empire and in growing mediævalism, and the irreconcilables ran from the world and hid their heads in hermitages and monasteries.

Exactly the same controversy arose at the time of the birth of Puritanism. The same raged at the beginning of this century between the Evangelicals and old-fashioned Churchmen.

For three centuries Christianity was tortured with perplexity as to this point. There were those disposed to soften asperities, to look upon social usages that may once have had a pagan origin as mere empty ceremonial, to consider the philosophers as searchers after truth, and old religions as containing sparks of verity, to reduce to a minimum all resistance.

A century after Paul appeared the first Latin Christian writer of note, Tertullian, and his energies were directed to answer the questions that boiled up in the community, bred schisms, and vexed consciences. He answered them from the puritanical standpoint.

There is hardly a sign in St. Paul's writings that any clash of duties had taken place, or was expected would take place. The conclusion to be drawn from this seems to be that no converts had been made from any of the respectable classes, that no pagan households of the smallest moment had been agitated by the breath of the new faith.

In Asia Minor, in Syria, in Macedonia, very probably the State religion was not so exacting as in Italy. Nevertheless, a citizen who had house and property, who was eligible to a municipal office, could not fail to find himself immersed in a sea of difficulties if he accepted Christ, and to need a hand to direct him. He would require instruction as to how far he should give way to custom and where he should draw the line and make a stand.

Tertullian declared that no Christian could accept a magistracy, which obliged him to be continually going to the temples, assisting at sacrifices, giving games; in a word, to be daily showing his adhesion to the established religion. And he added—that to nothing was the Christian more strange than to the political affairs of his country.[1] And yet he had but just said: "We fill the senate and the forum."[2]

[1] *Apol.* 38. [2] *Apol.* 37.

What he meant was that there were a considerable number of believing decurions and duumvirs in the provincial towns and in the municipalities of Italy, and that there were even some Christians in the Roman senate.

But all did not view the matter of compliance with the formalities of office in the same light as Tertullian. And it was because there was so lenient a spirit in the Church that this puritan seceded from it to Montanism.

The Church was well aware that unless some concessions were made she could hardly hope to gain admittance into the higher classes of the Roman world, she must be content to be the religion of a class only, and that the class of the Have-nots and Know-nothings. It is, however, to be presumed that the rich and noble and intellectual have souls as well as the rag-tag; and the Church would have proved almost as narrow as Mosaism had she confined her mission to the poor and ignorant. To be catholic she must appeal to and gain all classes.

Moreover, she saw that if some of her sons occupied high offices they might prove useful to their brethren. Towards the beginning of the reign of Diocletian the Council of Elvira was concerned with this delicate question. It maintained that those Christians who accepted the office of *flamen* and presided at sacrifices were excommunicate, but the bishops decreed that Christians might be invested with municipal offices, as duumvirs, and assist at the pagan ceremonies inseparable from the office. They required only that during their year of office they should not enter the assemblies of the faithful, but that on leaving they should be suffered to return to communion without any preliminary penance.

However, the question was one that gave great trouble.

We find that a number of noble houses in the second century disappear from official life, and we would have supposed that they had become extinct did we not find their names continued in the Catacombs. This shows that such households did hold aloof from all participation in the political and municipal life of their country as unsuitable for them in their new religion.

Nevertheless men of rank and wealth could not always, however much they desired it, thus withdraw into privacy. The municipal law of Salpensa, discovered a few years ago, contains a provision that such persons as were eligible, but shirked their responsibilities, should nevertheless be elected and required to discharge the duties of the office. It was, therefore, possible for a Christian citizen to be appointed magistrate against his will, and at once he was forced to decide whether he could at all yield to official ritual, or how far he could do so. A law of Marcus Aurelius, inserted in the Digest, mentions decurions who accept their functions voluntarily, and others upon whom these offices were forced.

It will, therefore, be seen that a case of conscience arose, and that of great importance, the moment that Christianity ceased to be a ferment among the baser sort, and among mere foreigners, Jews and Orientals.

We know what the result of the infusion of Christianity was into Roman society in the fourth century. The result was not what perhaps might have been anticipated; it was a compromise at every point. The Church made great concessions to the laws and usages of society; she was forced to this whether she liked it or not, and had St. Paul had the faintest anticipation that the old pagan *régime* would be supplanted by that of the Gospel in the Roman world, he would have given instructions for conduct at such an eventful period of transition.

Had he, indeed, been able to sow the seed of life in one single household of a respectable class, immediately the questions that have been noticed would have flashed out as sparks, when flint and steel are brought together.

But there are no indications of anything of the sort in his writings. No suggestions are made for guidance when the conflict began.

On all such matters he remained silent. That he should have passed these questions over, shows that they had not manifested themselves. If they had not, then it was due to the fact that the Gospel had not begun to ruffle even the surface of Roman life; that it was confined to such persons as were outside consideration, who were not citizens, were without means or standing. His converts can have consisted only of Jews, half castes, freedmen, pedlars, runaway slaves, vagrants from Syria and Anatolia who drifted from town to town, the scum of Levantine trade.

I repeat he cannot have even touched the settled classes, or at once the difficulties would have presented themselves which did appear later, and troubled the Church and divided men's minds. That the enormous bulk of the believers did belong to the unattached at a much later period is quite certain. Cæcilius says in the third century, "The Christians are made up of the very dregs of the population."[1] They are all of them ignorant, unlettered, and wholly devoid of culture.[2]

To such as these Christianity gave a hope, a home, and consolation, such as the selfish, cruel, and contemptuous

[1] Min. Felix, *Octav.* xxxi. 6. [2] *Ibid.* v. 4; vi. 4; xii. 7.

pagan world could not offer; and it was these ignorant and despised individuals who were predestined to carry the Gospel into every rich and noble household; even into Cæsar's family. This despised rabble would prove the lever that would upset paganism; and what I contend for is, that it was with this rabble of outcasts, and waifs and strays that Paul began, and that when he wrote his Epistles he had done nothing whatever to touch the lettered and settled population of the Roman world. He saw the Gospel sown only in such a population as may be found in Houndsditch and the Borough; not for three centuries did it work upwards to reach a class represented in London by the West End, nay, even by the villa residents of Lewisham and Putney.

That it worked upwards at all and smote paganism with death, and then transformed the face of the East and West, and created new social life, new political organisations, a new literature, new philosophy, new arts and sciences, and gave to hard-hearted mankind a new, pitiful—ay, and to sensuous mankind a clean heart—that is, in itself, a most cogent proof of the divine origin of Christianity. A wondrous thing indeed. The slave and outcast element that had been a festering moral ulcer in society became instead its spring of health and enlightenment. Where, when, beside, has such a moral miracle been seen?

CHAPTER XXI

THE VOYAGE TO JERUSALEM

APRIL AND MAY, A.D. 58

Paul's plans—A plot to murder him at sea—He arranges for a deputation from all his Churches to visit Jerusalem—Himself visits Philippi—Sails for Troas—The Agape and Eucharist—The origin of the former—The hour of supper shortly after midday—The guild meetings—The Synagogue service of Farewell to the Sabbath—The Agape service identical—Disorderly scenes—The Agape suppressed—Paul at Troas—Eutychus—The Lord's Supper—The traces of the Agape in the Eucharistic service—Doubtfulness of a miracle at Troas—Paul continues his voyage—Arrived at Jerusalem.

PAUL had hoped to have been in Jerusalem for the Passover, with the money collected in Galatia, Macedonia, Achaia, and the province in Asia, for the relief of the necessities of the poor at Jerusalem.

But he was prevented by the discovery of a plot for his assassination. He had purposed sailing from Cenchræa in one of the pilgrim vessels that started for Palestine from all parts of the Mediterranean in the early spring.

But the Jews, who hated him for precisely the same reason as did the craftsmen of Ephesus, because he damaged their business, had schemed to have him murdered on board ship and thrown into the sea. They dared not attack him on land after the rebuff they had met with from Gallio, but the captain of the pilgrim ship would be too much interested in his Jewish passengers, their fares, and the chance of taking them back again, to refuse such a trifle as to allow them to get rid on the way of an obnoxious companion.

Learning this, the faithful sent Paul hastily away into Macedonia, there to spend his Easter with his "true yokefellow," and other attached friends. He had with him a considerable party of delegates from the Churches, Sopater of Berœa, Aristarchus and Secundus of Thessalonica, Caius of Derbe, Tychicus and Trophimus of the province of Asia, Timothy likewise as the representative of the Macedonian Churches. He himself would conduct this train and marshal them. Paul evidently intended to make an impression on the Apostles and believers in Jerusalem by this embassy from all the Churches of his foundation, all furnished with liberal contributions. He gave orders to the delegates to make of Troas the place of assembly. He for his part went to Philippi to bid there a tender farewell to his dear friends, a farewell that might be for ever, as he had made up his mind to visit Rome after having been to Jerusalem, and even to go thence further west, into Spain.

If Professor Ramsay is right in believing the year to have been A.D. 57, then the Passover fell on April 7; as Paul could not be at Jerusalem for the highest festival he purposed arriving there for Pentecost, that fell on May 28. If, however, the year, as is more probable, was A.D. 58, then he would leave Philippi on April 3, the Monday when the eight days of the Paschal Feast concluded.

At Philippi Paul met again Luke, the physician, and induced him to accompany him to Jerusalem, and make an eighth in this demonstration with which he was likely to astonish the Judaisers of the Holy City.

Paul took ship at Neapolis, when the Passover was concluded, and sailed for Troas, the appointed meeting-place of the deputation. Instead of reaching his destination in two days, owing to contrary winds he did not reach Troas under five.

At Troas he encountered fresh delays, probably due to the necessity of taking in a cargo, and the vessel remained there seven days.

On the afternoon of the Sabbath there was the usual assembly of the faithful for the Agape, and for the Eucharist which would follow in due order on the Sunday morning.

The room employed was an upper chamber, such as in a Roman house was given over to be a common dormitory for slaves, but which in the East was reserved for receptions and meals.

At this point it will be of interest to sketch the liturgical service of the Apostolic Church, so far as can be gathered from early sources.

As soon as the Sabbath declined, at sunset the Lord's Day begun. The Christians who had broken with the Synagogue began their service with the Agape, or Cæna Domini, at about 3 P.M. a substitute with them for the Sabbatical afternoon feast of bread and wine in the Synagogue, which closed the services for the seventh day.

The *cœna*, which we have in our version translated as supper, was the Greek δεῖπνον.

The ancients usually contented themselves with two or, at the most, three meals a day. Only gluttons like Vitellius took four. Old people were advised by their doctors to eat thrice in the day, and labourers in the fields also had three meals. But generally speaking there were but two, the *jentaculum* or breakfast, eaten between the hours of 7 and 9 A.M., and the *cœna*, the great meal of the day, that was taken at 1.30 P.M. in winter, and an hour later in summer.

The *prandium* or lunch at 10.30 A.M. was a very light meal, and was partaken of casually. It was followed by the siesta and bath, that preceded the *cœna*. With this meal all the business of the day was over, and amusement began. The tables sometimes remained spread all the afternoon, and the hours of relaxation were spent in talk, in reading, in looking at mimes, and in listening to music. Sometimes a sort of dessert was served as evening fell, and this was called the *vespertina*.[1]

When the Goths overran Europe, they had no taste for idling the entire afternoon, and what they were accustomed to was a heavy meal and a carouse at the close of the day, and then, and then only, did the *cœna* become an evening meal. So St. Isidore of Seville in the seventh century says: "The *cœna* is now the evening meal, in the place of that which the ancients were wont to call the *vespertina*."[2]

The *cœna* was moreover the great feast held by all the clubs or sodalities formed among the freedmen, tradesmen, and artisans of the Roman world. To evade observation and repression the Christians accommodated themselves to the methods of these societies, and escaped observation accordingly. Soon after noon, we must suppose that the believers came from all sides bearing bottles of wine, baskets of bread, grapes, citrons, and oil for the lamps, perhaps also joints of cold boiled or roast meat. When all were assembled, at 1.30 P.M. in winter, never later than

---

[1] See on this Mommsen and Marquardt: "Handbuch d. Römischen Alterthümer," vol. vii.; "Privat Leben d. Römer" (Leipzig, 1879), pp. 257-9, 289.   [2] *Orig.*, xx. 2, 14.

3 P.M., all would adjourn from the *atrium*, where they had saluted each other and inquired about the news, to the upper room where the tables were spread.

In the Roman guild meetings it was customary for the members, as in a modern picnic, to contribute towards the common meal; but sometimes each member brought his own portion and consumed that. This was the objectionable practice at Corinth which Paul forbade. It was no doubt there as elsewhere caused by the Jewish members of the Church desiring to eat only such food as they knew was according to legal prescription, as also to avoid legal impurity by eating with the uncircumcised.

But although the Agape grew up out of a condition of affairs in the Churches of the provinces that were separated from the Synagogue, a condition which provoked such an institution as a substitute for the Sabbatical farewell meal of the Synagogue, it was given a deeper signification, and was treated as a weekly commemoration of the Last Supper which our Lord had eaten with the Twelve, and which had preceded the institution of the Eucharist. As the Synagogue eating of bread and drinking of wine was a farewell to the Sabbath, so was His Last Supper a farewell to the closing dispensation, and His institution of the new rite the inauguration of the new covenant. The service of the conclusion of the Sabbath in the Synagogue was this.

The Psalm of Degrees (cxxviii.) was recited or sung; then ensued a prayer: "Behold, the Almighty is my salvation, Him will I trust and will not fear, for my victory and song are God the Lord, and He will be to me salvation. Ye shall drink water out of the wells of salvation. With the Lord is deliverance, and Thy blessing is upon Thy people. The Lord of Hosts is with us, the God of Jacob is our castle. With Jewry were at one time light and gladness, joy, and happiness. So may it be unto us once more.[1] Therefore I lift up the cup of salvation and call upon the name of the Lord." The chalice is then elevated and blessed in these words: " Praised be Thou, O Lord our God, King of the world, who hast created the fruit of the vine."

The benediction of the bread follows : " Praised be Thou, O Lord our God, King of the world, who hast brought forth bread out of the earth." Next follow blessings pronounced over fragrant herbs, over fire, and over the Sabbath that is waning.

Now, as already indicated, at Antioch, and elsewhere out of Jewry, the believing Jews could not partake of this Sabbath feast and also of the Eucharist with uncircumcised Gentiles, and the latter were altogether excluded from the Sabbatical meal. Accordingly, in synagogues of the Dispersion, on the introduction of the elements, those not qualified to drink of the cup and eat of the bread in the synagogue walked out to some private dwelling, and then and there ate their love feast, independently of the Jews, but with close imitation of the Synagogue rite.

How close this imitation was we know from the "Didache," or "Teaching of the Apostles." When all were present, and the table was spread, then the president blessed, first the cup and then the bread. Over the chalice he said: " We thank Thee, O our Father, for the sacred vine of David, Thy servant, which Thou hast revealed unto us by Thy servant Jesus. Glory be to Thee in all ages." Over the bread he said : " We thank Thee, O our Father,

---

[1] A reference to the delivery of the Jews through Esther and Mordecai.

for the life and the knowledge that Thou hast given us through Thy servant Jesus. Glory be to Thee in all ages. As the particles of this bread were scattered on the mountains, yet have been gathered into one loaf, so may Thy Church also be assembled out of every quarter of the earth into Thy kingdom; for to Thee is glory and power by Christ Jesus in all ages."[1]

To each benediction the congregation responded Amen.

The Sabbatical supper, δεῖπνον, took place before set of sun. No doubt that at first it was so with the nonconforming Jews and the believing proselytes. They had their supper on the Saturday afternoon, at the same time that the Judaising believers along with the true Israelites in the synagogues were partaking of the farewell supper that saluted the retiring Sabbath and the closing week.

But when the Jewish day ended, that of the Christians began, so that their religious exercises commenced on Saturday afternoon with the *cœna*. And when the Church became wholly composed of Gentiles, they doubtless accommodated their hour for the *agape* to that of their ordinary δεῖπνον, or *prandium*, or *cœna*—i.e., from 2 P.M. to 3 P.M.

The work-day was over with Greek and Roman at noon, and the entire afternoon was devoted to amusement, eating and drinking, or lounging. The Christian Agape, beginning some time in the early afternoon, lasted on in a desultory way till dusk, when, as Tertullian says, lights were introduced.[2] Then ensued the singing of hymns, speeches and recitals, much like a harvest-tea or a Yorkshire parish convivial meeting. Some, no doubt, related their experiences, with all the exaggeration calculated to produce an

[1] "Didache," ix.   [2] Tertull. *Apol.*, xxviii.

impression on the audience. In Roman society, poets, orators, and historians read their compositions to an often yawning audience. In the Christian assemblies there were undoubtedly talkers who loved to hear their own voices, and could with difficulty be kept within bounds. At Corinth, and certainly elsewhere, among excitable people, the wine, the heat, the exaltation of emotions led to orgiastic ravings, the jabbering of disconnected unintelligible words, to fits, convulsions, pious exclamations, and incoherent ravings.

Du Chaillu, in his " Land of the Midnight Sun," mentions very similar phenomena as occurring among the Lutheran Laps and Finns on the visit of a schaman.

Among the Greeks the same sort of thing was familiar at the mysteries. At these the initiated took part in a sacred feast, and this was followed by ecstatic raptures and hysterical utterances.

In fact, precisely identical exhibitions take place in all religions, and it would indeed have been extraordinary if something of the sort had not attended the sacred convivialities among the early Christians.

In process of time it was found terribly trying to flesh and blood to continue religious exercises from the afternoon of one day to early morning on the next. The strain on the elders to maintain order and keep down the more effusive members on one side, and to prevent the more stolid from going to sleep, was great; added to this, the actual scandals that occurred forced on a change. In Bithynia the Agape was moved to Sunday afternoon. But it was generally abandoned, and all that has remained of it is traces in the liturgies of all the ancient Churches.

On the occasion of Paul's visit to Troas, nothing

objectionable took place. All were desirous to hear what the Apostle had to say rather than to make their own voices heard.

The evening, instead of being enlivened by hysterical exhibitions, proved to some of the younger members so dull that one, Eutychus, fell out of a window, having gone to sleep. "Paul," we are told, "preached unto them, ready to depart on the morrow, and continued his speech until midnight."

It was during this discourse that Eutychus fell down, and was taken up as dead.

Paul at once broke off his address, descended, embraced him, and assured the friends and relations that he was stunned only. "Make ye no ado; for the life is in him."

As soon as Paul had satisfied himself that the youth was not actually dead, he reascended to the upper room and continued speaking till past midnight. Then, after the prayer of midnight, he celebrated the Eucharist, consecrating the bread and wine set apart from the Agape some hours previously, and this he did about the time when men were wont to take their *jentaculum*, and probably it was as a *jentaculum* that Christ consecrated and distributed to the Apostles before leaving the upper chamber.

But although, as I have shown, the institution of the Agape grew out of circumstances at Antioch, as a substitute for the Sabbatical feast in the Synagogue, yet it is very likely that it had a further and a deeper meaning, and was kept in commemoration of Christ's Last Supper before His death, as already intimated. In the Gospel narratives, both the Supper and the Eucharistic institution are combined, as the sacred rite continued through the evening and night till early the following morning; and so in the

Apostolic Church the rite was all one; it began with the love feast at between 2 P.M. and 4 P.M. on the Saturday and lasted on till dawn on the Lord's Day.

Thus the events of that awful night were represented in sequence:

1. The Paschal or Last Supper was reproduced in the Agape on Saturday afternoon.

2. The foot-washing by Christ continued to be represented by the washing described by Tertullian and following on the Agape.

3. The exit of Judas found its analogy in the expulsion of demoniacs, the excommunicated, and the catechumens.

4. The great address by Christ has become the sermon.

5. The intercessory prayer made by Christ has left its trace in the analogous prayers that find a place in every liturgy. In the English Communion Service it has been displaced.

6. The institution of the Eucharist remains unaltered, save that the great thanksgiving of the primitive liturgies takes the place of the Hallel.

It is hardly necessary to point out that the Eucharistic service, as we have it, as used in the Latin Church, and as it is in the Oriental Churches, shows everywhere indications of being composed of two separate services that have been stitched together, precisely as does our Marriage Service.

These parts are variously called the Pro-Anaphora, the Mass of the Catechumens, and the Ante-Communion Service; and also the Anaphora, the Missa Fidelium, and the Communion Service with Canon.

The reason is that originally they were distinct; the first occupied the Sabbath afternoon, and the second was the service of the Sunday morning.

THE VOYAGE TO JERUSALEM 377

The liturgies of all Christendom preserve this feature. But now the service, instead of lasting thirteen or fourteen hours, is compressed into one short liturgy of the two parts welded more or less incompletely together, but always showing the line of junction.

There were good reasons for this.

1. The long night service gave great umbrage to the heathen, perhaps even to orderly Christians.

2. It was forbidden by Trajan, at least by Pliny in Bithynia, and probably by other proconsuls elsewhere.

3. It was a fruitful source of scandals.

Consequently the entire eating and drinking portion was exscinded, or removed to Sunday evening.

Simultaneously the first portion of the service was thrust forward and made to immediately precede the Eucharistic celebration in the morning.

The Agape consisted of three essential parts.

1. The oblation of the gifts.
2. The blessing of them by the president.
3. The distribution of the gifts.

(1) The oblation, reduced to one of bread and wine, has continued to this day. In the Oriental and Gallican Churches the gifts are then (2) blessed, and sufficient is taken off for the Eucharist.[1] Then (3), in the Gallican Church, on great festivals, the congregation eat of the

---

[1] Since the eleventh century, when wafer bread was introduced, this has not been done in the French Church. In the Eastern Churches and in the Russian Church the portion to be used for the Eucharist is cut off with a lance head. The blessed but unconsecrated bread was called the eulogia. In the fourth century the breads were given to catechumens. They are also called antidora, compensations for the Eucharistic gift, by the Council of Antioch in 341. The same usage continued in England through the Middle Ages, and in the thirteenth century it was forbidden to give them to priests' wives; but at Durham women who

gifts—*i.e.*, partake of the Agape—*before* the Eucharist proper. The wine, indeed, is suppressed, but the blessed bread, taken from the one loaf, is distributed to all, and is eaten seated. But in the Oriental Churches the eating of the blessed bread is deferred till after the conclusion of the Eucharist, when it is handed round to the congregation.

In the ancient Celtic Church in Ireland, and in the Northumbrian Church, and undoubtedly also in Scotland, the same usage prevailed, as we learn from Adamnan's "Life of St. Columba," *d*. 597; and Bede also refers to it in his "Life of St. Cuthbert," who died 687.

Such then is the history of the Agape and of its connection with the Eucharist. I have dwelt somewhat lengthily on it, because this is a matter that has not been made clear by ecclesiastical historians. Writers have formed their conjectures concerning it without any regard to traditional usage, which is often the only means of arriving at the explanation of customs alluded to rather than described at an early age.

We are now able to understand the scene in the upper chamber at Troas, and to follow the entire function from the Sabbath afternoon to the early morning of the Lord's Day.

At daybreak Paul sent on his companions. The ship having to double the promontory of Lectum, would take longer in making the journey than if the road were taken to Assos.

Paul stayed on to the last moment, probably to be assured of the recovery of Eutychus; and the other dele-

were churched received them. These holy breads were often sent from the Cathedral to its dependent parish churches in token of communion and fellowship. It is remarkable that nothing of the sort exists in the Roman Church. Probably the Agape was speedily abolished at Rome.

gates went on by ship. It was only, however, just as he was about to sail, "while they were bidding farewell," as the Bezan reading has it, that "they brought the young man alive, and were not a little comforted."

The temptation to Luke to represent this incident as miraculous must have been great, but his honesty stood the test; he did no more than record the circumstance. We hear nothing further of Eutychus, whether he died in consequence of the injuries he received or whether he recovered.[1] Luke was never again at Troas, as far as we know, and therefore unable to supplement the narrative with further information.

Paul now took the high road, eighteen miles long, through rich oak woods, till he reached the precipitous coast of Assos on the Gulf of Adramyttium. There he rejoined the ship. The vessel stopped every evening because of the wind in the Ægean, which in summer generally blows from the north and dies away in the evening. From Assos the vessel sailed to Mitylene, remained there the night, and next day was wafted to a point on the mainland over against Chios. On the morrow she struck across to Samos, and after making a halt at Trogyllium, came next day to Miletus. She did not put into the port of Ephesus, which was visible at the head of the bay, the great temple gleaming in the sun. The ship passed through the narrows separating the Isle of Samos from the continent, and let down her anchor in the harbour of Trogyllium, under Mount Mycale. Next day it required a very few hours to fan her over to Miletus, where the Mæander pours into the sea.

[1] A Eutychus or Eutychius, was Bishop of Melitene in Armenia, but whether the same is quite unknown.

Here the vessel made a considerable halt, and Paul took advantage of it to send a message to Ephesus to entreat the elders of the Church there to come to him. They at once obeyed. It had been at his own desire that the ship had not halted at Ephesus, as he was in a hurry to reach Jerusalem at Pentecost, and he thought that what business he had to transact would be done more expeditiously at a little distance.

At Miletus occurred that touching parting with the elders, which is so graphically described by Luke.[1]

At length Tyre was reached, where there had been a little colony of believers since the dispersion consequent on the martyrdom of Stephen. Here the vessel unloaded, and for this seven days were taken up. Disciples there "said through the spirit to Paul that he should not set foot in Jerusalem."[2] He, however, disregarded the warning, and went on board ship again, after a day at Ptolemais, and on the morrow reached Cæsarea. Here again a prophet, named Agabus, announced to him bonds and imprisonment at Jerusalem. It needed no prophet to assure him of this.

"After these days, we, having equipped horses, proceeded on our way to Jerusalem. And there went with us also some of the disciples from Cæsarea, conducting us to the house of one Mnason, an early disciple, where we should lodge."[3]

---

[1] Acts xx. 18–38. [2] *Ibid.* xxi. 4. [3] *Ibid.* xxi. 15–16.

CHAPTER XXII

THE RIOT AT JERUSALEM

MAY, A.D. 57

Paul holds that the Day of Grace for the Jew was closed—The Apostles had left Jerusalem—James clings to the first hope—The condition of Judæa—The *Sicarii*—Rebellions—The Sadducæan High-priesthood—The real reason of antagonism against Paul entertained by the Sadducees—The falling off of the Temple toll—Paul's reception by the Brethren—No hostility felt towards him by the Jewish Christians—The proposal made by James—Kindly intended—The Nazarites—Riot caused by the Asian Jews—Paul delivered by the Roman legionaries—The Tribune Lysias—Paul's defence—Before the Council—Attempted assassination—Sent to Cæsarea.

TWICE twelve years had passed, and even more, since the ascension of the Lord, and now none of the Twelve were at Jerusalem, where the Church was presided over by the Lord's brother, James.

Had the original thought of the salvation of Gentiledom through Israel been given up as impossible of attainment? In other words, was the period during which the offer was made to the Jews closed for ever?

Paul thought so, but he stood alone in that conviction. Till the destruction of Jerusalem, we have no reason to conclude that the original design was altered; that is to say, granting that in the divine mind such was the original scheme of salvation for the world.

In his Epistle to the Romans Paul had but recently shown that such a possibility had been, as also his conviction that the Jew had finally closed the door against the accomplishment of this glorious work through him. Paul saw the rise of the tide on every side, and the inevitable disappearance of Jerusalem beneath the flood. It was like the enactment of one of those Celtic myths in which a sealed fountain in a guilty city is opened, whereupon the water issues and continues to flow in ever increasing volume, till the city is sunk beneath it, and all that can be seen of it is by the watcher in certain favourable lights, who perceives the ruin at the bottom of the lake under the crystal waves.

The fact that the Twelve had left Jerusalem shows that they had begun to realise that the time of the extension of the offer to Israel was drawing to its close, and that the whole scheme of evangelisation of the world was about to be profoundly modified.

That James still clung to the hope that yet, before their day of grace closed, the heart of Jewdom might relent and turn to Christ, is natural. It would have been strange had he not hoped on against a growing conviction that the hope was vain.

And till the final signal was given, James continued to combine Christian faith with Mosaic practice. Still the Temple service was attended and the Sabbath observed, but the Sabbath worship preluded that of the Lord's Day.

The condition of affairs in Judæa was, however, becoming intolerable. Felix, the freedman, brother of Pallas, the influential creature of Claudius and Agrippina, was procurator of Judæa. He was a cruel, avaricious and sordid wretch, with the mind of a slave, and untrained like a Roman in the school of governing peoples.

THE RIOT AT JERUSALEM

The land swarmed with pretended Messiahs, or with heralds announcing the coming of the Redeemer of Israel.

Ananias, son of Nebaios, had been nominated by Herod in A.D. 48 to the High-priesthood, but had been deposed, and the place given to Ishmael Ben-Phabi. Nevertheless, on account of his wealth, he possessed great power. His son Jonathan had been assassinated in the Temple by some ruffians hired for the purpose by Felix. Assassins had become an institution in the Holy City. Each faction either maintained its gang of bravoes or hired professional cut-throats as required to get rid of such as were obnoxious. These men penetrated everywhere, into private houses, into the Temple courts, with daggers concealed under their mantles. As Josephus says, every man went in fear of his life.

In the country bands of robbers roamed over the land. At various points rebellion flamed up. Felix sent his troops to repress it, but no sooner was one rising quelled than another broke out.

The most formidable leader of insurrection was an Egyptian Jew who collected a multitude of the dissatisfied in the desert, and led them to the Mount of Olives with intention to capture Jerusalem. But Felix massed his troops in the valley of Kedron, carried the height, and slaughtered thousands of the insurgents as they fled. Others he reserved for crucifixion along the highways.

Those who had managed to escape rallied and inaugurated a guerilla warfare, vastly irritating and difficult to suppress. The bands swept the champagne, burning the mansions of the Sadducees and the villas of the Roman residents. The sons of Ananias were men of wealth and power, and resented their exclusion from the High-priesthood and other positions of emolument about the Temple. The regnant and the deposed priestly families had their gangs of bravoes, and street fights were of daily occurrence, and people and Levites took sides in the frays.

The Sadducæan priesthood considered that it was defrauded of its tithes, and sent bodies of men armed with clubs to carry off the grain from the barns and threshing-floors of the defaulters. No reverence was felt by the people for the ambitious rival prelates. They commented on their pride, their lavish expenditure in dress, their gluttony and their licentiousness. All knew them to be alike disbelievers in the sacredness of their office.

The state of affairs in Jerusalem was much like that in Liège, Mayence and Cologne, when rival prince-bishops contested, sword in hand, for the episcopal chair, or like Rome when Damasus and Ursicinus were rival pontiffs, cursing and excommunicating each other.

Such was the condition of the Holy City when Paul arrived there for the feast of Pentecost. He well knew the dangers that awaited him. Those men of Corinth who had sought to compass his murder on the seas were there. Pilgrims from Ephesus were there also; so likewise the men whom he had affronted in Galatia.

When Paul had written to the Romans, he had begged them to pray that the alms he was bringing from the Churches might be well received.[1]

He had good cause for misgiving.

The Temple toll, usually mounting to a considerable sum, sent annually from all parts, wherever there was a colony of Jews and a cluster of proselytes, was vastly reduced in amount. It was now but a moiety of what it had been.

[1] Rom. xv. 30, 31.

For some time the fund had been dwindling, and it could not fail to be noticed that the falling off was from precisely those places where Paul had laboured.

The Sadducæan High-priesthood was not slow to note this, and at once instituted inquiries. Those who handed in the diminished toll had their ready explanation. Paul of Tarsus everywhere drew away the entire body of believing Gentiles, and even some of the Jews, so that these no longer shed their contributions into the Temple chest. Not only so, but he was outbidding them everywhere, and making it impossible for them to gain any converts to Judaism.

Paul was conscious that this would be a cause of irritation against him, but he hoped that the large sum collected for the poor of Jerusalem might meet with consideration and disarm resentment. He was much mistaken. The Sadducees did not care for the poor; what they wanted was the fingering of the Temple toll.

"And when we were come to Jerusalem," says Luke, " the brethren received us gladly."[1]

Next day, Paul and the delegates of the Churches went to the house of James, where he and the presbyters of the Church of Jerusalem were assembled to receive them.

After the usual Oriental salutations had been exchanged Paul "declared particularly what things God had wrought among the Gentiles by his ministry. And when they heard it, they glorified the Lord."

Dean Farrar says: "As we read the narrative of the Acts in the light of the Epistles, it is difficult to resist the impression that the meeting between the Apostle and the elders of Jerusalem was cold. It is, of course, certain that

[1] Acts xxi. 17.

the first object of the meeting was the presentation of the contribution from which Paul had hoped so much. . . . It must have been a far larger bounty than they had any reason to expect, and on this occasion, if ever, we might surely have looked for a little effusive sympathy. Yet we are not told about a word of thanks, and we see but too plainly that Paul's hardly disguised misgiving as to the manner in which his gift would be accepted was confirmed.[1] Never in any age have the recipients of alms at Jerusalem been remarkable for gratitude."

Renan goes further. He even hints that Paul's action in presenting the alms, which he had been asked by James to collect, was construed as an attempt to purchase acknowledgment of his apostleship: that the story of Peter and Simon Magus at Antioch, and the endeavour of the latter to buy of the Apostle the grace to give the Holy Spirit, was a thinly disguised account of Paul's proceeding on the two occasions of his presenting contributions to the Church at Jerusalem, and that Luke was too dull to perceive this, and incorporated this Judaic slander into his history without a suspicion that it was levelled against his hero. Renan is led to this by the gross assumption that the Magus of the Clementines was intended for Paul.[2]

James showed the gratitude of his Church and his own regard for Paul in a much better way than in " effusive sympathy"; by at once suggesting measures for the safety of the Apostle, which he knew was menaced by the dagger-men of the Sadducæan High Priest, savage at the diminution of the Temple tax, of the Corinthian, Asian, Macedonian, and Galatian Jews, all equally exasperated, and all exasperated from the same sordid cause that had

[1] Rom. xv. 31.   [2] " Vie de St. Paul," p. 514.

THE RIOT AT JERUSALEM

roused the craftsmen of Ephesus and the traffickers in the ventriloquism of the pythoness of Philippi.

But Paul, as James perhaps knew from Agabus, sent to forewarn him, was not to be daunted by any fears for his own person. That fearless spirit had looked death in the face too often to feel any terrors at its menace now. Therefore James used subtlety with him. He appealed to him in the way in which he knew he could be reached, through his charity.

"Thou seest, brother," said James, "how many thousands of Jews there are which believe; and they are all zealous of the Law; and they have been diligently informed of thee that thou teachest all the Jews which are among the Gentiles to forsake Moses, saying that they ought not to circumcise their children, neither to walk after the customs. What is then to be done? It is certain that a crowd will assemble, because it will be bruited about through all Jerusalem that you have come." And James knew well what a crowd thus gathered meant. It would be an assembly not only of the Judæo-Christians who had been worked upon by lying Hellenic Jews to doubt Paul, but also of those bent on his destruction, the agents of the Sadducees, and also his mortal foes the Hellenic Jews. "Now then," said James, "do what I propose. We have here four men who have a vow upon them. Take them, be purified with them, and pay their expenses, so that they may have their heads shaved and have done with their vow. Then all will recognise that these calumnies that have been so diligently spread about you are calumnies only, and that you do observe the Law. As regards the Gentiles that have embraced the faith we hold to the same rule that was laid down some years ago—

they are held exempt from all this sort of thing, only we enjoined that they should abstain from things offered to idols, and from blood, and strangled, and from fornication."

The suggestion was one as delicate as could well be made. On the very last visit of Paul to Jerusalem, four years before, he had himself taken on him the vow of the Nazarite, consequently James and the Elders knew that this proposition would not jar with his feelings. They did not ask him to take the vow, only to assist these poor men to accomplish the sacrifices, without which they could not escape from their Nazariteship.

In the eyes of James the great advantage of this step was that for seven days, the most thronged period of the feast, Paul would have to keep within the precincts of the upper court of the Temple, unable to leave it, and so be secure against danger.

James did not put it in this way, partly because he did not wish to place Paul in the position of one who shirked danger, partly, also, because he shrank from exposing even to Paul in plain words the disgrace of the High-priesthood, surrounded with hired assassins and actuated by the most sordid motives. James hoped, moreover, by this means to reassure the Jewish believers by an outward exhibition of the harmony of feeling that existed between himself and Paul.

I venture to think that the proceeding is explicable by this means, without having recourse to the interpretation put on the conduct of James by a whole series of commentators, beginning with Baur and tailing off with Farrar.

Here is what Renan says: "So these narrow spirits have no other answer to make to him who brought them the homage of a world—but a mark of mistrust. Paul must be set to expiate his prodigious conquests by a bit of mummery. He must pay his tribute to meanness of intellect. Not till he has accomplished a formality commanded by vulgar superstition, and has had four beggars' heads shaved, too poor to stand the cost themselves—not till then will he be recognised as a brother!"[1]

Paul raised no objection. James would not have made the suggestion had he supposed it would have gone against his conscience. "Though I be free from all men," said the Apostle once before, "yet have I made myself servant unto all, that I might gain the more. And unto the Jews I became as a Jew, that I might gain the Jews; to them that are under the law, as under the law, that I might gain them that are under the law."[2] Paul accordingly entered the Temple with the four Nazarites.

The chambers reserved for the Nazirs who sought purification were on the second terrace in the court reserved for the Israelites. The general congregation went there only at the hours of sacrifice, and in preference frequented the lower esplanade that was open to the Gentiles. Mount Moriah, on which stood the Temple, was actually composed of three stages. The lowest was the vast thronged court of the Gentiles. North-west of this, raised thirty feet above it, was the second terrace. And here stood notices in Greek warning off every one save an Israelite from passing further. One of these notices has been found of recent years built into the wall of a school near the site of the Temple. It runs: "Let no stranger penetrate beyond the balustrade that encloses the holy place and

[1] Renan: "Vie de St. Paul," p. 515.
[2] 1 Cor. ix. 19, 20.

enter within. He who doeth this will have none to blame save himself if he meets with what ensues—death."

For seven days Paul was condemned to live in retirement with the four paupers on the platform; and then to pay for twelve animals that would have to be sacrificed, four he lambs of the first year, four rams, four ewe lambs.

By the end of the week probably a good many of the pilgrims would have departed, other matters would have arisen to occupy the attention of the Sadducees, and James and the Elders hoped to be able to smuggle Paul out of the city, and send him away to some place of security.

But this plan was not destined to succeed.

When the seven days were almost ended, some of the Jews of the province of Asia having caught sight of Trophimus the Ephesian in the city, whom they knew by face well enough, and having heard that Paul was actually within the sacred precincts, at once saw their opportunity, and rushed about among the mob assembled in the court for the sacrifice, crying out: "Men of Israel, help! This is the man that teacheth all men everywhere against the people and the law and this place; and further hath brought uncircumcised Greeks into the Temple and hath polluted this holy place."

An immense commotion ensued, extending into the town, and there ensued a general rush to the Temple from all parts. The Jews of Asia, perhaps led by Alexander the coppersmith, laid hold of Paul, and dragged him down the steps from the court of the Israelites, as this latter might not be polluted by murder. Thereupon the Levites closed the doors behind, to shut out the rabble.

On reaching the court of the Gentiles, the fanatics who had been beating the Apostle would have killed him, had not the Roman soldiers, kept on the alert in expectation of an uproar, swept the crowd to left and right and come to his assistance.

The legionaries arrived from the tower of Antonia, on the north-west side of the Temple enclosure. The tribune to whom the procurator of Judæa had confided the guardianship of the city made that his headquarters. The moment he heard the tramp of feet rushing towards the Temple he was ready, and gathering together a few centurions and a detachment of soldiers, he entered the court of the Gentiles, which was reached by a stair leading directly into it from the tower.

The mob, overawed by the soldiers, made way for them, and the most violent desisted from beating Paul. The officer very speedily delivered him from the hands of those that held him.

The tribune was called Lysias. He was a Greek by birth, but he had purchased his citizenship of the Emperor Claudius, and had thereupon assumed the name of Claudius.

He at once concluded that this disturbance was a recrudescence of that which had recently given so much trouble, the rising under the Egyptian Jew; and Lysias thought he had succeeded in laying hands on the man himself, who, after the defeat on the Mount of Olives, had effected his escape. He at once had him chained, and then asked of the crowd who he was and what he had done.

Some cried one thing and some another, and the tribune, despairing of getting any definite information out of the rabble, was about to convey Paul into the fortress, when the mob, disappointed at the thought of being baulked of their revenge, plunged up the stairs, forcing the legionaries together, and howling "Death! death! away with him to the execution!"

Paul, encumbered by his chains, could not move. Lysias ordered the soldiers to lift Paul on their shoulders and carry him through the gate. Then the Apostle, leaning down to the tribune, said in his ear: "May I speak?"

"What!" answered Lysias; "Do you know Greek? Are you not that Egyptian who made such a disturbance a month or two ago?"

Paul replied: "I am a Jew of Tarsus, a citizen of no mean Cilician city. I pray you suffer me to address a few words to the mob."

Lysias gave his consent.

The platform at the top of the stairs was cleared, and space made for Paul, who now signed with his hand that he desired to address the multitude.

Presently some sort of quiet was obtained, and he at once began the story for the thousandth time repeated of his conversion. In that story everything was contained, evidence of his sincerity, evidence of the Resurrection, and evidence that Jesus was the Christ. The mob was not in a condition to listen to an argument, but it would hearken to a narrative.

After having told how he was miraculously converted, Paul went on to explain why he went to the Gentiles; not, indeed, that he had gone directly to them, but to excuse the way in which he had detached the masses of converts from the Synagogue and cut off the stream of their contributions to the Temple. This was what really touched and irritated those connected with the Temple, just as disengaging their *clientèle* touched and irritated all the mercantile Jews in the Greek cities.

"It came to pass," continued Paul, "that when I was come to Jerusalem, whilst I was engaged in prayer in the Temple, I fell into a trance, and saw Jesus the Lord standing and saying unto me, Make haste, and get thee quickly out of Jerusalem, for they will not receive thy testimony concerning me. . . . . Depart, for I will send thee far hence to the Gentiles."

The mob had listened with tolerable impatience up to this point. Now they burst into a roar of disapprobation, for he had come to the very point which made them uneasy.

It must be clearly understood that in, probably, every synagogue efforts had been made to bring in the Gentiles. Every Jew had made a point of striving to go to the Gentiles. All had compassed sea and land to make one proselyte. It was not this, it could not have been this which angered the entire rabble of Jews and Hellenists. Unless it be understood as I suggest, I fail altogether to be able to explain the exasperation. It was not the religious prejudices of all these people that was wounded, it was their common interest.

When a manufacturer has had an extensive connection throughout Europe, and one of his travellers has employed his opportunities in attracting to himself all those who had given orders and sent money to this manufacturer, and then sets up a factory of his own and appropriates to himself all the connection which formerly gave commissions to his previous master, will the latter love him? Will he not seek his ruin by every means in his power?

This is no mere conjecture. It was so. Paul had started an opposition sect which had paralysed the trade of the Jews in Asia Minor and Greece, and threatened to destroy it altogether. The elements for exasperation were there—religious fanaticism may have served as a cloak, but it was such a transparent veil, that it is amazing it has not hitherto been seen through.

The mob yelled out : " Away with such a fellow from the earth : for it is not fit that he should live."

And as they cried out, and cast off their clothes, and threw dust into the air, the tribune commanded that Paul should be taken into the tower and examined by scourging.

But as he was being bound, Paul said to the centurion who stood by, " Is it lawful for you to scourge a man that is a Roman citizen, untried and uncondemned ? "

On hearing this the centurion immediately communicated with the chief officer, who ordered that no further attempt at torture should be made.

On the morrow, because he desired to have some certain knowledge as to what the accusation was that would be formulated against the prisoner, the tribune summoned the chief priests to assemble the Sanhedrim, and then brought Paul before the council.

The accusation of having taken Greeks within the sacred precincts was at once dropped. It could not be proved. No one had seen Trophimus in the court of Israel. The Sanhedrim was awkwardly placed, and so demanded of Paul that he should give an account of himself.

"Men and brethren," he said, "I have lived in all good conscience before God until this day."

Then Ananias, the ex-High Priest, commanded some of his ruffians, who had worked their way to within reach of the prisoner, to smite him on the mouth.

At once the indignation of Paul flared forth: " God

shall smite thee, thou whited wall!" he exclaimed; "Sittest thou there to judge me after the law, and commandest me to be smitten contrary to the law?"

Thereupon some that stood near said: "What! revile the High Priest of God!"

Paul answered: "I was not aware, brethren, that he was the High Priest," and in fact he was not such; he had been replaced by Ishmael, but he enjoyed as much dignity and influence as if he still were so, owing to his commanding will, and his power over the cut-throats. "It is written," continued Paul, "thou shalt not speak evil of the ruler of thy people."

Then he proceeded with his defence.

"Men and brethren, I am a Pharisee, the son of a Pharisee——" that was his answer to the vague and no longer pressed charge of his having violated the holiness of the sanctuary. "Of the hope and resurrection of the dead I am called in question." There in a nutshell was his position. The resurrection of Jesus Christ formed the basis of his teaching. If Christ be not risen, our faith is vain, we are false witnesses.

He did not indeed name Christ. There was no occasion for him to do so—he went to first principles. Is there such a hope as resurrection, or not? I assert that there is; and I have evidence to prove it; that was what he would proceed to say. Then further, the evidence is this, Christ is risen. I have seen Him since His death, so have the twelve elect witnesses, so have about five hundred brethren, whom you may question. Now if we have this mass of evidence in favour of the resurrection of One whom you all know to have been crucified and slain, why are we not justified in arguing that we also may rise in our bodies?

But the council would not hear more. It was quite enough for him to have laid the first step of his thesis for disputes to break out. At once there arose dissension between the Pharisees and the Sadducees on the council; and the Scribes on the former side stood up and strove, saying: "We find no evil in this man. If a spirit or an angel hath spoken to him, let us not fight against God." This was the starting of a tumult, and the chief captain, fearing lest Paul should be pulled in pieces between the rival parties, sent the soldiers into the court to remove the prisoner, and reconvey him to the castle.

The strength of the Apostle, never great, had been tried to the uttermost by the scenes of these two days, and on the night of the second, alone in his prison in the tower of Antonia, he fell into discouragement, very natural after the strain on his nerves, to which he had been subjected. Then in vision he saw the Lord, who said to him, "Be of good courage. As thou hast testified of me in Jerusalem, so also must thou bear witness at Rome."

For the moment Paul had escaped, through the interposition, first of the Pharisees, and then of the Romans. But the Sadducees were not to be disappointed of their revenge. And here it may be noted that throughout what follows, it was the Sadducee High Priest and superior clergy who sought the destruction of Paul. This is absolutely inexplicable on the grounds usually alleged, zeal for the Law, resentment at the incalling of the Gentiles. For the Law the half infidel Sadducees cared not a rush, except so far as it supported their claims to power and money through the Temple; they had acquired an hereditary right to the High-priesthood. As to the Gentiles, in heart they were Gentiles themselves, just as before the

French Revolution half the great wealthy prelates were rationalists and infidels.

But if we allow that Paul's activity had reduced the Temple toll to a miserable fraction of what it had been, then their resentment is at once to be accounted for.

Now the zealots, the *sicarii*, whom Ananias was accustomed to employ, agreed to make away with Paul. There were forty of these, and they took oath to assassinate him; Ananias approved of their design. They proposed that he should ask the tribune, in the name of the Sanhedrim, to send the prisoner once more into the court, under the plea that further examination was desired, and then, instead of smiting him on the mouth, they would silence him effectually with their stilettoes.

The plot was not kept so secret but that it was heard of by the nephew of Paul, who went to the castle and divulged it.

Then Claudius Lysias, glad to be rid of the responsibility, and for the purpose of removing from Jerusalem an occasion for riot, sent off Paul with the utmost precaution to the procurator at Cæsarea.

CHAPTER XXIII

CÆSAREA

A.D. 57—59

Paul sent to Cæsarea—Heard by Felix—The orator Tertullus bungles the case—Paul remanded—How Paul now appears to be rich—Conjectures—Recall of Felix and arrival of Festus—Charge made against Paul of high treason—Paul appeals to Nero—The composition of the Gospel of St. Luke—Epistles written at this period—Represent a new phase of Paul's mind—He combats Chaldean Gnosticism—The Magian system—Containing some truth—The celestial hierarchy of Dionysius—Danger to early Christianity from Gnosticism—Paul assumes a conservative position—The doctrine of Redemption—Paul begins to perceive that a philosophy of Christianity was needed—No dogmatism in the primitive Church—But doctrine was certain to be evolved in time.

THE captain of the company which conducted Paul to Cæsarea delivered to Felix the *elogium* of the prisoner. Paul was at once conducted before the procurator, who questioned him and gave orders that he should be consigned, not to prison, but to custody in the residence he occupied himself, the old palace of King Herod the Great.

At Jerusalem Lysias had informed the accusers of Paul that the matter was remitted to the proconsul, and Ananias resolved that he would go in person to Cæsarea, accompanied by some other Sadducæan members of the Sanhedrim, to press the condemnation of Paul. Antagonism to the Apostle on the part of the Pharisees no longer shows; it is the Temple party, the wealthy Sadducees profiting by the

Temple, that appear now as his implacable and irreconcilable enemies.

Ananias took down with him a Roman barrister who would prosecute for him, as he himself was not a fluent speaker in Greek, and, moreover, did not understand the procedure of a Roman court.

Tertullus, the lawyer, was probably a young man, one who had come into the province to pick up a living, because there was a glut of such persons in Rome. His address made to Felix shows inexperience and want of tact. He represented Paul as a mover of sedition, a ringleader of a sect, whose object was to profane the sanctuary, and whose case would have been disposed of in the Jewish court had not the tribune Lysias meddled and "with great violence" taken him away from the court. It was easy for Paul to answer so bungling an accusation.

Felix had already heard sufficient of the facts from Lysias not to be prejudiced against that officer by anything the orator might say. No actual crime was alleged to have been committed by Paul, merely an *intention* to desecrate the Temple; that he was a leader of sedition was the only charge at all serious, and this was incapable of proof.

Paul at once answered. He began with a compliment to the procurator, which he did not deserve, but which was a formality expected and demanded by custom. Then he proceeded to deny every count in the charge.

"I went up to Jerusalem, not to commit sacrilege, but to worship. The Jews cannot prove that they found me disputing in the Temple, nor addressing the people either there or in the synagogues, nor in the streets. What evidence can they produce? They have none. As to the charge that I belong to a sect—well, I admit that I belong to that sect which believes in a resurrection, which these Sadducæan priests deny, but which is held by the vast bulk of the people and by all their Scribes. So far from being a fomenter of riots, I came to Jerusalem to bring alms to the poor of my nation. Those who stirred up the riot were some Jews of Ephesus, but they are not here to substantiate what they then said against me. As they are not here—so be it, let those who are here bring evidence that I stirred up the riot. I did nothing of the sort; the only controversy I provoked was in the heart of their own council, when I declared my belief in the resurrection."

Felix at once remanded the prisoner.

"When Lysias the tribune arrives, I will hear the case again," said he.

Informally he did hear him again, but only to give pleasure to Drusilla, a Jewess with whom he was living in adultery.[1] He also had conversations with him occasionally, and he retained him in arrest, without chains, under the responsibility of a soldier, in the hopes that Paul would give him a bribe to release him.

A very interesting matter for speculation has been mooted by Professor Ramsay.

Hitherto Paul was miserably poor, dependent on what he could earn and on the remittances he received from Philippi. Twice in Thessalonica,[2] once in Athens,[3] and once in Rome[4] did he receive money to relieve his necessities; from Philippi and from no other Church, from no one else but an inhabitant of Philippi, would he receive a penny. And now, immediately after having paid a visit to

[1] She had eloped from her husband, Aziz, to Felix, who had employed Simon Magus as go-between. She was aged but twenty.
[2] Phil. iv. 16.   [3] 2 Cor. xi. 9.   [4] Phil. iv. 10.

Philippi, we find him so well provided with money that he is able to command respect and consideration from the Roman officer; not only so, but also to pay the charges of clearing four men of their Nazarite vow.

It is quite inadmissible to suppose that he had used some of the contributions of the Churches for the latter purpose. But in addition to this heavy item, several facts show that during the ensuing four years Paul had at his command a good deal of money. "Imprisonment and a long suit are expensive." Now, it is clear that Paul, during the following four years, did not appear before the world as a penniless wanderer, living by the work of his hands. A person in that position will not, either at the present day or in the first century, be treated with such marked respect as was certainly paid to Paul at Cæsarea, on the voyage, and in Rome. The governor, Felix, and his wife, the Princess Drusilla, accorded him an interview and private conversation. King Agrippa and his queen Berenice also desired to see him. A poor man never receives such attentions or rouses such interest. Moreover, Felix hoped for a bribe from him, and a rich Roman official did not look for a small gift. Paul, therefore, wore the outward appearance of a man of means, like one in a position to bribe a Roman procurator. The minimum in the way of personal attendants that was allowable for a man of respectable position was two slaves; and, as we shall see, Paul was believed to be attended by two slaves to serve him. At Cæsarea he was confined in the palace of Herod, but he had to live, to maintain two attendants, and to keep up a respectable appearance. Many comforts, which are almost necessities, would be given by the guards so long as they were kept in good humour. In Rome he was able to hire a lodging for himself, to live there, maintaining, of course, the soldiers who guarded him.

"An appeal to the supreme court could not be made by everyone that chose. Such an appeal had to be permitted and sent forward by the provincial governor, and only a serious case would be entertained. But the case of a very poor man is never esteemed as serious, and there is little doubt that the citizens' right of appeal to the Emperor was hedged in by fees and pledges. There is always one law for the rich man and another for the poor; at least, to this extent, that many claims can be successfully pushed by a rich man in which a poor man would have no chance of success. In appealing to the Emperor, Paul was choosing undoubtedly an expensive line of trial. All this had certainly been estimated before the decisive step was taken. . . . . Where, then, was the money procured? Was it from new contributions collected from the Churches? That seems most improbable, both from their general poverty, from Paul's general character, and from the silence of Luke on the point."[1]

Professor Ramsay answers: "There seems no alternative except that Paul's hereditary property was used in those years."

But there is another alternative. Had Paul come in at this time for his father's savings, he would almost certainly have gone to Tarsus to recover his inheritance. He did not do so. He became easy in his circumstances after his last visit to Philippi, whence he had already frequently drawn money. Is it not more probable that he had the necessary supplies from Lydia, who had a flourishing business and who, if not his wife, was yet sincerely devoted to him? If

[1] "Paul the Traveller and the Roman Citizen," pp. 310-2.

we admit that she was his wife—the Fathers declare that he was married, and there is no other trace in the Acts or his epistles of any other woman having been closely associated with him—then his reception of remittances from Philippi, of which she furnished the bulk, is perfectly explicable, as well as his having plenty of money at his disposal now, after having paid her a visit but a short while before his imprisonment.

For two years Paul remained in prison. Then Felix was recalled in disgrace, and Porcius Festus appointed in his room. He was an honest man and a good governor. Three days after his arrival at Cæsarea he went up to Jerusalem, when at once " the High Priest and the chief of the Jews informed him against Paul." Their resentment was kept alive by the continued diminution of the funds sent from the Hellenistic synagogues. Festus ordered the accusers to come down to Cæsarea and there lay their accusation against Paul.

" And when he had tarried among them no more than eight or ten days, he went down to Cæsarea; and the next day sitting on the judgment seat commanded Paul to be brought."

The usual charges were made against him of doing an injury to the Temple, but to this was added the more serious one of high treason. Then when Festus proposed to move the venue of the trial to Jerusalem, Paul appealed to Cæsar. After a little consideration Festus acceded to this request.

During the two years that had passed Paul had been allowed free intercourse with his friends. Luke, Timothy, Aristarchus of Thessalonica, Tychicus, Trophimus, were with him, at all events for a part of the time.

It is probable that to this period is due the writing of the Third Gospel. Paul must have felt a practical inconvenience when founding his Churches in having only a few oral records of the acts and sayings of the Lord to communicate to the disciples. Often he was with one of these Churches for only two or three months, and he might never see them again. He could repeat to them only what he had heard about Christ in the brief interviews with Peter and James, and a good deal of what was only third-hand information. At Cæsarea he was near the scene of the great events of the Lord's life, he had with him a man of education and literary power—Luke—and there was leisure in which he might collect the requisite material. At no other time, as far as we are aware, had Luke this opportunity. The precision of details regarding the Law and Mosaic customs, and concerning the topography of Palestine, all point to the writer having been in the Holy Land at the time when he composed his work. And the restless spirit of Paul could ill brook two years of enforced idleness; he must be doing something for God. And what more useful and splendid result could have been achieved than the inspiration of this Gospel and the supervision of the text as written by Luke?[1]

But besides providing a Gospel record for distribution among the Churches founded by him, Paul was also concerned for their continuance in the faith.

We have three Epistles belonging to this period. One —that to Philemon—need not concern us, as, beautiful

[1] "Nomine suo ex opinione ejus (Pauli) conscripsit."—*Fragment ap. Muratori*, 170. "Lucæ digestum Paulo adscribere solent."—Tertull. *cont. Marcion*, iv. 5. "Lucas, sectator Pauli, quod ab illo prædicabatur evangelicum in libro condidit."—Irenæus, *adv. Hares*. iii. 1.

though it be, it contains nothing doctrinal; the others are that to the Ephesians and that to the Colossians.

As they exhibit a third phase of his mind it is necessary to consider them here.

At Miletus, in bidding farewell to the pastors of the Church of Ephesus, Paul had forewarned them that a new trouble was looming before the Church. "I know this, that after my departing shall grievous wolves enter in among you, not sparing the flock. Also of your own selves shall men arise, speaking perverse things, to draw away disciples after them."[1] These false teachers, emerging from the heart of the Gentile believers, would be something different from the Judaisers insisting on the observance of the Law. To understand what they were we must look back to what were the elements out of which this Church, as well as the others in the Asian province, were composed.

We can hardly think that the unreasoning, superstitious rabble that adored Artemis, and were excited by the processions of dancing priests and priestesses, felt much drawn to the Church. In the repulsion caused by the grossness and stupidity of the idolatry practised at Ephesus, the Gospel would find access to the hearts and minds of those who had been groping after something better, even among the lowest class. Such were the men who had turned to the Chaldean Magi. And when, some time after Paul had founded the Church, the incident of Sceva and his sons occurred, a number of those who had professed their belief and had been baptized produced unexpectedly their old magical books, which they had secreted, and after which they still hankered, and

[1] Acts xx. 29, 30.

burned them. This was the result of a sudden impulse. When this was past, many of these men would assuredly regret what they had done, and procure for themselves fresh copies of the treatises they had destroyed; or, if they did not exactly do this, they would begin, perhaps unconsciously, to fuse their old convictions into one amalgam with their new faith. The new faith was a belief in facts, and, as yet, not in doctrines. Being men of brains and activity of intellect this would not suffice them, and they would naturally, inevitably attempt to work out a philosophy of Christianity; and so long as there was no definite Christian dogma there was absolutely nothing to prevent them from so doing.

Now the system of the Magi was one of emanation from the Pleroma (the Fulness) of Existence in the One Supreme God. From Him extended a ladder of existences, some fuller of light and perfection than others, in descent through matter to the mere inert, inanimate dead lump itself. And the envelope of matter degraded the spiritual existence wrapped in it. Man was double, and man to follow his higher nature must seek emancipation by asceticism from his carnal appetites. But above man, rank on rank, up into the ineffable light, the Fulness of All, extend the æons, those nearest the summit fullest of perfection, those nearest man the most debased. So all creation is one vast progression towards absorption in the Fulness of Life, and all religion consists in the struggle upwards out of the material and carnal to the immaterial and spiritual.

In later times the pseudo Dionysius took this doctrine and worked it out into a splendid system. According to him this ladder of life does exist. There is an angelic hierarchy. There is also an ecclesiastical hierarchy. All political, all social life is made up of hierarchies. But then, according to Dionysius, these hierarchies are ordered for the sake of illuminating what is in darkness. The higher orders reflecting the glory of God turn and cast down the light they have received on the stage below, and so the light descends, dancing from stair to stair, flashed from face to face into the infinite abyss.

So on earth the ecclesiastical hierarchy is ordered that the bishops should convey grace and enlightenment to the priesthood, and they in turn to their flocks, and so on and on down to the lowest depths of ignorance, all are partakers in a priesthood of light and emanation of grace, in that all partake and partake only to give to those who have not.

The period was one of speculation. In Egypt Philo had endeavoured to evolve a philosophy of Judaism out of the sacred texts by allegorising every historic narrative and transforming every positive precept into a vaporous idea.

The comprehension of the great doctrine of Emanations was entitled the *Gnosis*, the knowledge. Those who understood it were in the way of light, for they knew the scheme of the universe and the method of mounting the scale.

In the first century the system was far from perfected, but it was in process of elaboration. The doctrine was so fascinating, was so intelligible, contained such obvious truth, and was so practical that its acceptance was ensured.

Various names were given to the emanations from the Pleroma, as thrones, lordships, powers, æons. And these Paul alludes to, and accepts.[1] There was sufficient truth

[1] Col. i. 16.

in the Gnostic system for him to admit some of its assumptions. But a great menace lay in this doctrine—that of transforming Christ into an emanation, an æon of a high order indeed, but still only one in the scale; a single member in the interminable genealogies.[1] In this Gnosticism the fundamental doctrine was a duality between matter and spirit. In the second century it would assume shape in conflicting Gods; the God of this earth, of all nature, evil, and evil only, over against a God in whom all the fulness of spiritual existence was to be found. And these would be represented as in incessant antagonism.

We can trace the origin back to Zoroasterism in Persia.

It was about to produce a Mithraic cult that would spread throughout pagan Europe. It would develop into the Manicheism of the West; and mixed with Christianity in so far that it adopted Christ as one of the æons, it was about to produce infinite trouble to the Asian Churches and to invade Egypt as well.

This was the menace that Paul now saw clouding the sky. Somewhat later he would give to this philosophy its historic name.[2]

At this time it was associated with a certain amount of Judaic formalism: it professed circumcision as symbolical of emancipation from the flesh, it observed Sabbaths and new moons.[3]

Hitherto Paul had been something more than an innovator; he had been revolutionary. But now, in face of this new danger, he began to fall back on tradition, and

[1] 1 Tim. i. 4; Tit. iii. 9.
[2] 1 Tim. vi. 20. "O Timothy, keep that which is committed to thy trust, avoiding profane and vain babblings, and oppositions of *Gnosis* falsely so called." [3] Col. ii. 11, 16.

to exhibit a conservative tendency.[1] If once the audacious spirit of religious speculation were allowed full play, there was no knowing whither it would lead.

In his first Epistle to the Corinthians, when under the domination of conviction that the end was at hand, he had counselled abstention from marriage ; but now he extolled the social virtues, and the excellence of domestic life.[2] Asceticism, which he had once favoured, he now regarded as dangerous, as something to be condemned in principle and in its precepts.[3]

But now, especially, he insisted on the doctrine of redemption, and represented Christ, not as an æon, but as containing in Himself the Pleroma, the fulness of divine perfection, and as the manifestation in the body of the divine plenitude. God is in Christ, and Christ is not an emanation from God. Christ was conceived in eternity, the world was prepared for His reception, and then finally He was revealed, to fill all things and to be all in all ; and through Him, in the Church, the redemption of mankind was to be accomplished.

The Epistles to the Ephesians and the Colossians should be read with the understanding of the danger from Gnosticism and of the effort made by Paul to substitute something like a philosophy of Christianity in its place. Never having received a philosophic education, it was but an attempt ; he saw certain possibilities, he perceived mysteries behind the facts of Christ's life, and these he suggested, but he had not the discipline of mind, acquired by education other than that of rabbinic schools, to think out a complete system of theology.

---

[1] Eph. iii. 2-5 ; ii. 20 ; Col. ii. 2-5.
[2] Eph. v. 31-33 ; vi. 1-9 ; Col. iii. 18-22 ; iv. 1. [3] 1 Tim. iv. 1-5.

We find no more struggle against Judaism. All his energies are now devoted to the growing Gnosticism of the Asiatic Churches, the natural, inevitable result of the overlaying of Magian dogmatism with a layer of Christianity, very thin and unconsolidated.

Paul was now beginning to perceive that men sought in Christianity something more than hopes of a resurrection and triumph in a Messianic kingdom. From that he had been forced, by unpleasant experience, to learn that they further insisted on a moral system based on a revelation. Now he was finding out that they needed a system of theology as well. They had minds as well as souls, and the minds had begun to work on the material he had supplied.

The primitive Church is sometimes extolled for being undogmatic. It was so only because the members were in daily anticipation of the second advent. But already, while Christ walked the earth, the question was asked, "Who art thou?"

The human mind must ask the reason of things it receives, as certainly as a child will begin to build when given a box of bricks. The facts enunciated by the Apostles were not packets of mixed seeds carefully sterilised, but living truths, each containing a mystery enfolded but undeveloped within it.

In the Gospel of St. Mark and probably the first edition in Hebrew (Aramaic) of St. Matthew there was no record of the birth of Jesus Christ. In the first years of the Church all that believers asked was, "How are we to prepare for His second coming?" But when the Messianic perspective became distant, then men began to ask, "Who is Christ? Is He a prophet, or is He divine?

Is He the Word incarnate, or an emanation from the Pleroma?"

It was the function of the Church to answer these questions; and she could do so only by showing that the doctrinal truths she now began to formulate were based on legitimate deductions.

CHAPTER XXIV

ROME

A.D. 59—61

The voyage and shipwreck of Paul passed over—The Church in Rome —How formed—The *ghetto* in Rome—Position of Jews in Rome— Their number—Inorganic condition of Christianity in Rome—The only conceivable manner in which Peter can be regarded as connected with this Church—The idea of Paul as an Apostle to the heathen demands great modification—What his real wish was— The appeal of Paul to Cæsar—Its real purpose—Strained relations between the Synagogue and the Church—Paul hopes to obtain imperial recognition of the independence of the Church—Paul as a prophet—Unfortunate result of this attempt—The persecution of Nero—The third book by Luke not written—Paul in Rome—Epistles written from Rome—Acquittal of Paul.

THE narrative of the voyage and shipwreck of St. Paul has been so fully illustrated archæologically, geographically, and nautically, and is of so little importance towards the development of his character and the modelling of his ideas, that I venture to pass it over completely. The masterly treatise of Mr. James Smith,[1] followed up by that of Professor Ramsay,[2] leave no space for such as myself. Moreover, it is not my object in this work to do more than consider, from my own point of view, the growth of ideas in the mind of Paul, and the true character of his work. Before he reached the imperial city, in fact

[1] "Voyage and Shipwreck of St. Paul" (London, 1866, third edition).
[2] "St. Paul the Traveller and the Roman Citizen" (1896), cap. xiv.

on his landing at Puteoli, Paul was met by believers. And they came to meet him as he approached Rome.

Already had he written to the Church there a pastoral epistle, and so was known. How came there to be in Rome a large colony of believers? M. Renan has answered this question admirably. "We must rid ourselves of the idea, bred in the imagination only, that the propagation of Christianity was due to a series of missions, and to a set of preachers similar to the missionaries of modern times, going about from town to town. Paul, Barnabas, and their companions, were the only Apostles who acted on this principle. The rest was accomplished by workers whose names have remained unknown. Beside the Apostolate which became so illustrious, there was another that was obscure, whose agents were not teachers by profession, but who were, nevertheless, quite as efficacious as if they had been such.

"The Jews at this period were eminently nomadic. Merchants, servants, artisans, they ran about seeking all the great littoral cities, where to carry on their business. Active, diligent, honest, they carried with them their special convictions, their good example, their exaltation; and through these dominated the masses, degraded religiously, by means of that superiority which an enthusiast always exercises in the midst of those who are indifferent. Those affiliated to the Christian sect travelled about like the other Jews, and carried the glad tidings with them.

"This was a sort of secret propaganda, and was far more efficacious than declared missionary enterprise. The gentleness, cheerfulness, the good humour, the patience of the new believers, made them everywhere welcome and won to them all hearts.

"Rome was one of the first places thus reached. The capital of the Empire heard the name of Jesus long before the intermediary countries had been evangelised, precisely as a lofty mountain top catches the sun before the valleys are illumined."

Already about the year 50 the controversy relative to the Messiahship of Christ had caused commotions in Rome, and this had resulted in a decree of banishment against the Jews. It was in consequence of this that Paul encountered Priscilla and Aquila in Corinth, and from them acquired an interest in the unorganised Church in Rome. But this edict fell at once into abeyance, and Christians and Jews again settled in Rome. Their quarters were on the Etruscan side of the Tiber, in the most squalid and poverty-stricken portion of the city, the modern Trastevere, near the Porta Portese, where has been found the principal Jewish catacomb.

The Jews of Rome were in constant relation with those of Palestine; the chain of communication was interrupted only during the winter months. In early spring numerous pilgrims, Jewish and proselyte, hastened to Puteoli, where several vessels were ready to convey them to Cæsarea, in time for the Passover.

The monuments in the Jewish cemeteries show that the languages in general usage were Greek and Latin. The Jews possessed their schools and their synagogues, which were thoroughly organised, and they were strict in observance of the Law.

But all the Jews were not poor, nor confined to the despised quarter beyond the Tiber. Many, owing to their rectitude, were in enjoyment of positions of trust, some were physicians, others stewards. Their influence extended to the imperial household. Poppæa, the wife of Nero, listened to the doctrine of the One God, and greatly favoured the Jews. The captives carried away and sold as slaves by Pompey had been manumitted, and had acquired both wealth and influence.

The Jews in Rome numbered eight thousand men,[1] which is the present number in the *ghetto*, and the total population of the capital was about two millions and a half. The first colonists from the Holy Land had arrived probably at the time when Judas Maccabæus concluded a treaty with the senate (B.C. 157). The settlement of Jews had been swelled by prisoners of war who had been freed by their masters. Emboldened by the licence accorded by the conflict of parties in Rome, these new comers played a part in the assemblies in the forum, where they excited disturbances. Cicero complained of them as acting in concert on whichever side they threw their weight.[2] Augustus allowed them to share in the gratuitous distribution of corn, and ordered that they should receive their portion on the morrow should the day of distribution fall on the Sabbath.

They had fallen into disgrace under Caligula and Claudius, but held their own, and made themselves necessary on account of their industry, honesty, and intelligence. But though the bulk of the Jews were engaged in small trades and peddling, they then, as now, felt an irresistible attraction to the stage, which they supplied with actors. And they ministered to the popular craving after initiation into the secrets of the future, by setting up as interpreters of dreams and fortune tellers.

---

[1] Joseph. *Ant.* xvii. 12.
[2] Pro Flacco. "Scis quanta sit manus, quanta concordia, quantum valeant in concionibus."

Among these resident Jews, Christianity had made its way, but as yet the Christians had not dissociated themselves from the Synagogue. They held their Agapæ, but only as enjoying the same licence as the clubs. It was illegal to establish an independent religion with independent rites, without State authorisation. Consequently in Rome, as in Jerusalem and Judæa, the Christians existed as a faction in the Synagogue; but did not, as in Asia Minor, constitute an independent Church. When Paul wrote to the believers in Rome, he made no allusion to any apostolic founder of the Church there. When he arrived in Rome, he learned that no Apostle had preceded him.

And yet, as already intimated, it is quite possible that there may be some basis in fact for the tradition that the Roman Church had Peter as its founder. Not, indeed, that this Apostle had been there, but in the partition of work at Jerusalem, whilst the charge of preaching the word to the Edessian neophytes may have been committed to Thaddæus, and that of ministering to those of Pontus and Bithynia to Andrew, and to those of Parthia, to Thomas, it is conceivable that Peter may have specially interested himself in the Jews and proselytes from Italy who visited Jerusalem at the feasts or on business. Assuming that the early tradition is founded on fact—that at least twelve years elapsed since the Ascension before the Twelve separated—common-sense would show us that they would arrange among themselves for some partition of spheres of work. And I venture to think that, on the supposition that Peter took it upon him to look specially after the Latin Jews and their converts, we have a satisfactory solution of a problem that has been a point of controversy upon which as much is to be said on one side as on the other. Romanists can assert, and have a right to assert, that Latin Christianity was due in a measure to the teaching of Peter. What they cannot prove is that he was in Rome previous to his death, nor that he founded an episcopal throne there. On the other hand, the generally entertained idea of St. Paul as the Apostle to the Gentiles, preaching to the unconverted, drawing the net of the Church in untried waters, must be greatly modified. He did not carry the Gospel to the heathen, though he certainly travelled among them.

The character of his Epistles, as I have already pointed out, tells the same thing. Is it possible to conceive of them as addressed to raw converts from paganism? They presuppose not merely an intimate knowledge of the Law, but a prejudice in its favour that can have grown up only by long association with the synagogue and a novitiate under the rabbis.

Conceive of a man educated in a Roman Catholic seminary on St. Thomas Aquinas and Alphonso Liguori sent among Scotch Presbyterians or long-headed Yorkshire Dissenters. He would be absolutely incapable of any argument that would convince their cool, clear brains, and they would be as unable to understand the quirks and twists of his dialectics. So was Paul among Greeks and Romans.

Undoubtedly there is much in these epistles which would delight and edify a converted Greek or Roman: the splendid descriptions of faith, of charity, of the Resurrection; but these are pearls set in a tissue of tangled argument relative to the Law and the Promises, faith and works and illustrations drawn from Mosaic practice and rabbinic symbolism absolutely unintelligible to any save Jews and Judaised converts of long standing. It is possible that at the outstart Paul may have thought of going directly to convert Gentiledom, but he soon abandoned the attempt as impracticable.

The Americans send out and maintain missions to the Mohammedans in Mesopotamia and Asia Minor, but the missionaries have long despaired of making one convert of the disciples of Islam, and they poach for congregations among the historic Christian Churches.

These missionaries, I dare say, give themselves out as labouring among the unbelievers, but all their efforts are directed in quite another direction.

Unquestionably Paul would have liked to convert the heathen, but he could not do it; he had not the faculty. He proposed it more than once, but there it all ended.

At Antioch in Pisidia Paul had declared in the synagogue: "It was necessary that the word of God should first have been spoken to you; but seeing ye put it from you, and judge yourselves unworthy of everlasting life, lo, we turn to the Gentiles. For so hath the Lord commanded us, saying, I have set thee to be a light of the Gentiles, that thou shouldest be for salvation unto the ends of the earth."

Nevertheless Paul did not do what he declared was his intention and his mission. He went directly to Iconium, and there began the same course again in the synagogue; it was the same in Derbe, the same everywhere.* It is quite true that at Antioch we are told that the Gentiles heard him in the synagogue; but if we look at the sermon they listened to, it is simply an address to Jews and Jews only, that would be entirely unintelligible to one who was not familiar with the history of the Jews, and suitable only to such as could follow an argument built up on texts, and none of these texts to the point except to a rabbinical mind.[1] Besides, Paul began his sermon: " Men of Israel, and ye that fear God, give audience," showing that those to whom he addressed himself were either Jews by birth or proselytes of righteousness.

It is quite true that Paul did prove himself to be an Apostle of the Gentiles, but it was by wrenching his converts apart from association with the Jews, and giving them an independent articulate life. That was his achievement. The Twelve kept the Church and Synagogue together, making of the former a higher order of life to the other. Their disciples stepped up a stage in the same edifice. But Paul's work was one of separating his converts and organising them into independent communities. By so doing he was violating Roman law. He exposed every one of these Churches to great danger. The Jews might at once inform against them, and the magistrates had no option, they must close them and punish the elders.

There is more than appears on the surface in the appeal of Paul to Cæsar. He might have been set at liberty, he would have been discharged as innocent of the charge of stirring up revolt had he desired it. That he feared the plot of the Jews at Jerusalem to assassinate him does not explain his appeal; the nature of his accusation does not explain the proconsul allowing the appeal.

It is absurd to suppose that Paul appealed to Nero for protection against the plots of the Jews at Jerusalem, as though the proconsul were not perfectly able to secure his

[1] Acts xiii. 16-41.

safety. A centurion had done that before. He had but to intimate to Festus that his life was menaced, and the governor would take ample provision for his protection. His appeal to Cæsar must have had some other purport, and that Festus must have understood. It was as the latter said, "unreasonable to send a prisoner and not withal to signify the crimes laid against him." All he could write concerning the charge was that there was a contention of opinion between the prisoner and the accusers as to whether a certain man Jesus were dead or alive. Festus must have had a reason for allowing such a frivolous case, as he would regard it, being referred to the Emperor. And Paul must have been able to furnish him with a good reason which induced him to allow the appeal.

The reason probably was this:—

Paul desired to have the Christian Church legally recognised as separate from the Synagogue. That was his cherished object, and that could only be done by the question being examined and decided at Rome.

He could represent to Festus that were his congregation separated from the Jews and acknowledged as independent they would be under the protection of the magistrates, and one main occasion of disturbance among the Jews would be cut off.

Festus knew well how turbulent the Jews were, how touchy about everything that concerned their religion, and he would at once be convinced that this proposal was an important one.

So long as the believers in Christ used the synagogue they were safe. The law allowed the Jews the full exercise of their religion. There would doubtless exist in all synagogues some who would stand up and show how that the prophecies were fulfilled in Christ; how that the prophets spoke of a suffering Messiah. When these occupied the pulpit there would ensue a disturbance, or those who dissented from this opinion would walk out. When, however, the exponents of the Law had the place of exhortation they would take pains to explain away all the passages in Isaiah that spoke of suffering in the Messiah, and disprove the views of the newly arisen party. Then the latter would either loudly express disapproval, or ostentatiously march out.

Something of the same sort exists in the Evangelical churches of Germany, where some pastors are rationalists and deny the divinity of our Lord, dispute the Incarnation, and deny and even ridicule the Resurrection. Others again are orthodox, and in large towns it is customary to have a pastor and a vicar appointed to the same church holding and teaching diametrically opposite views. To escape a brawl each party is forced to have its service at a different hour; the orthodox lecturer preceding or following immediately on the heterodox preacher, so that one an hour after denies the fundamental tenet insisted on by his predecessor, or seeks to reconstruct a doctrine thrown down into the dust by the occupant of the pulpit from whom it is still warm.

Some sort of compromise must have been reached in Jerusalem, or Pharisee animosity would not have lost its virulence. But Paul was not the man to relish a compromise. Besides, the action of the synagogues in Asia had made a reconciliation impossible.

The time had not arrived when Christianity would be regarded as a *superstitio*, a non-Roman religion, unauthorised, and opposed to the well-being of the State.

It appeared to the Roman magistrates what it appeared to the Jews and Christians themselves—a split of opinion in the same body, a question of names and of the Law. So far, moreover, the Christian sect was made up of Jews very largely, and of the proselytes, attached to them more or less loosely, a number in Rome not sufficiently large, nor influential, to cause any alarm.

The situation was about to alter, and alter rapidly, but no suspicion that there was anything other than a party quarrel among the Jews had as yet entered the minds of the Roman authorities.

That Christianity was looked upon as something more than this was due to the action of Paul in erecting his clusters of converts into Churches in separate houses, holding their meetings on separate days from the Jews.

It is somewhat remarkable how respectful Paul shows himself towards the Roman imperial power, and to Nero, in whom it was personified and centred. In the Epistle to the Romans he tells the believers of the Eternal City that "no power" is other than "of God," and that to resist the power is to resist "the ordinance of God." "Rulers," he asserts, "are not a terror to good works, but to the evil." This, it is true, was written in the fourth or fifth year of Nero, before he had broken out in his career of crime, but it was on the eve of his union with Poppæa, and the murder of his wife Octavia, and very shortly before the assassination of his mother. Paul does not seem to have entertained the smallest anticipation of what Nero would become. In a hesitating manner Paul had claimed possession of the gift of prophecy,[1] but he must soon have lost confidence in his prophetic power.

[1] 1 Cor. xiii. 9; Rom. xii. 6.

He had asserted that Christ's second coming would be shortly, and that he would himself live to see it,[1] but after a few years found out his mistake. If, as is conjectured, his appeal to Nero was for the sake of obtaining recognition for the Church assemblies apart from the Synagogue, it was a short-sighted policy. In direct contrast to Paul's estimate of the Roman imperial power and of Nero, is that of the author of the Apocalypse. With the latter this power is that of the beast; and Nero is the crowned head of the beast, wounded to death, but returning again as the eighth head, in Domitian. Paul, badly sighted as to the future, speaks highly of Nero in 58, and the author of the Revelation can scarce find words and figures enough in which to execrate him in 95.

So little did Paul conceive of the possibility of Nero becoming a persecutor, that apparently he took the occasion of his appeal to detach the Christian community from the Synagogue, to organise it in independence, and so place it in such a position that, after the fire, the tyrant was able at once to put his hand down on it, and select his victims, to wrap them in tarred bands, and set them up as living torches in the circus. But for this step taken by Paul it would have been difficult to distinguish them from the Jews.

Probably Paul gained his point, and for two years enjoyed freedom from annoyance, but in A.D. 64 the Neronian persecution broke out.

Doubtless Paul had already determined the line of his defence, which would be this : that he was not allowed to give his interpretation of the prophecies as he understood them ; that he and others could not accept the traditional

---

[1] 1 Thess. iv. 15-17; Rom. xvi. 20.

interpretation; that the Jews everywhere had recourse to violence against him: that he had been delivered from their violence only by the interposition of the provincial magistrates; and that therefore he asked leave, in the interests of peace, to draw away his followers from the established synagogues to synagogues of their own. He advocated the founding of no new religion, only a different interpretation of the common formularies and texts.

It is most unfortunate that Luke never wrote the third book of his meditated trilogy. The Acts of the Apostles finishes abruptly with Paul in prison at Rome, or rather under surveillance; awaiting his trial. Certainly Luke never designed this as a finish to his work. In the Second Book of the Acts, he would have gone back in his record to the year 52, after the Council of Jerusalem, and have told of the work of the other Apostles, and have brought up his narrative to the death of Peter and Paul in Rome.

Three days after the arrival of Paul in Rome, he sent for the chief of the Jews to come to his lodgings, as he was precluded from going to the synagogue. To them he said: "Men and brethren, though I have committed nothing against the people, or customs of our fathers, yet was I delivered prisoner from Jerusalem into the hands of the Romans, who, when they had examined me, would have let me go, because there was no cause of death in me. But when the Jews spake against it, I was constrained to appeal unto Cæsar; not that I had aught to accuse my nation of. For this cause, therefore, have I called for you, to see you, and to speak with you; because that for the hope of Israel I am bound with this chain."

The elders of the synagogue at once replied that they had received no letters from Judæa concerning him, nor had any of the brethren returning from Jerusalem spoken against him.

This is remarkably confirmatory testimony to what has been advanced, that the movement in Jerusalem against Paul was entirely one which—after it had been started by Asiatic Jews out of revenge—was taken up and pursued by the Sadducean Temple party alone. The Pharisees, if not sympathetic, were neutral. They were not prepared to accept that *because* Jesus was risen from the dead, that *therefore* He was the promised Messiah, and would come again; but they were delighted to have the instances of Lazarus, dead and buried, Christ dead and buried, and both risen, to cast in the teeth of their adversaries who denied the possibility of any resurrection at all.

When Paul went on to "expound and testify the kingdom of God, persuading them concerning Jesus, both out of the Law of Moses, and out of the prophets"—then some believed, and some believed not, as might have been anticipated.

The elders of the synagogue at Rome said to Paul: " We desire to hear of thee what thou thinkest: for as concerning this sect, we know that everywhere it is spoken against."

These words of the elders go some way to exclude the notion of Peter or any other preacher of the Gospel having as yet been in Rome. It would seem as though, awed by the sentence of Claudius in 50, both parties had agreed not to ventilate their differences in public. The good will entertained by the Pharisees in Jerusalem towards the Church had extended to Rome. Differences were in a fair way to be smoothed and faith in Christ to be smothered. Or, perhaps, as suggested in a former chapter, one synagogue may have been abandoned to such as believed the promises to have been accomplished, whilst another was held by such as expected their accomplishment. At the same time tidings reached Rome that there had been disturbances in several provincial towns, caused by the spread of these opinions. The way in which Paul expounded the doctrine of the Messiahship of Jesus was to them a surprise, and staggered them, it was to them so absolutely novel.

For two whole years Paul continued in Rome, under the guard of a soldier, who was responsible with his life for his being present when the trial came on. The delay was doubtless caused by the difficulty of collecting the evidence.

The charge preferred against Paul was one of stirring up of revolt, and therefore of high treason. Paul had as companions the amiable and docile Timothy, and his admirer Luke. Aristarchus was a fellow-prisoner. Tychicus was with him off and on. Epaphroditus brought him news from Philippi of the dear and close friends there, and with the news, money contributions. Mark also, cousin to Barnabas, was now in Rome, and Paul learned to value him; Demas also attended him for awhile.

During this period Paul wrote and despatched the Epistle to the Philippians, perhaps the finest of all his letters. It is not polemical. Among the simple Macedonians heresy had not made head; it is practical, and full of sweet and tender touches. In it are allusions to the agnosticism that was corrupting the purity of the faith of the Asian churches, but no argument is attempted in refutation.

At length the prisoner stood before the judgment seat, was heard, the charges were investigated, and he was honourably acquitted.

With that acquittal the right of the Christians to form independent churches was established. It was probably for this, it may be conjectured, that Paul had contended, and this was now gained. Had he not appealed to Cæsar then his Churches with their worship, independent of the Synagogue, would have been exposed to incessant danger from the Jews, who could represent them as unauthorised, and therefore illegal.

CHAPTER XXV

THE LAST YEARS

A.D. 62—65

Course taken by Paul after his release—Did he go into Spain?—Numbers of Jews in Spain—The Neronian persecution—The separation of the Church from the Synagogue unfortunate for the former—Second imprisonment and martyrdom—Epistles written at this period—Differences of character—What Paul's great achievement really was—Is there a future work for the Jews?—Last words of Paul—Paul an Apostle *among* the Gentiles—His position in the mind of the Church.

AFTER his release and the vindication of his right to form independent Churches, Paul turned his face eastward, to his beloved Philippi, and then went on to Troas, and so to the Churches in Asia. Thence, perhaps, he bent west again, revisited and founded the Church in Rome, communicating to it the special grace of organisation, which he had promised it before. From Italy he may have gone on to Spain. This had been his ambition for some time,[1] and Spain was sufficiently Judaised for him to hope to achieve some success there.

Strabo says: "The natives of Spain submitted so completely to the Phœnicians that the descendants of the latter occupy most of the towns in Turdetania and the neighbouring country to the present day." And, "So fortunate were the Phœnicians in the planting of Carthage, and of other towns as far as Iberia, and beyond the

[1] Rom. xv. 24, 28.

pillars of Hercules, that to this day they hold possession of the best situations of Europe on the mainland and on the islands."[1] The oft-recurring occasions for colonisation at length induced the Jews to seek the coast towns of Spain and Gaul on the Mediterranean, and perhaps also the old Phœnician settlements in the province of Bætica at the then confines of the world. In this land they found a no less active trade by sea than in their old fatherland. They spread from Tartessus to Bætis and Anas, so that at length they were at home in the entire southern half of the peninsula.

During the first century the Jews had become so numerous and powerful that they attempted to completely Judaise the country. Consequently there was here everything to invite Paul to visit Spain. With synagogues in every city, and the Jews active in proselytising, he might count on a harvest. Clement of Rome, in his First Epistle to the Corinthians, says that Paul had been the herald of the faith in the east and in the west, even to the extremities of the latter,[2] and this may imply such a visit.

In A.D. 64 occurred the Neronian persecution. The city had been consumed by fire, and popular opinion, certainly without reason, accused the Emperor of having set it on fire. To divert unpopularity from himself he accused the Christians of having been the incendiaries. It is possible enough that their expectation of the end of all things, and references to the sayings of the Lord relative to the final burning of the world, may have been rumoured about and so gave occasion for suspicion to attach to them

[1] Strabo, iii. 2; xvii. 3.
[2] "Having *come* to the boundary of the West" is his expression. It has been objected, with force, that had Clement meant a mission beyond Italy he would have said "gone" in place of "come."

that they had attempted to force on the fulfilment of the prophecy.

The measure adopted by Paul, well intended though it had been, enabled Nero at once to put his hand on the Christians as distinguished from the Jews. They had increased in numbers, and had assumed a very different colour from what they bore when melted in with the Jews of the Synagogue, distinguishable only by their private opinions. Now they had separate conventicles and separate worship on different days. They were no longer to be classed with the Jews.

The persecution raged from A.D. 64 to 66, when Nero quitted Rome for the East. Behind him were left the infamous Tigellinus as prætorian præfect, and Helius, præfect of the city. Persecution then became intermittent. Paul was now in Rome; so also perhaps was Peter. Paul now suffered a martyr's death by the sword, and Peter either now or later died on the cross.

To the period of the second imprisonment belong the Pastoral Epistles, repudiated as not authentic by the German critics because of the difference in tone between them and the Controversial Epistles.

But the condition of Christianity had completely altered. From being held in suspense in Judaism it had been precipitated and removed to another vessel. What was polemically necessary at one time was needed no longer. Now that the Churches were formed, organisation and discipline became requisite. The active, restless energy of Paul was no doubt relaxed by old age, but also by the fact that his argumentative powers, such as they were, were no more called upon to meet Judaism and Gnosticism. There were heretics when the Pastoral Epistles were written, but Paul contented himself with denouncing them; he had, perhaps recognised his incapacity to refute them. There is a tone of exhaustion of strength, of decline of mental power, noticeable in these letters, but then Paul's never very strong constitution had been severely tried, and the body reacts on the mind.

The Pastoral Epistles represent the last phase of Paul's energy, not engaged in fighting, but in constructing; he is no longer revolutionary, he has become conservative, even ecclesiastically minded. But for that reason we have no right to reject these Epistles, but rather to recognise them as exactly suitable to the new condition of the Church on the one hand, and to the state of Paul's mind on the other.

It was a Cæsarean process, the disengagement of Christianity from the womb of Judaism. When Paul had accomplished that, then it was his duty to care for the infant Church he had freed, to feed it with milk, and provide it with nurses.

Finally, we may ask once again whether the great work of Paul was of that permanent character usually attributed to it, whether indeed it was not a working out the ends designed by God on a lower level, and one less perfect than that plan, which design of God to evangelise the world through Israel was rendered nugatory by the stubborn refusal of the Jew to undertake the task set before him; and whether the hesitations and scruples of the Twelve were not justified. It is not always possible to judge when the right moment has arrived at which to change front.

They may have thought that Paul was precipitating a conflict, and irritating the Jews in place of convincing them, forcing on a disruption which need not have occurred.

But Paul understood the hopelessness of the prospect of bringing over the entire Jewish nation to the obedience of Christ; to a large extent because of the Sadducæan hold on the priesthood and occupation of the Temple. When the head was unredeemably bad the body was past salvation. It had lost organic unity. The utmost that could be done was to convert individuals or sub-sections of parties. Even had the whole body of Pharisees come over to a conviction that Christ Jesus was the fulfilment of the Law and prophecies, yet still the Temple, the centre of the nation and its religion and polity, was irreclaimable.

And Paul saw, moreover, that the elements for a schism existed in the Diaspora. One large section, the largest, was impatient of the restraints of the ceremonial law, and was ready at a word, when sufficient excuse was given, to break away altogether. It was with this section that he constituted the Church, not with Gentiles, except only such as hung on to the skirts of this impatient, grumbling section of the Jewish community.

Is it unwarrantable to hope that the primary scheme of Providence may find at the end its fulfilment? That the Jewish people, so marvellously preserved, so richly endowed, may yet be the means of salvation to the world?

Had the Gospel streamed forth from Jerusalem, and had it possessed in the Jewish nation the treasure-keeper of sacred tradition and perhaps also of the ministry, what a unity there would have been in the Church! Rome has been but the ape of this primitive, divinely schemed unity, a cruel ape, murdering and betraying. May it not be that in the restoration of Israel, in its conversion to Christ will be found the bond of unity for which, alas, the rent Church of Christ sighs and almost despairs?

"Hath God cast away His people?" asked Paul; and he answered, "God forbid. God hath not cast away His people which He foreknew. Have they stumbled that they should fall past recovery? God forbid. If their tripping be the riches of the world, and the diminishing of them the riches of the Gentiles, how much more their fulness? If the casting away of them be the reconciling of the world, what shall the receiving of them be but life from the dead?"[1]

But the future is in God's hands. If we entertain this hope, we may take this confidence that it was shared by the great Apostle.

What in the meantime the Church has to do is not to petrify into dead conservatism, but to let the divine life that is in her develop itself organically, logically.

Legend says that when Paul was about to receive the fatal stroke he thus addressed a female convert who looked on, but through her spoke to the entire Church: "Fare thee well, Plantilla, thou plant of eternal life. Recognise thine own nobility of birth. Behold, thou shall become whiter than the snow, if thou, stepping into the ranks of the soldiers of Christ, attainest to heavenly life."

"It is of the nature of tradition," says Sabatier, "especially of religious tradition, to transform the figures of men it has consecrated into types and symbols. Those of the first Apostles of Christ have thus assumed, in process of time, a character as unalterable and hieratic as have those statues which one sees ranged in stiff symmetrical order under the portals of our cathedrals. Yet they were real men, those daring missionaries of the Christian idea, men belonging to their race and to their

[1] Rom. xi. 1-15.

age, each carrying into the accomplishment of his work such as fell to his lot his peculiar temperament and individual talents. To rediscover this distinct and original physiognomy under the envelopes of legend and dogma, to find the personality hidden by tradition, in a word, to see the man in the Apostle, such should be the effort of history, and such unconsciously or avowedly is the aim of criticism during the last fifty years. Such a historical resurrection is not possible for the majority of the first Apostles, who, so to speak, wrought anonymously at a common work, leaving behind them nothing concerning their personalities save vague traditions. It is other with the last on the scene, the thirteenth, Paul of Tarsus."

Recognising, as one cannot fail to do, the sincerity, the enthusiasm, the indefatigable energy of St. Paul, his singleness of heart, his strength of purpose, his devotion to his Master, and his breadth of charity, I have not dwelt upon these characteristics, because these have been written about a thousand times, now with grave admiration, then in frothy verbiage. What has been attempted in these pages is to supplement the work of his eulogisers by filling in their omissions.

I have endeavoured to the best of my poor abilities to throw myself back into the period in which the Apostle lived and laboured, and to endeavour to understand both what his methods of work were and also why, on the one hand, they aroused such bitter hostility, and, on the other, such guarded approval. I have tried to work out the development of his ideas from their first genesis; and to weigh in the scales of common principles of logic the arguments that St. Paul employed.

His method of procedure was one, I have shown, that

he was justified in adopting, if the Gospel was to be offered first to the Jew; that it was exasperating to the Jew was inevitable; but this mode of preaching was not possible for the Twelve in Jerusalem, where the Sanhedrim was all-powerful to stop it.

The generally received opinion that Paul was an Apostle *to* the Gentiles I conceive requires some modification. He was an Apostle *among* the Gentiles, and if the Gentiles were converted, it was not due to his direct action, but to the proselytes whom he convinced.

. That his method of reasoning should be quite other than would be pursued by Greek or Roman was inevitable, unless inspiration be taken to supply to a man an entirely new set of brains. It may be asked, How is it that St. Paul has taken so commanding a position in the mind of the Church, that he so dominated thought in the first age that even St. Peter and St. Jude fell under his influence and reproduced his thoughts in their Epistles, and that he was quoted as of infallible authority throughout the Church, and that, although his success was so limited and his argumentative power so defective?

We have but to pass from reading the Pauline Epistles to the writings of Justin Martyr, the pseudo-Barnabas and the Pastor of Hermas, to understand this. It is a change from the breezy mountain top to the atmosphere of a cabin in a valley; the difference is the same as that between the canonical and the apocryphal Gospels. To compare great things with small the difference is as wide between the best plays of Shakespeare and the productions of Colley Cibber, Bickerstaff, and Colman; or between an oratorio by Handel and a "service" by a musical scribbler of the present day; or between Plato and Porphyry.

The Church did not for some centuries possess men of commanding ability. Everything in the decaying Empire was mediocre, but there was still veneration for real power and originality such as had been manifested in the past. Not till Augustine rose did any genius appear above the Christian horizon. There had been writers, writers in plenty, but all of the third or fourth order.

This was one reason why St. Paul's writings were held in such admiration. Another was that it was felt that he had been truly inspired in the direction he took. The fall of Jerusalem was the closing of the door to the Jew. Then it was seen that the Gentile Church was to rise into universality, and that the Jews must seek salvation in it, and that the idea of a Jewish Church expanded to catholicity was impossible. Paul's forecast had come true, his work had prepared for this change, he was justified in his conduct by events. This was recognised, and with the recognition came his exaltation. To this, again, must be added the great good fortune he enjoyed in having a biographer who admired him beyond measure. Almost nothing was known of the other Apostles, their work in the East was unrecorded, and in the great dearth of authentic history of their doings, those of Paul were fastened on and their importance perhaps magnified unduly at the expense of the rest.

Yet his strong personality, the intense individuality of this Apostle, told above all. And in his wonderful Epistles he had a word for every one in all times—a word that went deep into every heart, met every experience, comforted in every sorrow, cheered in every discouragement, that braced every tired soul. And so—in all time—Paul has been, and will be, looked on as a personal and very dear guide and friend to every Christian who seeks things spiritual. It is the humanity of Paul that meets us and makes us cling to him, listen to, and love him. That, I conceive, is another reason why he has obtained so high a place in the esteem of the Church.

If there was a moment when his position was risked, it was that when he launched forth against the Law. But, if careless in his language, his real meaning was made abundantly clear, and apologists and controversialists in the ensuing centuries spoke the mind of the Church in limiting his term "Law" to the ceremonial ordinances, or in shelving his argument altogether.[1]

Altogether Paul's position had been unique. The only man of ability among the Apostles, who, though last called, laboured more abundantly than they all, striking out a line for himself and maintaining it, and sealing his testimony with his blood.

" *We were dreamers, dreaming greatly, in the man-stifled town,*
  We yearned beyond the sky-line, where the strange roads go down;
  Came the Whisper, came the Vision, came the Power with the Need,
  Till the Soul that is not man's soul was lent us to lead.

        .   .   .   .   .

" *Follow after—we are waiting, by the trails that we lost,*
  For the sounds of many footsteps, for the tread of a host.
  Follow after—follow after—for the harvest is sown:
  By the bones about the wayside ye shall come to your own."[2]

----

[1] See what is said in the Addenda on "Pauline Anomia."
[2] "The Seven Seas," by Rudyard Kipling, 1896.

ADDENDA

THE APOSTOLATE (p. 65).—The question as to the signification of the Apostolate is not very easy to solve, as so many later ideas have been imported into it, and this affects our mind when considering it. An Apostle is, as the word signifies, *One who is sent.* The sender is, of course, Christ. But sent for what purpose? I take it for two : 1st, to carry the Gospel throughout the world. "Go ye into all the world, and preach the Gospel to every creature" (Mark xvi. 15). But in the form of commission recorded by St. Matthew something further is implied. "Go ye and teach all nations, baptizing them in the name of the Father, and of the Son, and of the Holy Ghost ; teaching them to observe all things whatsoever I have commanded you" (Matt. xxviii. 19, 20). Here the commission is seen to include, 2ndly, a ministerial act, that of initiation into Christ's spiritual kingdom. Primarily the mission is to preach the Gospel. But what is the Gospel? The word occurs about a hundred times in the New Testament. One half of the book is occupied by the four Gospels. That is to say, four out of the eight or nine writers have put on record what the Gospel was, according to their opinion. St. Mark commences his narrative with the words, "The beginning of the Gospel of Jesus Christ, the Son of God." Matthew, Luke, and John agree with him in considering the Gospel to be the record of the acts and words of Jesus Christ. It is a narrative of facts, and not a scheme of salvation.[1]

[1] See Hammond: "Church or Chapel, an Eirenicon" (Lond. 1890), pp. 335-40.

Now the special mission of the Twelve seems to have been to give testimony to Christ, and He showed them in what their Apostleship was to consist. "He opened their understanding, that they might understand the Scriptures; and said unto them, Thus it is written, and thus it behoved Christ to suffer, and to rise from the dead the third day; and that repentance and remission of sins should be preached in His name among all nations, beginning at Jerusalem. *And ye are witnesses of these things*" (Luke xxiv. 45-48). And again: "Ye shall receive power, after that the Holy Ghost is come upon you; and *ye shall be witnesses unto me*, both in Jerusalem, and in all Judæa, and in Samaria, and unto the uttermost part of the earth" (Acts i. 8).

When Judas by transgression fell, then it was proposed to fill his place from among those only who had witnessed Christ's life "beginning from the baptism of John, unto that same day that he was taken up from us," and he was to be, especially, " a witness—of His resurrection" (Acts i. 21-22). Matthias was chosen. But the limitation shows that the Eleven understood the Apostolate to consist primarily in witnessing to the facts of Christ's life, death and resurrection. That, as they understood it, was the Gospel and that the Apostleship.

But had St. Paul any other conception of the Gospel than that entertained by the Twelve? Let us look at his Epistles. In Romans i. 1 he writes that he was "separated unto the Gospel of God," and then he proceeds to inform us that his Gospel was "concerning His Son Jesus Christ." He mentions indeed only two facts in our Lord's history, the Incarnation and the Resurrection, but in these two everything is comprised. So again in 2 Tim. ii. 8, " Remember that Jesus Christ, of the seed of David, was raised from the dead, according to my Gospel," *i.e.* his witness. In 1 Cor. xv. 1-5 he declares to the Corinthians what his Gospel was—" That Christ died for our sins .... and that He was buried, and that He rose again .... and that He was seen," &c. It is the same still, a record of facts. We have a sermon of St. Paul's in Acts xiii. In that he says (v. 32) that he is preaching the Gospel: " We bring you the Gospel of the promise," &c., and that is, testimony to the resurrection of Jesus Christ.

It is very generally assumed—understand, assumed only—that Paul's Gospel is a proclamation of free justification, is, in fact, a scheme of salvation. I can see no warrant for this in his writings. In his final address to the elders of Ephesus, Paul spoke of his having testified " the Gospel of the grace of God " (Acts xx. 24), but this grace or favour of God was precisely shown in this, " That God sent His only begotten son into the world, that we might live through Him " (1 John iv. 9). The word Gospel means glad tidings, and I contend that in its *primary* sense, in that employed by the Apostles, Paul included, it meant the announcement that Christ was come of the seed of David, the promised Messiah, that He died and rose, and would come again. It was a dogma of facts and not a scheme or theory of salvation.

I take it, then, that St. Paul's employment of the term Gospel was the same as that of the Twelve. It was not a plan of justification by faith, not a scheme at all, but a testimony to the advent of the Messiah, and to His resurrection.

St. Paul did not receive his Gospel of men, that is to say he did not go to Galatians, Macedonians, and Achaians, &c., with testimony at second hand; he did not go to report that he had heard the Twelve declare that Christ was come, and by wicked hands had been slain, but had risen again; he went as a first hand witness, for he had seen Jesus Christ at his conversion. He dated his Apostleship from the vision at Damascus (Acts ix. 6, 15; xxii. 21; xxvi. 17; Rom. i. 1; 1 Cor. i. 1; 2 Cor. i. 1; Gal. i. 1, 12; ii. 7, 9).

Paul was qualified to give testimony that Christ was alive from the dead, but was not qualified to give witness as to what He had done and taught during His ministry, for in fact he had not been in Palestine at the time, but at Tarsus in Cilicia. The elder Apostles may have hesitated whether to widen the term *Apostle* into comprehension of a witness not qualified according to the definition given by Jesus Christ. They had not only been with Christ during His ministry, but also after

His resurrection, and they had further received an outpouring of the Holy Ghost "to bring all things to 'their' remembrance" (John xiv. 26). There was no evidence that the Spirit had fallen on Paul, they had but his unsupported word that he had seen Christ and received commission from Him in a vision. What guarantee had they that he did not deceive himself? What guarantee that any number of vain, ambitious, and hysterical persons might not set themselves up as Apostles on the same plea, which was one impossible of verification? (See further, p. 462.)

They understood by the Apostleship a witness to certain events that took place in Jerusalem and Galilee between A.D. 28 and 30. At that time Paul was not in the country. They were required not merely to take his word for it that he —of whom they knew very little—had received his mission from Christ, but also very greatly to alter their conception of what Apostleship meant.

As to Paul's legitimate claim to the ministry, that was quite another matter. That they recognised, for he had been ordained by imposition of hands (Acts xiii. 2, 3).

What the qualification of Barnabas was to be regarded as an Apostle or witness, that we do not know, but almost certainly he must have been one of Christ's disciples, for the Twelve did not question his suitability.[1]

So far from the Twelve being blameworthy in the reserve with which they received St. Paul, and in hesitating to allow his claim, they really seem to have gone to the extreme limits of concession. Would any court now listen to a man who entered the witness-box, and who, after having been shown to have been many hundred miles away at the time when a certain event took place, yet asked to be heard because five years after the event he had dreamt of the circumstances?

St. Paul speaks of the Apostolate as one of the *charismata*, the extraordinary gifts of God. So it was in his case especially, for he saw Christ by revelation, and consequently was able to bear testimony to Him. But so also in a different degree was

[1] The early Fathers say he was one of the Seventy.

it with the Twelve, for they had been miraculously endowed with the Spirit to bring to their remembrance all that Christ had taught and done.

RELIGIOUS ECSTASY (p. 116).—Elevation from the ground and illumination of the face are not phenomena, or supposed phenomena, peculiar to Christianity. In the life of the Neoplatonist philosopher Jamblicus, by Eunapius, the heathen author says: "It is related that when they (Porphyry and Jamblicus) prayed, they appeared to be lifted some two cubits above the ground, and their bodies and garments gleamed like unto gold." The Neoplatonist school was that of pagan mystics; the philosophers belonging to it endeavoured by ecstatic devotion to elevate their souls into absorption into the divine light. Asterius Urbanus, in a passage quoted by Eusebius, says that a Montanist ecstatic, in one of his transports, was "pitched like a quoit" into the air, and falling, was killed (Euseb. *H. E.* v. 17). There is a very curious and instructive account of the "conversion" of Thespesios of Soli given by Plutarch (*De sera Numinis vindicta*, xxvii.), which, though not exhibiting the phenomenon of elevation, may be compared with the ecstasies of St. Paul and St. Theresa.

"Thespesios of Soli, an acquaintance and friend of Protogenes, now living with us, lived at one time in an extravagant and dissolute manner. Then when he had wasted his fortune, driven by necessity, he became a great rogue. . . . . . What chiefly discredited him was a prophecy of Amphilochos. He had turned to the god with the question whether he would fare any better later, and the oracular answer given was he would be better after his death. And this happened shortly after. He fell off a height on his neck, and, though not wounding himself, he died of the fall. On the third day, however, as he was about to be buried, he recovered his vigour, and from that time a marvellous change took place in his life. For the Cilicians knew no man of the time leading a more sober life, more pious towards the divinity, more difficult to the foes and more reliable to the friends of the gods, so that they who were acquainted with him asked the reason of this extraordinary change. Thespesios answered that when he fell his soul separated from the body, and felt like a boatman who was upset from his skiff and was struggling in the water. But presently his soul recovered itself, and then all at once it seemed to inhale the full plenitude of its existence, and to see all things as though it were but one eye. Of created things it perceived nothing save the greater stars, at an infinite distance apart, in ineffable splendour, and musical tones of infinite sweetness, and the soul seemed to glide in space softly in all directions as in a calm." The whole account is most interesting, but too long for quotation.[1]

David Joris, of Delft, founder of an Anabaptist sect, had his first ecstasy in November 1536, whilst in his workshop, and standing; and was, as it were, rapt away and up and saw visions—not very decent, by the way, but he was a most immoral man—and received a revelation as to "angelical marriage." When he came back out of ecstasy he was as exhausted as if he had run for two miles, and was gasping for breath. He at once took pen and paper and wrote his visions. His "Wonder Bok," with its indecent pictures, is somewhat rare. The man was perfectly sincere, and fell into real ecstasies, but his visions were indited by his natural thoughts.[2] In A. Moller's *Beschreibung Freibergs* is an account of a Lutheran woman, in 1620, whose case closely resembles that of the girl mentioned in the text, only that it was more pronounced. "In the presence of the deacons Dachsel and Waldburg she was raised out of her bed, in all her body, head, hands and feet, to the height of an ell and a half, so that she remained no more in connection with the bed, but floated freely above it, so that it almost seemed as though she might drift out of the window. Waldburg laid hold of her, and he and all present cried out to God, and so she was brought

[1] See also the story of Hermolienus of Clazomenæ, in Pliny, *H. N.* vii. 53, and that of Eximenides by Suidas.
[2] Nippold: *David Joris*, in "Zeitschrift f. Historische Theologie," 1863, p. 61 *et seq.*

down again." Other instances are given by Dom Calmet in his *Apparitions des Esprits*, 1750.

Very similar phenomena are reported among the Brahmins, and indeed the contrivance whereby an ascetic supports himself in a seated position on a small rod is an attempt by art to represent what a Brahmin saint can attain to if in a sufficiently ecstatic condition.

Whatever may be the occasion of ecstasy and its manifestations, it seems clear that the person rapt sees, hears, speaks, only in accordance with preconceived ideas. The revelations of St. Bridget contain nothing but the notions she had received from sacred pictures. A Calvinist visionary sees, hears, naught but what is in accord with his prejudices; a Roman Catholic that only which confirms his belief; a foul-minded mystic like David Joris beholds only tainted visions; a Brahmin is confirmed in his Brahminism; and a Mussulman in his Mohammedanism. It is a condition of body and mind and soul that may be employed by God, or may be left to prey on already assimilated ideas. Some of St. Theresa's revelations are grotesque—some of St. Bridget's silly; those of Joris a blend in equal proportions of religion and obscenity; those of some prophets certainly false (Jer. xxiii. 29, 32). I take it then that ecstasy is a natural though unusual condition into which a man or woman may fall, through overwrought nerves, or due to hysteria, and that God may make use of this condition for direct commune with the soul, and for giving direction to it; but that in general the mind in such cases, just as in dream, feeds on material already received. It is very noticeable that both in the case of St. Peter and in that of St. Paul, at his conversion, the visions went clean *against* preconceptions, which never takes place in natural ecstasy.

ANATOLIAN POLYANDRY (p. 160).—I cannot help thinking that anthropologists and writers on primitive marriage make a great mistake in attempting to prove that monogamy is a late development, and that all mankind passed through the social phases of promiscuity and the various forms of polyandry. It seems to me that the social phenomena, of which there are so many remains, in which a woman is either common property, or in which she belongs to several brothers, or to a class, may be explained simply by other means than supposing them to be relics of primeval conditions. For instance, the high plateau of Tibet will not support more than a limited population. It is therefore the object of those inhabiting it to limit the supply of children. They do this in two ways: *First*, by making one woman the wife of all the brothers in a family; and *secondly*, by the institution of monasteries of Buddhist celibates. "Buddhism, which enjoins monastic life on 11,000 out of a total population of 120,000, farther restrains the increase of population within the limits of sustenance by inculcating and rigidly upholding the system of polyandry, permitting marriage only to the eldest son, the heir of the land, while the bride accepts all his brothers as inferior or subordinate husbands, thus attaching the whole family to the soil and family roof-tree, the children being regarded legally as the property of the eldest son, who is addressed by them as Big Father, his brothers receiving the title of Little Father."— Bishop (I. L.), "Among the Tibetans," London, 1894.

That this custom is purely based on economic grounds can hardly be doubted. If questioned, then here is another instance. In Tyrol, the narrow strip of alluvial land in the valleys and limited amount of pasturage in the Alps make it impossible for the population to greatly increase and find subsistence in their native mountains. It is also impracticable to divide up dairy farms, as tillage farms are parcelled in the flat land. A farm must be kept together. Now when a father dies and leaves, say, five sons, what is often done is this. The brothers draw lots as to which of them is to marry, then he on whom the lot falls alone takes to him a wife, and the four brothers, one or more may be elder, serve the married one and assist in the farm work. Can it be doubted that were these Tyrolese not good Christian men, and so forbidden by their religion, the woman would be the wife of the five? I believe that it has been economic causes which have disturbed and altered the primitive institution of monogamy, and not that monogamy, or more exactly monogyny, should be a late outgrowth after ages of promiscuity and polyandry.

After circumstances have produced polyandry, when the determining causes have ceased, then there will be a reversion to monogyny, but in the marriage ceremonies a trace of the condition of affairs, in which the woman was common property, may survive. It is so in the South Pacific Islands. But I fail to see, because there and elsewhere where monogyny is becoming customary, that promiscuity was the primordial condition out of which it is developing, but rather that this condition of promiscuity was an interruption of the original condition and order, and that which we now encounter is a reversion to the primitive type before polyandry arose, bred out of temporary economic necessity.

Very generally religious rites preserve features of common life that have passed out of general use. Thus the use of flint knives for circumcision and for embalming remained on in Egypt long after bronze and iron had come into common usage. So also in the Church, flint and steel are employed in East and West for kindling the Easter fire; and the use of lucifers is regarded as unlawful for the purpose. So also, in the Roman Communion, the Congregation of Rites orders that only beeswax shall be employed for altar candles, although vegetable wax and mineral oil composites have come into general employ. I have supposed that Anatolian promiscuity in the temples is due to such a survival. But it may have risen from another cause, that of sexual hospitality. Some of the temples in the East were served by large bands of priestesses, who were harlots; others had not these fixed bands, but called on all virgins to pass through a period of service of this description, previous to becoming marriageable; and again others were supplied by women in fulfilment of vows.

At the same time I cannot but suspect that the reason for these abominations being practised in the temples of the East was that it was a conservative protest against the change of custom in the relations of the sexes and the organisation of the family consequent on the necessity for the temporary check imposed on the growth of the population having come to an end. The plateau of Central Anatolia is like that of Tibet; the rigorous winters ensue on burning summers; the vast salt tracts growing nothing, make it impossible for a large population to be maintained on tillage or to exist as nomads. But when the fertile valleys were occupied, and when the mountains were worked for metal and for statuary marble, then at once there was a demand for workmen, and all occasion for artificially hindering increase came to an end. Why are we to imagine that human beings began in a more gross and grovelling condition as regards the sexes than the anthropoid apes, and than almost all birds?

We see in all races where the need for limitation of the population ceases that there is gravitation towards monogyny. Surely this indicates that man, unless under imperious necessity, is a monogamous animal. The same cause that produces polyandry produces infanticide. Is it so that the original, primordial condition of man is one in which he kills his children? Is it not that infanticide grew out of a supposed necessity to keep the population down to the number which a barren soil would sustain? And promiscuity or so-called " communal marriage " is, I take it, a similar barbarous expedient of savage life. To my mind, Westermarck, in his " History of Human Marriage" (Lond. 1891), has cut away conclusively every prop on which McLennan, Morgan, Sir John Lubbock, and those who follow them like sheep, have endeavoured to rear the fabric of promiscuity as the initial condition of mankind out of which monogamy slowly emerged.

THE GREEKS (p. 165).—The importance of the Hellenes in Christian times has been wofully misunderstood and misrepresented. Gibbon did his best by sneer to discredit the Byzantine Empire, and we have not yet escaped from the influence he has exerted. That Empire lasted a thousand years, and formed a mighty breakwater against the barbarian tribes from the North, and also against Persians, Saracens and Turks from the East. It covered Asia Minor and North Africa with excellent roads, and established commercial *entrepôts* throughout the Levant. Anatolia, now a desert, was a thriving and peopled region under the Byzantine sceptre. It did more, it preserved to the West, sunk in barbarism, the treasures of classic literature and culture. True, it was not creative, but it was conservative.

The strength of that Empire was sapped by the Latin conquest of Constantinople; and destroyed by the Turk, because the Pope, seeing his Christian brethren in need, shut up his bowels of compassion against them, and hailed the Moslem who would ruin Oriental Christianity that stood in the old paths and refused to submit to his pretensions built up on forged decretals. As said in the text, Where now is the Roman? The Italian does not represent him in character or blood. But the Greek is indestructible. In Greece proper and in the Isles of the Ægean and in Crete, "the entirely and exclusively Hellenic character of all the features, physical and intellectual, presented by the present inhabitants of the country is a most striking fact, almost unique in history, a glorious mark of our race and a wondrous proof of the intensity of our national vitality" (D. Bikelas: "Seven Essays on Christian Greece," translated by the Marquis of Bute, London, 1890). The same writer says: "From the time of the fall of Constantinople until the present day, through all the agonies of a slavery which lasted four hundred years, and amid all the trials of better days, the Greeks have never lost hope for the future. This national hopefulness is not the mere vanity which remembrance of the past inspires in a fallen race. We have hoped, and we do hope, because—even during the first two centuries of our bondage, when the hand of the Turks was still full of strength and lay so heavy upon us—we have always known what were and are those things which give us our true life and strength."

Recent events have shown us how Greece can dare and do, and such a nation has before it a future. And may it not be that just as the Greek nation has its mission in the future, so may the Greek Church, as a reconciler of the discord among Christians in the West? This may be a dream, but I cannot conceive such a body as a Church being preserved in suspended animation without a purpose in God's providence.

MULIERES SUBINTRODUCTÆ (p. 174).—There is a significant passage in Irenæus ("Adv. Haer.,' I. vi. 3), which shows that the practice of "leading about sisters" prevailed in his time (the book was written between A.D. 182 and 188), and that it by no means conduced to edification. In connection with this the story of Glycerius the Deacon may be considered. It has been given with some fulness by Professor Ramsay ("The Church in the Roman Empire") About A.D. 372 Glycerius led after him a body of young women, "and scandalised the country by wandering about with them in a disorderly manner, dancing and singing hymns, amidst the jeers of the coarse rustics. When their fathers came to rescue the girls, Glycerius ignominiously drove them away. Finally, the whole band took refuge with a bishop," probably St. Gregory Nazianzen the elder, and St. Basil had to write very strongly to his brother bishop not to encourage this sort of thing. Gregory evidently accepted the conduct of Glycerius as quite in accordance with the custom of clerics taking unmarried women about with them, and calling them sisters; and he hesitated to forbid Glycerius proceeding in a manner, not then very extraordinary, and not without sanction in the past.

In this case of Glycerius we have simply the practice of taking about a female companion, linked in pure spiritual relationship, magnified into sweeping through the country with a troop of enthusiastic girls in attendance. No charge of immorality was made against Glycerius, only one of following a usage that gave a handle to the blasphemers. We see that there was a tendency to this sort of thing early, for St. Paul had to give Timothy his advice to keep the young widows at arm's length (1 Tim. v. 11-13). Two Epistles, erroneously attributed to St. Clement of Rome, yet certainly not later than the second century, are addressed to the Virgins, and condemn the practice of young people of different sexes living together under the pretence of religion, and specially warn virgins against cohabiting with the clergy, lest offence be given " to the Jews, the heathen, and to the Church of God " (i. 10; ii. 5). The author speaks of the "shameless men who, under pretext of the fear of God, dwell with virgins and (wilfully) expose themselves to danger." Manes, who took about with him twenty-two youths and damsels, did but follow the lead of men in the Church like Glycerius (Archelaus, "Disput." 12). St. Cyprian had occasion to write very peremptorily on the matter, and to threaten excommunication if persisted in ("Ep." 4). In the Synod of Antioch in 210, Paul, Bishop of Samosata, was condemned for this practice, which prevailed among the priests and deacons of his Syrian diocese, and which he encouraged by his own example (Euseb. " H. E.," vii. 30). In the Council of Nicæa (A.D. 325) the third canon forbade ecclesiastics having any *mulier subintroducta* in the house with them except a near relation above suspicion. Some twenty years before that, the Council of Elvira had passed a very similar canon. Yet the practice died hard, for as late as A.D. 538 (*circ.*) it was condemned by a *novel* of Justinian. It was not unknown in the Middle Ages, for it was revived by Dolcino, the heretic, and by the Fraticelli, and by St. Robert of Arbrissel. Indeed, "spiritual wives" have become an institution in some Protestant mystic sects. The origin of the custom can be well understood; it was a reaction against the prevailing licentiousness. Those who were converted, and set themselves up to be saints, endeavoured to make a show of their ecstatic purity by putting themselves into dangerous associations and passing through unharmed, just as some fanatics have endeavoured to establish the truth of their mission by marching through flames. In all times of religious excitement there are to be found men with small brains and lively enthusiasm, who rush into extravagances, and who are more troublesome to deal with than open enemies.

The canons of the councils and condemnations of the practice have been largely used by Romanists to justify the papal condemnation of clerical marriage, that is to say, they have employed denunciations of objectionable extravagances to forbid a legitimate divine institution.

CIRCUMCISION (p. 199) as practised in the Coptic Church. For this see Zaborowski: *Bulletin de la Société d'Anthropologie*, 1896, p. 500; and *L'Anthropologie*, 1896, p. 656.

THE ROBUR (p. 219).—An illustration of the Tullianum at Rome will make it more easy to understand what a Roman prison was like. This is from an engraved slab of marble,

executed by M. Cocceius Nerva, consul with Vespasian, A.D. 71, and with Domitian A.D. 90, and afterwards emperor. The upper portion is the *Robur* or *Lignum*, in which were the stocks, and where prisoners were executed. The lower portion is the Tullianum, in Greece and the East called the Barathrum. Into this Jugurtha was lowered and there allowed to die of starvation in darkness. Usually this lower portion was a great cesspool, with a drain outwards. St. Ferreolus of Vienne, A.D. 304, was cast down into this cesspool, but managed to escape through the outfall into the Rhone. In the Acts of the Scillitane Martyrs (Ruinart: Act Martyr. sincer. 77) we read of the proconsul giving sentence, " Let them be thrown into prison; let them be put into the *Lignum* till to-morrow." The utter darkness, the heat, and the stench of this miserable place, are often dwelt on by the martyrs and their biographers. " After a few days," says St. Perpetua, " we were taken to the prison, and I was frightened, for I never had known such darkness. O bitter day ! The heat was excessive by reason of the crowd there." In the Acts of St. Pionius and others of Smyrna, we read that the jailers "shut them up in the inner part of the prison, so that, bereaved of all comfort and all light, they were forced to sustain extreme torment, from the darkness and stench of the prison." See also Tertullian, " Ad. Martyras," 2.

THE UNKNOWN GOD (p. 233).—Had St. Paul landed in Delos, he would have seen, not merely an altar, but a temple dedicated to the unknown stranger gods. Tozer (H. F.) " The Islands of the Ægean," 1890, p. 8. At Athens there were many altars to the unknown gods.

PROPHECIES AND UNKNOWN TONGUES (p. 249).—The danger to religion in these indecent exhibitions must have very speedily made itself felt, for when Asterius Urbanus wrote against the Montanists, *circ.* 213, he condemns their ecstasies and prophecies, which were but a recrudescence of these disagreeable performances at Corinth, but transferred to Mysia; and he does this on the grounds that this is " contrary to the custom of the Church, as handed down from early times and preserved thenceforward in continuous succession." Indeed we see by St. Paul's words to the Thessalonians (1 Thess. v. 20) that prophecy was already discredited among the soberer heads, probably because associated with these scenes.

Prophecy is one of the *charismata* (1 Cor. xii. 10, 28), a supernatural divine gift. But then in what does it consist? First, it is an illumination from above revealing the truth. In such manner was St. Paul a prophet, for he was inspired to know the truth as it is in Jesus. But secondly, it was a revelation of the future. Some prophets, no doubt, did not possess this gift of seeing and foretelling what was to be. Thirdly, it was the gift of exhortation, and perhaps of composition of psalm and hymn. Consequently we must discriminate. It was in the third case an exaltation of natural faculties and not extraordinary. But in the two first it was miraculous. Yet so great is the vanity of man, and so liable is he to deceive himself, that very soon many pretended to have the miraculous prophetic gift who had really no right to it. Moreover, hysteria and nervous disorder, which are very infectious, produced conditions resembling that which was miraculous, and so difficult was it to distinguish the true from the spurious that the Church suppressed the whole exhibition. We get an idea of the sort of phenomena that occurred at Corinth, from that which attended the revolt of the Calvinists in the Cévennes.

A Sieur du Serre, master glass manufacturer at Peyrat in Dauphiné, was ordained prophet by a "school of prophets" at Geneva, and he set to work to inspire his wife and children and all the young hands working in his factory by fasting, long prayers and sermons, and reading of the Apocalypse, so as to superinduce ecstasies. Then these young girls and boys ordained by him scattered through the country seeing visions and prophesying. The most conspicuous among the prophetesses of this period (1689) was *la belle Isabeau*, a shepherdess, daughter of a wool-comber near Crest, aged from sixteen to eighteen. She began to have trances and speak in small gatherings of the Huguenots, but her fame spread and crowds came to hear and see her.

Gerlan, a Dauphinois lawyer, was captivated by her, and followed her everywhere, noting down her words as though the oracles of God. She was a thin girl, short, with irregular features, a broad head, and dark intelligent eyes. Gerlan thus describes the first meeting he attended: "I am by myself incapable of speaking," said she, but falling on her knees, she added: "O God, unloose my tongue, if it be Thy good pleasure, that I may announce Thy word to console Thy afflicted people!" Immediately the Spirit seized her, and she made a long prayer. "I thought," says Gerlan, "that an angel was speaking." After having made all sing a psalm which she started, she preached in a loud tone. Sometimes she fell into a trance, and it was in vain to touch, call, shake her. She was then insensible to pain, to being pinched, to needles run into her, or to fire applied to her. During these trances she spoke, sang, and prophesied. On recovering from the fits she could remember nothing that she had said or done in them. By breathing on others she communicated the same powers, and women and children went into raptures, saw visions and prophesied. She converted a Mme. de Baix, widow of a *Conseiller du parlement*, at Grenoble, and made her and her daughter ecstatics and prophetesses. When the handsome Isabeau preached, the inspiration came on all. "A man who had no thought of prophesying was returning from an assembly one night with some companions, when all at once he fell flat and went into spasmodic contortions on a bed of snow. Then, with his eyes closed, like one asleep, he began to preach and prophesy."[1]

Finally *la belle Isabeau* was taken and lodged with some other prophetesses in prison, where they were kindly treated, well fed, and visited by numerous ladies, and humoured and favoured as if they were off their heads, and so completely cured, and the beautiful Isabeau was married to a good-looking, sturdy, young peasant, and prophesied no more. Gabriel Astier, aged twenty-two, was another prophet. He promised the Cévennes Calvinists invulnerability, which however was not granted them. Hardly one of the prophecies came true, but that did not greatly affect the fanatics who followed these leaders. Those possessed with the Spirit numbered thousands, and they wandered about eating only nuts and apples, and falling flat on their backs and going into convulsions at intervals. "In his ecstasies Gabriel saw heaven open, and some who had suffered sitting on shining clouds. He also saw paradise and the angels, hell, and Satan. Sometimes a great pain invaded his bones, and his soul seemed to be a prey to mortal agony. Then he summoned a child to

[1] Jurieu: "Lettres Prophétiques."

sing a psalm to him." (Peyrat: "Hist. des Pasteurs du Désert," i. p. 194.) Another prophetess, Isabeau Charras, was wont to strip herself stark naked when prophesying. (Fléchier: " Rélation des Fanatiques.")

The phenomena attending these attacks were as follows. Usually those taken fell flat. Indeed Gabriel Astier was wont to cry, "Go down! the Spirit is on you"; when perhaps a thousand people tumbled backward in a rigid condition. They were then taken with convulsive trembling, and with contortions of the muscles; at once they broke out into more or less unintelligible exclamations, but always in French, and this was thought to be miraculous, as those thus taken were often children of five or nine years, who ordinarily spoke only the Languedoc *patois*. Here is a description of one of these attacks which came on a shepherd named Pierre Bernand. "He remained about two hours on his knees, and then fell as one dead; then his body became much agitated. On the morrow he fell again, and his convulsions became more violent. As he lay on his back his body lifted itself and bounded as if heaved about by a strong man. We were afraid he might hurt himself, and three of us tried to hold him, but it was impossible to control him. He continued in this condition, beating himself, and bathed in sweat. The same occurred two or three times before he spoke, then the Great Master having opened his mouth, the first thing he said was that he was tormented because of his sins. Afterwards his convulsions became less, and his discourse turned on urgent solicitations to amendment of life." ("Théâtre sacré des Cévennes," p. 151.)

Precisely similar phenomena took place during Wesley's preaching, and a very curious book, "The Autobiography of Peter Cartwright," London, 1862, gives an account of identically the same exhibitions accompanied with barking as of dogs, when the revivalist preached in Kentucky and Tennessee. See on this my "Strange Survivals," London, 1892, the article on "Revivals." For a full account of the Cévegnol prophets see Figuier (Louis), "Hist. du Merveilleux," Paris, 1860, ii. 179 *seq.*

The speaking with tongues, or glossology, has given rise to the most varied opinions. Some have thought that those affected jabbered unintelligible sounds, which it required others to make sense out of. Some have supposed that a single language was spoken by those with the gift; others again that they reverted to barbarous tongues with which they were acquainted in their youth or childhood, but which were not spoken in towns among the civilised. In all probability, judging from recent examples, both first and last are right. In Kentucky, at Cartwright's preaching, the people barked like dogs when in ecstasy, and in some of the Irvingite *séances* the possessed gabbled unintelligible nonsense. But it is also likely that those coming out of wild, barbarous lands should, when in a fit produced by nervous excitement, pour forth words in a tongue familiar to them in childhood. A very old lady I knew, in fact a kinswoman, had been brought up as a little girl in Portugal, which she left at a very early age, and she had almost completely forgotten Portuguese. Many years later, when suffering from fever, in a paroxysm she left her bed, knelt down and prayed in Portuguese, a thing she could not have done when well. Does it not seem that Paul suggests as much when he says that one so speaking seems to be a barbarian, *i.e.*, one from beyond the civilised world? (1 Cor. xiv. 11.)

PAULINE ANOMIA (p. 310).—The unfortunate effects of Paul's argument on the abrogation of the Law bore fruit very quickly. We see in the Epistle of Jude that already there were those in the Church who turned "the grace of God into lasciviousness," and this apparently at the Agape, "spots in your feasts of charity." But Paul indeed saw the evil start up under his own eyes, in Churches of his own founding, as in Corinth and Ephesus, where some of his disciples gave themselves over "to work all uncleanness with greediness" (Eph. iv. 19). Somewhat later this came to a head and infected entire Churches. So in the message to the Church of Pergamos, Christ says: "Thou hast them that hold the doctrine of Balaam—to eat things sacrificed unto idols, and to commit fornication" (Rev. ii. 14); and to the Church of Thyatira the same rebuke is administered. There a prophetess took the lead in urging to Anomia, "Thou sufferest that woman Jezebel, which calleth herself a prophetess, to teach and to seduce my servants to commit fornication, and to eat things sacrificed unto idols" (ii. 20). This *teaching* of immorality in the Church is a startling feature, and it seems to have been deliberately pursued by some who called themselves apostles (Rev. ii. 2), as well as by those who assumed to be prophets. In the Corinthian Church even the elders encouraged incest. Now, it is not possible to explain this phenomenon except on the ground that Paul's argument as to the Law being overridden had been laid hold of and elevated into a principle. These teachers did not wink at lapses into immorality, but defiantly urged on the converts to the Gospel to commit adultery, fornication, and all uncleanness, "such as is not so much as named among the Gentiles" (1 Cor. v. 1), as a protest against those who contended that the moral law as given on the tables was still binding upon the Church. Paul had not discriminated between the ceremonial and the moral law, and it was entirely open to the judgment of his converts whether he did or did not intend to throw both overboard. If his argument was good for anything, it applied equally to both.

In the first epistle on Virginity by the pseudo-Clement, a very early production, the immoralities committed at the Agape are admitted. The writer says: "Others eat and drink with them [*i.e.*, the virgins] at feasts [and indulge] in loose behaviour and much uncleanness, such as ought not to be among those who have elected holiness for themselves" (i. 10). Tertullian admits the worst Agape scandals (*De Jej.* 17).

Irenæus shows us how that the anti-legists coupled together licence in morals and laxity in the matter of the eating of sacrificial food. "They make no scruple about eating meats offered in sacrifice to idols, imagining that they can in this way contract no defilement. At every heathen festival celebrated in honour of idols these men are the first to assemble. Others yield themselves up to the lusts of the flesh with the utmost greed, maintaining that carnal things should be allowed to the carnal nature, while spiritual things are ordained for the spiritual" (*Adv. Hæres.* I. vi.).

These sectaries pretended that they were *in* the world, but not *of* the world, and that whatever indulgence they allowed to their natural lusts in no way stained the soul.

Because St. Paul, with great good sense, declares that an idol was nothing, and that meat offered in sacrifice was not actually defiling, and that consequently a Christian was not polluted by eating such meat, his most zealous followers thrust themselves forward at the altars of the gods, ostentatiously to eat of the sacrifices. So, in precisely the same manner, because he had pronounced the supersession of the Law, which was blotted out by the blood of Christ, and nailed to the Cross, the enthusiasts of free justification plunged into licence, working all uncleanness with greediness, in token of their emancipation from the Law.

The Church trembled on the verge of becoming an immoral sect. It was high time that the Gospels should appear and show that Christ had given His sanction to the moral law, nay had extended its application. Till the Gospels appeared there was no law in the non-Jewish Churches, except customary, and that based on the sentences pronounced by the Apostles. Charges of shameless immorality were, as we know, repeatedly made against the Christians; the heathen accused them of converting their nocturnal meetings, after the convivialities of the Agape, into scenes of hideous debauchery.[1] Nor were they wholly unjustified in making this charge, for, in the first place, these things actually did take place among some of the heretical anti-Judaic sects,[2] and the heathens were not capable of nicely distinguishing the sects from the body of

[1] Justin Martyr, 1st *Apol.* xxvi.; 2nd *Apol.* xii.; *Adv. Tryph.* x.; Athenagoras, *Apol.* iii. xxxi.; Min. Felix, *Octav.* ix.; Tertull. *Apol.* ii. iv. viii.; *Ad Nationes*, i. ii. vii. xvi.; Euseb. *H. E.* iv. 7; Theoph. *ad Autol.* iii. 4.

[2] Iren. *Hær.* i. 6, 25, 26; Clem. Alex. *Strom.* iii. 2, 4, 5; Epiphan. *Hæres.* xxxiv. 1.

the Church; but, in the next place, there is too much cause to fear that such abominations did actually occur among those Christians in the Church who were infected with hatred of the Law. St. Paul shows us this in Corinth and Ephesus, taking place immediately his presence was withdrawn; that it was rampant a little later is shown by the Epistle of St. Jude, and by the messages to the Seven Churches. It was probably not till St. John took the Asiatic Churches in hand, that this antinomian spirit, that rose out of St. Paul's argument like the Jin from the sealed flask of the fisherman in the " Arabian Nights," could be laid.

Gnosticism and Manicheism were not in reality heresies formed in the Church and breaking off from it, but were Oriental systems based on the dualism so dear to Eastern minds, which saw in all creation an eternal conflict between light and darkness, good and evil, spirit and matter. When these systems came in contact with Christianity, they at once absorbed some of it. The promulgators of this fusion caught at the antitheses propounded by St. Paul between the Law and the Promise, works and faith, the carnal mind and the spiritual, and worked them into their dualistic creed, and appealed to his authority on its behalf. The moral outcome or application of this religion of opposition of spirit and matter was diverse. Some became ascetics, forbade marriage and to eat meat (1 Tim. iv. 3), and sought, in conquest of all the instincts and appetites of the body, to attain to absorption in the Pleroma, the fulness of the divinity. On the other hand, others, contending that the spirit was emancipated by faith from the body, held that nothing done in the flesh could pollute the soul, and made of that an excuse for immorality. It seems to me that we have a refurbishing of this heresy by some of the new school of novelists who deal with the sex problem.

The Gnostics first, and then Manes, taught that, as the world was full of evil, lawlessness, pain, and death, it was manifestly the creation of an evil power, the Demiurge. And as, according to Paul, the Law was given to accentuate the power of sin, it also was given by the same evil principle; whereas free grace and peace come by Jesus Christ, the mouthpiece of the good principle, who is benevolence only.

Irenæus (*circ.* A.D. 190), in his "Refutation of Heresies," answers this contention by asserting that the Law of Moses was but the reaffirmation of the natural law imposed by the Creator on man when he was made, and that Christ reasserted the divine authority of this eternal law. But each re-edition extended the provisions and intensified the application as mankind progressed and was able to bear it (iv. 14–16). This is what I have maintained in the text (p. 280).

The very instructive "Disputation of Archelaus with Manes" (*between* A.D. 276–282) shows us the heresiarch representing himself as a follower of St. Paul, who, he says, "is held with us to be the most approved apostle" (xiii.), and on his authority maintaining that "the Law is to be destroyed and rejected." By a series of quotations Manes proceeded to demonstrate that the Law was evil and the source of evil. Till the Law came there was no sin. He therefore concluded that it must emanate from the great antagonist to God, *i.e.*, from Satan. The answer of Bishop Archelaus is precisely that of Irenæus. The Mosaic Law was the reassertion of the natural law. Owing to man's ignorance and the force of bad example, the binding authority of the natural law became weak and was forgotten, thence the need for its solemn re-imposition on Sinai (xxx.). And the new law as given by Christ is none other than the same made perfect.

Archelaus uses similes to illustrate his doctrine. "The truth," he says, "is simply this, that just as we trace the purple in a robe, so we discover the New Testament in the texture of the Old." In fact, it is like shot silk, showing in one light one colour and another in another light, because both are contained in one fabric; or, again, the New and the Old are the web and woof in the one fabric (xli.). Or, again, the old Law was the milk on which the sons of God were reared till they were capable of digesting and assimilating the more solid nutriment of the new law.

Justin Martyr (*d.* A.D. 165) takes another line. He represents the new law as completely abrogating the old, but then he is careful to limit this old law to one of ceremonies, and not to include in it the Two Tables.

St. Hippolitus (A.D. 222–239), in his "Refutation of all Heresies," derives the Gnostic tenets from the speculations of the Greek philosophers. He was mistaken in that; undoubtedly much was derived from these philosophers, but far more from the categories of emanations drawn out by the Chaldee Magi, the dualistic principles of Zoroaster, and the eternal revolution of existence of the Brahmins and Buddhists.

Tertullian, in his "Confutation of Marcion" (A.D. 208), argues that the giving of free will to man by the Creator impetrated the giving also of a law, for without a law the will would be inoperative, unable to make an election. Then he shows that the law imposed by the Creator was the revelation of what was necessary for man's happiness; that, therefore, the Creator and Lawgiver was good. He goes on to demonstrate that the Mosaic Law and the new law of the Gospel are reaffirmations of this primordial law (read the whole of Book II. and also IV. xvi. ; also *Adv. Jud.* ii.).

In a striking passage on Paul's apostleship, Tertullian argues against Marcion, who set up St. Paul as the *one* Apostle (*hæreticorum apostolus* Paul had become, says the writer, III. v.), that Paul in agreement with the Twelve is justly esteemed as an Apostle, but that if he be dissociated from them, and opposed to them, then Marcion must be called on to supply evidence that Paul was an Apostle, better than the unsubstantiated assertion of Paul himself, for that in every court two or three witnesses are required to confirm a claim (V. i.).

INDEX

ACTS OF APOSTLES, when written, 20; second book never written, 424; supposed purport of, 90, 261
Adoption, 69, 270-2
Agabus, a prophet, 16, 380, 387
Agape, 114-6, 124, 140, 188, 190, 253, 262, 264-5, 369-78, 416, 458
Alexander the coppersmith, 240, 390
— the Great, 38
— Jannæus, 22
Alexandria, 38, 50
Amphipolis, 221
Ananias, disciple, 89
— high priest, 383, 394-5
Anaphora, 376
Anastasis, 237
Anatolia, Jews in, 168-9; social condition in, 160-1
Anatolian plateau, 155, 157-9, 168; religion, 161-4 303-5; women, position of, 160, 445
Animals, callousness to their sufferings, 327-8
Antinomianism, 304, 307-10, 350, 457-62
Antioch in Pisidia, 169, 293, 418
— in Syria, 14-17, 19, 38, 47, 113-8, 140-2, 175, 181, 185-8, 197, 204, 287
Antiochus Epiphanes, 96
Antonina, tower of, 391

Apamæa, 288-9
Apollonia, 221
Apollonius, 63
Apollos, 311, 313, 337
Apostles, function of, 27-9, 65, 71-2, 85-6, 101, 107-10, 154, 190, 259-61, 439-43; whence drawn, 21
Apostleship, definition of, 85-6, 439-43; Paul's claim to, 85, 101, 103, 129; disputed, 306-8, 441-2
Appeal to Cæsar, 126, 419-21
Appuleius, 243, 252
Aquila and Priscilla, 243, 245, 258, 295, 344-5, 414
Arabia, 91-3, 101
Aratus, 45, 234
Archelaus, Bishop, 451, 461
Areopagus, 230-1
Aristarchus, 225, 368, 403, 426
Asceticism, Gnostic, 460; Pauline, 409
Asiarchs, 340
Assos, 379
Athens, 225-38, 240-1
Augustus, cult of, 163

BAAL, cult of, 45
Babylon, 199, 200
Barnabas, 14-17, 19, 101, 114-5 117, 124, 141-3, 148, 152 153, 175-6, 181, 185, 189, 190, 198

Berenice, 229
Berœa, 182, 223-4, 225
Byzantine Empire, 448-9

CÆNA DOMINI, 369, 373-5; hour of cæna, 369-70
Cæsarea, 258, 397, 398-411
Caius or Gaius, 245
Captivity, Jewish, 24
Cenchræa, 258, 367
Cévennes, prophets of, 454-6
Chaldee religion, 292; *see* Magianism
Charismata, 373-4, 442, 453-7
Chloe, 246, 311
Cilicia, province of, 41, 43-4, 47, 112-3, 204, 288
Cilician gates, 158, 205
Circumcision, 113-4, 120, 177, 199, 262, 309; in the Coptic Church, 199, 452
Classic knowledge, Paul's defect in, 61, 151, 226-8
literature, difficulties of early Christians about, 358-9
Claudius, decree of, 19, 243, 344, 414, 425
Clement of Rome, 215, 429; pseudo-Clement, 450-1, 458
Columbus, 88
Colossæ, 288, 293
Colossians, Epistle to, 409
Conversion of St. Paul, 81-91, 392; discrepancies, 82-4, 122
of Cornelius, 36, 90-1
Corinth, 182, 241-56, 290, 310, 312, 344, 371; Isthmus of, 242
Corinthians, Church of, 311-6, 458; Epistle (First) to, 311-2, 313; (Second), 313-5, 317; 343
Crispus, 245
Customary law, 282-3, 459
Cyprus, 19, 148-52, 154, 198

DALMATIA, 344
Damaris, 338
Damascus, 47, 81-2, 92, 101-2, 105, 181
Daniel, 97
David Joris, 444-5
Defects in St. Paul's mind and education, 61, 151, 226-8, 233, 236, 318-36
Demetrius, 339, 341
Demiurge, 274, 460
Derbe, 168, 174, 181, 205, 287, 418
Development in the Church, 250-6; *see* Evolution
Diaspora, 38, 40, 48-9, 120, 175-7, 179-80, 300, 301, 305, 432
Didache, 252, 372
Dionysius the Areopagite, 338
Discourses of St. Paul, 146-8, 151, 169-70, 232-7
Dogma, evolution of, 410-11
Drusilla, 400
Durham, 377
Duumviri, 363

ECSTASY, 118, 127-39, 443-5
Education, difficulties relative to, 358
Elevation in ecstasy, 134-6, 443-5
Elvira, Council of, 363
Elymas, 150-2
Epaphroditus, 215, 426
Ephesus, 138, 258, 288-98, 299, 312, 337-41, 343, 367, 379-80, 405
Ephesians, Epistle to, 409
Epilepsy, 137
Equity, 285
Erastus, 245
Essenes, 93
Eucharist, 114, 375-8
Eulogiæ, 377
Euodias, 215
Eutychus, 375, 378-9
Evolution in religion, 106-7, 109-10, 250-6, 410-1

INDEX 465

Excommunication, 184, 300, 311, 317
Ezra, reform by, 25

FAITH and works, 332-6, 460
Famine in Judæa, 14-17, 19, 117
Farewell to the Sabbath, 187-8, 371-2
Felix, 382-4, 398-403
Festus (Porcius), 403, 420
Fever, malarial, 155-7, 208; remedies for, 208
Foreign religions, 355
Fortunatus, 246
Fulvia, 223

GALATIA, 154-75, 198-206, 287-8
Galatians, Epistle to, 306-10, 347
Gallio, proconsul, 247-9
Gamaliel, 53-6, 59, 60, 78, 143
Gauls, 167-8
Gemara, 26
Genealogies of Christ, 69; endless, of Gnostics, 408
Glycerius, 450-1
Gnosis, 407-8
Gnostics, 274-5, 405-8, 460-1
Goats'-hair cloth, 73
Gospel of St. Luke, 404
  meaning of the term, 439-41
Gospels unwritten, 281, 304
Greek, quality of the, 165-7, 240, 448-50

HEBREWS, Epistle to, 349
Hellenic Jews, 23, 73, 80, 114, 121, 144, 152
Hieropolis, 293-5
High-priesthood, 26, 32-3, 39; 383-5
High treason, 248
Hillel, 53-5
Hippolitus, St., 462

ICONIUM, 170, 174, 181, 206, 207, 287, 418
Illyricum, 343-4
Incestuous Corinthian, 310-3
Inspiration, 276, 319-23
Investiture, 263
Irenæus, 458, 461
Ishmael Ben Phabi, 383

JAMES, ST., 62, 63, 102, 186, 189, 193, 195, 258-9, 262, 381, 385-90
Jason, 221, 226
Jazates, K. Adiabene, 178
Jentaculum, 375
Jerusalem, Paul's visits to, 102, 111, 189-95, 258, 381-97
  Church at, 61-6, 69-75, 117, 183-5, 385
  council at, 190-6
  taken by Pompey, 98
Jewish influence over the heathen, 34, 37, 165, 414-15
  narrowness, 46-50, 53
  nation designed as centre of the Christian Church, 22, 64-70, 120, 352, 431-3
  schools, 22, 23-4, 27, 29, 51-2
Joan of Arc, 90
Judaisers, 178, 183-6, 188-92, 262-76, 296, 299-303, 304
Judas Maccabæus, 97-8
Jus Civile, 277-81
  Gentium, 277-81, 284, 286
Justin Martyr, 462
Justus, 245

KINSMEN of St. Paul, 112

LAODICÆA, 288, 294-5
Lares et penates, 356
Law, strife about, 53, 178, 183-6, 188-92, 262-76, 296, 299-303, 304-5, 309, 314, 458-62.

Lex Porcia, 220
Luke, St., 15, 150, 152, 172, 208-9, 220-1, 236, 249, 258, 368, 403, 424, 426; Gospel of, 404, 424; Acts written by, 20, 424
Lycaonia, 155, 169, 288
Lydia, 213-6, 220, 296, 402
Lysias, 391-2, 397, 399
Lystra, 174, 181, 205-7, 287

MACCABEES, 69, 97-8
Macedonia, 208-12, 225-6, 337, 341, 343, 368, 426
Magianism, 150-1, 292, 405-8
Malarial fever, 155-7, 323-4
Manicheism, 408, 460-2
Mark, John, 124, 153-4, 157, 198, 426
Meats, rule of, 177; offered to idols, 177, 193, 459
Memory, training of, 27-8
Messianism, 66, 93-100, 108, 144, 222-3, 255, 316, 346, 425-6
Miletus, 379-80, 408
Military service, difficulties connected with, 360
Mishna, 26
Mithras, 408
Moments of development, 124-6
Mulier subintroducta, 173-4, 450-2
Municipal offices, difficulties connected with, 363-4

NAMES, Hebrew and Greek, 48-9, 152
Natural laws, 268-9, 272, 278-81, 286, 461-2
Nazarites, 257-8, 387-9
Nero, 419, 422, 423

OLIVE grafting, 275
Ordination of Barnabas and Saul, 142-3

PAMPHYLIA, 153-4
Paphos, 150-2, 153
Pastoral Epistles, 430-1
Patria potestas, 69
Paul, St., birth, 18, 47; education, 48-9, 51-5, 59; at Jerusalem, 53, 58-9; returns to Tarsus, 60; again at Jerusalem, 75; at the trial and sentence of Stephen, 75, 79; persecutes the Church, 81; conversion of, 82, 84; goes into Arabia, 92; returns to Damascus, 101; visits Jerusalem, 102; goes back to Tarsus, 105; summoned by Barnabas to Antioch, 115; visits Jerusalem again, 118; vision in the Temple, 123; returns to Antioch, 124; ordination, 142; qualifications of Paul as a missioner, 145; goes to Cyprus, 148; preaches at Paphos, 151; crosses into Pamphylia, 153; malarial fever, 154; at Antioch in Pisidia, 169; association with Thecla, 170; at Perga, 175; returns to Antioch in Syria, 175; disputes with Peter, 186; goes up to Jerusalem, 190; returns to Antioch and quarrels with Barnabas, 197-8; re-visits Cilicia, 204, and Galatia, 205; reaches Troas, 208; associates with him Silas, 197, and Timothy, 206, and Luke, 208; in Macedonia, 210; at Philippi, 211; imprisoned, 219; at Thessalonica, 221; leaves Berœa, 224; goes to Athens, 225; leaves for Corinth, 241; disturbance there, 247;

Paul, St., leaves Corinth, 249; goes again to Jerusalem, 257, 287; goes to Antioch, 287; re-visits Anatolia, 287; arrives at Ephesus, 288; riot at Ephesus, 338; escapes to Macedonia, 343, and goes again to Corinth, 344; again re-visits Jerusalem, 367; riot at Jerusalem, 390; taken to Cæsarea, 397; in prison at Cæsarea, 398; before Felix, 399, 401; appeals to Cæsar, 403; sails for Rome, 412; in prison in Rome, 424; acquittal, 427; re-visits Philippi, 428; second imprisonment, 430; death, 433

Perga, 153, 155, 157, 175

Persecution, Herodian, 16–18, 20; Neronian, 423, 429–30

Persis, 246

Peter, St., at Antioch, 119, 186–7; at Babylon, 198–9; baptizes Cornelius, 16, 90–1; at Jerusalem, 192–4, 345; at Rome, 416, 424, 430; disappears, 190; papal claims resting on, 85, 200–4; speeches of, 64, 77, 78, 110; strife with Paul, 186–7

Pharisees, 31–2, 34, 49, 72, 394–6, 421, 425

Philemon, Epistle to, 404

Philippi, 182, 208, 210–21, 222, 226, 244, 249, 296, 344, 368, 426, 428

Philippians, Epistle to, 20, 426

Philo Judæus, 50–1, 407

Phœbe, 246

Piræus, 225, 228, 233

Plantilla, 433

Pleroma, 292, 407, 460

Polyandry, 160–3, 303–4, 445–8

Poppæa, 415, 422

Priscilla—*see* Aquila

Prodigies, 222–3

Promise opposed to the Law, 270, 325–6, 460

Prophecy, Paul's claim to the gift of, 422–3; falls into discredit, 453

Prophecies, 223, 249, 453–7

Prophets, 114, 117, 123, 141–2, 380; in the Cévennes, 454–6

Proselytes, 35, 36, 37, 113–5, 144, 166, 170, 179–80, 182, 190, 193, 212, 224–5, 244, 259, 261, 265, 301–2

Proseuche, 182, 212

Purification, rule of, 178

Puritanism, 361

Pythoness, 216–8

QUARTUS, 245

RABBINISM, 23–7, 29–31, 54–5, 60, 271–2, 318, 323–4

Roads, Anatolian, 157–8

Robur, 219, 452–3

Rome, Church of, 344–6, 413–6; claims of, 85, 200–4; Jews in, 39, 344–7, 414–6; Paul in, 424–7, 430, 433

Romans, Epistle to, 344–66

SABBATH, 116

Sabbatical feast, 187–8, 190, 195, 372–3

Sadducees, 32, 33, 53, 72–3, 383–8, 396

Sanhedrim, 75, 79, 81, 394

Sceva, 293, 297, 405

Secundus, 225, 368

Semo Sanchus, 201

Sergius Paulus, 150–2

Seven Sleepers, 298

Sicarii, 383, 397

Silas or Silvanus, 197, 204, 206, 218–21, 223, 244

Simon Magus, 87, 88, 201, 307, 400
Sopater, 368
Spain, 428–9
Stephanas, 245, 249
Stephen, St., 74–9, 81, 100, 121
Stoic philosophy, 285–6
Superstitio, 421
Synagogue, its importance, 39; used by Paul, 121, 145, 148–9, 169, 180–2, 212, 244, 260, 296
Syntyche, 215

Tarsus, 42–8, 60, 111–2, 157–8, 204–5
Temple, courts, 389; toll, 384; vision in, 104, 122–4
Tennyson, 132–4
Tertius, 245
Tertullian, 360, 362–3, 399, 462
Thecla, St., 170–2, 174
Theresa, St., 127–32, 137–8
Thessalonica, 182, 221, 226, 244, 249, 290

Thessalonians, Epistle to, 225, 247
Thorn in the flesh, 155–7
Timothy, 205–7, 220–1, 226, 244, 249, 312, 337, 368, 403, 426
Titus, 119, 124, 196, 312–3
Tralles, 288
Troas, 343, 368–9, 374–6, 428
Trophimus, 368, 390
Tryphæna, 246; Queen of Pontus, 171
Tryphosa, 246
Tübingen school, 261
Tychicus, 368, 403, 426

Unknown God, 232–4, 453
tongues, 249, 453, 456–7

Vision at Antioch, 118, 121–2; at Corinth, 246; at Ephesus, 138; at Jerusalem, 83, 104, 122–4
Visions not regarded as trustworthy, 88, 307, 308

Zelots, 383, 397

www.ingramcontent.com/pod-product-compliance
Lightning Source LLC
Chambersburg PA
CBHW022101300426
44117CB00007B/540